CATHOLIC RECORD SOCIETY
PUBLICATIONS

RECORDS SERIES
VOLUME 83

Little Malvern Letters

I: 1482–1737

Edited by

AILEEN M. HODGSON and MICHAEL HODGETTS

PUBLISHED FOR

THE CATHOLIC RECORD SOCIETY

BY

THE BOYDELL PRESS

2011

First published 2011

ISBN 978 0 902832 26 8

A Catholic Record Society publication
Published by The Boydell Press
an imprint of Boydell & Brewer Ltd
PO Box 9, Woodbridge, Suffolk IP12 3DF, UK
and of Boydell & Brewer Inc.
668 Mt Hope Avenue, Rochester, NY 14620, USA
website: www.boydellandbrewer.com

A CIP catalogue record for this book is available
from the British Library

Information about the Catholic Record Society
and its publications may be obtained from the Hon. Secretary,
c/o 114 Mount St, London, W1X 6AH

The publisher has no responsibility for the continued existence or accuracy
of URLs for external or third-party internet websites referred to in this book,
and does not guarantee that any content on such websites is, or will remain,
accurate or appropriate.

Papers used by Boydell & Brewer Ltd are natural, recyclable products
made from wood grown in sustainable forests

Printed and bound in Great Britain by
CPI Group (UK) Ltd, Croydon CR0 4YY

CONTENTS

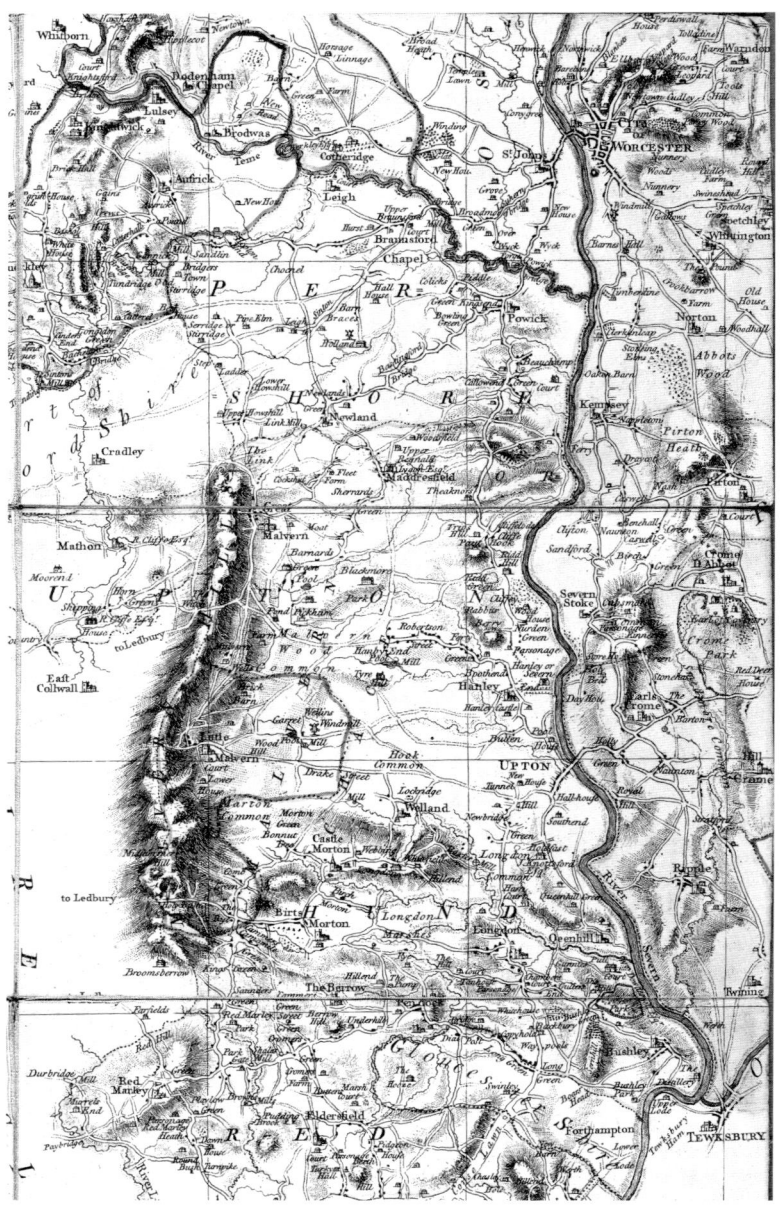

Sections of Isaac Taylor's Map of Worcestershire, 1772,

Little Malvern is due west of Upton, immediately east of the Malvern Hills.

reproduced by kind permission of Worcestershire Record Office.

ABBREVIATIONS

Anstruther	Godfrey Anstruther, OP, *The Seminary Priests*, 4 vols. (Great Wakering, Essex, 1968–77)
Berington	Berington Collection: Worcestershire Record Office, BA 81, 705:24
CRS	Catholic Record Society, Records Series
CSPD	*Calendar of State Papers, Domestic Series* (organised by reign)
Foley	Henry Foley, ed., *Records of the English Province of the Society of Jesus*, 7 vols. in 8 (London, 1875–83)
HMC 2nd Report	*Second Report of the Royal Commission on Historical Manuscripts* (London, 1871)
L&P Henry VIII	*Letters and Papers, Foreign and Domestic, of the Reign of Henry VIII, Preserved in the Public Record Office, the British Museum, and Elsewhere in England*, 23 vols. in 38 (London, 1862–1932)
Lechmere Box	Little Malvern papers, Lechmere MSS: Worcestershire Record Office, BA 1546, 899:169
ODNB	*Oxford Dictionary of National Biography*, 61 vols. (Oxford, 2004)
OED	*Oxford English Dictionary*
VCH	Victoria County History (organised by county)
Worcs. Hist. Soc.	Worcestershire Historical Society

INTRODUCTION

(Numbers in boldface type refer to documents in this volume.)

Little Malvern Court, ten miles south-south-west of Worcester at SO 770404, was a small Benedictine priory that was acquired after the Dissolution by the recusant Russells and is still the home of their descendants the Beringtons. It is perched on the east side of the Malvern Hills, facing towards Upton-upon-Severn across the flat meadows that were once Malvern Chase. Behind it the road climbs steeply towards the gap through the Hills to Herefordshire at Wind's Point. Mass is claimed to have been said at the Priory and Court from the twelfth to the twentieth century; and although the house chapel was closed in 1954, the Victorian church of St Wulstan is still the centre of a parish served by Benedictines from Downside, a link that goes back to 1828. J.H. Shorthouse's romantic novel *John Inglesant* (1866) was inspired by the portrait in the dining-room of Prior Joseph Williams of Sheen Anglorum at Nieuport, who at the French Revolution returned to England and was given a home here by his niece, the then owner of the Court. The churchyard of St Wulstan's is well known to musicians as the burial place of Sir Edward Elgar.

The Berington Collection, now in Worcestershire Record Office, runs to about 7,000 items, made up of papers of the Russells and Beringtons from the Dissolution onwards and records of the Priory from the reign of Stephen onwards. It is a remarkable series, both for recusant and for national history, with correspondents not only in Worcestershire and Herefordshire but also in Oxford and London and, during the eighteenth century, on the Continent as well. Apart from Prior Williams, two other cousins of the Beringtons were in religious houses (at Rouen and Bruges) at the time of the French Revolution and have left vivid descriptions of its impact and of their escapes to England. The Russell letters begin with those of John I, who was secretary to the Council of the Welsh Marches from 1525 until his death in 1540. He was the first of nine Russells who held Little Malvern for the two hundred years from 1538 to 1737. The others were Henry I (1540–58), John II (1558–88), Henry II (1588–1608), John III (1608–41), Thomas I (1641–70), John IV (1670–1701), John V (1701–34) and Thomas II (1734–7). Henry II was a brother of John II, and Thomas II was a brother of John V; otherwise succession was from father to son. The nine are indicated below by boldface sub-headings. They are, however, very unevenly represented in the Collection, and, although the two hundred documents printed here range from 1482 to 1737, all but forty are from the century between 1580 and 1680.

Little Malvern Priory

The Priory of St Giles at Little Malvern was a cell of Worcester Cathedral, not of Great Malvern Priory (which depended on Westminster Abbey), though the tower seems to have been designed by the same mason as that of Great Malvern.[1] Among its medieval benefactors were King Henry III and Gilbert de Clare, the Red Earl of Gloucester (1243–1295), who built Caerphilly Castle, owned Hanley Castle near Upton-upon-Severn, and constructed the Red Earl's Dyke to mark the western boundary of Malvern Chase. There was also Giles de Berkeley, who in 1294 stipulated that he and one of his horses were to be buried in the chancel at Little Malvern, and his heart and his horse Lombard in the church at Coberley near Cheltenham in Gloucestershire.[2] The fourteenth-century seal of the Priory, which is now back at Little Malvern, shows St Giles vested in apparelled alb, amice and chasuble and seated within a triple-canopied niche. His left hand holds his crozier, and his right rests on the head of a fawn wounded through the neck by an arrow. Behind the fawn, a tree suggests the Chase.[3]

In 1480 the Priory underwent a visitation by Bishop John Alcock of Worcester, who was also President of the Council of the Welsh Marches and subsequently bishop of Ely and founder of Jesus College, Cambridge. At Hartlebury Castle, the ancient home of the bishops of Worcester, there is a portrait of him: a small, ascetic man with penetrating eyes and a firm jaw. He was shocked at the decrepit and undisciplined conditions that he found and sent the prior, John Wittesham, back to Abingdon Abbey and the other three monks to Gloucester Abbey (now the Cathedral) for two years for 'reformacion'. Meanwhile, he wrote in 1482 (**1**), 'I have builded your church [and] your place of your lodging is sufficiently repaired'. Alcock pulled down the nave (if indeed it was ever finished) and left a small church consisting of chancel, tower and two side chapels, one of which served as the parish church. The east window he filled with stained glass portraying Edward IV and his family.[4] Similarly he reduced the domestic quarters to the H-plan of a small

[1] For the Priory, see Thomas Habington, *A Survey of Worcestershire*, ed. John Amphlett (Worcs. Hist. Soc., 1895–9) II. 189–94; Treadway Russell Nash, *Collections for the History of Worcestershire* (London, Oxford and Worcester, 1781–2), II. 140–56; Sir William Dugdale, *Monasticon Anglicanum*, ed. John Caley, Sir Henry Ellis and the Rev. Bulkeley Bandinel (London, 1846), IV. 446–57. Nash prints forty-three documents relating to the Priory and the *Monasticon* fifteen.

[2] Habington, *Survey*, II. 190; *Register of Bishop Godfrey Giffard, September 23rd, 1268, to January 26th, 1302*, ed. J.W. Willis Bund (Worcs. Hist. Soc., 1902), II. 449; VCH *Glos.*, VII. 176, 182.

[3] C.H. Hunter Blair, 'Some Medieval Seal Matrices', *Antiquaries' Journal* 4 (1924), 245–6.

[4] Habington, *Survey*, II. 190–2. Bishop Alcock's letter is also printed in *Monasticon An-*

medieval manor house, consisting of the fourteenth-century Prior's Hall on the west side of the former cloister and cross-wings at each end. Despite later additions and reconstructions, most of this building still survives. The three-storey stone cross-wing and the round tower at its south end are also medieval. The Prior's Hall, with its magnificent arch-braced roof, is open to the public and in regular use for social and other functions.[5] Finally, as second founder, Alcock had a new seal made for the Priory, which included his own arms and figures of his patrons Our Lady and St John the Evangelist as well as that of St Giles.[6]

On 31 August 1534 this seal was appended to the subscription to the Royal Supremacy by the prior, John Brystow, and his five monks (John Malvern, Robert Hanley, Richard Kethminster, Robert Cavoloc and Robert Lye).[7] According to a survey made two years later, there were then seven monks including the prior, five of them priests and all of good conversation and living; two of them asked for capacities, but the others 'desireth . . . they may continue their religion there'. The house had an income of only £101 6s 1½d and was therefore suppressed under the Act of 1536. But the survey also noted that nineteen yeomen, hinds and servants depended on the Priory, which was 'very necessary for the relief of poverty': it recommended that, if the house was suppressed, at least the church should be saved (**24**). After the Dissolution the number of families within the parish of Little Malvern did in fact drop from thirty-six to only six.[8] But the church survived and still contains some of Alcock's stained glass, a fourteenth-century screen and richly-carved rood-beam and a fourteenth-century bell, probably by John Rudhall of Gloucester.

John Russell I (d. 1540)

In 1538 the Priory was granted for twenty-one years to John Russell of Bedwardine in Worcester and Elmley Castle on the northern slopes of Bredon Hill, four miles south-west of Evesham. This was a reward for service as secretary of the Council of the Welsh Marches, which otherwise was poorly remunerated (**12, 17**).[9] Although the Council was

---

glicanum, IV. 452–3 (Appendix XII). Throughout the Introduction, boldface numbers are those of documents in the text.

[5] VCH *Worcs.*, III. 449–450; Alan Brooks and Sir Nikolaus Pevsner, *The Buildings of England: Worcestershire*, 2nd edn (London, 2007), 431–4.

[6] British Museum Seals Catalogue, no. 3605.

[7] *Monasticon Anglicanum*, IV. 447; Blair, 'Some Medieval Seal Matrices', 246. See *L&P Henry VIII*, VII, no. 1121 (60); see also no. 891.

[8] Nash, *Collections for the History of Worcestershire*, II. 142.

[9] Russell's colleague Sir John Pakington similarly regarded his grant of the nunnery of Westwood, near Droitwich, as compensation for his 'painful office' in the Marches, which had led to a loss of fees from his practice in London and Westminster Hall: *L&P Henry*

primarily an instrument of 'good rule', it was also, in 1525–7, the household of Princess Mary. Its headquarters was at Ludlow Castle, but the princess also used Tickenhill House near Bewdley (**3, 11, 12**) and Thornbury in Gloucestershire (which had been seized by the Crown when the duke of Buckingham was executed in 1521). The Treasurer's accounts from July 1526 to December 1527 include £543 7*s* 6d for building and repairs at Tickenhill and Ludlow.[10] Since the records of the Council are mostly lost, John Russell's papers (**2–33**) are useful evidence for its workings and for the relationships between Church and State in the years just before the break with Rome. The correspondents include Wolsey (**2**), who twenty years before had been chaplain to Sir Richard Nanfan at Birtsmorton Court, near Little Malvern (cf. **131**); Thomas Cromwell (**21, 23, 25, 26, 29, 33**); Lord Chancellor Audley, who was Russell's brother-in-law (**9, 23, 30, 32**); Bishop John Vesey of Exeter, who was President of the Council (**3, 5, 12**); the abbots of Evesham and Westminster (**13, 22**); and Prior More of Worcester (**18**). Items **25–6** are the missing half of a correspondence with Cromwell incompletely documented in the *Letters & Papers of Henry VIII*. They give an unpleasant picture of how mutterings by a parson in an alehouse about the dissolution of a local priory were promptly reported to Cromwell and to the King himself and led to his arrest, imprisonment and examination under torture.

Henry Russell I (d. 1558)

John Russell's tenure was only a lease, at £10 6*s* 8*d* a year, and it is not certain that he lived at Little Malvern. In his will of 1540 he still described himself as of Bedwardine and in 1543 Little Malvern was granted to a pair of speculators named Richard Andrewes and Nicholas Temple.[11] Later, however, it reverted to the Crown, and in 1554 Queen Mary granted it outright to John's son Henry Russell (I) for £413 18*s* 6*d*, on condition that he and his heirs paid £5 a year to the curate of Little Malvern—an obligation that lasted until the 1960s. The purchase price was paid jointly by Henry Russell and his brother-in-law Charles Brocton or Broughton of Henley, two miles east of Ludlow.[12] There is

---

VIII, XII/2, no. 775; XIII/1, no. 1520 (38b). John Russell was secretary of the Council from 1525 until his death in 1540: *L&P Henry VIII*, XVI, no. 107g (39).

[10] Frederick Madden, *Privy Purse Expenses of the Princess Mary* (London, 1831), pp. xliv–xlv; Caroline A.J. Skeel, *The Council in the Marches of Wales*, Girton College Studies 2 (London, 1904), 49–80; E.A.B. Barnard, *A Vanished Palace* (Kidderminster, 1929), 3–10 (though behind a Georgian façade much of Tickenhill survives).

[11] *Index of Wills Proved in the Prerogative Court of Canterbury, 1383–1558*, comp. J. Challenor C. Smith, Index Library 10–11 (London, 1893–5), I. 459; VCH *Worcs.*, III. 451.

[12] The Letters Patent, dated 26 September 1 & 2 Philip & Mary, are MS Berington 83. They are printed in *Monasticon Anglicanum*, IV. 456–7 (Appendix XVII).

a glimpse of the priory church in his time in the inventory of 1552 (**34**); the furnishings of the former domestic buildings are listed in the probate inventory of his wife, Milburgha Brocton, in 1575 (**36**). Henry himself died in 1558, only five years after the Queen's grant of Little Malvern.[13] But in the previous eighteen years he and Milburgha had had four sons and seven daughters,[14] and they seem to have extended the northern wing to the west and to have added the three Tudor garderobes, one in the north wing and two in the south. The mention in Milburgha's inventory of seven upstairs chambers, including a 'great chamber', suggests also that by 1575 the hall had been floored across half-way up. So the couple may already have been living at the Court before 1554.

John Russell II (1540–1588)

Henry Russell I was succeeded by his eldest son John II, who was still a minor in 1558. In 1570, at Great Malvern Priory, he married Jane Lumley, whose father, George Lumley, had been executed in 1537 after the Pilgrimage of Grace. Her brother John, seventh Lord Lumley (1534–1609) of Lumley Castle in County Durham, was imprisoned in the Tower; he was later a patron of William Byrd and connived in the harbouring of priests. Jane had come to Worcestershire when she married Geoffrey Markham of Astwood in Feckenham, who was sheriff in 1564: after his death in 1568 she had moved to Great Malvern to live with her mother, whose second husband, John Knotsford, had acquired and converted the former Prior's Lodging there.[15] But John II and Jane Russell are a rather shadowy couple: no letters of either have survived, they had no children, and after her death in 1582 John did not remarry. He seems, however, to have conformed: in 1587 Bishop Freke of Worcester described him rather dismissively as 'commended for forwardness in

---

[13] The grant of administration to his widow is Berington 276.
[14] John (1540–1588), Henry (1540–1608), Charles, Rowland (b. 1552); Elizabeth (Hayward), Maud (Mintridge), Ann (Chelmick), Margery (Berrow), Mary (Blathwaytt or Braithwaite), Jane or Joan (Cowarne) and Frances, who died unmarried. *The Visitation of Worcestershire, 1634*, ed. A.T. Butler, Harleian Society 90 (London, 1934), 84–5; Henry Sydney Grazebrook, *The Heraldry of Worcestershire* (London, 1873), II: (M–Z), 484–6. Maud had died by 1575, when her mother's will (**35**) mentions 'my six daughters' and 'my son-in-law James Mintridge'. Milburgha is also spelt Milbora and Milborowe.
[15] G.E. C[okayne], *The Complete Peerage*, ed. Vicary Gibbs (London, 1910–59), VIII. 275–9; James Nott, *Some of the Antiquities of 'Moche Malverne'* (Malvern, 1885), 117–18, 136, 138. By 1558 Markham and Jane Lumley had a son, John: VCH *Worcs.*, III. 115. Markham's inquisition post mortem (C.142/167/113) was taken in 1573–4: *P.R.O. Lists and Indexes 26: Inquisitions, Elizabeth* (London, 1908), 232, though VCH *Worcs.*, III. 119, gives the date of his death as 1568. Knutsford was Sheriff of Worcestershire in 1550: Nash, *Collections*, I, p. xviii.

religion but not so for discretion'.[16] He died a year later, on 20 November 1588, and was succeeded by his brother Henry.

Henry Russell II (1540–1608)

In 1588 Henry Russell II was forty-eight and had spent most of his life at St John's College, Oxford. He was one of the original members of the College in 1555, and is named in the second foundation charter of 5 March 1557/8. He supplicated for his BA in 1559 and, with Edmund Campion and Gregory Martin, incepted as Master of Arts in 1564. In September that year he became vice-president of the college, in 1568 'Greke Reader', and in 1579 bursar. The statutes provided that normally fellows must be ordained within three years of taking their Masters' degrees. But there could be twelve lawyers, who need not be ordained for fourteen years, and one student of medicine, who did not have to be ordained at all. After the Elizabethan Act of Uniformity in 1559 this clause provided a loophole for dons with recusant sympathies, and Russell accordingly obtained a 'lawyer's place' and took his BCL in 1570. In 1574 the 'commissaries' of the College Visitor, Sir William Cordell, 'warned Mr Russell not hereafter to resort to any suspect or lewd [*infamem*] house, and that he should in all things conform to the religion now established in England and sincerely profess the same'.[17] Two years later, in 1576, he became principal of Gloucester Hall (formerly the Benedictine Gloucester College and now Worcester College), which after the Dissolution had become an annexe to St John's and a notorious haunt of papists. George Blackwell, the future Archpriest, had been a fellow there from 1572, and between 1581 and 1588 eleven graduates from St John's and Gloucester Hall were executed as seminary priests. In 1577 the bishop of Oxford reported that 'Gloucester Hall . . . is greatly suspected and yet the Principal there presented nothing to me. One Sir William Catesby lieth there.'[18] This was Sir William Catesby of Ashby St Ledgers in Northamptonshire, who in 1581 was tried before Star Chamber for harbouring Campion;[19] his son Robert, the future Gunpowder Plotter, was an undergraduate at Gloucester Hall.

In 1568 Henry was joined at St John's by his younger brother Row-

---

[16] John Strype, *Annals of the Reformation* (Oxford, 1824) III/2. 457. In 1564, on the other hand, Geoffrey Markham had been 'an adversary of true religion': Mary Bateson, 'Collection of Original Letters from the Bishops to the Privy Council, 1564', *Camden Miscellany* 9 (1895), 6.

[17] W.H. Stevenson and H.E. Salter, *The Early History of St. John's College, Oxford*, Oxford Historical Society n.s. 1 (Oxford, 1939), 213, 222, 327, 412 and *passim*.

[18] Patrick Ryan, SJ, 'Diocesan Returns of Recusants for England and Wales, 1577', in *Miscellanea XII*, CRS 22 (London, 1921), 100–101 (SP 12/118/37).

[19] Godfrey Anstruther, *Vaux of Harrowden* (Newport, 1953), 119–32.

land, who in 1577 incepted as Master of Arts and was appointed lecturer in rhetoric. On 30 March 1579 Rowland was given permission by the college to travel abroad. On 7 April 1580 (Easter Thursday) the spy Charles Sledd met him at Bayonne College in Paris, in the rooms of Allen's agent there, Thomas Covert, and on 25 November that year he was at Douai. He returned to Oxford in June 1582, where he lectured on law for a month before resigning in 1583 as he had not been ordained.[20] Subsequently he became attorney to Sir Francis Willoughby (c.1546–1596) at Wollaton Hall, near Nottingham.[21] In 1598, after the death of Sir Francis, he was described as of London, gentleman, but it is not known what he was doing there or when he died.[22]

In 1580, while Rowland was abroad, his brother Henry resigned from Gloucester Hall and instead was offered a post by Sir William Cordell at Melford Hall, Long Melford, in Suffolk, a house now owned by the National Trust. Despite the comments of his 'commissaries' in 1574, Cordell was a friend of both Russells and had earlier described Rowland as 'my scholar'. 'If Mr Russell', he wrote, 'shall be clearly discharged of his place in Gloucester College to his own good liking and shall have disposition to serve me, I will never forsake him until he can be better provided, and I mean to place him in the office of the steward of my house, if he will accept it, wherein his only pains shall be to control and oversee the clerk of my kitchen and my other officers that have charge of my house. . . . I do confess that I do like and love the man very well, and I trust, that if it shall be his hap to serve me, I will give him occasion to do the like to me.'[23] Nine months later, however, in May 1581, Cordell died, and on 14 August 1581 the Privy Council wrote to the vicechancellor of Oxford (**39**), having been informed

> that three Masters of Arts, namely one Russell, Stubbs and Yate, at the time of the apprehending of Campion the Jesuit at the house of one Yate of Lyford in that shire were then in the said house . . . and that they and likewise one Jacob, a musician taken in Campion's company, have been tolerated there many years without going to the church and receiving of the Sacrament.

This was Henry Russell; the other two were almost certainly Justinian Stubbs and Robert or James Yate. Stubbs and Robert Yate were colleagues of Henry Russell at Gloucester Hall; Stubbs and James Yate both

---

[20] Thomas Francis Knox, ed., *The First and Second Diaries of the English College, Douay* (London, 1878), 173; Stevenson and Salter, *St. John's*, 164, 220, 240–1, 242, 321, 341–2, 478; Clare Talbot, ed., *Miscellanea: Recusant Records*, CRS 53 (London, 1961), 241.

[21] Berington 581; cf. Lechmere Box, A.13. The present Wollaton Hall was built by Sir Francis between 1580 and 1588; the older Hall continued in use until some time between 1616 and 1637: John Howard Hodson, 'The First Wollaton Hall', *Transactions of the Thoroton Society of Nottinghamshire* 72 (1968), 59–67.

[22] Berington 604; *HMC 2nd Report*, no. [35] (see Appendix II below).

[23] Stevenson and Salter, *St. John's*, 486, 496–7.

occur in subsequent family correspondence. Moreover, from 1583 onwards Henry was involved in a protracted lawsuit over Lowches Farm,
Long Wittenham, near Dorchester. The farm belonged to St John's, and
the case ostensibly arose from the dismissal of an unsatisfactory tenant,
the widow Maud Sawyer, and the transfer of the lease to Russell. But
behind this there were insinuations that he had connived with Francis
Willis, then president of St John's and from 1586 dean of Worcester, to
harbour Campion, apparently at Lowches—which would have formed
a useful base for his work in Oxfordshire and Berkshire during the late
summer of 1580. In the Collection are three long and rambling letters
from a cousin of Russell's named West, referring to his capture with
Campion and warning him about an action to be brought by a Captain
Bourne who was in Leicester's force in Flanders and about 'two ladies
of honour of the Court . . . [who] speaks unto the Council for Sawyer
odiously against you and your President . . . and . . . wait daily on the
Queen's Majesty and are of kindred to the Lord Admiral'.[24] West also
noted (41) that 'There is in London one Mr Russell, Sir John Perrot's
man, that may do much with Borne.' This was Charles Russell, another
of Henry's brothers, who was in the service of Sir John Perrot at Carew
Castle on Milford Haven (42). Perrot was Lord Deputy of Ireland from
1584 to 1588 but incurred the enmity of Lord Burghley, was convicted of
treason and died in the Tower in November 1592. The Lowches lawsuit
went first, in June 1583, to Lord Chancellor Bromley, who urged the
College to deal charitably with Mrs Sawyer and allow her to stay until
Michaelmas 1584, when Russell would pay her £100. She refused this
offer and petitioned the queen, who referred the matter to Toby Matthew,
then dean of Durham, later archbishop of York and formerly a fellow
of St John's. Later, Henry Russell wrote (43) to Sir Christopher Hatton,
by now Lord Chancellor, that 'the plaintiffs are still continuing with
clamorous complaints, never yielding unto authority but still delighting
in continual troubles and desirous to dwell and spend their whole lives
in causeless complaints and endless suits'. The case was not settled
until 1592, when Henry was required to pay Mrs Sawyer £120. It seems
unlikely that a poor widow could have afforded such a protracted and
costly suit without powerful backing from someone determined, as the
fellows wrote to the Privy Council, 'to bring our College to obloquy and
to be hardly reported of'.[25]

---

[24] Berington 29 (1). 29 (2) is included in the text below (41).
[25] Berington 26 (10). The whole correspondence is Berington 20–41, of which the West
letters are 29 (1–3). See also Michael Hodgetts, 'Campion in the Thames Valley, 1580',
Recusant History 30 (2010–11), 26–46.

Henry Russell at Little Malvern, 1588–1608

Henry Russell inherited Little Malvern in November 1588 on the death of his brother John II and was its owner for the next twenty years. In view of his activities at Gloucester Hall and Lowches, there can be no doubt that he harboured priests there too. The Court certainly had a secret chapel and is said to have had priest-holes, though none survive.[26] The chapel was on the top floor of the three-storey porch at the southeast corner of the Prior's Hall and was approached from the gallery at the screens end of the Hall. The priest's room was on the top floor of the adjoining south cross-wing and was approached by a medieval newel staircase of stone. It has been supposed that the gallery and the lath-and-plaster partition that divided it from the Hall were inserted in Henry Russell's time to camouflage the position of the chapel. But both chapel and gallery may already have existed before the Dissolution, as at Ashbury in Berkshire (a former grange of Abingdon Abbey) and at Cothay in Somerset, where the lath-and-plaster partition dividing the gallery from the hall is still (unusually) in place and the oratory over the porch retains its fifteenth-century wall paintings.[27] If the gallery at Little Malvern was of late-medieval construction, it could have been the 'chapel chamber' mentioned in Milburgha Russell's probate inventory of 1575 (**36**). This chapel continued in use until 1791, when Mary Williams, daughter of Elizabeth Berington and Thomas Williams and niece of Prior Williams, converted the lower half of the Hall into a more commodious chapel with plasterwork and Gothic sash windows. The Georgian chapel, the gallery and the partition were all removed in the 1960s to reveal the medieval roof of the Hall, and access to the earlier chapel over the porch is now by a small modern staircase at the south end.

In 1591, three years after succeeding to Little Malvern, Henry Russell married Elizabeth Pakington, the eldest of the three sisters of Humphrey Pakington of Harvington Hall, twelve miles north of Worcester. In consequence, the Collection contains a most important five-cornered correspondence between Henry and Elizabeth Russell, Humphrey Pakington, the Worcester physician John Halsey, and John Grove, who acted as banker and man of business to the other four (**44–126**). Although the letters are mainly concerned with leases and financial arrangements, they sometimes touch on politics and religion, and they also give an agreeable picture of Elizabethan and Jacobean social life, with references to gifts of puddings, fat hens, cheeses, capons, loaves of sugar and collars

[26] Granville Squiers, *Secret Hiding-Places* (London, 1933), 66; Aileen Hodgson, 'Story of Little Malvern' (unpublished), 69–70; Hodgson, 'A History of Little Malvern Court: II', *Worcestershire Recusant* 39 (June 1982), 11; Michael Hodgetts, 'A Topographical Index of Hiding-Places: II', *Recusant History* 24 (1998–9), 49 (no. 288).

[27] Hodgetts, 'Index of Hiding-Places: II', 5, 38 (nos. 178, 262).

of brawn. To make sense of them, however, something needs to be said about each of the other four correspondents, about Humphrey Pakington's two wives and about Henry's nephew Alderford Russell.

Elizabeth Pakington (1556–1623)

In 1591 Elizabeth Pakington was thirty-five.[28] Henry Russell was not her first suitor: a love letter has survived from one George Selby to his 'Sweet Bess' (**37**). For many years she suffered from poor health, and the Collection includes prescriptions by John Halsey, with diagnoses of her humours and quotations from Galen in Latin and Greek (**44–5, 50–52, 54, 57–8, 60, 64**). The nauseous concoctions that she was to take at the full of the moon and other propitious times have recently served as a guide to the planting of the moat-side herb garden at Harvington Hall. About 1601 she lost the sight of one eye, and the other became so weak that in desperation her husband was induced to allow a London surgeon named Eager 'to preserve the sight of the better eye by taking up with needle and thread an artery, and so by cutting it asunder in time to divert the course of any hot blood or humour that by that passage were likely to annoy the eye'. Henry reported to Humphrey Pakington (**63**) that 'she hath had very great pain therewith night and day, where he promised the contrary'. On 6 June 1607 John Grove wrote to Russell (**80**), enclosing a pair of spectacles that Humphrey, 'being lately in town, prayed me to cause conveyed to her'. Nevertheless, she outlived her husband by fifteen years, dying on 8 February 1622/3 at the age of sixty-six.[29]

In 1613 Elizabeth Russell gave five shillings towards the organ built by Thomas Dallam at Worcester Cathedral and enthusiastically described by Thomas Habington of Hindlip in his *Survey of Worcestershire*. The donors also included her brother Humphrey Pakington, who gave £5, and other recusants, such as Ralph Sheldon of Beoley, Sir Thomas Russell of Strensham, John Hanford of Woollas, Charles Stanford of Abbots Salford and William Coles of Hallow. There were also William Sebright, who had been tenant of Humphrey Pakington's sequestrated lands; Sir William Walsh, who had rounded up the Gunpowder Plotters at Holbeach on 8 November 1605; Sir Henry Bromley, who had carried out the great search at Hindlip after the Plot; and his sister the redoubtable Meriel Lyttelton, who restored the fortunes of the Lytteltons after their disastrous involvement in that and the Essex Plot. Habington records that the donors were acknowledged by having their arms displayed on

---

[28] She was christened at Chaddesley Corbett on 6 September 1556. The marriage settlement (Berington 93) is dated 6 November 1591.

[29] Her probate inventory is printed in Malcolm Wanklyn, ed., *Inventories of Worcestershire Landed Gentry, 1537–1786*, Worcs. Hist. Soc. n.s. 16 (Worcester, 1998), no. 47.

the case of the organ, which stood on the screen.[30] It is clear that the new organ was a matter for legitimate pride throughout the county and that local gentry were willing to subscribe for it, whatever political and religious divisions there might have been between them.

Humphrey Pakington (1555–1631)

Humphrey Pakington was educated at Shrewsbury School from 1565 onwards and is first recorded as a recusant in London in 1585. In 1591 he was convicted of recusancy in Worcestershire, and his estates were sequestrated—only to be leased a month later to his friend William Sebright, who was member of Parliament for Droitwich and town clerk of London. They remained in the hands of the Crown until 1607, when James I granted them to John Grove. Nevertheless, at least from 1604 until 1613 Pakington had a post in the household of Sir Thomas Egerton, who in 1603 became Lord Ellesmere and Lord Chancellor. The coincidence of dates makes it possible that he succeeded John Donne in 1602 as Egerton's secretary.[31] Egerton's third wife, the former Lady Derby, was herself a recusant; in 1586 the spy Nicholas Berden reported that she and her sister Lady Compton had been at the French ambassador's, attended by John Gerard's elder brother Thomas, later Sir Thomas.[32] The letters include several written from or referring to the Egerton houses at Ashridge in Hertfordshire and Harefield in Middlesex (**65, 67, 71, 73, 75, 78**) and one from Lady Derby herself about a footman recommended to her by Humphrey (**67, 68**). They suggest that Egerton, despite his official position and contrary to his reputation, may have been a discreet protector of papists, like Lord Treasurer Buckhurst and the earl of Worcester.[33]

Ashridge Park is now a Regency house by Wyatt (1808–14) but contains remnants of the thirteenth-century college of the Bonshommes. After the Dissolution this was turned into a house, where both Mary I and Elizabeth I stayed before their accessions. Half a mile north is the Elizabethan manor house of Little Gaddesden, which now houses a collection of early keyboard instruments. At the south end of the village is a third manor house, Lucies, which was built by the Dormers in 1576. Ellesmere bought Ashridge and Little Gaddesden from Jane, Lady Cheyne; Lucies from the Dormers; and Great Gaddesden, two miles to

---

[30] Michael Hodgetts, 'Recusant Contributors to the Worcester Cathedral Organ, 1613', *Midland Catholic History* 1 (1991), 28–33.
[31] Lionel Anderton Webster and Veronica Anderton Webster, 'The Pakingtons of Harvington', *Recusant History* 12 (1973–4), 203–15; Michael Hodgetts, *Life at Harvington, 1250–2000* (Archdiocese of Birmingham Historical Commission, 2002), 21–39.
[32] *CSPD Elizabeth I, 1580–90*, 373 (SP 12/195/75).
[33] Anthony G. Petti, ed., *Recusant Documents from the Ellesmere Manuscripts*, CRS 60 (London, 1968), pp. xii–xiv; Geoffrey de C. Parmiter, *Elizabethan Popish Recusancy in the Inns of Court*, Bulletin of the Institute of Historical Research, Special Supplement 11 (London, 1976), 10, 11, 12, 14, 23.

the south-east, from the Stanleys, the family of his third wife. All these purchases were made in or soon after 1602 and provide a *terminus a quo* for otherwise undated letters. Towards the end of the seventeenth century Great Gaddesden was bought by the Halseys, the family of John Halsey.[34]

Humphrey Pakington was also a 'deare frynd' of Thomas Habington of Hindlip, where Henry Garnet, Edward Oldcorne, Ralph Ashley and Nicholas Owen were all arrested in 1606. The Collection includes a letter from Thomas Habington's wife Mary to Elizabeth Russell, written shortly after the search (**103**). A copy of Philippe d'Oultreman's *Le Vray Chrestien catholique* (Saint-Omer, 1622), formerly at Harvington and now at Oscott, contains the ownership mark 'Baronne Brookesby' as well as those of both Humphrey Pakington's daughters. This is almost certainly Eleanor Brooksby, who, with her sister Anne Vaux, was Garnet's housekeeper for twenty years but was not at Hindlip during the search and afterwards 'lay hid so secretly that her whereabouts has never come to light'.[35] It is tempting to wonder whether she lay hid at Harvington. The priest-holes there are the finest surviving series in the country, and on the top floor are two secret chapels and three rooms used by the priests, mostly with their original Elizabethan decoration. It is likely that the later and more cunning hides, which are sited round a Great Staircase of soon after 1600, are by Owen. They are so closely associated with the Staircase as to suggest that they were inserted at the same time as it was. A possible context for them is the papal ruling on the Archpriest Controversy in October 1602, under which Blackwell was no longer to consult the Jesuits. Until then it is clear that Hindlip, though a Jesuit house, had also been a 'receptacle' for seculars, whom Oldcorne 'stationed in many places'.[36] The number of hides at Harvington implies that it too was a receptacle for priests coming from abroad and their siting round the Staircase suggests that it became one soon after 1600.

There may be a clue to all this in a letter written by Henry Russell's nephew Walter Cowarne (1579–1607) in February 1604 (**66**), just before he went abroad to Saint-Omer, *ab archipresbytero Angliae missus*, and from there to Valladolid.[37] It mentions Halsey, who had treated him for

[34] VCH *Herts.*, II. 201–15; Nikolaus Pevsner, *The Buildings of England: Hertfordshire*, 2nd edn, rev. Bridget Cherry (Harmondsworth, 1977), 150–52, 236–40.

[35] G.F. Pullen, *Catalogue of the Bible Collections in the Old Library at St Mary's, Oscott, c.1472–c.1850* (New Oscott, 1971), no. 1075B; Anstruther, *Vaux of Harrowden*, 343–4, 348, 349.

[36] Michael Hodgetts, 'Elizabethan Priest-Holes, III: East Anglia, Baddesley Clinton, Hindlip', *Recusant History* 12 (1973–4), 171–97; Hodgetts, 'Elizabethan Priest-Holes, IV: Harvington', *Recusant History* 13 (1975–6), 1–55; Hodgetts, *Secret Hiding-Places* (Dublin, 1989), 70–75, 82–99, 170–77.

[37] Edwin Henson, ed., *Registers of the English College at Valladolid, 1589–1962*, CRS 30 (London, 1930), 83. Cowarne was born at Ross-on-Wye and educated at Worcester before

a surfeit, and Humphrey Pakington, who was with him, and has a post-script that runs, 'No news but that some young gentlemen that were going beyond sea (amongst whom is Mr George Berington) have and do lie in prison here, unless they be, as the speech was they should be, delivered today upon bail.' George Berington (1576–1664) had been at Valladolid from 1596 to 1600; he subsequently became a Benedictine and returned to work in Herefordshire. The martyr Roger Cadwallador, who was born at Stretton Sugwas in Herefordshire in 1567 and executed at Leominster in 1610, had also been at Valladolid, in 1592–3.[38] His alias of Greenway suggests a link with Oswald Tesimond alias Green-way, who was in Worcestershire from 1598 to 1606. A copy of Molina's *Exercicios espirituales* (Burgos, 1622), formerly at Harvington and with Humphrey's initials in it, shows that he understood Spanish.[39] Did he too have links with Valladolid?

Bridget Pakington (1572–1606) and Abigail Pakington (c.1577–1657)

Humphrey Pakington's first wife was Bridget Kingsmill (1572–1606), the fourth daughter of Sir William Kingsmill of Sydmonton in Hamp-shire and of Bridget Raleigh of Farnborough in Warwickshire. About 1589 she had married Sir Thomas Norris, the fifth of the six sons of Sir Henry Norris of Rycote in Oxfordshire. From 1585 onwards Sir Thomas was first vice-president and then president of Munster, where he took part in much fighting. He died at Mallow Castle, County Cork, in September 1599 'by the neglect of a small wound' sustained in ac-tion. Bridget had married Humphrey by the summer of 1601, and that November she was said by John Chamberlain to have 'become a great Catholic and takes great pains to convert her sisters'. But by June 1602, when their child was born, there were already 'variable reports and censures of [the] marriage' (**59**). In 1598 the astrologer Simon Forman had noted that she was 'an enemy to herself' and 'in danger of the pox';

---

going to Oxford; he died at Valladolid in 1607 (ibid.). In 1605, at the time of the Whitsun Riot in Herefordshire, his father, also Walter, Henry Russell's brother-in-law, was tenant of the recusant centre at The Darren in Garway, a mile from Whitfield, where Cadwallador 'usually said Mass': John Hobson Matthews, 'Records Relating to Catholicism in the South Wales Marches, 17th and 18th Centuries', in *Miscellanea II*, CRS 2 (London, 1906), 292–3; Talbot, *Recusant Records*, CRS 53, pp. 138, 143.

[38] Henson, *Registers of the English College at Valladolid*, CRS 30, pp. 22, 43.

[39] G.F. Pullen, *Recusant Books at St. Mary's, Oscott, Part I: 1518–1687* (New Oscott, 1964), no. 586. There is also a copy of Ribadeneyra's *Traicté de la tribulation* (Paris, 1599) inscribed, 'Esto libro fue de Marco Parcelo y fiole a su herm fray Antonio Porcelo en el año de 1623. Esto es de mi Sa Doña Maria Pakington' (Pullen, *Recusant Books at St. Mary's, Oscott, Part II: 1641–1830* (New Oscott, 1966), no. 1097). Humphrey Pakington's elder daughter Mary married Sir John Yate in the second half of 1630, which fixes the date of the inscription as between 1623 and 1630: Michael Hodgetts, 'The Yates of Harvington, 1631–1696', *Recusant History* 22 (1994–5), 155.

the details recorded in his casebook are consistent with gonorrhoea and treatment by mercury sublimate. In July 1602 she arranged a transfer of Humphrey's sequestrated estates from William Sebright to Sir Richard Verney of Compton Verney in Warwickshire, and John Grove was anxious that she should not be allowed to see her husband's papers (**59**). In February 1604 he referred to her bluntly as 'the lewd madam' and told Henry Russell that Humphrey was to allow her £120 a year on condition that she made no further claims on him (**65**). She was buried at Chaddesley Corbett on 14 April 1606.[40]

In the summer of 1607, Humphrey married a second wife, Abigail Sacheverell. She was one of the daughters of Henry Sacheverell (1547–1620) of Morley and Hopwell in Derbyshire and his wife Jane Bradbourne.[41] Like Russell, Henry Sacheverell was a graduate of St John's College, Oxford, and a friend of Campion, who in 1581 stayed with him and said Mass 'about the Wednesday after Twelfth Day' (11 January). Later that year, he was said to be keeping both a minister and a priest, William Harrison, who was 'short of stature and very decent of body and behaviour, his beard of a flaxen colour, cut short'. (This was the Harrison who was later Archpriest.) 'The minister is to say the common service for the household, and the priest doth say Mass secretly in their chambers for themselves and such other their secret friends.' A spy's report of February 1595 mentions an old carpenter and mason named Green who was then dwelling on Mr Sacheverell's land at Morley. He had made 'a secret place in Mr Bentley's house at Lea [probably the Lea Hall a mile from Bradbourne Hall] with a door of freestone that no man could ever judge there were any such place, and he made all the secret places in recusants' houses in that country'.[42]

There are no letters of Bridget Pakington's in the Collection, only references to her in those of Grove. But Abigail is represented. Born about 1577, she was about thirty when she married Humphrey and survived until 1657. After Humphrey's death in 1631 she was a vigorous champion of her sons-in-law, Sir John Yate and Sir Henry Audley, and of her

[40] C.D. Gilbert, 'Bridget Pakington (1572–1606)', *Midland Catholic History* 8 (2001), 7–13.

[41] Abigail is probably the 'Mrs Pakington' who in late July or early August 1607 had a part in the performance at Ashby-de-la-Zouch Castle of *The Entertainment of the Dowager Countess of Derby*, a masque written by the satirist John Marston to mark the engagement of the Countess's eldest daughter, Anne, to Lord Chandos. See Michael Hodgetts, 'Mrs Packington and a Shakespearian Emblem, 1607', *Midland Catholic History* 2 (1992), 42–5.

[42] British Library, MS Lansdowne 30, no. 78, ff. 201–2; Talbot, *Recusant Records*, CRS 53, pp. 187, 189 ('Henrie Sir Cheverell'), 209; Anstruther I. 152; Foley IV. 470–71; Anstruther, *Vaux of Harrowden*, 253–5. See also Michael Hodgetts, 'Campion in Staffordshire and Derbyshire, 1581', *Midland Catholic History* 7 (2000), 52–4; Hodgetts, 'A Topographical Index of Hiding-Places: II', 11, no. 194.

nephew John Russell, when they were indicted for recusancy; and her letters are rewarding to read, both for their delightful, personal syntax and for their robust common sense about bribery of juries and informers (**134, 135–6**).

John Halsey (d. 1605)

John Halsey was probably the man of that name who was a fellow of St John's College, Oxford, in 1555 and later of its neighbour Trinity College. He was in practice in Worcester by 1570, and by the late 1570s Henry Russell's brother-in-law Richard Hayward was 'in hand with Mr Halsey' about his wife's cough.[43] He was in trouble for recusancy by 1580 and in 1582–3 was imprisoned with Lord Vaux and Sir Thomas Tresham in the Fleet, from which he was moved to the Clink on 15 February 1582/3. About 1585 he occurs in a list of 'knaves, Papists and harbourers of priests' that also includes servants of Henry Vaux and of Lords Montague, Lumley and Compton. On 18 March 1586/7 the decipherer Thomas Phelippes reported that Anthony Tyrrell's 'book' had been 'perused and allowed' by various prisoners in the Clink and the Marshalsea, including William Weston, and that 'Dr Halsey the physician was acquainted with the same'. By 1592 he was in prison in Worcester Castle but was later released. He died of a stroke in London on Easter Sunday 1605 while examining a patient's urine at the Angel outside Temple Bar.[44] Some of the letters mention an attempt by one Zachary Field to get his hands on Halsey's property, which was eventually foiled by a letter from the earl of Derby to the secretary of the Privy Council, Sir Julius Caesar (**73, 79, 80–81, 87, 88**). As a doctor, Halsey could go anywhere at any hour of the day or night and it is likely that he escorted priests, as Vaux's and Montague's servants certainly did.[45]

John Grove (1560–1616)

John Grove lived in St Mildred, Poultry, London, and at Pool Hall, Alveley, which is east of the Severn between Bridgnorth and Bewdley. His brass in Alveley Church records that he died on 11 December 1616 aged fifty-six, and that he was a freeman of the Grocers' Company. In his will, made the day before his death, he appointed 'my good friend Mr Humfrey Pakington' as one of his executors and left £40 to him and

---

[43] Berington 562 (7).
[44] C.D. Gilbert, 'John Halsey, Recusant Physician', *Midland Catholic History* 3 (1994), 4–7; 'The Official Lists of Catholic Prisoners during the Reign of Queen Elizabeth', II: '1581–1602', in *Miscellanea II*, CRS 2, pp. 223, 227, 229, 230; John Morris, ed., *The Troubles of our Catholic Forefathers*, II (London, 1875), 454. In the prison lists Halsey is three times described as of Tewkesbury, which is eight miles south-east of Little Malvern.
[45] Michael Hodgetts, 'The Owens of Oxford', *Recusant History* 24 (1998–9), 415–30, esp. 418–19.

£10 each to Humphrey's brother John and wife Abigail.[46] He then still owed the Crown £650 on behalf of John Halsey.[47] Thirty-six of his letters have survived, all but three of them written in 1605–8. Apart from the content, they are important for dating the whole series, as, unlike the other correspondents, he always included the year in the date. It is also worth adding that, in a letter to Anne Vaux written from the Tower on 3 March 1606, Garnet 'desyre[d] to know if the money be transported for my debts and what money Richard [Blount] hath of ye Society and of ye grocer's money [*sic*] and the hundreth pound that was given me of curtesy'.[48] Was 'ye grocer' John Grove?

Alderford Russell

Throughout his life Henry Russell remained in touch with his Oxford friends. After the death of Francis Willis in 1596, his widow, Catherine Willis, consulted him for advice on a possible second marriage, to Anthony Harford of Bosbury, five miles north-west of Little Malvern (**47–8**). Justinian Stubbs's references to 'my two chamber-fellows' suggest that he acted as tutor to Edmund and John, the two sons of Henry and Elizabeth Russell (**99, 100, 114, 118**), and in his will (**70**) Henry left some of his books to St John's, adding: 'If my poor ability would have extended further, I would have dealt with . . . that College and company . . . more liberally.' From 1602 his nephew Alderford, son of his brother Charles, was also at Oxford, though maybe not at St John's, and, as well as his battels (**61**), there is a letter of March 1603 from him to Henry Russell (**62**) asking 'how I should scape receiving the Communion now at Easter, since I did not take it at Christmas'. Subsequently there are references to unpaid tailors' bills, mounting debts and irresponsible management of the estate at Greenhill in Pembrokeshire that Alderford had inherited from his father (**70, 75, 77–8, 80, 82, 85, 88, 101**).[49] John

---

[46] *Index of Wills Proved in the Prerogative Court of Canterbury, V: 1605–1619*, comp. E. Stokes, Index Library 43 (London, 1912), 202 (6 Weldon).

[47] John J. LaRocca, ed., *Jacobean Recusant Rolls for Middlesex*, CRS 76 (London, 1997), 40–42, 111–12.

[48] Foley IV. 108 (SP 14/216/242). The John Grove who in 1585 resorted to the Cornish priest John Brushford in a village on Salisbury Plain near Amesbury is probably John Grove of Donhead St Andrew in Wiltshire. But the two families must have been connected, as the arms of the Groves of Alveley were *Ermine, on a chevron engrailed gules three escallops or*, and those of the Groves of Donhead differ only by having *one escallop or between two argent*. Foley III. 277–8; Anstruther, I. 56–7; Hugh Bowler, ed., *Recusant Roll no. 2, 1593–1594*, CRS 57 (London, 1965), pp. lxxxix–xciv, 185, 187; Sir Bernard Burke, *The General Armory of England, Scotland, Ireland and Wales*, new edn (London, 1884), 432.

[49] Charles had died in 1588, and his widow Eleanor had married a second husband, John Smythe of Ripple. On 1 April 1590 Smythe devised lands belonging to him and his wife to Henry Russell for Alderford's maintenance: Berington 285. See Aileen Hodgson, 'A Prodigal Son—Unreturned', *Worcestershire Recusant* 29 (June 1977), 15–23.

Grove complained that his good advice had been met with nothing but abuse (**87**): 'For me to accomplish your request will neither pleasure Mr Alderford Russell, nor stand with my safety, nor yet save him from ruining his estate.' John Pakington, Humphrey's brother, gave him a hawk, 'in hope it might have detained him from worse company' (**95**). In the end he was 'slain with Captain Baugh at the taking of a Frenchman',[50] perhaps, as Aileen Hodgson suggested, during Buckingham's expedition to La Rochelle in 1629.[51]

John Russell II (1594–1641)

Henry Russell II died on 4 March 1607/8, leaving two sons, John and Edmund, the elder of whom was only fourteen and therefore a ward of the Crown. Henry, who was fifty-three when John was born, had anticipated that he might not live to be seventy-four and had taken steps accordingly. On 27 October 1604, Humphrey Pakington informed his sister (**68**) that 'My Lord of Cranborne [Sir Robert Cecil, later earl of Salisbury] hath granted to my most honourable good lady the Countess of Derby that you shall have a wardship of your son if my brother Russell chance to die before he come of age and you live'—though 'my lord . . . passeth none absolutely before they fall'.[52] In 1609 the wardship was in fact granted to Thomas Marbury (1568–1636), of Marbury and Great Budworth, Cheshire,[53] and from then until John came of age in 1615 the payments were made both by him and by Elizabeth Russell. Marbury and Richard Cartwright, who often appears with him, seem to have been London scriveners who acted both for Humphrey Pakington and for the earl of Salisbury. Letters from Grove to Elizabeth Russell in the second half of 1608 show that it was he who made this arrangement (**101**, **105–8**), so that Marbury's connexion with the Russells is likely to have been only professional. These letters also show that Grove was obstructing a prosecution of Lady Russell of Strensham for recusancy,

[50] Quoted by Hodgson, 'A Prodigal Son—Unreturned', 22, from 'a scrap of paper (undated) in the Berington Collection', without a reference. The 'scrap' was probably in the Lechmere Box, but I have not found it.

[51] In March 1616 Captain Baugh was described as 'a pirate', in a note of payments made to him since December 1613 in part of a sum of £2,586 16s 8d: *CSPD James I, 1623–25, with Addenda, 1580–1625*, 581.

[52] In 1594 Lady Derby's brother-in-law William Stanley (1561–1642), later 6th earl of Derby, had married Elizabeth de Vere, daughter of Edward, 17th earl of Oxford, and of Salisbury's sister Anna Cecil. Both he and his brother, Lady Derby's first husband Ferdinando, the 5th earl, matriculated at St John's College, Oxford, in 1572: Cokayne, *Complete Peerage*, IV. 212–13.

[53] Birmingham Archdiocesan Archives, C.7; *Cheshire Visitation Pedigrees, 1663*, ed. Arthur Adams, Publications of the Harleian Society 93 (London, 1941), 76–7.

though her husband, Sir Thomas, the overseer of Shakespeare's will, was convicted in 1610.[54]

In 1615, shortly before John came of age, Elizabeth began negotiations through Justinian Stubbs for a match between him and one of the sisters of Benedict Hall of High Meadow, four miles south-east of Monmouth on the western side of the Forest of Dean (**118**). (It is not clear whether she was Cecily, who by 1623 had married Edward Morgan of Pencoyd, or Mary.)[55] But instead John made a runaway marriage with his cousin Mary Lutley, daughter of John Lutley of Broncroft Castle in Shropshire and of Mary Pakington, Elizabeth Russell's sister. Elizabeth was furious, and a tactful letter from her brother Humphrey (**123**) was needed before she would receive her daughter-in-law (and niece). It is likely that the Halls could offer better terms than the Lutleys, though we cannot be sure, as the marriage settlement has not survived, nor have any letters of Mary Lutley. In any case, as Humphrey wrote,

> If he had married to your desire and choosing, yet is it uncertain whether the effect thereof would have been more profitable or not, or better for your quietness, so inscrutable are the designments of Almighty God and so chargeable are the maintenances of gentlewomen that bring great portions.

The Lutleys were recusants, and two of Mary Lutley's brothers, Philip and Humphrey, later became priests.[56] Humphrey, who was named after his uncle Humphrey Pakington, was at Harvington Hall from some time in the 1630s until his death in 1653,[57] and he too occurs in the family correspondence (**165**).

Having married in haste, John Russell then had scruples about it, possibly from prudishness, possibly because of the impediment of consanguinity between two first cousins, or possibly because the couple had been married before the parson but not before a Catholic priest.[58] He also had scruples about his prayers and the time he ought to spend over them. Whatever the reasons, there is a forthright and practical letter from a priest who acted as his spiritual director (**127**). The signature has prudently been cut away, but the writer mentions three priests known to John Russell who would take the same view: 'Mr Clendock, your cousin, Mr Martyne . . . and Mr Walpole'. Clendock was probably

---

[54] *CSPD James I, 1603–10*, 593.
[55] *The Visitation of the County of Gloucester, 1623*, ed. Sir John Maclean and W.C. Heane, Harleian Society 21 (London, 1885), 73–4. The negotiations were with the girls' brother Benedict because their father, William, had died in February 1615/16 (ibid.).
[56] Anstruther, II. 205–6; *Visitation of Worcestershire, 1634*, 84–5; *The Visitation of Shropshire, taken in the year 1623*, ed. George Grazebrook and John Paul Rylands, Harleian Society 29–30 (London, 1889), II. 343–5. Mary Lutley's sister Magdalen married William Berington of Moat Hall, Shropshire, an ancestor of the present owner of Little Malvern.
[57] Hodgetts, 'The Yates of Harvington, 1631–1696', 158–60.
[58] Though see John Bossy, *The English Catholic Community* (1975), 132–42.

Morgan Clennock (1558–1620), who was ordained in Rome in 1582 and was in Wales from 1588 onwards. Walpole was probably Edward Walpole (1562–1637), who in 1621–2 was Jesuit superior in Worcestershire.[59] 'Mr Martyne' cannot be satisfactorily identified. Together with the *Manual* of 1614 from Little Malvern (now at Oscott), the letter gives a vivid glimpse of recusant devotional practice, on which Mrs Hodgson commented:

> So every night the prayers went up from the family gathered by candlelight in the attic chapel or by the glow of the fire in the great hall . . . [while] across the yard the tower of Little Malvern Priory stood silent against the night sky.[60]

There is also a letter, addressed to 'most loving and dear cousin John', from a priest in London, written on the day when he was to be banished, perhaps in 1618 (**130**). Again the signature has been cut away, but the writer may have been Ralph Stamford alias Palmer, who was in Staffordshire in 1610 and was ordered to be removed from the Clink on 5 June 1618 to go into exile with Gondomar.[61]

John Russell III was an able classical scholar. His neat account books served also as commonplace books with Latin and Greek quotations, and in the Collection there is a hilarious and ambiguous tribute to James I written in Latin hexameters and signed by him (**92**). While on the surface it is a conventional tribute to the king, Russell shows considerable skill in making his compliments double-edged; when, for instance, he says that 'no Scot' (*nemo Caledoniae*) would deplore the death of Elizabeth, or when he describes James himself as 'unique in form and more unique in deeds' (*egregius forma, magis egregius virtute*). Since a prose translation must lose much of the verve and bite of the original, I have put it into heroic couplets with as much of the mock solemnity of the Latin as I could.

There is also a long letter to an unnamed lady, discussing the merits of an author of Greek verses who had sent some of his work to Russell through Humphrey Lutley and whom he would like to meet (**132**). 'If he shall have occasion to come into this country and shall please to vouchsafe me that great favour as to see poor Little Malvern, he will find in my poor closet store of books not everywhere obvious.' Was 'your Ladyship' one of the daughters of Edward Somerset, fourth earl of Worcester? Justinian Stubbs, who had been with Henry Russell at Gloucester Hall,[62] seems now to have been practising as a physician, and his letters indicate

---

[59] Anstruther, I. 79–80; Thomas M. McCoog, *English and Welsh Jesuits, 1555–1650*, CRS 74–5 (London, 1994–5), II. 323.
[60] Hodgson, 'Story of Little Malvern', 82; J.D. Crichton, 'The *Manual* of 1614', *Recusant History* 17 (1984–5), 158–72.
[61] Anstruther I. 330–31.
[62] Stevenson and Salter, *St. John's*, 306.

not only that he was visiting Raglan Castle but also other connections with the earl's family (**100, 114, 119**). Among the houses that he mentions are those of Lady Petre, 'Mistress Cassey', 'Mistress Gootheridge', 'Mr Morgan of Llantarnam', 'my Lady Winter', 'Mr Crowper' and Benedict Hall's at High Meadow. Of these, Lady Petre, wife of William, second Lord Petre, was Lady Catherine Somerset; Edward Morgan of Llantarnam married Lady Frances Somerset; Lady Winter, wife of Sir Edward Winter of Lydney in Monmouthshire, was Lady Anne Somerset; and Benedict Hall married the Winters' daughter Anne.[63] The priceless collection of manuscripts at Raglan Castle made it almost a national library of Wales, and it would be a great attraction for a man with John Russell's scholarly tastes. His claim about his own books is borne out by the contents of the Little Malvern library, now at Birmingham University, and there are also letters (**153–4**) from the Worcestershire antiquary Thomas Habington and the Warwickshire antiquary Sir Simon Archer about a rent roll from the archives of Worcester Cathedral.[64]

Despite John Russell's early scruples over his marriage, he and Mary (Lutley) had three sons and six daughters: Thomas (I), John and Martin; Elizabeth, Mary, Anne, Helena, Margaret and Susan.[65] Martin (*c*.1633–1711) became a Dominican at Bornhem under Philip (Cardinal) Howard and later returned to work from Little Malvern;[66] Margaret (1638–1712) and Helena (1632–1700) were professed in 1657 as Dame Hilda and Dame Mildred at the English Benedictine convent at Brussels.[67] The contact with the Benedictines was probably through George Berington OSB, the 'Mr George Berington' of Walter Cowarne's letter of 1604, who was back in Herefordshire by 1626, when the Privy Council ordered the bishop of Hereford to make diligent search for him and the Jesuit Francis Hanmer (1593–1666); he died in Hereford at the age of eighty-eight in 1664.[68] His brother John Bernard Berington OSB (*c*.1574–1639), prior of St Edmund's in Paris and provincial in France for eighteen years,[69]

---

[63] Joseph Alfred Bradney, *A History of Monmouthshire*, II/1: *The Hundred of Raglan* (London, 1911), 26–7.

[64] For Archer, see Philip Styles, *Studies in Seventeenth Century West Midlands History* (Kineton, 1978), 1–41; for Habington, C.D. Gilbert, 'The Composition of Thomas Habington's Survey of Worcestershire', *Recusant History* 26 (2002–3), 415–25.

[65] *Visitation of Worcestershire, 1634*, 85.

[66] *Dominicana*, CRS 25 (London 1925), 173; see also pp. xxxiv–xxxvi below.

[67] 'The English Benedictine Nuns of Brussels and Winchester, 1598–1856', in *Miscellanea IX*, CRS 14 (London, 1914), 187. They were the first of twenty-two nuns from the related families of Russell, Berington and Monnington.

[68] Henson, *Registers of the English College at Valladolid*, CRS 30, p. 43; Justin McCann and Hugh Connolly, eds., *Memorials of Father Augustine Baker and Other Documents Relating to the English Benedictines*, CRS 33 (London, 1933), 195, 217–18; Foley, IV. 397–9.

[69] Henson, *Registers of the English College at Valladolid*, CRS 30, p. 21; McCann and Connolly, *Memorials of Father Augustine Baker*, CRS 33, pp. 195, 211, 218, 258.

had reconciled Walter Cowarne, and, like Cowarne, both Beringtons had studied at Valladolid.

Until 1632 there is no evidence that any of the Russells of Little Malvern had been prosecuted for recusancy. The enforcement of the fines in Worcestershire is something of a puzzle: although nearly two hundred men and women from the county are already recorded as convicted in the first Recusant Roll of 1592–3, none at all were presented at Quarter Sessions from 1591, when the surviving Rolls begin, until 1634, with one sole exception, Samuel Randoll of Martley in 1608.[70] The most likely guess is that they were presented at sessions of the Council of the Marches at Bewdley or Ludlow, though it is unclear now, and seems to have been unclear to the Privy Council then, what authority the Council had in religious causes.[71] Between 1595 and 1605 only three or four Worcestershire recusants in any one year paid anything at all that reached the Exchequer: John Talbot of Grafton the full £20 a month, Humphrey Pakington £26 13s 4d a year, and one or two others the odd pound here and there.[72] Under James I and Charles I the receiver of Recusants' Revenue at the Exchequer, Sir Henry Spiller of Eldersfield, five miles south of Little Malvern, was himself a Church Papist with a wife who was 'a great Papist and zealous to convert Protestants'. As early as 1606 information was laid against him 'touching his abuses of the business of the recusants', and in the Parliament of 1621 he was charged with misdemeanour for failing to collect the full fines.[73]

These charges are amply proved by letters in the Berington Collection. On 29 August 1632 Sir Henry Audley, one of Abigail Pakington's sons-in-law, was indicted in Middlesex as of 'Harrington in Chadgley Corbett' and St Giles-in-the-Fields.[74] On 20 February 1632/3 he was indicted there again, together with Abigail herself, her other son-in-law Sir John Yate, John Russell, John Weedon of Feckenham and Francis Hanford of Woollas Hall in Eckington on the slopes of Bredon Hill.

[70] Ronald Halstead, 'Worcestershire Recusants from the Quarter Sessions Papers', *Worcestershire Recusant* 1 [April 1963], 14–17; 2 [December 1963], 1–17; 3 (July 1964), 10–24.
[71] Penry Williams, *The Council in the Marches of Wales under Elizabeth I* (Cardiff, 1958), 87–99. The records of the Council have not survived. 'They were kept in a room at Ludlow Castle and they are not there now' (ibid., 362).
[72] Michael Hodgetts, 'Elizabethan Recusancy in Worcestershire, I', *Transactions of the Worcestershire Archaeological Society*, 3rd ser. 1 (1965–7), 69–78.
[73] Aileen M. Hodgson, 'Sir Henry Spiller of Eldersfield', *Worcestershire Recusant* 1 [April 1963], 25–9; Wallace Notestein, Frances Helen Relf and Hartley Simpson, eds., *Commons Debates, 1621* (New Haven, 1935), IV. 102–3; V. 410; Michael Questier, 'Sir Henry Spiller, Recusancy and the Efficiency of the Jacobean Exchequer', *Bulletin of the Institute of Historical Research* 66 (1993), 251–66.
[74] John Cordy Jeaffreson, ed., *Middlesex County Records, III: Temp. 1 Charles I to 18 Charles II* (London, 1888), 43. The Worcestershire entries from this book are summarised, not quite exactly, in J.W. Willis Bund, comp., *Calendar of the Quarter Sessions Papers, I: 1591–1643* (Worcs. Hist. Soc., 1899–1900), pt 2, pp. ccxv–ccxvi.

According to Abigail (**135**), the indictment was at the instigation of 'one Bee, sometimes the King's servant', but 'was prevented by way of the jury (although with some charge to us), which pleaded we stood already indicted and they had no reason to indict us again'. On the same day five Warwickshire recusants were indicted, all said to be of St Andrew's Holborn.[75] 'A friend of yours and mine', who must have been Spiller, spoke to the under-sheriff of Middlesex, who promised to obstruct further proceedings (**135**), and also advised Abigail and her sons-in-law 'to deal underhand with Bee his two creatures Avery and Hayton (by whom he first indicted us) to take them off'. On 29 August 1634, however, there was another indictment of six Worcestershire recusants as of St Giles-in-the-Fields: Russell, Weedon and Hanford as before; Francis Acton of Stoulton between Worcester and Pershore; Rowland Bartlett of Castlemorton; Francis Hanford; and John Hornyold of Hanley Castle.[76] Spiller happened to be in court, discussed the case with the Recorder, and on 10 September, after his return to Worcestershire, wrote to Russell from Eldersfield (**137**), informing him of the indictment and offering to come over to Little Malvern 'and second this testimony of my well wishes . . . by any further good office resting in my power'. He also enclosed a note quoting a pronouncement by James I and an order in Council against indicting recusants in places where they did not live (**138**). This formed the basis of a petition by the six to the King, arguing that since they lived 'near eighty miles from London' they did not come within the jurisdiction of the London and Middlesex sessions (**142**). In 1637 one Morris Hughes of Old Radnor gave a written undertaking to 'surcease his prosecution' against Russell and others on payment of £20 (**145**): he was presumably a professional informer. John Russell was only indicted once more, in London in April 1640, when he was one of nine recusants cited from Worcestershire and St Andrew's Holborn.[77] He died ten months later, in February 1641.

Thomas Russell I (c.1620–70)

The papers of his son Thomas Russell I are largely concerned with the impact of the Civil War on himself and on the county. 'The period from

---

[75] Jeaffreson, *Middlesex County Records*, III. 45; cf. 134. The Warwickshire recusants were Anthony Dormer of Budbrook (Grove Park), Richard Middlemore of Edgbaston, Thomas Morgan of Weston, Anthony Sheldon of [Temple] Grafton and Sir Charles Smith of Wootton Wawen.

[76] Jeaffreson, *Middlesex County Records*, III. 136–7; Aileen M. Hodgson, 'The Actons of Wolverton Hall', *Worcestershire Recusant* 37 (June 1981), 26–35; Philip Panter, 'The Manor of Wollashall', *Worcestershire Recusant* 6 (December 1965), 1–6; Michael Hodgetts, *Blackmore Park, 1596–1846–1996* (Upton-on-Severn, 1996).

[77] Jeaffreson, *Middlesex County Records*, III. 145.

1640 to the outbreak of the Civil War saw a very determined drive to convict recusants, and higher numbers were reached than at any other time.'[78] In Worcestershire, however, only thirty-five parishes sent in returns, and the one hundred and seventy recusants presented at the Quarter Sessions in April 1641 did not include either Thomas Russell, John Hornyold or Abigail Pakington.[79] Two months before that, on 26 February, Charles Wright, a Messenger of the Commons, and John Bailey, apparitor of the deanery of Powick, signed a certificate (151) that they had searched Little Malvern 'for Jesuits, Romish priests, all Massing stuff, Popish relics and warlike ammunition but did not find any such in the house'. This apparently unique document may have been worded by Russell himself and no doubt had to be paid for. Perhaps the most significant sentence is the last: 'that the said Thomas Russell is and will be ready at all times to attend the pleasure of the honourable House'. But once the war began, Worcestershire was held by the Royalists,[80] and until 1646 it was they who caused his financial troubles.

The king raised his standard at Nottingham Castle on 22 August 1642. A commission of array for Worcestershire had already been issued on 14 July to Lord Coventry, Sir Thomas Lyttelton and Sir William Russell (155). On 8 August the high constable wrote to the constables of Little Malvern and the neighbouring parishes of Welland, Holdfast, Berrow and Pendock, ordering them to summon the train bands of their constablewicks to muster on 12 August 'in the great meadow called Pitchcroft', which is now Worcester racecourse (155). The constable of Little Malvern, Peter Tiler, made a 'note of such money laid out by me . . . for and towards the setting forth of a soldier' (156). It gives a vivid picture of the materials and making of 'apparel' and knapsack; arms were provided by the Commissioners. In 1643, a list of eighty 'gentlemen that find horse' included Thomas Russell, Thomas Hornyold, Rowland Bartlett and Abigail Pakington.[81] On 18 December 1643 Russell was required by Sir Rowland Berkeley of Cotheridge, a Royalist officer and member of Parliament for the county, to send in 'a man and horse armed for present service in the war' (159).[82]

By October 1642 the Royalists had troops but not the means to maintain them. Instead they turned to looting, one of the first victims of

[78] John Bossy, *The English Catholic Community, 1570–1850* (New York, 1976), 187; *Diary of Henry Townshend of Elmley Lovett, 1640–1663*, ed. J.W. Willis Bund, 2 vols. in 4 (Worcs. Hist. Soc., 1915–20), I. 6; II. 22.
[79] Willis Bund, *Calendar of the Quarter Sessions Papers*, pt 2, 698–700.
[80] J.W. Willis Bund, *The Civil War in Worcestershire* (Birmingham, 1905); VCH *Worcs.*, II. 218–24; Malcolm Wanklyn and Frank Jones, *A Military History of the English Civil War, 1642–1646: Strategy and Tactics* (Harlow, 2005), 56–7, 63, 85, 117, 167–8, 179, 191, 223, 235, 241, 254.
[81] *Diary of Henry Townshend*, II. 77–8.
[82] For Sir Rowland's part in the Civil War, see VCH *Worcs.*, IV. 257.

which was Thomas Russell. A party led by Colonel Dud Dudley, the illegitimate son of Edward, Lord Dudley, raided Little Malvern and helped themselves to food, sheep and cattle, and furnishings that included a jack and a copy of Gerard's *Herbal*. A neighbour of Russell's bought the jack and the *Herbal* from a soldier and offered to sell them back for what he had paid (**157**). In February 1643/4 Prince Rupert issued a proclamation against looting and instead increased the levy on the county (**160**). He offered restitution to those who had already suffered, but there is no evidence that Russell ever received any. Quartermasters could also demand immediate provision of supplies in kind, and the Collection includes a warrant dated 6 March 1644/5 for four quarters of oats to be delivered upon sight of it to Captain Bruerton at the Talbot in Upton-upon-Severn. (**164**). It was addressed to the constable of Little Malvern, but the receipt is to Thomas Russell, who clearly had to find the provisions.[83]

The strategic importance of Worcestershire to the king was that it lay between Oxford, his headquarters, and Wales, the source of much of his manpower and money. The royal mint, first at Aberystwyth and then at Shrewsbury, was run by a Worcestershire recusant, Thomas Bushell of Cleeve Prior near Bidford-on-Avon.[84] The first engagement of the whole war was at the bridge across the Teme at Powick, three miles below Worcester, when Prince Rupert prevented Fiennes's horse from intercepting the royal plate, which was being escorted to Aberystwyth by a force under Lord Byron. If Fiennes had been successful, the Royalist cause might have foundered at the outset for lack of money. By 1646 the fifth earl, now the marquess, of Worcester at Raglan Castle had contributed nearly £1,000,000 to the king. Forges in Worcestershire turned out swords, pikes, cannon and shot; salt came from Droitwich, and charcoal and timber from the Forests of Feckenham, Wyre and Kinver. Meanwhile, the Roundheads held Gloucester to the south-west, Birmingham to the north-east and Warwick and Banbury Castles to the east. So garrisons had to be maintained at Dudley Castle, which lay between Birmingham and the great road to Lancashire; at Bewdley, Worcester and Upton to command the bridges over the Severn; and at Evesham, downstream from Warwick and Stratford, where the high road from Worcester to Oxford crossed the Avon. The cost to the county was £3,000, sometimes £4,000, a month, of which Russell had to find £3 14*s* 8*d*, making £44 16*s* a year (**163**). The capture of Evesham in May 1645 by Parliamentary troops from Gloucester and Warwick was followed during the campaigning season of 1646 by the capture of Dudley Castle, Hartlebury Castle, the 'Loyal City' of Worcester, and finally Raglan Castle.[85] Among those

---

[83] Berington 633.
[84] *ODNB* s.v. Bushell, Thomas.
[85] Willis Bund, *The Civil War in Worcestershire*, 4, 5, 65.

recorded at Worcester in July 1646 at the end of the three-month siege
was one 'Russell de Malvern'.[86] This may be Thomas, but it may also
be one of his brothers, either John or Martin, the future Dominican, who
had returned from school at Saint-Omer in 1644 and claimed himself
to have fought at the Battle of Worcester in September 1651, when he
was nineteen.[87] Many other boys had been sent home from Saint-Omer
when he was because of the College's mounting debts and the ravaging
of Flanders by the French, but some had left of their own accord to join
the Royalist armies.[88]

After the surrender of Worcester in 1646 and the sequestration of Delinquents' estates in the county, Thomas Russell was in serious financial
trouble for fourteen years. His estates were sequestrated on 24 March
1647 (**184**). From 1 November 1647, for £80 a year, he was allowed to
rent two-thirds of an estate valued at £141 a year (**169, 172**). In 1650 he
was informed that, although there would be no further charge for Delinquency, two-thirds of his estates were still to be sequestered for recusancy (**174**). He had an increasing family to support, and in the summer
of 1655 he also had to find dowries for his sisters Margaret and Helena
when they entered the convent at Brussels (**186**).[89] His papers show how
desperate he was for money (**170–71, 173, 177, 185**). Thomas Fletcher,
a recusant linen-draper of London, lent him £50 and sent him 'twelve
ells of dowlas for shirts, which I pray you will accept and wear for my
sake'.[90] In October 1653 an Act was passed that allowed recusants and
Delinquents to contract for their sequestered estates for life, though if
they failed to pay they would lose even the right to rent them.[91] On 19
January 1653/4 Thomas petitioned to be allowed so to contract (**180**).[92]
The payments continued at the rate of £70 a year until his final discharge
in 1660 (**189**).[93] In April 1658 he was summoned to appear at the Talbot
in Sidbury, Worcester, and pay off all his debts to the Protectorate (**188**).
His uncle Edmund (the younger son of Henry II and Elizabeth Pakington) had to walk to Hereford and back on a sore foot to make a similar appearance (**187**). Even after the Restoration, Thomas Russell was

---

[86] *Diary of Henry Townshend*, I. 195.
[87] C.F. Raymund Palmer, OP, *The Life of Philip Thomas Howard, O.P., Cardinal of Norfolk* (London, 1867), 191.
[88] Hubert Chadwick, *St Omers to Stonyhurst* (London, 1962), 163–4.
[89] The payments for the dowries were made through 'Mr Halsey the goldsmith' (**181**). Was he a connexion of John Halsey?
[90] Berington 633 (47).
[91] *Calendar of the Proceedings of the Committee for Compounding, &c., 1643–1660*, ed. M.A. Everett Green (London, 1889–92), I. 657.
[92] Abstract ibid., V. 3197.
[93] The last payment was for the half-year to 25 March 1660: he was discharged on 11 July. There are ten receipts from the Commonwealth in Berington 635, dating from 1651 to 1655.

required to pay a royal aid imposed by Charles II in 1667 (**194**), and he was also harassed by begging letters from his uncle, who by 1665 was in prison for debt (**193**).[94] But otherwise the last few years of his life were reasonably prosperous and peaceful. The last entry in his account book was made on 23 July 1670, shortly before his death.[95]

At the end of 1643, or early in 1644, he had married Joan Smith,[96] who was probably the daughter (or sister) of Francis Smith of Aston in Shropshire. The identification is not certain but there are three arguments in its favour. First, Aston is close to Broncroft Castle, the home of Thomas Russell's mother; secondly, the Smiths of Aston were recusants;[97] and thirdly, one of their sons was christened Francis, a name no Russell had borne before. The date of the marriage can be fixed by a letter to Thomas Russell dated 19 February 1643/4, which congratulates him and his 'new spouse' (**161**). Altogether the couple had three sons and five daughters: John IV (1647–1701), Thomas and Francis; Mary, Katherine, Milburgha, Anastasia and Anne. The first seven are named in an indenture made on 3 May 1683 by Thomas's widow Joan;[98] Anne had already died. Thomas (1655–1724) followed his uncle Martin to school at Saint-Omer (**192**), became a Jesuit and was later chaplain at Little Malvern.[99] Milburgha (1665–1730) was clothed as an Augustinian nun at Bruges in June 1687 and professed a year later.[100] Another of the nuns there was Mary (Xaveria) Berington (1626–1704), a widowed daughter of John Berington of Much Cowarne in Herefordshire and Priscilla Middlemore of Edgbaston.[101] Thomas Russell was succeeded by his eldest son, John IV, who in 1670 was twenty-three.

Martin Russell (1633–1711)

Thomas Russell's brother Martin, the Dominican, deserves a section of his own. In 1655 Philip Howard, later the cardinal, was trying to revive

---

[94] Edmund had married Elizabeth Mintridge of Sherridge in Lea, Worcestershire, and was living at Coddington, four miles north-west of Little Malvern and just into Herefordshire: *The Visitation of Herefordshire, 1634*, ed. Michael Powell Siddons, Harleian Society n.s. 15 (London, 2002), 45.

[95] Berington 381 (1).

[96] Nash, *Collections for the History of Worcestershire*, II. 141.

[97] Two-thirds of the estates of Francis Smith of Aston, Shropshire, were sequestrated for Popish recusancy on 24 March 1645/6: TNA:PRO, C.203/4. Francis and his wife Audrey were Papists in 1680: House of Lords Record Office, Papists in the County of Salop, 1680, 321 (c.59).

[98] Berington 115.

[99] Geoffrey Holt, *The English Jesuits, 1650–1829*, CRS 70 (London, 1984), 216. See also p. xxxviii below.

[100] Bruges Convent Archives, I Annals, 145. To be published in Pascal Majérus, ed., *Windesheim Annals*, CRS 84 (Woodbridge, forthcoming).

[101] Ibid., 134, 142, 222.

the English Dominican province and found an English house in Flanders. He came to England, where he consulted the vicar general of the English Dominicans, Fr Thomas Catchmay, and David Kerrys, who was confessor to his mother, the countess of Arundel. Catchmay in turn spoke to a secular priest, David Morris, who in 1655 or 1656 went down to Little Malvern and met Martin Russell, who was then thinking of becoming a Jesuit. The two travelled back to London, where they met Howard, who in May 1656 sent Russell to the Dominican house at Ghent. He entered on 18 June and was professed a year later, on 18 June 1657, for the province of England and the convent of London. In April 1658 Howard established the house at Bornhem, with Russell as his first subject. Russell was ordained there in September 1658 and in 1659 he went to Brussels to study philosophy. In 1660, he was sent by Howard to Rome on a mission to the master general, after which he studied theology at Milan and then taught philosophy at Rimini until 1664. In 1665 he was sent to Tangier, where, after the marriage of Catherine of Braganza to Charles II, Portuguese Dominicans were to be replaced by English ones to serve the (mostly Irish) Catholic soldiers in the garrison. In fact, Russell, though dignified with the title of Prior, was alone there. In 1667 he converted two Protestant soldiers who had been sentenced to death, and the governor was so enraged that he had to leave. He crossed to Malaga and came on to London to see Howard, who appointed him prior of Bornhem. He arrived there on 26 November 1667, but during the voyage he had contracted a fever that left him permanently debilitated. In 1670 Joan Russell pressed him to return to Little Malvern to help with the administration of his brother's estate, and Howard released him to do so.

He seems to have remained there until the outbreak of the Oates Plot in 1678, when he returned to Bornhem. In August 1680, however, he came back to England and resumed work in the Welsh Marches. After the Revolution, on Christmas Eve 1690, he was arrested and imprisoned in Hereford gaol. At the Quarter Sessions in March 1690/1 he was brought before Bishop Herbert Croft (1614–91) of Hereford. Croft was the younger son of Sir Herbert Croft of Croft Castle in Herefordshire, who had become a Catholic and lived with the English Benedictines at Douai until his death in 1622. The Bishop himself had been a student at the English College in Rome and is the only Anglican bishop that it has ever produced. So, when asked, 'You were educated beyond seas, were you not?', Russell retorted, 'I hope, my Lord, that is no crime. You were so, too.' A true bill was found against him, but at the Assizes the Herefordshire gentry packed the jury and prevented witnesses from appearing. He was acquitted and continued to work for another twenty years, until his death on 8 September 1711 at the house of the Pickerings of Stanton Lacy, three miles north of Ludlow. He was buried in the parish church there with a ledger-stone inscribed 'D. Martinus Russel O.P. RIP'.[102]

The Berington Collection contains a landing permit for Martin Russell issued at Dover on 12 June 1655 (**182**), two letters to Thomas Russell about him of 1653 and 1655 (**181, 183**), another letter to Thomas Russell from Howard, dated from Arundel House on 22 September 1660 (**190**), and a mention in the accounts of John Russell IV for 1694 of payments to his 'uncle Martin' (**197**). The reference in the last of these to 'the charity moneys which I receive yearly from my brother[-in-law] Greenwood' suggests that by then the family had set up a regular fund for his support.

John Russell IV (1647–1701)

The most interesting document from the 1670s is a letter written to Thomas Russell's widow Joan by the martyr Blessed Anthony Turner, who was then superior of the Jesuit Residence of St George (Worcestershire and Warwickshire) (**195**). It is dated 17 March 1672/3, just after the passing of the Test Act, and was written from Gubbershill, a timber-framed house at Ripple near Tewkesbury, which belonged to the recusant Reeds and was used by the Worcestershire Jesuits. A list of stuff belonging to them in 1687 includes 'two trunks of books at Gubbershill'.[103] Although the letter is merely a brief note about a horse which he had borrowed to ride to Worcester, with a couple of sentences about the proclamation banishing priests, it shows that Turner was on close terms with the Russells. In a postscript he adds, 'Mrs Brent presents her services, and I desire mine may be presented to your good company.' The Brents lived at Lark Stoke, seven miles south of Stratford-upon-Avon: the connexion was that Catherine Brent married Thomas Bartlett of Hill End.[104] An item in Turner's account book shows that the Russells had contacts with the Worcestershire Jesuits at least forty years before:[105]

> John Russell of Malvern and Edmund Russell of Coddington, by bond dated 1 of November 1639 owe to Mr Brookes of Grafton and Mr Browne of Col-

---

[102] Palmer, *Life of Philip Thomas Howard*, 96–7, 105, 118, 135, 142, 146, 190–92. Berington 642 is a transcript of these passages by Edmund Bishop. See also Aileen Hodgson, 'A Worcestershire Dominican', *Worcestershire Recusant* 32 (December 1978), 24–9.

[103] Foley, IV. 282; V. 868. Richard Reed of Gubbershill contracted for two-thirds of his sequestrated estate on 17 January 1654/5: *Calendar of Committee for Compounding*, IV. 2708. For the house, David Verey, *The Buildings of England: Gloucestershire*, II: *The Vale and the Forest of Dean* (Harmondsworth, 1970), 393.

[104] Mrs Bryan [Mary Helen Alicia] Stapleton, *A History of the Post-Reformation Catholic Missions in Oxfordshire* (London, 1906), 45–9.

[105] Aileen M. Hodgson, 'A Jesuit Account Book', *Worcestershire Recusant* 4 (December 1964), 19–33; the quoted entry is on p. 23.

ton £100 payable after the decease of Henry Barnesley of Barnesley Hall. Sealed and delivered in the presence of

Thomas Russell	John Russell
mark of Elizabeth Russell	Edmund Russell
Mary Russell her mark	

When the Oates Plot broke in 1678, Turner went up to London, where his brother Edward, also a Jesuit, was in prison. But he was unable to reach him or to find friends who would harbour him. In the end he surrendered to a justice, perhaps hoping that by confessing his priesthood he might escape implication in the plot. He and four others were condemned in the trial of the Five Jesuits before Chief Justice Scroggs and executed at Tyburn on 30 June 1679.[106] His brother died in the Gatehouse in 1681. Other victims of the plot included St John Wall, who had worked in Warwickshire, Worcestershire and Staffordshire, and St John Kemble, who had worked in Herefordshire. Both were executed on the same day, 22 August 1679, Wall at Worcester and Kemble at Hereford. On 26 November 1678 one of Thomas Hornyold's servants, Thomas Palin, was arrested at Pixham Ferry, four miles downstream from Worcester, on the way back from escorting a priest named Henry Barnesley across the Severn to Cookhill, near Alcester and Coughton Court. Barnesley himself was arrested later and imprisoned first at Warwick and then in London. What happened to him after that is unknown, but he was seventy-four at the time of his arrest and may not have survived his imprisonment. He was one of the Barnesleys of Barnesley Hall near Bromsgrove and almost certainly the Henry Barnesley of Turner's notebook; Brookes and Brown were Jesuits. Palin admitted that Barnesley had been 'three or four days' at Blackmore Park, and he may have served regularly there and at Little Malvern, though of this there is no proof.[107]

So far as is known, John Russell IV did not marry until 1683, when he was thirty-six. But in 1676 he was 'infirm in body' and had to make provision for the estates and for his unmarried sisters in case he died. The will he made on 16 July that year (**196**) is very badly damaged, but enough is legible for his dilemma to be plain. The heir was his brother Thomas, born in 1655, who had been educated at Saint-Omer from about 1665 onwards (**192**) and now intended to become a Jesuit but might not persevere. John therefore bequeathed the estate to him, 'provided that he the said Thomas shall reside in England and live a secular life'. If Thomas 'disposed of himself to the service of the Church' or died beyond

---

[106] Foley, V. 44–60; cf. John Warner, *The History of English Persecution of Catholics and the Presbyterian Plot*, ed. T.A. Birrell, trans. John Bligh, CRS 47–8 (London, 1953), I. 109–12.
[107] C.D. Gilbert, 'Worcestershire and the Popish Plot, II', *Worcestershire Recusant* 48 (December 1986), 31–4; Anstruther, II. 17.

the seas before returning to England as a layman, the estates were to go to the third brother, Francis, who was still a minor. Thomas did in fact enter the Society two months later and was at Watten until 1678 and then at Liège until 1684 for his philosophy and theology. He was ordained in 1685 and sent to England in 1686. For most of his ministry he was in the Residence of St George (Worcestershire and Warwickshire) or in the College of St Francis Xavier (Herefordshire and South Wales), and he is recorded as being at Little Malvern about 1703 and in 1711, 1715 and 1724, the year when he probably died.[108]

These dates fall during the ownership of his nephew John V, not of his brother John IV. It is, however, possible to identify two of the priests who were at Little Malvern during the 1690s. One was Ralph Clayton (*c*.1663–1743), who according to a Chapter list of 1692 'lives sometimes with Mr John Russell of Little Malvern and sometimes with Mr Bartlett of Hill End'.[109] The other was Miles Davies alias Blount and Pollet (b. 1662), who was ordained in Rome in April 1688 and left for England that October. In 1705 he made a formal recantation in an eighteen-page sermon (**199**), which lists some of the houses where he had served, including Hill End, Little Malvern and Blackmore Park. Anstruther comments tartly, 'Judged by his sermon, he was no great loss.'[110]

The wife whom John IV married in 1683 was Elizabeth Greenwood (d. 1729) of Brize Norton in Oxfordshire.[111] They had five children: John V (1689–1734), Thomas II (1693–1737), Mary, George (b. 1694) and Elizabeth. John IV died in 1701 and was buried in the chancel of the Priory church with an inscription which concludes: 'Upon whose soul, sweet Jesus, have mercy'. He was the only Russell to be interred there, his burial is the first entry in the surviving parish registers, and with him there began the regular keeping of the Little Malvern Obits.[112] These form a valuable supplement to the registers from now until 1783, when the Catholic registers begin.[113]

---

[108] Holt, *English Jesuits*, CRS 70, p. 216.
[109] Raymund Stanfield, 'Particulars of Priests in England and Wales, 1692', in *Miscellanea VII*, CRS 9 (London, 1911), 113; Anstruther, III. 35–6.
[110] Anstruther, III. 47 and sources quoted; Myles Davies, *The Recantation of Mr. Pollet, a Roman Priest* (London, 1705). There is a copy of the latter in the British Library (1417 f. 50).
[111] *The Visitations of the County of Oxford taken in the years 1566, 1574, and in 1634*, ed. William Henry Turner, Harleian Society 5 (London, 1871), 256. The marriage settlement (4 May 1683) is Berington 625. For the recusancy of the Greenwoods, see Stapleton, *Post-Reformation Catholic Missions in Oxfordshire*, 168–70; Alan Davidson, 'Roman Catholicism in Oxfordshire, 1580–1640' (PhD thesis, University of Bristol, 1970), 199–202; there are copies of this in Bristol University Library and in the Bodleian (MS Top. Oxon. d.602).
[112] Berington 537.
[113] *Catholic Registers of Little Malvern in the County of Worcestershire*, ed. Mary Henderson and Lillian Lascelles (Malvern, 1975). These cover baptisms from 1783 to 1864,

John Russell V (1689–1734)

John Russell V was only twelve when his father died and did not come of age until 1710. On 15 August 1715 he and sixty-one other papists from the Middle and Lower Divisions of Oswaldslow Hundred were summoned to appear at the Talbot in Sidbury, Worcester, to take the Oaths of Allegiance and Supremacy and subscribe to the Declaration against Transubstantiation. Only seven appeared in person, of whom Russell was not one. Of those who did appear, only one took the Oath of Allegiance, and he refused the Oath of Supremacy and the Declaration.[114] How far the Russells were Jacobites as well as Royalists is uncertain. There are three interesting Stuart relics at the Court: a travelling trunk that belonged to Catherine of Braganza; a supposed portrait of James II; and a rosary given to Winifred Berington by her brother (or uncle) Bishop Hornyold, who assured her that it had belonged to Mary Queen of Scots.[115] But the trunk came into the family by marriage in 1796, and the identification of the portrait is doubtful. There is, however, an unsigned and undated Jacobite poem in the Collection, which is worth including for its heartfelt sentiments, if not as English literature (**200**).

Also in 1715 John Russell registered his estates in accordance with the Act of 1 George I. They consisted of Coddington in Herefordshire, worth £55 and charged with £1,000 for his sisters Elizabeth and Mary; an estate at Solihull worth £39 8*s* 4*d* and charged with an annuity of £30 for his brother Thomas under their father's will of 4 April 1701; and Little Malvern itself, worth £253 14*s* 2*d*, subject to an annuity to his mother of £50. He added, 'I maintain all the poor in the parish and the repairs of both church and chapel.' The gross income of his three estates was therefore just under £350, but with substantial obligations. His widowed mother registered an estate at Little Malvern worth £82 out of that of her son John.[116] These figures can be confirmed and filled out from the estate papers. In 1694 his father had calculated his rents as £241 12*s* 4*d* from Little Malvern and the adjacent properties, £55 from Coddington and £39 2*s* 4*d* from Solihull: altogether £335 14*s* 8*d*. Out of that he paid

---

confirmations from 1823 to 1857 and burials from 1826 to 1875. New registers were begun when the Catholic church of St Wulstan was built in 1862.

[114] W.E. English, 'Worcestershire Nonjurors in 1715', *Midland Catholic History* 4 (1995), 23–38. The entry for John Russell is on p. 24.

[115] The attestation, signed by Winifred Berington, is kept with the rosary. Winifred Hornyold married John Berington in 1734 and died in 1791, though, since there is no date, the signatory may be their daughter, also Winifred, who died unmarried in 1826 and was buried in Chapter House Yard, Hereford.

[116] Edgar E. Estcourt and John Orlebar Payne, eds., *The English Catholic Nonjurors of 1715* (1886), 80, 271, 276, 289, 291. On p. 276 Estcourt and Payne identify Thomas as 'probably' the Jesuit, who was in fact the uncle of John V and this Thomas.

£1 4*s* to the Crown, £7 to the parson, £1 10*s* to the constable and half the churchwardens' charges, usually about £2 (**197**). In 1708 John V's mother noted in the same book that the estate 'in all' was worth £350 a year, of which £213 came from Little Malvern, £40 from Castlemorton, £40 from Solihull and £55 from Coddington.

These accounts show that the shape of the estate had changed greatly since the grant of the Priory to the Russells a century and a half before. The core of it was still Little Malvern and the neighbourhood. But the lands at Coddington had been bought by Henry Russell II, while the letters patent of 1554 list much that had passed out of the Russells' possession by 1708: lands at Stokesay and Newton in Shropshire formerly owned by Haughmond Abbey; lands at Hailes, Little Wormington and Winchcombe in Gloucestershire formerly owned by Hailes Abbey; land at Wedmore in Somerset formerly owned by the executed duke of Somerset; and a lease of the manor of East Greenwich in Kent.[117] These may have been sold by Thomas Russell I in the 1650s, but further research would be needed to prove it.

Thomas Russell II (1693–1737) and the Beringtons

In 1720 John V married his first cousin Mary Greenwood, his mother's niece. They had no children, and on his death in 1734 Little Malvern passed to his brother Thomas II, who did not marry and is represented in the Collection only by some entries and astronomical calculations in account books. The third brother, George, born in 1694, had died before 1733, as he is not mentioned in John's will. So on the death of Thomas II the heiress was Elizabeth Berington (1685–1744), the elder of their two sisters. By 1715 she had married Thomas Berington (d. 1743), the third son of John Berington of Winsley House, Hope-under-Dinmore, eight miles north of Hereford, and of Elizabeth, daughter of Sir Thomas Wolrych of Dudmaston Hall in Shropshire. At the time of their succession they were living at Much Cowarne, eight miles north-east of Hereford, where in 1715 Thomas had registered an estate worth £278 5*s* 8*d*.[118] There was another family of Beringtons at Moat Hall, Pontesbury, eight miles south-west of Shrewsbury. Both had been recusant since the sixteenth century. Until 1768 the Beringtons of Moat Hall also owned Berington House in St Alkmund's Square in Shrewsbury itself, where Mass was said for the Catholics of the county town.[119] Apart from the two Benedictines mentioned above, the two branches had already produced a Jesuit,

---

[117] Berington 83.
[118] Estcourt and Payne, *English Catholic Nonjurors*, 81.
[119] Peter Phillips, 'A Catholic Community: Shrewsbury, I: 1750–1850', *Recusant History* 20 (1990–91), 239–61.

John Berington (1673–1743), and two Chaptermen, Thomas Berington (1673–1755) and his cousin Simon Berington alias Wolrych (1680–1755), who was Elizabeth's brother.[120] In the course of the eighteenth century they produced three more priests: another Thomas (1740–1805); his brother Charles (1748–1798), who in 1786 became vicar apostolic of the Midlands; and Joseph (1743–1827), the Cisalpine historian and controversialist, whose mother was Winifred Hornyold of Blackmore Park. George Slaughter, who taught at Lisbon from 1689 until his death in 1741, was a cousin through his mother, Winifred Berington of Winsley.[121]

The only surviving child of Thomas and Elizabeth Berington of Little Malvern was a daughter, another Elizabeth (1715–89). In 1749, after the deaths of both her parents, she married Thomas Williams (d. 1766), a Catholic druggist with business interests in London and estates and lead-mines in Flintshire. It was their only daughter Mary (1749–1828) who in 1791 converted the lower half of the Prior's Hall into a Georgian chapel. The Beringtons and Williamses had many cousins, sisters and aunts in religious houses on the Continent, and the Collection contains a fascinating correspondence with them, especially at the time of the French Revolution. In 1796 Mary Williams married Walter Wakeman, a widowed physician of Tewkesbury, who died only four years later. On her death in 1828 she left land near by to Downside Priory as the site for a future church. Little Malvern passed to William Berington I (1794–1847), who was a distant cousin of Mrs Wakeman and a nephew of the Rev. Joseph Berington. In the following year, at Bath, he married Mary Frances Brun (1796–1866): Mrs Alexandra Berington, who now lives at Little Malvern Court, is the widow of their great-great-great-grandson.

---

[120] Anstruther, I. 34; II. 12–13; Henry Norbert Birt, *Obit Book of the English Benedictines from 1600 to 1912* (Edinburgh, 1913), 20, 42; Holt, *English Jesuits*, CRS 70, p. 31.
[121] Anstruther, III. 12–13, 204; IV. 28–30.

EDITORIAL PROCEDURES

The Little Malvern papers were first sorted and labelled in the winter of 1865–6 by Daniel Parsons of Oriel College, Oxford.[1] They were already in poor condition, as he later recorded:

> Some of the documents were in a state of such advanced decay as to make complete reading of them most difficult or impossible. As I examined paper after paper, the room in which I sat became powdered with small fragments of yellow dust. These fragments and dust were the signs of injuries, in many cases irreparable. . . . The collection is not only extremely valuable as it stands but it represents a collection at one time much larger. It is known that during the present century a large number of documents have been intentionally destroyed, probably in entire ignorance of their value. Nothing is now known about them.

In 1871 a description of the Collection (Appendix II below) was published in the Second Report of the Historical Manuscripts Commission, pp. 72–3. It was, as Parsons complained, based 'upon the documents so arranged by me in 1865–6' but was not made by him, as he was in Germany in May 1869, when he received a circular from the Commission.[2] Instead it was made by Mr Joseph Stevenson, subsequently a distinguished Jesuit, who described the Collection as 'too extensive to be exhausted in the course of a single visit' and intended to make 'a more systematic investigation at some future period'. If he did, the results were never published by the Commission. In 1947 Mr W.J.C. Berington (1904–1957) deposited the Collection at Worcestershire Record Office, where it was excellently calendared by Miss Margaret Henderson with the class no. BA 81, 705:24. The 154 documents in this volume headed 'Berington' and followed by a number are from this series.

'Lechmere Box' / 'Lechmere f.899:169'

In 1846, however, about three hundred items had been borrowed by Sir Edmund Lechmere of Severn End near Upton-on-Severn, who intended to write a history of Little Malvern. But when he died in 1894, he had still not finished it or returned the borrowed papers. The Lechmere MSS are now also in Worcestershire Record Office, where those originally

---

[1] Daniel Parsons, *A Notice of the Little Malvern Collection of Manuscripts* (Oxford, 1876); also in his posthumous *Little Malvern Priory and House* (London, 1888). Fuller details of the deplorable state of the MSS are in a letter from Parsons published in the *Worcester Herald* of 9 September 1871, a copy of which is in Lechmere Box, Folder 22 ('Russell MSS—D').

[2] Parsons, letter in *Worcester Herald*.

from Little Malvern are in a box numbered BA 1546, 899:169. The nineteen documents in the text headed 'Lechmere Box' are from this series. When they came into the Record Office they were roughly divided into eight groups (i–viii), only one of which had any logic: (vi), which is a set of pen-and-ink drawings of Hanley Castle and Little Malvern. I have begun to sort them into folders in accordance with the numbering in a pink-covered notebook compiled by Sir Edmund and now kept in the same box. This contains notes on Bishop Alcock, a rather flowery description of Little Malvern and lists of 143 of the documents as (in that order) A.1–30; E.1–13; B.1–47, 73–77 (48–72 being numbered blank spaces); and C.1–48. Although most of the documents have numbers gummed on to the back, none have letters; many have numbers but are not listed, and some that are listed have not yet been found in the box. Moreover, the numbers on the back do not always agree with those in the notebook. To ease the work of future researchers, I have put items which are printed here but have no reference in the notebook into a separate folder labelled 'Items Included' (in this volume). In 1993, thirteen of the most fragile papers from the Lechmere Box were guarded and bound in a green binder with the class-no. BA 1546, f.899:169 (where 'f' stands for 'flat binder'). Nine of them are included here with the reference 'Lechmere f.899:169'.

William Berington and Aileen Hodgson

This volume has a long history of its own, having already outlived two editors. It was begun by Mr W.J.C. Berington about 1947 on his return from war service in the Army Intelligence Corps. But in 1957 he died suddenly of a heart attack while in London. By his will, made in 1955, he bequeathed his collectanea

> to the rector at the time of my death of Oscott College, Sutton Coldfield, near Birmingham, as a contribution to the history of various Catholic families in Worcestershire and the neighbouring counties. If for any reason the Rector is unable to accept the papers, then it is my desire that they should be added to the Berington Collection aforesaid. And I request the Rector to consult as to the desirability of completing the work and publishing the whole or part thereof.

Mr Berington had chosen Oscott College because many of the Midland District papers were then kept there. About the time of his death, however, Archbishop Francis Grimshaw of Birmingham appointed the first archdiocesan archivist, Fr J. Denis McEvilly, and later he had these papers moved to Cathedral House as part of a properly organised Birmingham Archdiocesan Archives.[3] Among the volunteers who were

---

[3] J. Denis McEvilly, 'Birmingham Diocesan Archives', *Catholic Archives* 1 (1981), 26–31.

helping with the necessary listings was Mrs Aileen Hodgson, who lived at West Malvern, only three miles from Little Malvern Court. She was therefore asked to collate Mr Berington's papers and complete his book. This was an excellent choice, as she had a wide and detailed knowledge of Worcestershire recusancy and was for many years secretary of Worcestershire Catholic History Society and a frequent contributor to its journal, *Worcestershire Recusant*. With this she combined an interest in art and architecture, which went back to her days as an actress at the Birmingham Repertory Theatre under Sir Barry Jackson.

By 1962 she had produced about 78,000 words of typescript covering the eight hundred years from the founding of the Priory to the centenary of St Wulstan's, which was celebrated that year. She had, however, unwisely been persuaded by a fellow member of the Malvern Writers' Circle that, in order to sell, the book should include much general history and speculation about the unrecorded thoughts and feelings of the characters in the story, especially the women. These additions doubled the length and therefore the cost of the book, the full text of which remains unpublished, though bound sets of the typescript are now at Little Malvern Court and in the possession of her nephew Fr Dominic Round. (There was a third set, dog-eared and sometimes torn, which I have used as a rough working copy.)[4] About 1970 Mrs Hodgson began to explore the alternative format of a volume of documents to be published by the Catholic Record Society. But the then editor, Mr Antony Allison, was unwilling to accept it, partly because of its length (600 pages of quarto typescript at a time when the Society was very short of money), and partly because much further editorial work was needed before it could go to the printer. So in 1981, when I became editor of *Worcestershire Recusant* on the death of Fr McEvilly, I commissioned Mrs Hodgson to put the gist of her narrative into a series of eight articles, which duly appeared between no. 38 (December 1981) and no. 46 (December 1985).

There were therefore three versions of her work on the Collection: the 'Story of Little Malvern' (1958–62);[5] the projected records volume (1970–72); and the articles in *Worcestershire Recusant* (1981–5). The 'Story' and the articles ended at 1962 (the centenary of the church); the volume of documents at 1828. The period down to 1737 was covered by 120 pages out of 300 of the 'Story' (about 31,000 words out of 78,000), by 350 pages out of 600 of the records volume (text and introductions) and by five of the eight articles. But there was much common material,

---

[4] There were occasional minor differences of wording in the typescript of the three copies, and all had MS corrections and interlinings. None of these were historically significant.

[5] The title was never finally settled: the subtitle was 'The Story of Little Malvern Court', which is how she cited it herself in Hodgson, 'A Jesuit Account Book', 31 (Introduction, n. 105); but in the typescript the main title, originally 'Brave Heritage', was amended in her handwriting to 'The Castell under the Hill' or 'The Book of Little Malvern'.

as the 'Story' and the articles contained substantial quotations, while the articles and the introductions to the documents were cut-down versions of the 'Story'.

The present book

After Mrs Hodgson's death in 1997, Fr Round asked me to sort and edit her papers. This was a long job, as there was much extraneous material, only one set of the 600 pages was numbered, nearly seventy pages of it were missing altogether, and there were up to four unpaginated carbon copies or redrafts of others. The notes were not attached to the documents to which they referred but were in separate groups, which were not included in the pagination. There were also miscellaneous jottings, transcripts, pedigrees and correspondence, together with typescript and published versions of *Catholic Registers of Little Malvern* (ed. Mary Henderson and Lilian Lascelles, Worcestershire Catholic History Society, 1975) and an annotated list of the portraits and a record of the condition of the Court about 1955, both by Mr W.J.C. Berington. Her papers did not, however, include Berington's Collectanea, nor are these now in Birmingham Archdiocesan Archives. She says explicitly that they were moved there,[6] and both in the 'Story' and in *Worcestershire Recusant* she sometimes quoted from specific notes ('WJCB') and transcripts.[7] At the beginning of the 'Story' she added that Berington had also dealt with other recusant families, 'much more thoroughly than I have been able to within the scope of this book', and that 'his full notes will be calendared and preserved in typescript for any research student who wishes to use them'.[8] But this latter project seems never to have been put into effect, and there is no record of what became of his manuscripts.

When the sorting was complete, an attempt was made to scan as much of the text as corresponds to this volume. This turned out to be impossible, even after it had been photocopied to convert quarto to A4 and to enhance the often faint typescript, so that I have had to retype it all. Aileen Hodgson's selection included 145 documents from this period. I have omitted eleven of these (some of which have been printed elsewhere) and added sixty-six (of which about thirty relate to John Russell I and about twenty to Humphrey Pakington) to make the round two hundred. Apart from the 182 Berington and Berington/Lechmere items, there are fourteen from other sources and four (**24**, **124**, **163**, **196**) that I have printed from Aileen Hodgson's transcripts as I have not been able

---

[6] Hodgson, 'A History of Little Malvern Court: I', *Worcestershire Recusant* 38 (December 1981), 4–5.
[7] Hodgson, 'A History of Little Malvern Court: I', 14; 'A History . . . : II', 13–14 n. 19; 'History of Little Malvern Court IV', *Worcestershire Recusant* 41 (June 1983), 35.
[8] Hodgson, 'Story of Little Malvern', 3.

to trace the original MSS. She had arranged the documents in groups corresponding to their reference numbers in the Record Office; I have rearranged them as far as possible in chronological order, though the dates of some remain conjectural. Where there was any doubt, her transcripts have been checked against the originals. She had kept the original spelling: modern spelling has been used here, except for surnames, to compensate for the frequent damage to the MSS and the obscure nature of some of the subject matter. Doubtful words are in italics followed by a question mark in square brackets. Conjectural restorations where the MS is torn are in italics within square brackets; where no plausible restoration is possible, the gap is marked by three points. Punctuation is editorial; in particular, to save space the openings of letters have been run into the first line and their endings and signatures into the last line, whether they are so in the MS or not. Exceptions to these procedures have been made in nos. **170** and **196**, where, because of very extensive damage to the MSS, the original spelling and in **170** also the original lineation have been reproduced, so that readers can judge for themselves how plausible my restorations are. Addresses and endorsements are normally included only where they add information not in the body of the letter. Every effort has been made to trace copyright.

The introductions to this volume and its sequel (1737–1862) have drawn on all three of Aileen Hodgson's versions and contain all matters of substance in them, either explicitly or by means of the necessary references. They have, however, been completely rewritten and brought up to date, and I alone am responsible for their wording and order, for various additions, and for any errors. Three of the supplementary papers appear as Appendices I–III. The remainder, the miscellaneous unused notes and the substance of the material after 1862 have also been transcribed on to computer: after editing, bound hard copy will be deposited at the Archdiocesan Archives. In this way, Mr Berington's original intention will be fulfilled, if belatedly and not in the form that he had in mind.

Finally, thanks to others who have helped in the making of this book: Mrs Alexandra Berington and Sir Nicholas Lechmere, Bt; Robin Whittaker and his staff at the Worcestershire Record Office; the staff on the sixth floor of Birmingham Central Library, where most of the annotating has been done; and my colleagues on the Council of the Catholic Record Society, especially Philip Harris, my predecessor, and Peter Doyle, my successor as editor of the series of Records and Monographs in which the volume now takes its place.

Michael Hodgetts

RUSSELL OF LITTLE MALVERN 1538 -1641

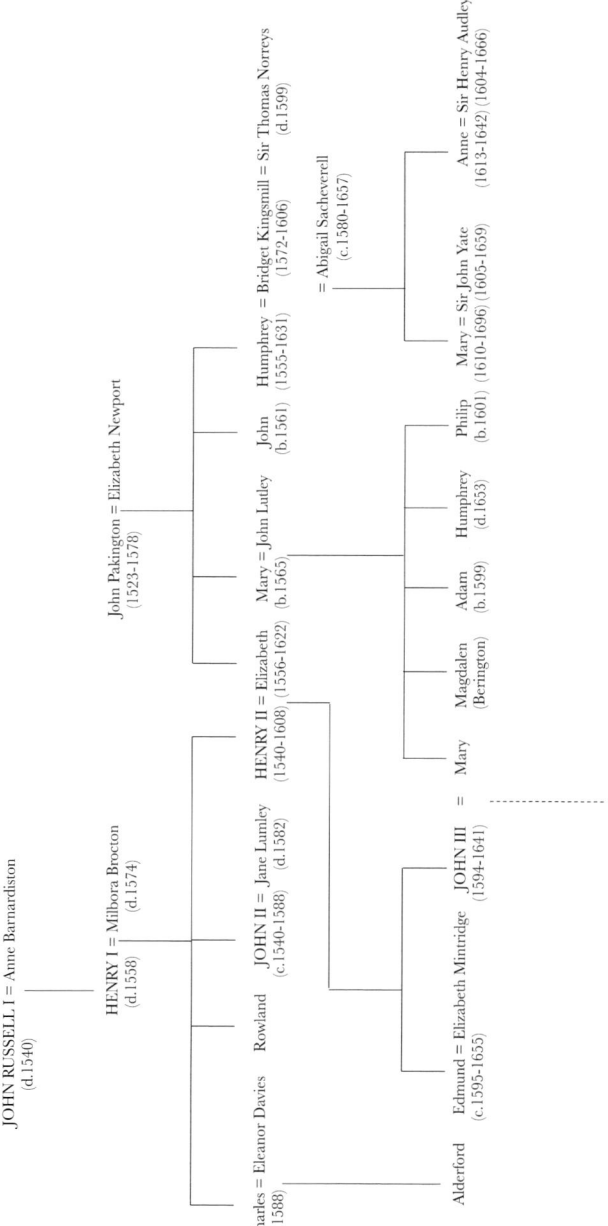

JOHN RUSSELL I = Anne Barnardiston
(d.1540)

HENRY I = Milbora Brocton
(d.1558)   (d.1574)

John Pakington = Elizabeth Newport
(1523-1578)

Charles = Eleanor Davies   Rowland   JOHN II = Jane Lumley   HENRY II = Elizabeth   Mary = John Ludey   John   Humphrey = Bridget Kingsmill = Sir Thomas Norreys
(d.1588)   (c.1540-1588) (d.1582)   (1540-1608) (1556-1622)   (b.1565)   (b.1561)   (1555-1631)   (1572-1606)   (d.1599)

= Abigail Sacheverell
(c.1580-1657)

Alderford   Edmund = Elizabeth Mintridge   JOHN III   =   Mary   Magdalen   Adam   Humphrey   Philip   Mary = Sir John Yate   Anne = Sir Henry Audley
              (c.1595-1655)   (1594-1641)   (Berington) (b.1599) (d.1653)   (b.1601)   (1610-1696) (1605-1659)   (1613-1642) (1604-1666)

Owners of Little Malvern are in capitals

RUSSELL OF LITTLE MALVERN 1641-1737

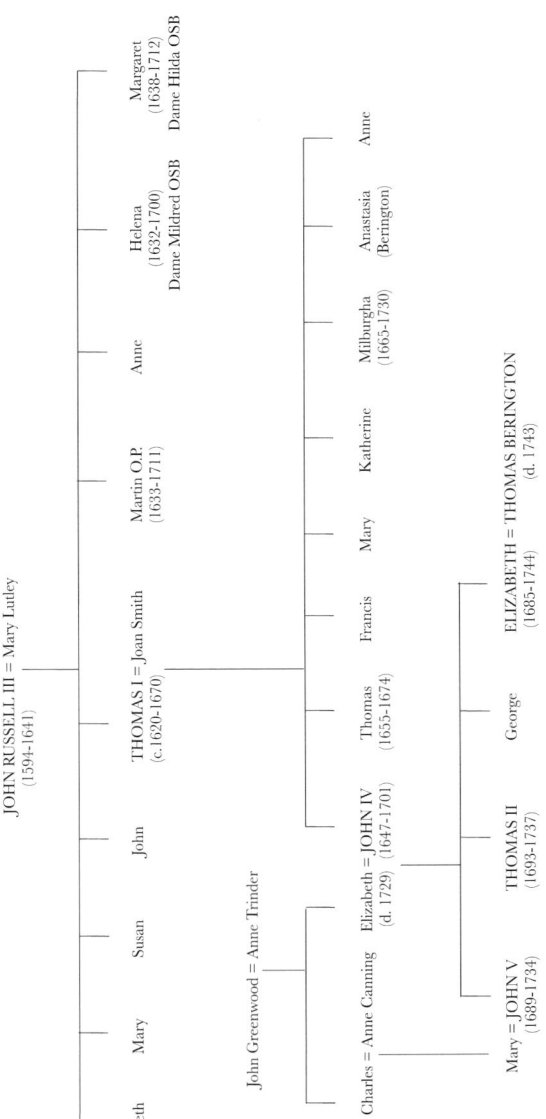

JOHN RUSSELL III = Mary Ludley
(1594-1641)

Elizabeth   Mary   Susan   John   THOMAS I = Joan Smith   Anne   Martin O.P.   Anne   Helena   Margaret
(c.1620-1670)   (1633-1711)   (1632-1700)   (1638-1712)
Dame Mildred OSB   Dame Hilda OSB

John Greenwood = Anne Trinder

Charles = Anne Canning   Elizabeth = JOHN IV   Thomas   Francis   Mary   Katherine   Milburgha   Anastasia   Anne
(d. 1729)   (1647-1701)   (1655-1674)   (1665-1730)   (Berington)

Mary = JOHN V   THOMAS II   George   ELIZABETH = THOMAS BERINGTON
(1689-1734)   (1693-1737)   (1685-1744)   (d. 1743)

Owners of Little Malvern are in capitals

THE DOCUMENTS

CHRONOLOGICAL LIST OF LETTERS

Unless otherwise stated, items are from the Berington Collection (Worcester Record Office, BA 81, 705:24): see pp. xliii–xlvii above.

1. Bishop John Alcock to the Prior and Convent of Little Malvern, 22 October 1482 (Alcock's Register, f. 111/129)
2. [Cardinal Wolsey] to the Marcher Council, 4 May [1517] (1)
3. Bishop John Vesey to the Marcher Council, 24 March [1526–7] (3 (5))
4. Marcher Council to John Russell, 1 April 1526 (4 (15))
5. Bishop Vesey to John Russell, 12 April [1526] (4 (7))
6. William Cholmley to John Russell, 30 April [1526] (3 (2))
7. The Sheriff of Caernarvon to the Marcher Council, 10 May [1526] (4 (4))
8. William Griffith to the Marcher Council, 28 May [1526] (4 (9))
9. Thomas Audley to John Russell, [20] December [1526] (4 (13))
10. Earl of Worcester to the Marcher Council, 21 January [1526/7] (3 (4))
11. Bishop Vesey to John Salter, George Bromley and John Russell, 23 February [1526/7], (7)
12. Bishop Vesey to the Household of Princess Mary, [March 1526/7] (3 (3))
13. Abbot Clement Lichfield to John Russell, April [1526–1538] (4 (1))
14. Bishop Vesey and others to the King's Council, 6 August [1527–33] (4 (6))
15. The King's Council to [?], [1528] (4 (3))
16. Lord Ferrers to Bishop Vesey, 16 June [1529] (3 (6))
17. Articles and Remembrances concerning the Marches, 1 November [1529] (8)
18. John Russell to Prior William More and Roger Wintour, 21 October [1530] (6 (3))
19. Roger Wintour to John Russell, 2 November [1530] (4 (12))
20. Sir John Russell to John Russell, 6 April [1533] (6 (2))
21. Thomas Cromwell to Sir John Russell &c, 18 July [1530–35] (5 (6))
22. Abbot William Boston to John Russell, 23 April [1534] (4 (5))
23. Thomas Audley and Thomas Cromwell to Sir John Russell &c, 20 July [? 1535] (5 (8))
24. Survey of Little Malvern Priory, [1535] (Hodgson transcripts: source unidentified)
25. Thomas Cromwell to Sir Gilbert Talbot and John Russell, 7 September [1536] (5 (3))

26. Thomas Cromwell to John Russell, 8 October [1536] (5 (4))

27. Edward Bache to John Russell, 28 November 1536 (4 (14))

28. John Russell to Sir Richard Rich, 25 September [1537] (6 (1))

29. John Russell to Thomas Cromwell, 28 September 1537 (*L&P Henry VIII*, XII/2, no. 769)

30. Thomas Audley to John Russell, 14 March [1537–40] (5 (1))

31. Thomas Cromwell to John Russell, 7 December 1538 (5 (5))

32. Thomas Audley to John Russell, 28 February [1538–40] (5 (7))

33. Thomas Cromwell to [John Russell], 18 February [1540] (5 (2))

34. Little Malvern church inventory, 1552 (National Archives, E.117/9/22/46)

35. Will of Milbora Russell, 27 June 1574 (278)

36. Probate inventory of Milbora Russell, 1575 (Worcs. R. O., I.1575/57a))

37. George Selby to Elizabeth Pakington [1580s?] (563 (3))

38. The Privy Council to the Vice-Chancellor of Oxford, 14 August 1581 (*Acts of the Privy Council, 1580–1*, p. 170)

39. Examination of John Felton, 24 December 1582 (National Archives, SP 12/156/29/i)

40. Henry Russell to Charles Russell, 29 March 1585 (C.29);

41. W. West to Henry Russell, 25 August 1585 (29 (2))

42. Henry Russell to Sir Christopher Hatton, [1587–91] (23)

43. Henry Russell to [Sir John Perrot], 2 April [1588] (623 (16))

44. John Halsey to Elizabeth Pakington [before 1591] (565 (1))

45. John Halsey to Elizabeth Pakington [before 1591] (565 (2))

46. William Savage and others to John Russell II, 4 June [1588] (Lechmere, 'Items Included', 1/2)

47. Francis Willis to Henry Russell, 14 April 1595 (Lechmere B.10)

48. Catherine Willis to Henry Russell, 31 July [1596] (Berington 562 (23))

49. ? to the Dowager Countess of Derby, 3 July 1596 (Lechmere, 'Items Included' 2)

50. John Halsey to Elizabeth Russell, 17 October 1597 (565 (3))

51. John Halsey to Elizabeth Russell, 25 January 1599/1600 (565 (4))

52. John Halsey to Henry Day, 2 February 1599/1600 (617))

53. Humphrey Pakington to Henry Russell, 23 February [1599–1600] (Lechmere f.899:169 (7)/C.7)

54. John Halsey to Elizabeth Russell, 17 April 1601 (565 (5))

55. Humphrey Pakington to Elizabeth Russell, 28 April [1601]: (576 (13)

56. Humphrey Pakington to [Henry Russell], 17 October [1601]: Lechmere f.899:169 (5)

57. John Halsey to Henry Russell, 2 January 1601/2 (565 (6))

58. John Halsey to Henry Russell, 19 March 1601/2 (565 (7))

59. John Grove to Henry Russell, 7 July 1602 (376 (2))

60. John Halsey to Henry Russell, 22 October 1602 (565 (7.1)

61. Alderford Russell's Oxford expenses, December 1602 (609)

62. Alderford Russell to Henry Russell, 27 March 1603 (565 (31))

63. Henry Russell to [Humphrey Pakington], 25 April [1603?] (570 (1))

64. John Halsey to [Henry Russell], 3 February 1603/4 (565 (8))

65. John Grove to Henry Russell, 5 February 1603/4 (Lechmere f.899:169 (6))

66. W[alter] Acutto [Hackett *vere* Cowarne] to Henry & Elizabeth Russell, 25 February 1604 (562 (36))

67. Humphrey Pakington to Elizabeth Russell, 27 October [1604] (576 (18))

68. Lady Derby to Humphrey Pakington, [November 1604] (815)

69. Will of Henry Russell, 29 November 1604 (Lechmere, 'Items Included, 3/1)

70. Sir Edward Blount to Henry Russell, 20 December 1604 (562 (34)

71. John Grove to Henry Russell, 6 April 1605 (376 (4))

72. John Grove to Henry Russell, 13 April 1605 (376 (5))

73. John Grove to Henry Russell, 4 May 1605 (376 (6))

74. John Grove to Henry Russell, 16 November 1605 (376 (7))

75. John Grove to Henry Russell, 21 March 1605–6 (376 (9))

76. Acquittance, Alderford Russell to Richard Middleton, 27 March 1606 (Lechmere, 'Items Included' 5)

77. Grove to Henry Russell, 22 November 1606 (376 (10))

78. John Bache to Henry Russell, 7 December 1606 (376 (39))

79. John Grove to Henry Russell, 10 January 1606/7 (376 (11))

80. John Grove to Henry Russell, 6 June 1607 (Lechmere f.899:169 (12))

81. Earl of Derby to Sir Julius Caesar, 12 July 1607 (Lansdowne 153, f. 241)

82. Henry Russell to ? Bowen [? September 1607] (570 (2))

83. John Grove to Henry Russell, 17 October 1607 (376 (14))

84. John Grove to Henry Russell, 15 November 1607 (376 (16))

85. Humphrey Pakington to Henry Russell [November 1607] (Lechmere f.899:169 (10))

86. Humphrey Pakington to Henry Russell [Nov.–Dec. 1607] (Lechmere f.899:169 (13))

87. Grove to Russell, 19 December 1607 (376 (17))

88. Humphrey Pakington to Henry Russell, 20 Dec. 1607 (Lechmere f.899:169 (4))

89. Humphrey Pakington to Henry Russell, 22 Dec. 1607 (Lechmere f.899:169 (3))

90. Grove to Russell, 26 January 1607/8 (376 (20))

91. Henry Russell to [Humphrey Pakington], 24 January 1607/8 (570 (3))

92. Long Live King James! (620)

93. John Pakington to Elizabeth Russell, 27 July [ ], (569 (2))

94. John Pakington to Elizabeth Russell, 4 March [ ], (569 (4))

95. John Pakington to Elizabeth Russell, 23 November [ ], (569 (7))

96. John Pakington to Elizabeth Russell, 3 Sept. [ ], (569 (8))

97. John Mintridge to Elizabeth Russell, n.d. (615 (2))

98. John Mintridge to Elizabeth Russell, 2 January [ ] (615 (3))

99. Justinian Stubbs to Elizabeth Russell, 5 March 1607/8 (616 (2))

100. Justinian Stubbs to Elizabeth Russell, 21 April [? 1608] (616 (1))

101. John Grove to Elizabeth Russell, 27 June 1608 (376 (23))

102. J[ames] Yate to Elizabeth Russell, 11 July 1608 (Lechmere C.8)

103. Mary Habington to [Elizabeth] Russell, 30 August [? 1608] (614)

104. Humphrey Pakington to Elizabeth Russell, 24 Sept. [1608] (Lechmere f.899:169 (8))

105. John Grove to Elizabeth Russell, 4 November 1608 (376 (25)

106. John Grove to Elizabeth Russell, 14 November 1608 (376 (27))

107. John Grove to Elizabeth Russell, 26 November 1608 (376 (28))

108. John Grove to Elizabeth Russell, 10 December 1608 (376 (29))

109. John Grove to Elizabeth Russell, [January] 1608/1609 (376 (22))

110. John Grove to Elizabeth Russell, 20 February 1608/9 (376 (31))

111. John Grove to Elizabeth Russell, 26 February 1608/9 (376 (32))

112. Lord Chancellor Ellesmere to [Francis Moore], 4 April 1611 (378)

113. Humphrey Pakington to Elizabeth Russell, 28 Aug. [1608–1615] (576 (21))

114. Justinian Stubbs to Elizabeth Russell, 10 July [1608–15] (616 (3))

115. Humphrey Pakington to Elizabeth Russell, 21 January 1614–15 (576 (22))

116. Humphrey Pakington to Elizabeth Russell, 2 January [1609–15] (576 (2))

117. Benedict Hall to Justinian Stubbs, 16 August [1615] (621)

118. Justinian Stubbs to Elizabeth Russell, 30 August [1615] (616 (5))

119. Justinian Stubbs to Elizabeth Russell, 4 September [1615] (616 (4))

120. Humphrey Pakington to Elizabeth Russell, 28 October 1615 (576 (4))

121. Humphrey Pakington to Elizabeth Russell [November 1615] (576 (11))

122. Acquittances for the Wardship of John Russell III, 1614–15 (377)

123. Humphrey Pakington to Elizabeth Russell, 12 January [1615/16] (576 (8))

124. John Grove to Elizabeth Russell, 2 March 1615/1616 (Hodgson transcripts: ? = Lechmere C.43)

125. Humphrey Pakington to Elizabeth Russell, 22 November [1615–22] (Lechmere C.32)

126. Humphrey Pakington to Elizabeth Russell, 3 February [1614–17] (576 (5))

127. [ ] to John Russell [1619–1620] (623 (1))

128. Humphrey Pakington to [John] Russell, 23 November [–1621], (576 (16))

129. Licence for Humphrey Pakington to travel, 22 April 1622 (*Acts of the Privy Council, July 1621–May 1623*, p. 199)

130. [Ralph Stamford] to John Russell III, 30 May [? 1623–] (648 (2))

131. Giles Nanfan to John Russell III [? 1628] (Lechmere B.8)

132. John Russell III to [ ], undated (619 (4))

133. Edmund Russell to John Russell III, undated. (623 (3))

134. Abigail Pakington to John Russell III [July 1632] (623 (19))

135. Abigail Pakington to John Russell III, 20 March 1632/3 (Lechmere C.44)

136. Abigail Pakington to John Russell III [1633] (648 (9))

137. Sir Henry Spiller to John Russell III, 10 September 1634 (623 (21))

138. Notes on Indictments of Recusants, [10 September 1634] (871)

139. Rowland Bartlett to John Russell III [October 1634] (623 (6))

140. John Hornyold to John Russell III [? 1634] (623 (13))

141. John Hornyold to John Russell III [October 1634] (623 (8))

142. Draft Petition to the King, 1634–5 (Lechmere [E.12])

143. John Hornyold to John Russell III [no date], (623 (9))

144. Thomas Rea to John Russell III, 28 January 1636/7 (623 (22))

145. Acquittance from Maurice Hughes to John Russell III, 12 July 1637 (Lechmere B.38)

146. Charles Stanford to John Russell III, 1640 (Lechmere B.1)

147. Charles Stanford to John Russell III, 16 September 1640 (623 (27))

148. Sir William Russell to John Russell III, 26 October 1640 (623 (30))

149. Order from the Long Parliament, 2 December 1640 (Townsend, *Diary*, II, p. 22)

150. John Russell III to [? John Hornyold], [no date], (619 (3))

151. Lord Keeper Littleton to Sheriff &c of Worcestershire, 18 November 1641 (Townsend II, p. 44)

152. Certificate of Search at Little Malvern, 28 February 1641/42 (631)

153. Sir Simon Archer to Thomas Habington, 23 April 1642 (632)

154. Thomas Habington to [ ] Cox, 19 May 1642 (Lechmere, 'Items Included', 4)

155. Order for Arraying of Soldiers for the King, 8 August 1642 (873).

156. 'The Setting Forth of a Soldier' [August 1642] (630)

157. Robert Cruse to Thomas Russell, 3 November 1642 (633 (21))

158. Three Letters on one sheet [? 1642] (633 (31)

159. Sir Rowland Berkeley to Thomas Russell, 18 December 1643 (Lechmere [C.2])

160. Proclamation by Prince Rupert, 10 February 1643/4 (876)

161. Richard Hopton to Thomas Russell, 19 February 1643/4 (633 (24))

162. Richard Dowdeswell to Thomas Russell, 28 May [1644] (633 (17))

163. Receipt for Monthly Contribution to the King's Army, 7 August 1644 (Hodgson transcripts: source unidentified)

164. Demand and Receipt for Contribution in Kind, 6 March 1644/5 (Berington 877)

165. Humphrey Lutley to Thomas Russell, 17 January [ ] (633 (12))

166. John Unett to Thomas Russell, 19 [ ] (633 (9))

167. Thomas Hornyold to Thomas Russell, 8 [1646] (633 (4))

168. William Dingley to Thomas Russell, 26 July 1647 (633 (29))

169. Demise to Thomas Russell by the Worcestershire Committee for Sequestration, 1 April 1648 (107)

170. Edward Berkeley to Thomas Russell, 1 May 1648 (633 (32))

171. Edward Berkeley to Thomas Russell, 1 July 1648 (Lechmere C.19)

172. Sequestered Estates of Papists and Annual Rents, November 1648 (British Library MS Add. 5508, f. 191)

173. Petition of Thomas Russell to the Worcestershire Committee for Sequestration [December 1649?] (108)

174. Certificate of the Worcestershire Committee to Thomas Russell, 3 January 1649/50 (Lechmere E.11/6)

175. Edmund Russell to Thomas Russell, 17 March 1649/50 (633 (35))

176. John Lingen to Thomas Russell, [ ] April [1649–50?] (633 (5))

177. Francis Ash to Richard Dowdeswell, 3 May 1650 (633 (36))

178. Edmund Russell to Thomas Russell, 20 December 1650 (633 (39))

179. Assessment of Little Malvern, June–December 1653 (Lechmere [A.24–25])

180. Petition of Thomas Russell to the Committee for Compounding, 19 January 1653/4 (SP 23/115/1)

181. John Weedon to Thomas Russell, [ ] 1655 (633 (48))

182. Landing Pass for Martin Russell, O.P., 12 June 1655 (641)

183. John Weedon to Thomas Russell, 22 August 1655 (633 (51))

184. Return by the Worcestershire Committee for Sequestration, May 1656 (National Archives, C.203/4)

185. Order to the Assessors and Collectors for Little Malvern, 8 October 1656 (891 (2))

186. Professions of Martin Russell and his sisters, 1657 (*Registrum Receptorum Conventus Gandav.*, f. 23; CRS 25, 173; CRS 14, 187)

187. Edmund Russell to Thomas Russell, 13 September [1657?] (633 (13))

188. John Nicholas, Receiver General for Worcestershire, to Thomas Russell, 3 April 1658 (633 (52))

189. Thomas Russell's Discharge by the Exchequer, 11 July 1660 (111)

1. *Bishop John Alcock[1] to the prior and convent of Little Malvern*
   22 October 1482
   Worcestershire Record Office, BA 2648/7(i), f. 111/129

Right well beloved brethren, I greet you well. And as it is notary known throughout all my diocese, to the great displeasure of God, disworship of the Church and slander to the religion of the blessed patron thereof St Bennet, and many other innumerable confessors of the same: the misliving and dissolute governance of the brethren that hath byn inhabit in the place of Little Malvern, being of my foundation and patronage; the rules of that holy religion not observed ne kept, but rather the said brethren in all their demeanance hath byn vagabond and lived like laymen to the pernicious example of all Christian men; and therefore it is a great presumption that the great ruin of the church and place, the decay of livelihood and the great poverty that the said place hath be now late in, was that God withdrew his grace and benefits and for the misguiding thereof was not pleased: and for as much as now by his grace and mercy I have builded your church, your place of your lodging is sufficient repaired and, as I suppose, a great part of the debt of the said place be content, and for that cause and by the cause ye should the better understand your religion, ye have byn this two years in worshipful and holy places of your religion: supposing that ye be now sufficiently instruct in the same, I am now content that everych of you that was there before now late, when I took the rule thereof into mine hands, except Dom John Wittesham, which by the law may not be there, resort to the said place of Little Malvern and there to abide and live after your holy profession: exhorting in the name of our Lord Christ Jesu, the blessed patron of your religion, and *virtute obediencie et sub pena excommunicationis* that fro henceforth ye keep your religion with the whole observance and discipline [and] rules thereof: the service of God *nocte dieque* devoutly be said and sung; your chapter, cloister, frater and dormitor be kept according, with due obedience unto your sovereigns; and that none of the brethren go into the town or the fields without an urgent cause, licence asked and obtained of the prior, and yet so that he that shall be so licensed have a fellow with him. And also I desire and will and pray you, for my recompense ghostly, to have every day a Mass at Our Lady altar said by one of the brethren for me, *videlicet*: *qualibet die Dominica de Trinitate; die Lune de Angelis; die Martis de Salus populi; die Mercurii de Requiem; die Jovis de Corpore Christi; die Veneris de Sancta Cruce; et die Sabati de Sancta Maria cum Evangelio Stabant iuxta crucem, cum collecta, secreta et post communionem de sancto Johanne Evangelista; ac in qualibet die post Vesperas cantetur antiphona 'O Maria et Johannes' cum versibus et collectis*; and also I will that in every Mass be said the collect *Rege quibus etc* with the secret *et post communionem, et post mortem meam in qualibet Missa oratio 'Deus qui inter apostolicos etc'.*[2] Which articles, and everych of them, be kept and observed under the pain above written, we will and charge you; and if ye so do, ye shall find me good lord to you and to your place, and ye shall have God's blessing and mine; and if ye do the contrary, I shall see the reformation thereof to your grievous punishment, in example of all other. Whereof I will be right sorry, as God knoweth, which enforce you to be his true servants and to do your duty, and ever have you in his blessed keeping. Written at Bewdley, in haste, the 22 day of October *anno Domino* 1482. John Worcester

To the prior and brethren of the Priory of Little Malvern.

[1] John Alcock (1430–1500) became bishop of Rochester in 1472, of Worcester in 1476 and of Ely in 1486. He was also Lord Chancellor (1485), tutor to Edward V, president of the Council of the Marches of Wales (1473) and founder of Jesus College, Cambridge, on the site of what had been the convent of St Radegund. As bishop of Worcester, he was nominal abbot of the cathedral foundation, of which Little Malvern was a cell.

[2] The Masses to be said at the Lady altar were those commonly assigned to fixed days of the week: on Sundays, of the Blessed Trinity; on Mondays, of the angels; on Tuesdays, for any need (beginning with the words *Salus populi*); on Wednesdays, for the dead (beginning *Requiem aeternam*); on Thursdays, of the Blessed Sacrament; on Fridays, of the Holy Cross; and on Saturdays, of Our Lady, with the Gospel 'There stood by the cross' (John 19:25). On each day to the collect were to be added the corresponding one for St John the Evangelist and that beginning *Rege quibus* or, after Alcock's death, that for a deceased bishop, and so with the two other variable prayers of the Mass. Every day at the end of Vespers the brethren were also to sing the antiphon *O Maria et Joannes*, with its responses and collects.

2.   *[Cardinal Wolsey] to the Marcher Council*[1]
      4 May [1517]
      Berington 1

Trusty and well beloved &c. And for as much as our Commissioners and Councillors in our Marches of Wales lately on our behalf, for the reformation of the great disorders, as robberies, murders and many other offences, used and committed in our said Marches, and for the weal and restfulness of our true subjects within the same and the shires adjoining, made and took certain necessary ordinances and directions, signed as well with their hands as with the hands of divers officers and the officers of [*the*] Lords Marchers of our said Marches, to remain from henceforth in custody with other records within every of the lordships of our said Marches, following in effect the old indentures heretofore devised and made for the intent before rehearsed: We, therefore, and our said Commissioners, intending that the same ordinances and directions shall be duly observed and kept, have at t[*his t*]ime sent [*inserted*: a true copy of] them unto you in parchment signed with [*the h*]ands of our said Commissioners enclosed with these our letters by our messenger this bearer, straitly charging you, not only to see them there safely kept with other the records and books of that lordship like as they so shall be in other lordships of our said [*deleted*: lordships] Marches, but also to see the tenor and effect of the said directions *to be* within your office there from time to time duly executed and performed, as we trust you and as you will answer therefor at your peril. Given &c. 4° die Maii . . .[2]

[1] This item consists altogether of eight pages. The first seven are a set of articles drawn up by the Council of the Welsh Marches at Shrewsbury on 27 September 1516 ('anno regni Regis Henrici VIII[i] viij°') and referred to in the letter printed here, which is the eighth page. At the end of the articles are the autograph signatures of the councillors, headed by the then president, Bishop Geoffrey Blythe of Coventry and Lichfield (d. 1525), and of nearly twenty officers of the Marcher lordships. The letter itself is in the name of the King, but must have been drafted by Wolsey. It refers to the articles as having been 'lately' drawn up, which means that the year is 1517. The whole document must have been among the papers at Ludlow Castle that John Russell I took over when he became secretary to the Council in 1525; cf. no. **17** below. It has survived because Russell, contrary to the instructions in the letter, took it home.

[2] The bottom of the letter is torn off.

3.   *Bishop John Vesey[1] to the Marcher Council*
       24 March [1526/7][2]
       Berington 3 (5)

Addressed: To the right worshipful my lord abbot of Reading,[3] Sir John Port knight,[4] Mr Salter, Mr Bromley,[5] Mr Russell, with others of the Princess' Council at Bewdley.

After my best hearty commendations. Upon Saturday last my Lord Cardinal's Grace showed me that within this ten days will dispatch us [*sic*], saying that we and the Princess's household shall then return to Bewdley. Therefore I am disappointed of my journey to my diocese for this time. Moreover, his Grace would that ye should see condign punishment speedily done upon him or them that brought up the bruit of the King's death &c. Also inquired of me what was done in the commissions of sewers,[6] which [*inserted*: matter] I perceive his Grace much mindeth the reformation of. My good Lady of Salisbury[7] hath sent to you this bearer only for expedition of her matters, which I doubt me not [*inserted*: ye] would handle according to good justice with your lawful[8] favour for her sake. Thus our Lord God send you all long well to fare. From London, in haste, the 24 day of March, with the rude hand of Yours, Jo: Exon

[1] John Vesey (*c.*1464–1554), bishop of Exeter, 1519–51; president of the Marcher Council, 1525–34. A great benefactor of his native town, Sutton Coldfield, seven miles north-east of Birmingham, he is buried in the church there.

[2] This and other items can be dated by the references to Princess Mary, who was in the Marches only from September 1525 to April 1527: Skeel, *The Council in the Marches of Wales*, 52. For Bewdley, see the Introduction, p. xii above.

[3] The priory and town of Leominster in Herefordshire were owned by Reading Abbey. From 1520 the abbot of Reading was Hugh Cook alias Faringdon, who was executed in 1539 for denying the royal Supremacy.

[4] Sir John Port (*c.*1472–1540), justice of the Council. By his marriage to Jane Fitzherbert he acquired Etwall in Derbyshire, where his great-grandson the famous Jesuit John Gerard was born in 1564. *ODNB*; Skeel, *The Council in the Marches of Wales*, 58–9; Madden, *Privy Purse Expenses of the Princess Mary*, p. xxxix, from MS Harleian 6807, f. 3; John Morris, *The Life of Father John Gerard*, 3rd edn (London, 1881), 1–2.

[5] John Salter and George Bromley were lawyers attached to the Council (Madden, as above).

[6] To survey and repair watercourses.

[7] The countess of Salisbury, Blessed Margaret Pole, lady governess to Princess Mary.

[8] In the sense of 'loyal, faithful'.

4. *Marcher Council to John Russell I*
   1 April 1526
   Berington 4 (15)

[*Warra*]nt to seal warrants [. . .] household

Where heretofore it hath pleased the King's Highness and the Queen's by their general warrants dormant[1] to licence and to give authority unto the Princess' Grace as well to take her disport and pleasure in all their forests, parks and chases within the shires and marches limited in the authority of the Princess' Council and of deer and coneys within the same, and to this Council and the head officers of household with the said Princess' Grace to make out warrants from [*deleted*: to] time to time for such deer seasonably into all and every the said forests, parks and chases as shall be necessary and behoveful for the expense of the said Household:[2] And, for as much as the Steward, Treasurer and Comptroller, being head officers of the same House[*hold*], be much absent, whereby no such warrants from them can pass when need ariseth: Therefore it is agreed, ordered and assented by the said Council that all such warrants to be made at any time henceforth for the use of the said Household shall pass in our sovereign lord the King's name and under his Signet remaining towards the said Council in the charge and custody of the Secretary there; for whose discharge in that part we have to these presents subscribed our names the first day of April in the 18th year of the reign of our said sovereign lord King Henry the Eight. Jo. Exon, Ja. Denton,[3] Jo. Burnett,[4] E. Croft[5]

[1] A warrant dormant is one drawn out in blank for the name or particulars to be filled in.

[2] For more on the Council's right to take deer, see Skeel, *The Council in the Marches of Wales*, 245–6.

[3] James Denton, clerk to the Council: Madden, *Privy Purse Expenses of the Princess Mary*, p. xxxix.
[4] ? Sir John Burdett (*c*.1460–1528/9): *The Visitation of the County of Warwick in the year 1619*, ed. John Fetherstone, Harleian Society 12 (London, 1877), 100–101; VCH *Warks.*, III. 28–9; IV. 190; Sir William Dugdale, *The Antiquities of Warwickshire*, 2nd edn, cont. William Thomas (London, 1730), 847.
[5] See no. **12**.

5. *Bishop Vesey to John Russell I*
   12 April [1526/7]
   Berington 4 (7)

In our hearty manner we recommend us unto you. So it is we have at this time received from [*deleted*: you] the Abbot of Pershore[1] a letter mentioning in effect that upon the complaint of Roger Walton of Pershore, your household servant, Symond Pylkynton, William Mossey and Catherine Bayly, this Council have directed a commission to you for the examination of the same matters, ye being apted[2] in many of the same matters and no friend to the said abbot, nor to his church. And that the said commission is [*deleted*: ob] obtained to you at the only nomination of the said complainant, without consent or agreement of the said abbot or of any other on his behalf. Wherefore, in consideration of the premisses and for the more indifferency, we have appointed the said matters to be examined and determined by you and Mr Packington[3] or you or [*sic, for* and] Mr Bracey, whom we authorise to associate you concerning the same. Thus heartily fare ye well. At Bewdley the 12th day of April, Your John Exon, Ric. Herbert.[4]

To the right worshipful John Russell Esquire, Secretary to the Princess' Grace.

[1] Either William Compton or John Stonywell, who succeeded Compton in September 1526: VCH *Worcs.*, II. 134–5; *L&P Henry VIII*, IV/2, no. 2537.
[2] Suited, prepared.
[3] John, later Sir John, Pakington, lawyer in attendance on the Council; great-uncle of Humphrey Pakington of Harvington and of Henry Russell II's wife Elizabeth Pakington.
[4] Sir Richard Herbert, an energetic member of the Council; Bishop Rowland Lee, Vesey's successor, wrote that his death in 1539 was 'as though I had lost one of my arms': Skeel, *The Council in the Marches of Wales*, 68; cf. pp. 78, 82, 203.

6.   *William Cholmeley to John Russell I*
         30 April [1526/7]
         Berington 3 (2)

Addressed: To the right worshipful Master Russell, Secretary to my Lady Princess's Grace.

Right worshipful, In my heartiest wise I recommend me unto you. And according to your desire have delivered unto Dr Burbank such money as ye took unto me at my departure from Ludlow. For payment whereof ye shall receive from him acquittance here enclosed. And also have delivered unto Henry Posur of London, Grocer, 24*s*, which also ye took unto me.[1] As for acquittance for payment thereof, he judgeth there req[*uireth*] none, for that ye have redelivery of this bill whereby ye stood bound for payment of the same. As for news, here are none worth the sending, other than I have touched in my letter now at this time sent to your Almoner,[2] which, I doubt not, will declare unto you. And any favour or pleasure that I may do you here, your mind known, I shall be always ready at your commandment, God willing, who have you in his blessed tuition. Scribbled in haste at London the last day of April.

Pleaseth you that in most humble wise I may be recommended unto my good Lord President and to other my masters of the Council.

Assuredly yours to his power, W. Cholmeley

[1] In 1532 Henry Posyer, Grocer, was owed £46 18*s* 7*d* by the late Cardinal Wolsey: *L&P Henry VIII*, V, no. 1264. In the 1630s money from the Council in Ludlow was sent with the drovers, who were the only regular travellers between Wales and London: Skeel, *The Council in the Marches of Wales*, 156.
[2] The almoner to the Council in 1525 was Peter Burnell: Madden, *Privy Purse Expenses of the Princess Mary*, p. xxxix, quoting MS Harleian 6897, f. 3.

7.   *The sheriff of Caernarvon to the Council of the Welsh Marches*
         10 May [1526]
         Berington 4 (4)

Addressed: To the right honourable lords and masters the King's Commissioners and Councillors to my Lady Princess in the Marches of Wales.

Endorsed: Advertisement to the King's Council in the Marches of Wales for the better reducing in into [*sic*] good order and [*deleted*: reducing] keeping of good rule in North Wales.

With our reverences, as to your lordships and masterships appertaineth. Please it the same, I have perused the King's most honourable letter, to me and the Deputy Sheriff of Caernarvonshire conjointly directed, bearing date the twenty day of April. Whereby I perceive the King's Grace, with your lordships and noble Councillors, have been advertised that divers murderers, felons, outlaws and fugitives hath been succoured, aided and comforted within the limits of our offices, rooms and authorities with victuals, lodging and other necessaries contrary to the laws of our [*sov*]ereign lord the King; and that we be loath and remiss to put a good endeavour to repress and rep[*rove*] [*deleted*: the] such offenders as to our duties appertaineth. Please it your good lordships and masterships that I by protestation certify unto you that, as concerning the shires of Anglesey and Caernarvon (as far as I perceive) be in good rule and order and little hurt done in them. [*The*] names of such as be misorderly within the said shires, with their demeanours (if any such be) I shall [?*send*] unto you to the uttermost of my knowledge at the 24th day of May next according to the King[*'s*] commandment. As touching Merionethshire, there be divers and many misdoers (as I am informed), whose nam[*es*] I shall gather and put in a bill and certify unto you as far as I can, and of their offences at the said 24th of May. And in the mean time I shall endeavour me in the best manner and policy that I can, as far as to me can be possible, to obtain of the misdoers and commit them to ward according to the [*King's*] commandment and your lordships', and shall not fail with all diligence to publish the King's commandment to his subjects in these parts in any condition concerning his most gracious letters, and shall enquire of retainers accordingly, and in like [*word omitted*: ? manner] as I perceive certify to your lordships. But as touching my personal appearance afore ye at the said 24th day of May, I beseech you of pardon, for of very truth I am so vexed with sickness that I cannot ride without jeopardy of my life. And I will be glad to be bounden to stand to and obey all such orders as by your lordships shall be devised concerning the weal of the county in like manner as all other officers in the Marches shall be bounden, as well as if I should personally appear afore your lordships (if you think so convenient). And as touching such lands as Henry Smyth claimeth to have title unto, I have laboured to Mr Hales, one of the King's General Surveyors, [*and*] by his favour have obtained such records concerning the same ready with this bearer to be shown; whereby your lordships shall perceive that the King's Grace is substantially entitled in the same during the nonage of the Earl of Derby.[1] So that my very [*inserted*: trust] is in your good lordships that ye, upon sight thereof, will see that I shall be no further vexed by the said Henry Smyth. And I beseech your good lordships to give credence to my priest, this bearer, who can furtherly inform all my business afore your lordships, as Almighty God knoweth. Who ever preserve your good lordships and masterships with [*deleted*: incres] increase of honour. At Caernarvon the 10th day of May, Your humble servant, William . . .[2]

[1] Edward Stanley, the 3rd earl, was only twelve when his father died on 23 May 1521: Cokayne, *Complete Peerage* IV. 208–9.

[2] Damaged on the right side. The surname, partly torn, seems to be '*ydalle*' or '*ydakes*'. Sir William Uvedale died on 2 January 1525. He was a Councillor to Prince Arthur by 1501, and from 1504 until his death was steward of Abberley, Shrawley, Elmley Lovett and Salwarpe (all in Worcs.). See *ODNB*. But 'my lady princess' did not come to the Marches until September 1525.

8. *William Griffith to the Marcher Council*
28 May [1526]
Berington 4 (9)

Addressed: To the right honourable lords and masters the King's Commissioners in the Marches of Wales, Councillors with my Lady Princess.

Right honourable my singular good lords and masters, I recommend me to you in my most [*inserted*: humble] wis[*e and with*] all mine whole heart and service, thanking Almighty God that your wisdoms have well devised and sithence been fully determined to proceed for the confirmation of the peace and good rule, as well of North Wales, wh[*erein*] I am officer, as of all other places of your authority. For performation and effective execution whereof, sa[*ving*] alway your pleasure and better advisement, it were necessary that, among all other your good provisio[*ns for good*] order, it would please you by your strait order to command that every sheriff in North Wales, and specially of the county of Merioneth, shall, by himself or sufficient deputy, bring into the Exchequer of Caernarvon due returns of execution of all manner writs to them for the King's warrants and for the peace out of the said Exchequer directed, and the same returns to be made upon their oaths, which been of old time certified. And also the said sheriffs and keepers of the peace and all other officers by virtue of their offices do take and bring in all manner rest-owers[1] of distresses taken by the King's bailiffs and collectors, and disobeyers of the King's writs of *sub poena* or other precepts &c.

Also that the said Sheriff of Merioneth bring in all and every gentleman within his office to be bo[*un*]d[*en*] jointly and severally afore Justice or Chamberlain for the good rule and peace of the quarters or p[*laces*] of their inhabitations and abiding, upon pain of £100 to be forfeited by every of the[*m*]. And so shall commit neither murder nor felony nor other enormity or mischief but that may readily be reformed and punished according to the laws, and likewise to be done in the other two shires. And such of the said gentlemen as shall refuse to be bounden in manner aforesaid to be committed to remain in ward unto [*sic*] they shall undertake for the good rule of their countries as is aforesaid, or else shall never be good rule in North Wales, I think. Albeit your pleasure and commandments concerning the premises shall be observed to the utmost of my power.

Please it you also to advertise the Remembrancer and *Examinant*[?][2] of many and divers writs of *sub poena* and *capias* which have gone out of the said Exchequer, and many of them delivered to Humphrey ap Howell, deputy-sheriff of the said county of Merioneth, by mine own hand for the King's service, whereof none executed or return was made. And also the *Examinant*[?] of many writs of *sub poena* which were dissolved, into perilous example of contempt of the law and impediment of [. . .] levy of the King's money within mine office. Which I have not seen sithence I am officer exce[*pt in*] the time of the said Humphrey his being officer.

Like it you also to consider there been divers gentlemen—first, Howell ap David [*deleted*: and] ap Meyrick; William ap John ap Rhys; Ellis ap Howell ap Griffin ap Rhys; John ap Jevan ap David; William ap Jevan ap David; Thomas ap Jevan ap David; Lewis ap Jevan ap David; Rhys ap William Vychan; Hugh ap Howell ap Jenkin; Hugh Owen [*the*] elder; Morris ap Howell ap Griffyn ap Rhys; Morris ap Owen ap Jenkyn; Morris ap Rhys ap Robert; John [*ap*] Richard ap Robert; and John ap Jevan ap Jenkyn; and other—confedered to the said Humphrey to maintain the contempt and disobeisance of the said writs and other misdemeanours. Without reformation whereof, not only I myself but also every other the King's officers and ministers in the said county of Merioneth shall be without indemnity. As knoweth God: he [*sic*] have you in his blessed preservation. At my poor house in Penrhyn, the 28th day of May. Your h[*onours '*?] and his *service*[?], Will. Griffith Kt[3]

[1] Apparently 'those who still owe in part'. For 'ower' = 'debtor', *OED* quotes 'worst owers' from Ben Jonson.
[2] The officers of the Council included a Remembrancer and a Clerk Examiner: Skeel, *The Council in the Marches of Wales*, 288–9. The Justiciar and Chamberlain of North Wales were based in Caernarvon, where courts were held for the three shires of Caernarvon, Anglesey and Merioneth.
[3] The Griffiths of Penrhyn were great landowners, with connexions to the Tudors and the Stanleys of Hooton in Cheshire. Their fortified manor-house stood on part of the site of the Victorian Penrhyn Castle (now owned by the National Trust), halfway between Conway and Caernarvon.

9.   *Thomas Audley[1] to John Russell I*
           [20] December [1526]
           Berington 4 (13)[2]

Addressed: To the right worshipful Master Secretary with the Lady Princess.

Brother Russell, I right heartily recommend me to you and to my sister. So it is that I am lately advertised by my Lord C[*ardinal*] that [*the King's*]

Highness hath made me his General Attorney of his Duchy of Lan[*caster*] and discharged me of the Princess' service. Whereof I have advertised my Lord President and ye my good lords and masters of the Council, trusting that my journey there may be spared. Albeit my very duty were to see my Lady's Grace and you all, and to give her thanks, nevertheless, the journey is so far, and so cold and foul weather, and I not all the best at ease to ride there. If I [*mi*]ght be spared, I were singularly bounden to you and all ye my [*fellow*]s. I pray you of your further service, as ye shall hear or see the ti[*me*] be noted or advertised herein by any, please you to send me word [? *thereof by*] your letter; and if there shall be any pleasure I may do you, I shall always be glad [*from*] time to time. And thus Almighty *Iesu* send you long and prosperous life. Scribbled this Monday afore St Thomas, by yours to all his power, Thomas Awdeley

I [*deleted*: *illegible*; *inserted*: send] you a bill and an answer which my lord's grace commanded [*me*] to send to the Council out of the Star Chamber. The parties will send to you after Twelfth [*omitted*: Night]. *Fiat Justicia.*

[1] Thomas Audley (1487/8–1544), later Lord Chancellor, was one of six lawyers appointed to the Marcher Council in July 1525. On 11 December 1526 he became attorney general of the duchy of Lancaster (*ODNB*). About 1519 he had married Christina Barnardiston of Kedington, Suffolk, whose sister Anne was John Russell's wife: hence 'brother Russell' and 'my sister'.
[2] The top right and bottom left corners of the letter are missing; the postscript is written to the left of and very close to the signature, which at first appears to be part of it.

10.   *Henry, earl of Worcester,*[1] *to the Marcher Council*
         21 January [1526/7]
         Berington 3 (4)[2]

Addressed: To my special good lords the Princess Grace' Council.

Endorsed: These concerning Brecknock.[3]

My especial good lords, In my heartiest manner I commend me unto your good lordships. And where ye have directed unto me the King's most honourable letters, touching as well certain murders and felonies within my authorities and lands, as also the livering of the King's duties and arrearages being behind unpaid, as in the same letters more plainly appeareth: I advertise you that, albeit some of the said murders and felonies were committed before that I had any jurisdiction or rule, yet nevertheless I have to my great cost and charge endeavoured myself by the best means and policy that I could to attach the said misdoers, and also charged my officers to endeavour themselves to do the same, in so much that at my last being at Gower I made pursuit after such of the said murderers as were then in that country so nigh that they fled in their shirts from their beds to the sanctuary.[4] And the said offenders be so friended, kinned and favoured that there can no number of men be raised in the country where they be but that they shall have knowledge by some of them to avoid; and therefore it is hard for me or for any other to take them but by tract of time and good deliberation. And I have prepared and set for them that I trust within brief time to have some of them. Also, of the King's said arrearages and duties being behind and unpaid, I know none but that is supposed to be in Brecknock. For the which matter I called on John ap Howel, under-sheriff of Brecknock, who ought to liver the same, to make answer in that behalf; and he affirmed that he had attached and brought into the castle of Brecknock many men with much cattle and cheeses[5] for the King's said arrearages and duties. Which men, cattle and cheeses were enlarged and delivered out of the said castle by Hugh Mervyn, the King's Receiver there. To whom I wrote to advertise me upon what persons the said arrearages doth rest, to the intent I might charge the officers of Brecknock to liver and bring in the same. Howbeit I can in no wise as yet have answer from him thereof, and till I may know upon whom the said arrearage is I cannot compel the officers to liver the same.

Moreover, whereas I am now commanded by the King's honourable letters to appear before your lordships upon sight of the same, I advertise you that before the receipt of the same I had knowledge and advertisement from the King's Council attending upon his most noble person that I must, as shortly as I can, ride up to give my attendance upon his Grace according to my duty [*bounden*]; as well for the sealing and delivering to the same Council of certain writings and bonds for [*such*] great sums of money as I must pay to his Grace' use for the delivery of my lands and for m[*y*] relief, as also for other causes and matters to be shown and declared unto me at my coming there. Wherefore I beseech your lordships to be so good unto me as to accept and ta[*ke*] this my reasonable excuse for my appearance at this time. And after my return from th[*e*] King's Highness I shall appear afore your lordships when it will please you to command me, praying you not to take this my answer or excuse for any delay. For I shall [*?faithfully*] observe your commandments now and at all time, as any man living. As k[*noweth God, who*] preserve your lordships. At Chepstow, the 21 day of January, H. Wo[*rcester*]

---

[1] Henry Somerset, 2nd earl of Worcester. He succeeded his father in 1526 in the possession of Raglan and Chepstow Castles and the lordship of Gower, hence the reference to 'the delivery of my lands'. He died in 1548 and is buried, with a fine Renaissance monument, at Chepstow.

[2] The letter is damaged on the right side, especially towards the bottom, where most of the signature is missing.

³ Brecknock (Brecon) Castle. Owned by the duke of Buckingham until his execution in 1521, it was 'a good and strong hold with all houses of office and lodging, builded after the old fashion'. In 1528 'decrees and directions' were issued about the arrears complained of here. Skeel, *The Council in the Marches of Wales*, 35, 54; *L&P Henry VIII*, IV/2, no. 5098.
⁴ 'The sanctuary' would be that at Margam Abbey, near Swansea.
⁵ 'Siesses', apparently = 'seeses', the Welsh pronunciation of 'cheeses'. Dyce (1844) amended 'cheeses' to 'seeses' in *The Merry Wives of Windsor*, I.ii.12; see the Arden edn by H.J. Oliver (London, 1971), pp. xliv, 20.

11. *Bishop Vesey to Salter, Bromley and Russell*
    *23 February [1526/7]*¹
    Berington 7

Addressed: To the right worshipful Mr Salter, Mr Bromley and Mr Secretary at Bewdley.

. . . hearty commendations, certifying the same that my Lord Cardinal's Grace is well content with your being still at Bewdley, saying it was so contained in your [?*instructions*]. At my being yesterday in the King's Court, showed me Sir Anthony Ponys,² that lately was brought to him from us letters expressing that if he 'pear³ not, shall be declared the King's rebel, and saith he had never from us any other letters or tokens for his appearance in that matter. I am right sorry that any man of worship should be thus by us entreated. I pray you advertise the Clerks hereof, that they look better to such light *affidavits*[?] against men of worth and that the process be surceased. Thus fare ye heartily well. From London in haste, *crastino Cathedre Sancti Petri*.⁴ Your Jo. Exon

¹ This letter can be dated from the question about whether the officers of the Marcher Council should be at Bewdley (rather than Ludlow), also raised in letter **12**, which in turn can be dated from the reference to 'the *Princess'* Council abiding at Bewdley'.
² Sir Anthony Poyntz (*c*.1480–1532/3) of Iron Acton in Gloucestershire, sheriff of Gloucestershire in 1527–9. The theologian Robert Poyntz (*c*.1535–?1568) was one of this family, and the Blessed James Fenn, formerly of Gloucester Hall, Oxford, was steward to Sir Nicholas Poyntz II (d. 1585) at Iron Acton: see *ODNB*; Anstruther, I. 113–14; T.B. Trappes-Lomax, 'The Family of Poyntz and its Catholic Associations', *Recusant History* 6 (1961–2), 68–79. In 1538 a servant of 'Mr Poynes' was paid for bringing presents from his master and partridges to Princess Mary: Madden, *Privy Purse Expenses of the Princess Mary*, 74, 75. The present house, Acton Court, was built for Sir Nicholas Poyntz I (*c*.1510–1556): David Verey and Alan Brooks, *The Buildings of England: Gloucestershire*, II: *The Vale and the Forest of Dean*, 3rd edn (New Haven, 2002), 548–50.
³ 'Aphetic form of *appear*': *OED*.
⁴ 'The morrow of St Peter's chair'.

12.   *Bishop John Vesey to the household of Princess Mary Tudor*
      [March 1526/7]
      Berington 3 (3)

Addressed: To the right worshipful the Princess's Council abiding at Bewdley.

With hearty recommendations unto you and Mr Salter, Mr Bromley[1] and Mr Russell. And so to the contents of your letters dated at Bewdley the 23 day of Februarii [*and re*]ceived at Bridgnorth the third day of March. The truth is that the King and my lord Cardinal's Grace be well content with your abiding at Bewdley and business there, and would ye had your convenient allocations for the same. And upon my report to my lord Cardinal's Grace of the exility[2] of you, Mr Salter, Mr Bromley and the Solicitor's[3] stipends not sufficient to sustain your charge, his Grace said it shall be augmented, with many good words in your commendation, whereof the hearing was to my comfort; saying also that ye, with all other of the Council, should be better entreated in your lodging and other things, as his Grace yesterday declared the same more at large in the presence of my Lord Steward, Mr Comptroller, Mr Crofts, Mr Almoner[4] and me, with many other things for the good rule of Wales and of the Princess' household; as ye shall know at our next meeting. Which my coming to you, as I think, will be within these twenty days, unless I for a time will visit my diocese, which to do I am much desirous, for divers my business there, as knoweth our Lord God; who send you long well to fare. Desiring the same I may be entirely recommended to Sir John Port, knight, with other of the Council, Your own priest, Jo. Exon.

[1] For Salter and Bromley, see no. **3**.

[2] Latin *exilitas*: 'poorness', 'meagreness'.

[3] The Solicitor is identified in neither Madden, *Privy Purse Expenses of the Princess Mary*, nor Skeel, *The Council in the Marches of Wales*.

[4] The Lord Steward was Lord Ferrers (see no. **16**), Mr Comptroller was Sir Giles Greville, Mr Crofts was Sir Edward Croft (d. 1547) of Croft Castle in Herefordshire, and Mr Almoner, Peter Burnell: Madden, *Privy Purse Expenses*, p. xxxix, quoting MS Harleian 6897, f. 3. For Croft, who was seven times sheriff of Herefordshire, see also *ODNB* under his grandson Sir James Croft (*c.*1518–1590).

13.   *Abbot Clement Lichfield*[1] *to John Russell I*
      [April 1526–38]
      Berington 4 (1)

Addressed: Unto the right worshipful Master Secretary be these delivered.

Right worshipful, I heartily [*commend m*]e to you. And, where Mr Foly-att[2] will bring before you divers witnesses, the which will make for his title to be good, if it please you to call some other person to be [*deleted*: with] associate with you to hear the deposition—either Mr Ferirs,[3] Mr *W . . r*[?], the under-sheriff or some other at your pleasure—I think it would be taken to be very indifferent. Herein do you as it shall like you. And I have [*deleted*: made [*illegible*]; *inserted*: put in writing] the award for our tenants of Ombrysley[4] after the rude manner, but I [*have*] writ according to our mind, I trust. Wherefore it may [*please you*] seal it, and I will provide for the delivery thereof in convenient time or before St Mark's day. And so our Lord God preserve you. By yours, Clement, Abbot of Evesham.

[1] Clement Lichfield, last but one of the fifty-six abbots of Evesham (1514–39), built the detached bell tower that, apart from the almonry and the gatehouse, is now the only remaining part of the Abbey. The letter is badly torn but seems to be the only one surviving in his own hand: E.A.B. Barnard, 'Old Days in and around Evesham', *Evesham Journal*, no. 1093 (28 January 1950) (cutting tucked inside the MS).

[2] The nearest Mr Foliot would be Francis at Pirton, ten miles west of Evesham, between Pershore and Worcester: *The Visitation of the County of Worcester made in the year 1569*, ed. W.P.W. Phillimore, Harleian Society 27 (London, 1888), 55; VCH *Worcs.*, IV. 182.

[3] The nearest Mr Ferrers would be Edward (second son of Sir Edward of Baddesley Clinton, near Warwick), who by his marriage to Elizabeth Grey (some time after 1532) acquired Wood Bevington, six miles north of Evesham: VCH *Warks.*, III. 160; cf. H.S. Gunn, *History of the Old Manor House of Wood Bevington* (Great Alne, 1911).

[4] Ombersley. An outlying estate of Evesham Abbey, five miles north of Worcester: C.J. Bond, 'The Estates of Evesham Abbey: A Preliminary Survey of their Medieval Topography', *Vale of Evesham Historical Society Research Papers* 4 (1973), 1–62, esp. 12, 19, 27, 36–7, 40, 42, 44, 49–50.

14.   *Bishop Vesey and others to the King's Council*
        6 August [1527–33]
        Berington 4 (6)

Right honourable, Our due recommendations premised, please it you wete we have lately received the King's most honourable letters at the suit of Sir Piers ap Brenton,[1] clerk, directed unto this Council, whereby we apperceive the King's most noble pleasure and commandment touching the interest pretended by the same Sir Piers unto the parsonage of Oswestry and otherwise, as by a copy of the same letters here enclosed doth [*inserted*: appear] more at large [*deleted*: appear]. Before receipt of which letters, upon complaint made unto this Council against the said Sir Piers and his farmer of that parsonage for the occupation of the same, and after the due examination [*inserted*: of the matter] this Council, for divers considerations them moving and especially for conservation of the King's peace, considering else great inconveniences might like to ensue, according to our duties took such order therein the 21st day of July last past as by a copy thereof, also here enclosed, more plainly doth appear. And for that we doubt, the said parties being strong, on both sides wilfully disposed and in a wild country, what dangers might follow—namely this season of the year—if, according to the King's high commandment in his said most honourable letters, we should now discharge the bonds of the peace [*inserted*: which be all the bonds we have] taken of either party, we have therefore only spared so to do till we might thus advertise you in these premises, to the intent, after the King's high pleasure thereupon further known (which we require you by your good furtherance may be by this bearer), we may follow and obey the same as with our duties [*do*]th accord. And thus our Lord have you in his blessed governance. [*Writt*]en at Shrewsbury the 6th day of August. Your Jo. Exon, John Porte, John Salter, G. Bromley, John Russell

¹ Despite the first sentence, there seems to be no reference to Sir Piers in the *L&P Henry VIII*.

15. *The King's Council to [??]*
        [1528]
        Berington 4 (3)

Right honourable, We recommend us unto your lordship. And, where it hath pleased the King's Highness and the Queen's good Grace, as well for their consolation and comfort, as also for the erudition of the Princess's Grace, to have her presence and continuance in the court; whereby her great and chargeable late household in those parts, long continued in the absence of her Grace, was thought unto the King's said Highness and his most honourable Council superfluous and to little purpose in effect, and therefore his gracious pleasure was the same to be dissolved for the time (as it now is); by reason whereof some of the Princess's servants in office in the said late household be now destitute and unprovided of since and would be glad to find for their livings, which of themselves are not able in substance to continue and abide the time as others of her servants be (and for their parts are contented), until the King's pleasure shall be the said household to be newly set up: we therefore heartily desire you, for the good mind you bear unto the Princess's said Grace, to be so good lord unto the bringers hereof, John Williams and Thomas Savage, two of her said late household, which are now desirous to do you service and have been always reputed for honest persons, to accept them unto your service in household at competent wages; with whom we trust your lordship shall have good cause to be contented. And we doubt not but your lordship and all other honourable men of these parts to whom we semblably have written at this time for others of the said late household shall attain thanks of the King's Highness, the Queen's Grace and Princess accordingly.[1]

[1] Princess Mary spent only a year and a half (1525–7) in the Welsh Marches, after which her huge household at Ludlow, Tickenhill and Thornbury became 'superfluous'. On 25 March 1528 the Marcher Council wrote to Wolsey to say that it had been discharged and enclosed a draft letter to thirty-four abbots in the Marches asking them in the king's name to take in some of its former officers: Skeel, *The Council in the Marches of Wales*, 52–3; *L&P Henry VIII*, IV/2, no. 4096. This seems to be one such letter.

16.   *Walter Devereux, Lord Ferrers,*[1] *to Bishop John Vesey*
       16 June [1529]
       Berington 3 (6)

Addressed: To the right honourable and my very good Lord President of the Princess' Council. And to other my lords and fellows of this same.

My very good lord, My duty used in my most hearty manner, I commend me unto your good lordship, ascertaining you this same that I have dissolved the King's sessions at Carmarthen to the King's profit and advantage according to the old custom there used, albeit, my good lord, so it is I have been roughly handled during the said sessions. For Rice Gruffith, esquire, divers and sundry times hath raised divers of the King's subjects, as well of this shire of Carmarthen as of other countries adjoinant, to the greatest numbers that he and his friends might make, and caused open proclamations to be made in churches that any man that loved him should come armed unto Carmarthen for disturbance of the King's peace. For proof whereof, upon Tuesday the 15 day of this Junii, about the hour of seven o'clock in the evening, I being in communication with divers gentlemen of the county for the rule of justice, he and his servants, armed, came suddenly into my chamber in the King's castle and incontinent made quarrel unto me for an unthrifty fellow, one Thomas ap Owen, being his kinsman. Which I had committed to ward for divers his misdemeanours, where he hath forfeited to the King's Majesty the sum of 650 marks, as appeareth as well by recognizance taken in the King's Exchequer here as by bonds taken before your lordship. And then this same Rhys, after he had given me divers and many opprobrious words, made assault on me with his dagger and would have stabbed me therewith. Howbeit, I remembering God and the King, forbare myself, commanding my servants on pain of their lives that they should do no harm to him nor to his. And so took his dagger from him and took him as a prisoner and so committed him unto ward, where he remaineth without bail or mainprise till the King's high pleasure and my Lord Cardinal's

Grace be therein known; unto whom I have certified all this whole matter. Notwithstanding, he and his adherents in his meinie doth raise with
open cry all the King's subjects that he and they can make, albeit I trust
in God, through your good assistance and other my lords and fellows of
the Council, to be able to order him and his according to [*inserted*: the
King] my sovereign lord his laws and, as case shall require, shall certify
your lordship from time to time, as knoweth Almighty God, who have
your good lordship in his blessed tuition. From Carmarthen, the 16 day
of this Junii. And the farther ordering of this same I remit to your high
discretion and other my fellows of the Council and, your mind [*here*]in
known, I shall o[*rder* ?] myself thereafter accordingly &c. Assuredly
yours, Walter Devereux.

¹ Walter Devereux, 3rd Lord Ferrers (*c*.1489–1558), was Chamberlain of South Wales
and steward of Princess Mary's household (*ODNB*). The year is fixed by the similar letter
that he wrote the same day to Wolsey: *L&P Henry VIII*, IV/3, no. 5682. Carmarthen Castle
was the seat of royal government in south Wales, as Caernarvon was in the north. Rhys ap
Gruffydd (*c*.1508–1531) was the grandson and heir of Sir Rhys ap Thomas (1448/9–1525),
who had lived at Carew Castle (see no. **43**) and been the King's principal lieutenant in
south Wales ever since the Battle of Bosworth: *ODNB* s.vv. Rhys, Sir, ap Thomas; Rice
Family (Rhys ap Gruffydd). The younger Rhys's wife was Katherine Howard, daughter of
Thomas, 2nd duke of Norfolk. He was not allowed to assume his grandfather's position and
attempted to claim it by force. He was beheaded on 4 December 1531.

17.   *Articles and remembrances for the Marcher Council*
        *1 November [1529]*¹
        Berington 8

Articles and remembrances to be delivered unto my Lord President
concerning the good rule, [*inserted*: reformation] and coming well of the
lordships, marches and other the King's poor subjects in those parts &c.
    First, where sundry and many heinous murders, rapes, robberies,
felonies and other great enormities and offences have been and daily
be committed within the same lordships [*deleted*: and little] to the great
fear, inquietness and impoverishing of the King's true subjects in those
parts and [*little*] or no condign punishments can be had, for as much as
the chief officers there, who be bare and poor gentlemen having neither
lands nor fees but only their due perquisites, be made officers with
[*inserted*: in] the said lordships, and do support, maintain and favour
[. . .] malefactors, being patised² with them, as is supposed and alleged
[*deleted*: thought], whereby it is thought that all such enormities doth
proceed and follow, impossible to be reformed [*deleted*: un] unless such
head officers be changed and better ordered.
    Item, it is thought that if it would please the King's Highness, being
advertised of the premises, by the assent of the lords marchers, by

authority of this Parliament to enact and divide the said lordships [*deleted*: marchers] in the Marches into sundry counties and shires, as the same do lie and be adjoint, and that the law of England may be [*inserted*: there] current [*deleted*: there] and officers as in all other counties there ordered and established, that the same countries and lordships should be in good order and [*inserted*: that] the King's true subjects inhabiting the same should live [*inserted*: in] restful quietness [*deleted*: as] in like manner as other the King's subjects do live in all other counties [*inserted*: as well] within South Wales [*deleted*: and; *inserted*: as] North Wales, where good laws and good customs be used: And that also [*inserted*: that] the said lord marchers should thereby have more profit, having the royalty within their several lordships (as all fines, amerciaments, wards, marriages, escheats, waifs, strays, cattles, [*inserted*: felonies], *fugitivours*, *dampnandours*[?],[3] utlegators[4] and such other forfeitures as reason requireth), than they now have.

[*The whole of the following paragraph is deleted.*]

Item, if such divisions [*inserted*: of the said lordships] into shires cannot be had and made as above mentioned, it is thought by this Council [*inserted*: for; *deleted*: the] good rule of the country to be had, that as well the King's Highness as all other lords marchers should and must appoint and depute sufficient sad and discreet approved persons to be the chief and head officers within their several lordships under them, having sufficient and reasonable fees or wages for the exercising their said offices, whereby they may live truly without any bribery, extortions or corruption, and that also as well the same lords marchers as all other such head officers to be bound in great bonds to the King's use truly and indifferently to minister justice without any redemption, fine or unlawful favour.

Item, where at this day more than in times past great numbers of mares, foals and other cattles, as well oxen, kine, sheep and other young beasts, be engrossed, bought and driven out of these parts into the [*deleted*: fr] countries of Kent, Southfolk and Southsex, and so conveyed by water, as well quick as barrelled, over sea into Flanders, France and other parts [*deleted*: beyond the sea]; whereby not only poor [*inserted*: ? the] husbands [*inserted*: ? in especial] the inhabitants [*deleted*: ? do of] in boroughs and towns, being craftsmanlike, in great penury and scarceness; for, whereas a fat ox of late [*deleted*: by; *inserted*: time] was bought for 12 or 13*s*, a fat cow for a noble, a veal [*deleted*: at] for 2*s* and a fat mutton [*deleted*: at] for 16*d*, at this day a fat ox is at 33*s* 4*d* or 40*s*, a cow at 20*s*, a veal at 40*d* and a mutton at 3*s*; by occasion whereof as well victuals as corn be at such high prices that boroughs and towns be decayed and the inhabitants thereof in such poverty that they [*deleted*: can] be not able to find their children and servants meat and drink. It is thought, if a restraint were made that no such cattles should pass over sea, and also that such persons as be great drivers of cattles and engross all the cattles in any fair and market to the intent aforesaid should be sequestered and put to silence, that such scarceness of victuals should be converted into plenteousness.

Item, it is to be remembered that the Council at Ludlow have at this day, being the first day of November, no money in their hands of the King's cofferers to sustain and keep the Household together. Wherefore the Council either must be drawn of necessity to dissever and *dishous. yold*[?][5] themselves, which to do they be not minded, or else short provision must be had for money to maintain, sustain and continue the said Household; for a great wearinesses [*sic*] to the Council it is to be unpaid their fee, as some of them be, and to give their attendance also upon their own costs and charges. Which known to the King's Highness by the good inducement[6] and information of my Lord President, the Council doubteth not will be shortly holpe[*n and*] remedied.

[The rest, including any signature, is torn off.]

[1] The year can be fixed by the reference to 'this Parliament'. The Reformation Parliament opened on 3 November 1529; in the previous fourteen years, under Wolsey, there had been only one session, from April to August 1523. In 1535, by an Act of this Parliament (27 Henry VIII c.26), the counties of Brecon, Radnor, Montgomery and Denbigh were created and the Marcher lordships of Clun, Chirbury, Oswestry and Whittington incorporated into Shropshire. See also no. **2** above and Berington 2, 'Articles wherein my lord legate's gracious pleasure is to be known', May 1526.

[2] Agreed.

[3] 'Goods of fugitives and condemned felons'? Neither word is in *OED*. But the *Dictionary of Medieval Latin from British Sources*, ed. R.E. Latham et al. (London, 1975–   ), s.v. *fugitivus*, quotes the Peterborough Chronicle: *catalla felonum, fugitivorum et dampnatorum.*

[4] Outlawries.

[5] 'Dishousehold': not in *OED*, but 'dishouse' was in use in the sixteenth century.

[6] 'Persuasion', but also 'statement of facts introducing other important facts (*legal*)'.

18.   *John Russell I to Prior William More of Worcester*[1] *and Roger Wintour*
        31 October [1530]
        Berington 6 (3)

Addressed: To my good lord prior of Worcester And to Mr Roger Wynter Esquire And unto either of them.

My most hearty commendations premised. For that ye have not subscribed, like as according to the appointment I did, the paper which by your assignment I left enclosed and sealed to be delivered you with Mr Sexton of Worcester at day among us accorded, I send now the same paper unto you again by this bearer, praying you to set your hand to the same and so to remit it unto me by this bringer, my said servant. And, and [*sic*] that for as much as accordingly as among us was agreed, the effects *comprised*[?] in the said paper be now at length drawn, devised and *engrossed*[?] [*inserted*: in indenture] in due form according to the law, as I am advertised by substantial men learned in the law named thereunto by my lord of Evesham,[2] as among us was accorded: therefore, upon sight of the same this day, indented and in both parts signed and sealed by my lord of Evesham, I have semblably either part of the same indenture of an award signed and sealed for my part, having a sure trust that you will do the same, according as among us was promitted.[3] For which [*deleted*: I] intent I perceive my said lord of Evesham hath now by his servant Thomas Watson sent the same indentures unto you which were brought unto me by the same Thomas this morning. Which award so signed and sealed I hear my lord of Evesham will, in our name and his, send unto both parties in manner as between us also was agreed, having a good trust for my part that we shall do a good [*inserted*: deed] therein, acceptable before God and to the great quietance of both shires, and also to the right good contentance of both parties and their friends at length, howsoever it shall appear to them at first sight. And thus I pray Christ have you both in his blessed tuition. Written at Elmley, the last day of October.

Mr Winter.[4] So it is that after my coming here from the Council late upon Saturday last, I was advertised that Mr William Neville[5] had left word that a great riot, by him suppressed, should be done at his house in Weke[6] the last week by Mr Vampage;[7] whereof I would be sorry if it be true. Nevertheless, I perceive, for our discharge, it shall be requisite it be inquired of as a-voiding[8] our indemnities in such cases. Wherefore, where ye shall please and when we shall have meeting therein, I pray you advertise me by my servant this bearer. And thus eftsoons[9] fare ye well, as I would myself. Your J. Russell.

---

[1] William More was cathedral prior of Worcester from 1518 to 1535. His day-book was edited, as *Journal of Prior William More*, by Ethel S. Fegan for Worcs. Hist. Soc. in 1914 and used by David Knowles for a sympathetic portrait in *The Religious Orders in England*, III: *The Tudor Age* (Cambridge, 1959), 108–26, repr. in his *Saints and Scholars* (Cambridge, 1962), 153–72. See also Julian M. Luxford, 'Flourishing the Register: The Worcester Monk-Artist Thomas Blockeley at Work', *Transactions of the Worcestershire Archaeological Society* 3rd series 19 (2004), 141–8. A copy of the award, dated 3 October 22 Henry VIII (1530), is Berington 272.

[2] Abbot Clement Lichfield: see no. **13**.

[3] Promised.

[4] Roger Wintour: see no. **19**.

[5] William Neville (1497–1545), poet and second son of Richard Neville, 2nd Lord Latimer (*c.*1467–1530). In 1532 he was accused of treason on the grounds that he had prophesied the King's death and his own elevation to the earldom of Warwick. *ODNB*.

[6] Wick. A village just across the Avon from Pershore; both Neville and Vampage (n. 7

below) had estates near by: *Visitation of the County of Worcester, 1569*, 138; VCH *Worcs.*, IV. 26, 168n, 170 (the last quoting *L&P Henry VIII*, V, no. 1679).

[7] Sir John Vampage of Pershore; possibly the John Vampage of Nafford in Birlingham (see no. **22**) who inherited in 1516 and had died by 1550 (VCH *Worcs.*, IV. 26).

[8] Invalidating, nullifying.

[9] Again.

19.   *Roger Wintour*[1] *to John Russell I*[2]
2 November [1530]
Berington 4 (12)

Addressed: To the right worshipful John Russell Esquire at Elmley deliver this.

In my heartiest manner I recommend me unto you. And, whereas I send you knowledge by your servant that I would make a presentment in your name and mine for a sessions to be kept at Worcester on Tuesday next for the entry committed at Wyke, at the which day I would a' be much desirous to have communed with you for divers causes which is here too long to write, and this Allhallows Day I received a letter from London that I must [*inserted*: be] there myself before Sunday next for a great matter, for the which I am sorry that I cannot keep 'pointment with you. Wherefore, because ye are next adjoining[3] it is requisite you do enquire of it: on Friday next ye shall have the Under-Sheriff at Bromsgrove. And thus fare ye as well as I would myself, this All Soulen day. Yours to his power, Roger Wynter.

[1] Roger Wintour (d. 1535). Of Huddington Court near Droitwich, and great-grandfather of the Gunpowder Plotters Robert, Thomas and John Wintour (VCH *Worcs.*, III. 409). Cf nos. **18**, [**13**]. His wife was Elizabeth, daughter of Sir John Hungerford; cf. Appendix IV. Their son Robert married Catherine, daughter of Sir George Throckmorton of Coughton.

[2] This letter is the reply to no. **18** above.

[3] Russell at Elmley Castle was three miles south of Wick, where the riot had taken place.

20.   *Sir John Russell to John Russell I*
6 April [1533]
Berington 6 (2)

Addressed: To the right worshipful Master Russell this be delivered.

Endorsed: Mr Russell's letter of the Court.

Right worshipful, In my heartiest manner I recommend me unto you, and have received your letter; ascertaining you I have been in hand with Mr Cromwell for your matters as effectuously as I would if they had been my own. And I perceive by him that he hath been laboured and persuaded by some manner against you, that he is very stiff in the other's cause and saith it were pity to put him out that is in possession already. Wherefore I think verily he is forelaboured by other. And, as touching the Abbot of Westminster,[1] as yet there is none nominate but I think that there shall be one shortly, and when he shall be known I will not fail to have you in remembrance and to do the best therein I can. Sir, I thank you for the pasty of lampreys you sent me, assuring you it was a very good dish. And there be any pleasure I may do you, you may command me as your own assuredly to the best of my little power, as knoweth our Lord, who send you good life and long. At Westminster, the 6th day of April, Your assuredly, J. Russell.

Since the writing of this letter, I spake with Mr Cromwell, and he saith he will do the best for you he can.

[1] Abbot John Islip died on 12 May 1532; his successor, William Boston, was not elected until April 1533: *L&P Henry VIII*, VI, no. 417/21. When Pershore Abbey was founded in 975, it was endowed with 300 hides, a quarter of Worcestershire. Edward the Confessor gave 200 of them to Westminster, but the lands of the two abbeys remained 'inextricably intermingled', and Pershore 'still retained some rights over all 300': Frank and Caroline Thorn, eds., *Domesday Book, 16: Worcestershire* (Chichester, 1982), note 8 (no page nos., about half-way through). So an interregnum at Westminster might affect leases etc. in much of Worcestershire.

21. *Thomas Cromwell to Sir John Russell and others*
     18 July [1533–5][1]
     Berington 5 (6)

I commend me unto you in my right hearty manner. And by the letters which I send to you here enclosed ye may perceive the complaint of Robert Symondes[2] of Pershore in the county of Worcester. Wherefore I heartily desire [*deleted*: you] and pray you groundly[3] to consider and ponder the contents of the same and, calling the parties before you, ye [*sic*] by such ways and means as ye can best devise examine the whole circumstances thereof and set a final end therein (if ye can). And if, through the obstinacy of either of the said parties, ye cannot conveniently so do, then my further desire is that ye write unto me the truth and plainness of the matter, with the circumstances thereof, to the intent that I may therein cause some means to be found as the [*omitted*: case] rightly shall require. Whereby ye shall do a very good and meritorious deed. And thus fare ye heartily well. At London, the 18th day of July, Your friend, Thomas Crumwell.

To my loving friends Sir John Russell knight, Roger Wynter, John Pakyngton and John Vampage esquires, or three [*deleted*: of] or two of them.

¹ The year is uncertain. Cromwell was acting Secretary from September 1532 while Gardiner was abroad and replaced him in April 1534. Roger Wintour (cf. nos. **18–19**) died in 1535: VCH *Worcs.*, III. 409.
² Mentioned on 16 April 1531 in *L&P Henry VIII*, V, no. 198.
³ Thoroughly.

22.   *Abbot William Boston¹ to John Russell I*
         23 April [1534]
         Berington 4 (5)

Addressed: To the right worshipful Master Russell Esquire, [*on*]e of the King's Council [*in*] the Marches of Wales.

Worshipful and good Master Russell, Most heartily I have me recommended unto you and have not forgotten my promise that whosoever should succeed you in my farm of Byrlingham² should in the same desire your good will. The truth is, I have letten the same farm to one William Tucke, a servant of mine own, on whose behalf I desire you to give him your good will, and at your coming hither he himself shall do the same. And, for as much as this year now to come he cannot occupy it in his own person, I also require and pray you to give your good will to that person, whosoever it be, that my receiver at his being in those parts shall name and appoint to occupy the said farm under the said William Tucke, promising you by these my letters that Robert Symondes, my bailey there, shall not have the occupation thereof, and the rather because I do not perceive him to be in your favour. And thus the Holy Ghost have you in his keeping. From my house at night this St George's day, Your own, William Ab[bot] of Westm[inster].

¹ See no. **20** above.
² Birlingham, three miles south-south-west of Pershore, was an estate of Westminster (VCH *Worcs.*, IV. 23–9); cf. no. **20** above.

23.   *Sir Thomas Audley and Thomas Cromwell to Sir John*
         Russell and others¹
         20 July [?1535]
         Berington 5 (8)

Addressed: To their loving friends Sir John Russell the younger, knight, John Pakington esquire and John Russell esquire, and to every of them be this given.

Endorsed: Wigorn.

After our right hearty commendations. Where the King's commission was directed unto you and other for the surveying and taxation of the clear yearly value of all the possessions of the clergy in the shire of Worcester, according to a book of Instructions assigned with the hand of the King's Highness annexed unto the said commission: we signify unto you that the King's pleasure is that ye, calling your fellows joined with you in commission, shall with all possible diligence accomplish the effect thereof, and to send to us to London all the books taken by you of the view and value of the said possessions, by one or two such of your fellows which were Auditors of the same, before the 12th day of September next coming, not failing this to do at your perils and as ye intend to advance the King's pleasure in this behalf. And thus fare you well. At London, the 20th day of July, Thomas Audeley, L. Chancellor, Thomas Crumwell

¹ This letter probably concerns the *Quarta Taxatio* of the clergy in July 1534. The assessment for the diocese of Worcester is bound into the Visitation Act Book of Bishop John Bell (1539–43), Worcestershire Record Office 2764/82. In the Vale of Evesham the £100,000 paid to the king by the clergy in 1531–5 seems to have been assessed at half of a Tenth for each of the five years. C.W. Clarke, 'Vale of Evesham Secular Clergy (1532, 1534, 1535, 1540) and their Payments for the Pardon of 1531', *Vale of Evesham Historical Society Research Papers* 2 (1969), 27–37.

24.   *Survey of Little Malvern Priory*¹
            [1535]
            Hodgson Transcripts; source unidentified

Articles of Instructions
[1] The names of houses, of what religion, to whom they ben cells, and of what value at the last valuation.
[2] The clear yearly value of the same at this new survey.
[3] The number of religious persons with their lives and conversations, and how many ben priests and how many will have capacities.
[4] The number of servants, hinds and other persons having their living of the same house.
[5] The value of bells, leads and other buildings to be sold with the estate or ruin of the said house.
[6] The entire value of the movable stock and store, with the debt owing to the house.
[7] The woods, with the age of them, parks, forests, commons belonging to the house and number of acres.
[8] The debts owing by the house.
[9] The houses of religion left out at the last valuation.

Answers to the said Articles

[1] The priory of Little Malvern, black monks of the order and rule of St Bennet, valued at £98 10s 9½d.

[2] £101 6s 1½d, whereof the due £10 6s 8d; the other rents, fees, woods, perquisites with the improperations *communibus annis*[2] £90 14s 5½d.

[3] Seven with the prior, all professed, whereof priests five, all of good conversation and living, both by report of the country and otherwise, desireth the King's Highness they may continue their religion there if his pleasure be that the same house shall remain unsuppressed or otherwise; two of them desireth capacities.

[4] Nineteen, whereof yeomen, two; hinds, servants, eight; persons having their living by convent seal, four; and other priests to serve the cure of Little Malvern aforesaid and persons having fees excepted, four.

[5] £17, the house being an old house and in decay, but it standeth very necessely [*sic* AMH] for the relief of poverty, and most specially the parish church, adjoining unto the priory church, both under one roof, being almost down, the parishioners there, oppressed with poverty, not able to repair the same. In consequence thereof, in case the house be suppressed it were a very gracious deed to preserve the poor church, being a [*illegible*].

[6] £41 9s 5d, as appeareth by an inventory thereof rendered.

[7] One hundred and six acres, whereof old woods of a hundred years' grow and upwards in Malvern Chase worth to be sold, £90; wood of ten years and under sixteen acres, which will be worth at fifteen years' grow 40s, and other woods in the Chase foresaid, where the Prior hath but fuels and attachments only, the quantity and value not upwards for because the said Prior may not sell the same commons in Malvern Chase with [*torn*] of cattles without any rate from other parks and forests more.

[8] £76 2s 5½d, as appeareth by a book of particulars thereof rendered.

---

[1] See *L&P Henry VIII*, IX, no. 1124; VCH *Worcs.*, III. 449–53. Little Malvern was in Oswaldslow Hundred; Great Malvern, Birtsmoreton, Castlemorton etc. were in Pershore Hundred.

[2] 'In normal years'.

25.   *Thomas Cromwell to Sir Gilbert Talbot[1] and John Russell I*
     7 September [1536]
     Berington 5 (3)

Addressed: To my loving friends Sir Gilbert Talbot knight and John Russell esquire and to either of them.

After my hearty commendations. I have received your letters touching the lewd communication of the vicar of Crowley[2] and have declared the contents of the same to the King's Highness. Who taketh your faithful diligences therein in very good part and for answer hath commanded me to signify unto you that his pleasure is you shall eftsoons examine the priest himself upon what ground he uttereth that communication, using all the ways ye can possibly devise to fish out of him whether he hath had any communication thereof with any other person, or whether he know any man minded or disposed, if he might get such opportunity, to such purpose, not sparing for the knowledge thereof to pinch him with pains to the declaration of it in case good advertisement will not serve to the same. And what you shall find herein, advertise, keeping him in the mean season in sure and sauf custody, your pains wherein his Grace will consider accordingly. And thus fare you heartily well. From Grafton, the 7th of September. Your loving friend, Thomas Crumwell.

I send you again for your better instruction the examination taken of this matter.

[1] Sir Gilbert Talbot II of Grafton near Bromsgrove succeeded in 1517 and died in 1543: VCH *Worcs.*, III. 126. According to *Visitation of the County of Worcester, 1569*, 134, his son Walter (or William) married Elizabeth, daughter of Roger Wintour of Huddington (see nos. **18, 19, 21**).

[2] Talbot and Russell had informed Cromwell that the parson of Crowle, Sir James Pratt, had spoken seditious words in an alehouse about the suppression of Studley Priory, near Redditch, and that they had committed him to Worcester gaol: *L&P Henry VIII*, XI, no. 407.

26.   *Thomas Cromwell to John Russell I*
     8 October [1536]
     Berington 5 (4)

Addressed: To my loving friend Mr John Russel, [*deleted*: *illegible*; *inserted*: one] of the Council in the Marches of Wales.

In my right hearty manner I commend me unto you, advertising the same [*sic*] that I have received your letters with also the information against the person that ye wrote to me of:[1] wherein, being at this [*inserted*: time] enbusied about other affairs of greater importance, I have no opportunity to answer you conveniently, but rather, giving you thanks for your pains taken in that behalf, do require and pray you for the time to commit the said person to ward and sauf custody till this troublous season[2] be a little quieted, that I may have leisure to order the matter accordingly: not doubting but or [*sic, for* ere] this ye have received the King's letters, the effect and tenor whereof I doubt not you will ensure according to such trust as the King's Highness hath committed unto you in that behalf. And so fare ye well. At Windsor, the 8th day of October. Your loving friend, Thomas Cromwell.

In your monastery I will do my best.

[1] Echoing Cromwell's wording in the previous letter, Talbot and Russell reported on 25 September that they had examined Pratt 'as well by advertisement as after by pinching with pain', but could get nothing more out of him: *L&P Henry VIII*, XI, no. 495. This is his reply. Pratt was still in Worcester Castle in January 1537, when he was described as 'aged and not like to live there': *L&P Henry VIII*, XII/1, no. 109.

[2] The Lincolnshire rising, which had begun on Sunday 1 October.

27. *Edward Bache[1] to John Russell I*
      28 November 1536
      Berington 4 (14)[2]

Addressed: To the right worshipful my especial good master John Russell esquire, Secretary to the King's Highness in the Marches of Wales, be these given.

Endorsed: My last bills and writing received for [*Mr Calph*]all at Wenlock by I. Parsons.

Right worshipful master, My duty used, these sha[*ll be to advertise*] you that, by warrant of your letter to Master Calphall[3] (who [*is now*] absent) and to me addressed, I have delivered to John Parsons, this bearer, your servant, the sum of ten pounds four shillings sterling comen to my hands and by me received of the profits of your mastership's office sithence the 18th day of October last past unto the present day. Thus I commit your mastership to the tuition and guidance of the Holy Trinity.[4] Scribbled at Wenlock, the 28th day of November in [*deleted*: the] anno 28° Regis Henrici Octavi. Your humble servant, Edward [*B*]ashe

[1] See also no. **31**. About 1600 a John Bache was one of Humphrey Pakington's servants (see nos. **73**, **78**, **101**), and Baches still live in Chaddesley Corbett, the village of which Harvington Hall is the manor-house: cf. nos. **39**, **59**.

[2] The top right-hand corner of the letter is missing.

[3] Probably Humphrey Caulfield (Callfild): see no. **31**.

[4] The commendation, though a common one, may have been suggested by the dedication of Much Wenlock parish church.

28. *John Russell I to Richard Rich*[1]
     25 September [1537]
     Berington 6 (1)

My duty unto your mastership premised. For as much as upon late
survey, among other, of the rents and possessions of Little Malvern in
Worcestershire certificate is now comen thereof to your hands; and to
avoid spoil and waste thereof, as well as to set forth forward necessary
tillage for this year in seasonable time therefor, now approaching: it may
please your mastership by this bearer to send me authority (like as the
King's Highness, as ye know, hath granted me therein preferment) to
enter and to put it into good use; and also of your favour to have further
preferment in such goods, cattles and implements meet for me as be
comprised in the inventory there late made; and thenceforth, because
the whole demesnes there (wherein is but small tillage ground) not able
to maintain households there; which considered—the ground [*inserted*:
very barren], the people there [*deleted*: very barren and poor; *inserted*:
very poor]—is much requisite there to be kept. And, for that the rent of
the farm, parsonage and tithes of Ellisfylde and Hardweyk Moor parish,[2]
three or four miles distant from Little Malvern, letten under covenant
sent ye by the same bearer, for better maintenance of households there
reserved in no money but in grains of divers kinds, as wheat, barley, oats
and peases and other necessaries for households, valued in the same certificate (over and above *100s*[?] out thereof yearly paid in pension to the
house of Shene, and with 17*s* 6*d* ob. reserved yearly thereof for rents of
assize and of tenements at will) at £14 19*s* 4*d* ob. by year: like as I have
been a suitor to your mastership heretofore, I needs eftsoons now require
you for the better maintenance of my poor house to be kept there, that,
charged for the same at King's Highness' pleasure [*sic*], I may of your favour therein have preferment *together*[?] with the demesnes, and also of
the rents and cottages of the village of Little Malvern set unto the . . . tion
of the late priory there. Wherein ye shall [*inserted*: *illegible*] shall much
bind me to requite therein your goodness, which shall not be forgotten,
God willing; who send you good accomplishment of your good and
worshipful desires. Written the 25 day of September, Your John Russell

To the right worshipful Master Rich, Chancellor of the Court of Augmentations.

---

[1] Richard Rich was appointed Chancellor of the Court of Augmentations when it was set
up in 1536.
[2] Eldersfield is about six miles south-south-east of Little Malvern; Hardwick was one of
the manors within it: VCH *Worcs.*, IV. 76–83; A. Mawer and F. M. Stenton with F.T.S.
Houghton, *The Place-Names of Worcestershire*, English Place-Name Society 4 (Cambridge, 1927), 197ff.

29.   *John Russell I to Thomas Cromwell*[1]
28 September 1537
L&P Henry VIII, XII/2, no. 769

Right honourable and my singular good lord, mine humble duty premised. Being of none power to thank your lordship for your manifold goodness showed to me and my poor son, I must as your bedesman further beseech your good continuance, as well to me in the late suppressed house
of Little Malvern, the village there and the farm thereto appurtenant
called Ellisfield, wherein I have ben a bold suitor by your commandment
to your good lordship before this time and found you in the same my
special good lord: that by your favour and good mean I may obtain such
grant thereof of the King's Highness to me and mine heirs, mine old true
service committed and to be done my life during graciously considered,
that I may thereby be more able to maintain my poor house and living
and mine heirs after me, ever to serve his Highness according to our
most bounden duty. Wherein, God willing, with your lordship's favour
I shall be a further suitor in the next term. As also that of your charity,
as ye have ben, [ye] will continue good lord unto my said son in his suit
for the reversion of mine office in the King's Signet in the Marches of
Wales, whereunto I trust with your lordship's favour he may be meet.
And he and I shall both account us therefor much bound to pray for your
good lordship, and, next the King our sovereign lord, to bear you our
hearts and service. It may further please your lordship of your blessed
disposition and charity to be so good lord unto the King's poor tenants
of Little Malvern, now suitors unto his Highness for their five bells that
have always served their parish church as well as the monastery there
late suppressed, amounting all in value (to be sold after 20s the hundred) to £45 0s 6¾d, make plaint, being else destitute of any bell to the
same parish, that by your good lordship's favour they may of the King's
especial grace obtain so gracious answer therein, or at least his most gracious favour to have before strangers preferment in the sale of the same
bells, as upon suit heretofore by me made to their use to the Chancellor
of the King's Court of Augmentation, was by him granted, with reasonable days of payment, their great poverty considered: wherein, in mine
poor opinion, your good lordship may do a full blessed deed, for I have
not seen so poor a sort so well and strong-hearted at their poor power to
charge themselves in such a good deed. And thus I pray Christ long to
preserve your good lordship in health and honour. Written the 28th day
of September. Your orator, John Russell Armiger

---

[1] This letter fixes the year of no. **28** and shows that Cromwell had not yet 'done his best'
(no. **26**) about Russell's petition. In the end, Russell was granted Little Malvern Priory and
the rents in kind of Eldersfield on 20 May 1538: *L&P Henry VIII*, XIV/1, 607. There is an
attested transcript in Berington 170 (32).

30. *Sir Thomas Audley to John Russell I*
      14 March [1537–40][1]
      Berington 5 (1)

Addressed: To my brother Russell these be delivered.

Endorsed: My Lord Chancellor's letter.

After my right hearty commendations. Where lately I addressed forth the King's writ of injunction to one William Cokke[2] of Keysend[3] that he, under a certain [*omitted*: penalty] in the same writ expressed, should in no wise make or cause to be done any scathe or waste in certain lands and tenements lying in Barowe, Rydmarley and other parishes in the counties of Wygorn and Gloucester until such time as the title thereof depending before me in the King's Court of Chancery between him and one John Cokke were fully ordered and determined, the said parties being also farther bound before me in recognisances of five hundred marks to abide and obey such award and *precipe*[4] as shall be taken therein by me and the said Court of Chancery this next term: the foresaid William Cokke, notwithstanding the said writ of injunction was delivered unto him accordingly, having little regard thereto, ne yet to the penalty therein contained, hath sithence the delivery thereof contemptuously, as credibly I am informed, made much scathe and waste upon the same lands in felling and cutting down many ashes and [*deleted*: hale] hazels which were there growing to a great number, and hath made several sales thereof to divers men, as to John Harvard[5] and William Harvard and other, in the manifest contempt of the King and Court of Chancery. Therefore, perceiving the man to be of such enormity, I require and pray you to call both him and the said Harvards before you, and so to give them in commandment upon certain pains in the King's behalf, to them to be limited, that they ne none of them meddle with any manner felling, cutting down or carrying away of any the said woods but suffer as well that that i[s] yet standing as that that is felled and cut down to remain there still according to the tenor of the King's said writ of injunction until such time as the matter [*be*] ordered by me and the said Court of Chancery, a[*s they*] will answer at their perils. And thus right heartily [*fare*] ye well. From Christ Church, the 14th of March. Your friend, Thomas Audley, Chancellor

---

[1] Christ Church (see address at end) was a priory in Aldgate, which Audley acquired as his London house in 1536 (*ODNB*); John Russell died in 1540. No. **32**, written to Russell nearly a year later, is about the same case. So this letter has been placed under 1538 and the later one under 1539, with a possible error of one year either way.

[2] Perhaps William Cokesey, who was auditor of Evesham Abbey, received a pension of £12 a year at its suppression and was one of the assessors of the Vale of Evesham deanery for the *Valor Ecclesiasticus* of 1535. Clarke, 'Vale of Evesham Secular Clergy', esp. 34.

[3] Now Chase End; at the southern end of the Malvern Hills (VCH *Worcs.*, III. 258) and close to the other parishes mentioned.

4 *Pr(a)ecipe*: a writ requiring something to be done. From *precipe quod reddat*: 'order him to render'.
5 Perhaps the John Harford of Bosbury who in 1549, with Richard Willison of Ledbury, acquired the possessions of a chantry at Ripple: VCH *Worcs.*, III. 496. See no. **48** below.

31.   *Thomas Cromwell to John Russell I*
       7 December 1538
       Berington 5 (5)

Addressed: To my loving friend John Russell Esquire, the King's Secretary of the Marches of Wales.

Mr Russell, After my hearty commendations. Whereas on the behalf of a right forward young man, Edward Bashe,[1] this bearer, I am informed that heretofore he hath exercised the room and office of your deputy or clerk in the King's Majesty's Signet in the Marches of Wales, and that upon certain controversies attempted betwixt your son and the said Edward you discharged him of any further intermeddling under you; and, for as much as he is advanced to the perfect knowledge of the said office and a person able to do the King's Highness acceptable service in that office and thereunto is well animated, I shall therefore heartily require and desire you, at the contemplation of these my letters and for my sake, to admit, accept and allow the said Edward into the said office as your deputy without further protraction of time, or at the least to admit the said Edward jointly occupier thereof with one Humphrey Calfilld,[1] now your deputy; and that, the said Edward receiving benefit at your hands as the moment of my requisition doth impart, doubt ye not I shall have your gratuity therein in remembrance, not to be forgotten, you may be sure, whensoever the time and case require. And thus heartily fare ye well. From London, the 7th of December, the thirty year of the King's Majesty's most noble reign. Your loving friend, Thomas Crumwell.

1 See also no. **27**.

32.   *Sir Thomas Audley to John Russell I*
       28 February [1538–40][1]
       Berington 5 (7)

Addressed: To my loving brother Mr John Russell be this given.

After my right hearty commendations. Whereas before this time I have taken travail and pain in the ordering of the matter in variance between Cocke and Cocke, and with great diligence reduced them, as me thought, to an honest indifferent order; who nevertheless, like cumbrous[2] people inclining rather to trouble and vexation than to quietness, have eftsoons disagreed upon mine award which I made for them in that behalf: whereupon, the said parties being here with me again, for as much as upon the declaration of their griefs I have eftsoons reformed my first award and declared my mind and intent therein, I heartily desire and pray you, in case you may apperceive that they vary again, that you will, in contemplation of these my letters, call them before you and, by such ways and means as you best can, cause them to obey, perform and accomplish my foresaid award according to the effect, purport and true meaning thereof: using them further in such wise therein that I be no more troubled with their clamorous suit. And in so doing you shall administer unto me right thankful pleasure, which I shall be glad at all times to requite with semblable friendship when occasion shall serve me. And thus as heartily fare you well as I would myself. Written at mine house of Christchurch in London the 28 day of February, Your loving friend, Thomas Audley Chancellor

I pray you have me commended to my sister your wife.

¹ For the dating of this letter, see no. **30** above. It is sealed with the Audley arms.
² Awkward.

33.   *Thomas Cromwell to [John Russell I]*
          18 February [1540]
          Berington 5 (2)

I commend me unto you. And whereas I am informed that without just cause or ground you do restrain and keep this bearer Richard Salwey, my servant, from the possession and use of the room and office of Peace in the county of Worcester, notwithstanding that he hath compounded and agreed with you for the same,¹ I require you that forthwith upon the receipt hereof you do permit and suffer my said servant to occupy, exercise and enjoy the said office with all the commodities and profits thereunto belonging, by himself or his sufficient deputy, according to the agreement and covenant concluded betwixt you and him for the same, making also unto my said servant delivery of all such records, remembrances and other writings as do remain in your hands and custody, whereby he may the better know the state of the said office; so as this bearer be not enforced and compelled to seek further remedy for recovery of his right in that behalf. Thus fare you well, from London the 18th of February, Your loving friend, Thomas Crumwell.

¹ In December 1539 Richard Salway, under-sheriff of Worcestershire, complained to Cromwell that, although he had paid John Russell and his son Henry £20 for the clerkship

of the peace, they had refused him admittance to it. At the same time he asked for two estates formerly owned by the Gloucestershire abbeys of Winchcombe and Hailes: *L&P Henry VIII*, XIV/2 (August–December 1539), no. 729. The intervention in this letter was effective: Berington 4 (8) is an undated letter from William Sheldon to 'my cousin Salwey, *Clerk of the Peace*, . . . or else to Mr Russell of the Council'.

34.   *Inventory of Little Malvern Church*[1]
       8 August 1552
       The National Archives, E.117/9/22/46

8 die Augusti in anno Regni Edwardi Sexti sexto.

This inventory indented of all bells, plate, [*and*] ornaments within the parish of Little Malvern, made and presented to the King's Majesty's Commissioners by Sir Thomas Bell, curate of the same parish, and John Marten, churchwarden there. Made *in anno sexto Edwardi sexti* as followeth, viz.

Imprimis, a chalice of silver by estimation nine ounces; Three old copes of coarse gear, not being silk; Two vestments and one alb of like art; One cross of copper; Two small bells,[2] whereof one is not our own.

      John Russell   W. Sheldon   G. Wall

[1] This inventory has also been printed in *Transactions of the Worcestershire Archaeological Society* n.s. 31 (1954), 23.
[2] At the Dissolution there were five, worth £45 0s 6¾d at 20s a hundredweight and so weighing about 2¼ tons. Despite John Russell's request to Cromwell (no. **29** above), this inventory shows that four of them had gone. Sir John Russell and others qcquired them in November 1537: Berington 170 (2), p. 28 (transcript). The survivor, cast in the fourteenth century, probably by John Rudhall of Gloucester, is inscribed *Ave Maria Gratia Plena Dominus Tecum* and may have been the Angelus bell.

35.   *Will of Milbora Russell*
       27 June 1574
       Berington 278

Milbarow Russell de Malvern Parva

In the name of God, Amen. I Mylbora Russell of Little Malvern in the county of Worcester widow, late wife of Henry Russell deceased, being sick in body but of whole mind and perfect remembrance, make this my last will and testament in manner and form following. First, I bequeath my soul to Almighty God and my body to be buried in the chancel of the church of Little Malvern. Item, I bequeath to my son John Russell all table boards, trestles, forms and all the hangings about the parlour walls, the furnace, the stone vat and all troughs in the bolt-house. Item, I bequeath unto my brother Charles Brocton the use of the bed and all that thereto belongeth that he now useth to lie in during his natural life, and after his decease to remain to my daughter Mary Russell for ever. Item, I give and bequeath to my son [*inserted*: -in-law] James Mintridge all such things [*deleted*: and cattle] that he hath in his possession which are mine, and further I release him and forgive him of all such debts as is betwixt him and me. Item, I give unto my daughter Elizabeth Russell that standing bedstead that I lie in. Item, I give Robert Davies my servant one of the best of my horses and [*deleted*: that is to say] six good sheep. Item, I bequeath all the rest of my goods [*and*] chattels, both movables and unmovables, my debts being paid and my funerals discharged, equally to be divided amongst my six daughters[1] at the discretion of my brother Charles Brocton and Henry Russell my son, whom I make my executors to this my last will and testament. Item, I will that if any of my daughters shall bestow themselves wilfully contrary to the mind of my executors,[2] then her part to be either distributed amongst the rest of her sisters or else to be employed to her use that hath so bestowed herself at the discretion of my [*deleted*: executors] executors. [*Deleted*: Item, I ordain my brother] Dated the 27 day of June in the sixteenth year of the reign of our sovereign lady Elizabeth [*deleted*: And further, and if it happen that any of my six daughters die before they [*be*] bestowed] witnessed as this my last will and testament [*sic*].

James Myntridge John Partriche Francis Brodford and John Russell and others.

[1] Altogether there were seven, but Maud had died by 1575 and her widower, James Mintridge, later married (2) Elizabeth Walwyn: cf. no. **113**. Berington 362 (see Appendix III, no. [6]) is an account-book, bound in leaves of plainsong notation, in which Henry Russell kept a record of these legacies (pp. 33–43) and ten times lists the six survivors in the order: Elizabeth, Joan, Anne, Margery, Frances and Mary. He also mentions 'my brothers' Cowarne (Joan), Chelmyck (Anne), Berrow (Margery) and Mintridge; Richard Hayward (*not* as 'my brother'); and 'portions of household stuff' for Frances and Mary. It seems that in 1574 Richard Hayward and Elizabeth were engaged but not yet married, and that Frances and Mary were still 'unbestowed'; Frances seems to have remained so. Only Anne and Margery seem to have survived until 1604 (no. **69**).

[2] The corresponding clause in an earlier draft will of 15 June 1568 (Lechmere Box A.14) runs: 'If it chance any of the said seven do die before they be bestowed, or abuse themselves in whoredom . . . , which God forbid, then I will her or their parts which so die or abuse herself or themselves equally to be divided amongst the rest of my daughters unbestowed.' It is not known what prompted this wording or why it was changed.

36.   *Probate inventory of Milbora Russell*[1]
1575
Worcestershire Record Office, I.1575/57a

An inventory of all the goods and chattels which were lately Milborowe Russell's of Little Malvern in the county of Worcester, widow deceased.

Imprimis, in the hall a table and form, old hangings, a bell and an old clock, 6s 8d

Item, in the parlour two tables with a bench backed with wainscot, three forms, a cupboard, an old coffer, three chairs, old hangings and a table of Henry the Eight, £1 13s 0d

Item, in the great parlour two beds with the appurtenances, three chests, gardevances, a round table, a truckle bed, £13 0s 0d

Item, in the buttery fifteen silver spoons, pewter and tin vessels, £12 1s 8d

Item, in the maids' chamber two beds and a coffer, £4 0s 0d

Item, in the men's chamber a standing bed with the appurtenances, a chest and a coffer, £4 0s 0d

Item, in an inner room [*deleted*: an woman's saddle] a pair of andirons, 3s 4d

Item, in the chapel chamber a down bed with the appurtenances, £6 13s 4d

Item, in the west chamber a feather bed with the appurtenances, £2 10s 8d

Item, in the great chamber two feather beds with the appurtenances, two coffers, a chair and a round table, £14 0s 0d

Item, in the east chamber a bed with furniture, £3 6s 8d

Item, in the men-servants' chamber two beds, £1 10s 0d

Item, in the cheese-house cheese, wool &c., £8 1s 6d

Item, in the kitchen pots, pans, broches &c., £10 0s 0d

Item, in a loft treenware and an old limbick,[2] 19s 6d

Item, in the brewhouse vats, skeels &c., £1 10s 0d

Item, in the bakehouse boulting tubs &c., £3 1s 10d

Item, in the deyhouse brass and other furniture, £8 15s 8d

Item, in the garner corn and malt, £11 15s 4d

Item, in the fields wheat and rye priced, £13 6s 8d

Item, in the field barley, £13 6s 8d

Item, in the barn wheat, £10 13s 4d

Item, in plough-gear, wains &c., £5 0s 0d

Item, in the larder-house a powdering-tub, barrels &c., 6s 8d

Item, poultry, 13s 4d

Item, goats, eight, £1 6s 8d

Item, eight horses, mares and colts, £20 0s 0d

Item, ten oxen, eighteen kine, two bulls, £80 0s 0d

Item, thirty-five swine of all sorts, £3 6s 8d

Item, thirty-six young beasts and thirteen calves, £60 13s 0d

Item, hay, £20 0s 0d
Item, two hundred and twenty sheep, £30 0s 0d
Item, hemp and flax, £3 0s 0d
Item, in the chapel chamber coffers, caskets, andirons, cushions, pillows
  for beds and windows [*sic*], pillow-beares, £7 6s 8d
Item, sheets: flax, hemp and hurden, 24 [*torn*]
Item, diaper, table-cloths, towels, napkins, £6 13s 4d
Item, flaxen and hempen table-cloths and napkins, £3 13s 4d
Item, silk coverlets and testerns, £6 13s 4d
Item, saddles, £2 0s 0d
Item, in the work-houses axes, bills &c., 16s 0d
Item, valleys[3] and spokes, £1 6s 0d

    Summa tota[*lis*] £427 9s 6d

[1] This inventory is also printed in Wanklyn, *Inventories of Worcestershire Landed Gentry*, 50–51. For the layout of the Court in 1575, see the Introduction, pp. xi, xiii, xvii, Appendix I; Brooks and Pevsner, *The Buildings of England: Worcestershire*, 431–4. The administration of his mother's will (no. **35**) and the division of the goods and chattels listed here caused Henry Russell much trouble. By the time that he started, his six sisters and their husbands had already helped themselves to livestock and household items that they fancied and had also paid current outgoings and made bridging loans to each other: Berington 362, pp. 33–43, and see note on no. **35**.
[2] Alembic.
[3] Felloes.

37. *George Selby to Elizabeth Pakington*
   [before 1580s?]
   Berington 562 (3)

        Jesus

Sweet Bess, The carrier stays, which makes me curtail my mind (most for that I have written wholly unto your brother) until my coming to Harvington. My only stay is my mother's trouble. With a thousand farewells and ten thousand k k k, Thine still assured, George Selby.

38. *The Privy Council to the Vice-Chancellor of Oxford*[1]
   14 August 1581
   Acts of the Privy Council of England, n.s. XII: 1580–1581, ed. John
    Roche Dasent (London, 1896), 170

A letter to the Vice-Chancellor and Doctors of the University of Oxford. That whereas their Lordships are informed that three Masters of Arts, namely one Russell, Stubbes and Yate, at the time of the apprehending of Campion the Jesuit at the house of one Yate of Lyford in that shire, were then in the said house: Forasmuch as their Lordships find by experience that most of the seminary priests which at this present disturb this Church have been heretofore scholars of that University, and that they and likewise one Jacob, a musician taken in Campion's company, have been tolerated there manye years without going to the church and receiving of the Sacraments, they are required (finding the information to be true) to examine the said Masters of Arts touching their being at Yate's house, what company was there, and whether Campion said any Mass or no, together with such other questions as they shall think meet to be propounded in that behalf; and further, to cause diligent search and enquiry to be made in all the colleges and houses of learning within that University after such suspected persons in religion, and to certifye their names unto their Lordships, using in the meane time the best means that they can to reduce them to conformity.

¹ For the context of this letter, see the Introduction, pp. xv–xvi above.

39. *Examination of John Felton*¹
  24 December 1582
  The National Archives, SP 12/156/29/i

The confession and examination of John Felton, priest, being of the age of seventy-four years or thereabouts, taken before the Reverend Father in God John, Bishop of Wigorn. the 24th day of December 1582 Anno Reginae Elizabethe xxv^to.

First, he saith that, being demanded where he lived all Queen Mary's time, saith that he served at a place called Locking in Berkshire. And two years after the said Queen's Majesty that now is came to the crown he served at a place called Sileby in Leicestershire, and after that about one year at Stretton-in-the-Dale in Com. Salop. From thence he went to Nether Wallop in Hampshire, where he served also for the space of seventeen weeks. After which time he gave over to serve and went from that place because he was threatened by one Lambert, a gentleman for citing of him. And from thence he went to one Mr Fowler's house near unto Stafford, where he found Dr Poole, late Bishop of Peterborough, who reconciled him to the Catholic Church again (meaning the Church of Rome). And, being demanded in what manner he reconciled him, he saith, by shriving him, absolving him and enjoining him penance of fasting &c. After which time he wandered abroad among his friends, and sometimes was with Mr William Gattacre at a place called Gatacre in the parish of Claverley in Com. Salop; sometimes with one Mr Thomas Farmer at Hoords Park near Bridgnorth in Com. Salop; sometimes with

Mr Jerome Hoord of Bridgnorth aforesaid; and sometimes with one Hilton in Com. Stafford.

And for the space of this ten years last past he hath been most in Worcestershire, Gloucestershire and Herefordshire. In Worcestershire, with one Robert Stringer of Upton Warren; with one Brooke near unto Hindlip; with one Mr Jeffreys of Ercombe [Earl's Croome];[2] with one Thomas More of Ripple.[3] And a little before harvest last with Mr Reginald Williams of Throckmorton;[4] since Michaelmas last with the Lady Throckmorton of Feckenham;[5] about four years ago with Mrs Heath of Alvechurch; within this two years at the Lady Windsor's; since Easter last with Mr Middlemore of Hawkslow; about a twelvemonth ago with Mrs Pakington of Chaddesley [Corbett]; within these two years at Mrs Talbot's of Grafton; about four years ago with John Badger's of Poolhouse, gent;[6] and within this twelvemonth at Hugh Lygon's of Upton, gent. To all which places he resorted as occasion served. In Gloucestershire, about four years ago at Forthampton with Mr Blount; in Herefordshire, at one George Fydoe's in the parish of Rochford. And being examined how often he hath said Mass within this twelvemonth, he answereth he cannot tell, but he saith peradventure he hath said Mass sundry times.

And being further examined where he hath said Mass, he answereth that he hath said Mass sundry times within this twelvemonth: at Thomas More's of Ripple, and namely on Tuesday last was a fortnight, where there was present at the said Mass the said Thomas More, Rhys More and Frances More, their sister; and being demanded who were all at his Masses there, he answereth he cannot tell. And further saith that, either in July or August last past, Mrs Sheldon, the wife of Ralph Sheldon esq., sent for him to the house of one Reginald Williams of Throckmorton to come to her to Strensham in Com. Wigorn. Which he did accordingly, and at his coming, being likewise requested by her, said Mass there, finding at Strensham such vestments and other furniture as is usually occupied in the celebrating of Mass. At which Mass were present the said Mrs Sheldon, Mrs Russell, and one other gentleman, whose name he knoweth not, and one man who helped him to say Mass, whose name he knoweth not. And further saith that at the same Mass Mrs Sheldon and Mrs Russell received the sacrament, and when he had said Mass, he was sent away; and saith also that Mrs Sheldon gave him two shillings and Mrs Russell gave him five shillings for his pains taken. And being demanded where else he hath said Mass, he answereth he cannot tell. And being further examined, whether at his Mass said at Strensham (where Mrs Sheldon and Mrs Russell received the sacrament) he shrived them before they received it or no, answereth he did shrive and absolve them; and so hath he likewise also shriven the said Thomas More and Rhys More.

Being demanded whether he knoweth any Popish priests, Jesuits or others coming from beyond sea, he saith that he knoweth none, but only one Barnes, son of one Barnes of Hanley Castle in Com. Wigorn., who is a priest and with whom this examinate once spake at Thomas More's aforesaid. And being demanded whether he have authority to reconcile or no, he answereth, if the Indulgence or Jubilee do continue, he hath authority so to do; and further saith that he reconciled the said Mrs Russell, if it were within the time of the aforesaid Jubilee. And being examined whom else he hath reconciled within this twelvemonth, he answereth that he hath reconciled one William Jeffreys of Warwick at *Coughton*[?] in Com. Warwick. Being demanded whereunto he did reconcile the said Mrs Russell and William Jeffries aforesaid, he answereth that he did reconcile them to the Catholic Church; and being asked who is the head of that Catholic Church, he saith he cannot tell. And further saith that Mrs Russell confessed unto him that she was reconciled to the Catholic Church by another all before that time, the cause whereof was because she had been at the service now used in the Church of England. And being further examined by what authority he did reconcile the persons aforesaid, he answereth that he received authority by word from Dr Allen beyond sea.

[1] The 1577 returns for Worcestershire are fairly thin, as Bishop Whitgift was too busy at Ludlow as Vice-President of the Marcher Council to collect many names in the time allowed: Ryan, 'Diocesan Returns of Recusants', in CRS 22, pp. 63–6. But on 24 December 1582 he took examinations of 'two old and very ignorant Massing priests', John Felton and Simon Southern, which do much to fill the gap. His covering letter to Walsingham (SP 12/156/29, printed in VCH *Worcs.*, II. 51), mentions searches in Worcestershire by 'Munday and his fellow', this being Anthony Munday, the spy and playwright who gave evidence against Campion. Of the two examinations, Felton's is much the longer, and the few names mentioned by Southern are all mentioned by Felton as well, except that Southern had been 'at Birlingham with a nephew of his, sometimes at Charlton with Mrs Dingley [see no. **168** below] . . . and at one Frewen's of Hanley Castle'. Neither mentions the Russells of Little Malvern, but Felton has a vivid account of saying Mass for Mrs Russell of Strensham and her sister Mrs Sheldon and mentions other names and houses that will recur later, including the Pakingtons of Chaddesley Corbett (Harvington).
[2] See no. **101**.
[3] The Mores of Ripple were watermen who worked a ferry across the Severn. Thomas had been Bishop Bonner's porter 'in Queen Mary's time': Whitgift to Walsingham as in n. 1 above.
[4] The timber-framed Throckmorton Court near Pershore was owned by Robert Throckmorton (d. 1581), who married Elizabeth Hungerford (VCH *Worcs.*, III. 356–7; cf. Appendix IV below). Was Reginald ('Rignall') Williams their bailiff there?
[5] Margaret (Puttenham), widow of Sir John Throckmorton, justice of Chester and vice-president of the Marcher Council. On 15 January 1578 she and others were reported to have heard Mass in the house of John Edwards of Chirk in Denbighshire. For details and extracts from both their wills, see A.L. Browne, 'Sir John Throckmorton of Feckenham', *Birmingham Archaeological Society: Transactions and Proceedings* 59 (1935), 123–42. One of their sons, Francis, was the plotter (1583); another, Edward, died at the English College in Rome in 1582: his lengthy panegyric by St Robert Southwell is in Foley, IV. 288–330.
[6] Pool House. John Badger's wife Eleanor was convicted of recusancy in 1588; in 1603

Elizabeth Badger married Francis Sheldon. See Diane Jennings Walker, 'Elizabethan Recusancy in Hanley Castle, I: The Gentry', *Midland Catholic History* 13 (2006), 12–13.

40.   *Henry Russell to Charles Russell*
   29 March [1585]
   Lechmere Box, C.29

Addressed: To his very loving brother Mr Charles Russell give these at his house, Greenhill in Pembrokeshire, with speed.

Endorsed: My brother Henry's letter of the 29th of March Ao. 1585.

Your letters (although long before they came to my hands), which you sent by Mr Maurice Canon his son,[1] were no less welcome unto me than your courtesy, plentifully uttered in them, deserveth, and the good affection of brotherly love desireth, or rather requireth. I am glad of your recovered health and wish you the long continuance thereof. As for Mr Canon his son, I would be ready to do him any pleasure; but what way my good will may be extended towards him, being placed both in house and with a reader and tutor chosen, I know not. But if I may any way be employed to friend him or forward his study, I shall be most heartily ready and willing. Your excuse I must receive of your slow writing to proceed not of your slackness but of want of messengers, lest that, if I should condemn you of reckless regard of your friends, I might be charged, by the same show of reason, with the like fault—although I might justly say I more seldom know of travel into those parts than I conjecture that you know of coming to Oxon. Mr White's son,[2] whom you commended, left Mr Gawyn,[3] his tutor, in the lurch of debt, at the least £7 or £8. I wrote unto his father by Mr Lorte.[4] Pity it were that the poor gentleman accepting him upon our recommendations should sustain any loss by our means. As you may, if you may be a means to procure him his money from Mr White, as also me £3 from Warreyn,[5] a scholar likewise recommended to me by you. Thus, thanking you and my sister for my good cheer, I commit you to God this 29th of March, Oxon. Yours to use as nature bindeth, Henry Russell.

[1] A Thomas Canon entered Jesus College in 1584/5. See Joseph Foster, *Alumni Oxonienses, 1500–1714* (Oxford, 1891), I, for all those noted here.
[2] A William White entered St John's College in 1582.
[3] Mr Gawyn has not been identified.
[4] Thomas Lorte entered Gloucester Hall in 1578 and took his BA in 1581/2 and his MA in 1584. Canon, White and Lorte were from Pembrokeshire.
[5] A William Warren entered Gloucester Hall in 1578.

41. *W. West to Henry Russell, 1585*[1]
23 August 1585
Berington 29 (2)

Addressed: To his loving cousin Mr Henry Russell of Long Wittenham deliver this letter at the worshipful Mr Willis, President of St John's College in Oxford, or at his house, with speed.

Mr Russell, I wrote at large the better to instruct you of Captain Borne's dealing for Sawyer and his mother great wrong, which will be revealed before the Lords against you and others with &c. Which prevent by foresight, that it comes not into question. For Borne and a preacher hath been in Holland with my lord of Leicester, his master, and obtain of his honour a very large commission unto the Lords of the Council, as well for Papistry as the wrongs of Sawyer, his mother and others; and for the examination of you and others Borne hath chosen commissioners, whose names I may not learn, nor your adversaries that are witnesses against you, but some are and hath been of your College, that says, if they be put unto their oaths, they will tell a truth of your base dealings of your charter, and hath written ten articles to be sworn and examined of, for their conscience pricks them of your inconscionable dealings: alleging [*inserted*: if] you, two of the Paynters and three more be put into close several prisons and well examined, ye will bring forth a nest of secret [*inserted*: Romish] Papists and where they long time have been succoured &c. I dare not write my knowledge, but I think my Lord Norris[2] is their head commissioner, for that Borne received sundry letters of General Norris unto my lord his father, as the like of my Lord of Leicester. Take heed and prevent those sequels, but if you had followed the instruction of my first letter these troubles had been ended and Borne your friend. But then you stumbled at a straw. Note: if Borne gives over the suit or absents himself, Sawyer and she is overthrown to your credit; for Borne is all in all to do you good and them hurt, for that he hath so long dealt therein and is so well known with the Lords. For if he give it over, no man will take it in hand without Borne's consent or advice; and Mr [*inserted*: Willis'] slanderous base speeches openly used against Borne doth aggravate Borne the more against yourself. Which words I would had been unspoken, and Borne laughed at the twenty shillings you proffered him and of your stout words in Fleet Street, of the which I was ashamed, for that he is a gentleman and the only man that may overthrow your enemies to your credit and profit. For ye have many privy enemies that both write and comes unto Borne, for he deals both cunningly and closely with ye, and he told me that you should marry Mr Willis' wife's sister. Also I am assured that Borne hath been three times in Oxford and in the country, learning of your doings and companions and conferring with your enemies, which greatly hath instructed and boldeneth him, for that there will be old hidden matters revealed and odious articles objected against ye. And beware of this troublesome time, for Borne hath a perilous head and is stout and well-founded, and nothing to be had of Borne but by courtesy and friendly dealings. Therefore deal so with him that your [sic] comes not into question this troublesome time. But what will ye answer when you, Mr Willis, two gentlewomen, Paynter and others be put to your oaths before these commissioners (and also certain others that now are and hath been of your College), sworn and examined on your charter, and your lease and Sawyer's conferred and praised with your charter? I think your whole College will then curse ye all, and prove it a cozening lease contrary to your charter, equity and right, to all your shames and reproach for ever. Beware it comes not into question, for this is the preacher desire, for that ye all are very evil spoken of many men in the country for sundry oppression to divers, and worse. And alleging, if you be suffered, you will [inserted: with] Papist cautels[3] put all the farmers out of College lands, to the starving of thirty of her Majesty true subjects. For God sake, let not these odious complaints come in question against you and others before the Lords, which is Borne and the preacher's only desire, and stay to have it to come into question at the Council table in this troublesome time. For they are well-known and friended with the Lords, and I fear you will be examined first of your familiar dealing with your old College fellow, traitor Campion, and of others that they and you little think of &c., and that cause why you were not sent up as prisoner with Campion unto the Lords. Also that your bond is forfeited unto the Queen's Majesty and cancelled, and the Justice and Willis will come into question, and the preacher said that Willis' fruit shows what he is in [deleted: mal] maintaining Russell, a proved Papist many years and traitor Campion's companion, wrongfully to take away other men's leases and goods. And I marvel by what means Borne came by the copy of your bond and sureties' names, and I fear Borne hath gotten the forfeiture of your bond. And where you did [deleted: a] allege that you did appear before the Lords at the Council table for Campion his cases and there answered the same and, discharged by their honours, they gave you their honours' warrants of discharge to show; but it is justly proved to the contrary. Take heed, for these are very bad dealings and concealments as the world is now, and would go hard against you and others if it come in question and breed further troubles to you and your friends than I will write. Also you [inserted: and] two of the Paynters and four more hath used very bad speeches in sundry places since Campion's death in his defence. Take heed, for you have a Judas that keeps both you and Mr Willis company that is Borne's friend, but the Justice' friendship and others' towards you is not so cunningly done, but it is seen into; and it is reported that Mr Willis got to be my Lord Chancellor's chaplain to be a defence and terror unto others not to complain of him. But all will not serve his turn, for there will be odious supplications put up unto the Council table against him and others with &c. And your lease is counted but a cunning cozening to defeat the poor from their right. For the which a thirty are agreed to come up unto the Court to exclaim of all your sundry base dealings and afore the Queen's Majesty call you Campion's companion both before and after the proclamation was for the apprehension of the traitor Campion, and a succourer for Romish and seminaries travellers, with more &c. These are the preacher's request: that [*sic*], and these will come up when Borne writes for them. Mr Russell, use the matter in time in such order with prevention that it comes not in question, for, on my faith, if it do, it will bring you, your friends and others into great dangerous troubles. Which is the mark that they shoot at—you and your friends—in these odious troubles: who dares speak for you, they an easy matter [*sic*] for the preacher to obtain his desire and Sawyer his farm and the widow her goods again with recompense. Also they saith that your coming unto the church is but as a counterfeit Papist that hath some dispensation from Rome for the same; also that you should be suspected to have conference with divers that came from Rome, and hath counselled the same, and [*inserted*: their] names, [*inserted*: and] how many years you did not come unto the church, like unto these stubborn Papists. Beware this come not into question; also there are divers that require to be put unto their oaths to declare their knowledge against your charter and all your doings. Good cousin Russell, consider of this troublesome world and follow my instructions; **[verso]** although you be clear of all in all, fire cannot be [*deleted*: there] without smoke. Let it not come into question, although it be chargeable; and by *cue*[?][4] make Borne so your friend that he speed no more in any of these actions against you. For presently there will be great punishments of these Papist traitors, as also of any that is suspected. The least articles will be credited, or cause of long troubles and imprisonments, and chiefly of Campion's companions and religion, with you long time known to be of both and a great succourer of Papists after his death and a wicked member towards God's Word and the commonwealth. And Borne hath in Oxford many gentlemen of his kindred and countrymen, and two scholars very often cometh unto Borne with letters. And, on my faith, for love and good will I bear unto you, I [*deleted*: and] have caused divers to take pains herein, and with much ado have persuaded Borne once more to stay his suit and to be your friend; and so hath he faithfully promised me. Consider well hereof my doings and stumble no more at a stone, but deal liberally with him that he go over again into Flanders and there to tarry. And by this token speak unto him that at the Brill he gave me his hand to be your friend in word and deed; and on the same I gave him two great maps for the lease and a case of musket daggs with snaphances.[5] And also in our coming over together from Gravesend unto Flushing[6] we were like to be drowned; and how the preacher that came with him wept for fear; and then I promised Borne that you should deal liberally with him if he would give over his suit and be your friend. He answered that he did know your twenty-shilling liberality and would not buy a bird in the bush. The preacher is a lord's chaplain, and of him also [*inserted*: he is] to be well recompensed. You need no more instruction but to bind him in good bands for all performance not to deal against you and the President in no kind of actions or matters concerning Sawyer, his mother or any other matter or cause against you, whatsoever [*inserted*: is or] hath been since the beginning of the world until this present day. And also have his general quittance and release, for ye were better spend £200 as this world is now than this matter should come in question against ye [*inserted*: and] others, Borne being your enemy and you in suspect and evil name. And two of the Paynters will come in great troubles if Borne be not your friend; and among ye all use the matter so with Borne that he go over into Flanders and there remain and deal no more against ye; and then may you end all in all unto your desire. By this token tell Captain Borne from me that, as he took passage at Flushing to come over, the wind served him not, and then he gave me his hand and saith, using him friendly he would not deal against ye, nor yet let Sawyer nor his mother know what he hath obtained of my lord his master in Flanders before he hath talked with you, and would say that he had lost his commission and writings, and also would tell you your privy adversaries' names and which way to overthrow your enemies. Herein I have showed myself your friend: therefore slack not time with him. Also I have caused divers captains and gentlemen in Flanders to speak unto Borne in your behalf to be your friend. Consider now well hereof and lose him not for saving of a £20, for there is further [*deleted*: actions] matter in these actions as the world is now than I dare write; which wisdom wills to prevent in time, for if it comes into question there will be great troubles and charges. Take heed thereof [*deleted*: for thereof] for there are that gapes for your living; and, for that I have made Borne once your friend, lose him not again, and with all speed take his band and general quittance [*inserted*: and cause him to go over]. Trust unto it, he will have no conference of talk herein but only with you: therefore use my instruction, which at large I have written for the faithful goodwill I bear unto you and our name. Also there is in London one Mr Russell, Sir John Perrot's man,[7] that may do much with Borne; and I and my friends have so dealt with Captain Borne that in word and deed you shall find him your faithful friend, unless the fault be in yourself, and will neither in word nor deed deal in any kind of matter or actions against you, Mr Willis or the Paynters during his life. Therefore let them have good consideration of him, for none of ye all are to come into question in this troublesome time. And Borne told me that he had removed his lodging and lies at one Mr Ratcliffe house at the sign of The Swan in the great sanctuary in Westminster. Thus God have us always in his keeping and defend us from all our enemies. In haste, for want of time, from Flushing, the 23 of August 1585. Your faithful friend for ever, W. West

¹ See no. **38** and the Introduction, pp. xv–xvi above. This is the second of three such letters. The first, dated from London on 25 April 1584, is nearly twice as long as this one and interminably repetitious; the undated third is the shortest but is torn for most of the way down the left side.
² Lord Norreys, of Rycote in Oxfordshire. Of his six sons, 'General Norris' is probably the second, Sir John ('Black Jack'), who died in Ireland in 1597.
³ Deceits; cf. *Hamlet*, I.3.15; *Julius Caesar*, II.1.129.
⁴ A blot, an indeterminate stroke and -*wghe*: ? = 'cuwghe' = ? 'at the right moment'.
⁵ Flint-locks.
⁶ Sir William Russell, fourth son of the 2nd Earl of Bedford, was appointed governor of Flushing in 1585: *Calendar of the Manuscripts . . . Preserved at Hatfield House*, Historical Manuscripts Commission 9 (London, 1873–1979), III. 378, 427; *ODNB*.
⁷ Henry Russell's brother Charles: see no. **43** below.

42. *Henry Russell to Sir Christopher Hatton*
*[1587–91]*¹
Berington 23

Endorsed: Henry Russell prayeth your Lordship that the cause between him and Mawd Sawyer, which hath been adjudged against the said Mawd at the Common Law and ordered against her by the late Lord Chancellor, the Lords of the Council, the Lords in the Star Chamber, by Dr Mathew, Dean of Durham [*deleted*: and lastly by the Lord Norris and others upon your Lordship's letters directed to them] may be utterly dismissed and he no further vexed or molested by her.

There shall be no more suits suffered against him without his privity or ordinary course of proceeding.

To the right honourable Sir Christopher Hatton, knight, Lord Chancellor of England.

Whereas (right honourable), upon special petition preferred to your lordship by Maud Sawier, widow, and John Sawyer, her late husband's son (where they conceal from your honour what courses and orders have been heretofore taken in the cause), it pleased your lordship to address your honourable letters unto the honourable the Lord Norris and to the worshipful Thomas Parrye and John Doylie, esquires, to hear and determine a controversy betwixt the said parties and your lordship's humble orator Henry Russell: which indeed was many years since adjudged by law and afterwards, upon divers and sundry complaints, ordered by the right honourable Sir Thomas Bromeley, knight, lately Lord Chancellor of England, the lords of her Majesty's most honourable Privy Council the lords in the High Court of Star Chamber and by Dr Mathew, dean of Durham, unto whom at the parties' humble suit her Highness committed the hearing and ordering of the cause; all which orders (whereof some are subscribed with your l[*ordship* ']s hand) your said orator is ready to show forth: your said orator humbly beseecheth your lordship (the said former judgments and orders considered) wh[*o*]lly to dism[*iss*] the cause so many times so determined and not to suffe[*r the s*]aid [. . .] to be any further vexed and molested, or his settled estate in his poor living to be any more questioned by the said clamorous complainants, never yielding unto any authority but still delighting in continual troubles and desirous to dwell and to spend their whole lives in causeless complaints and endless suits. So shall your lordship's poor orator during his life be bound continually to pray to God for the long preservation of your honourable and happy estate. Your lordship's most bounden and daily orator, Henry Russell.

---

[1] Undated: Hatton succeeded Bromley as Chancellor in 1587 and remained so until his death in November 1591.

43.   *Henry Russell to [Sir John Perrot]*[1]
         2 April [1588]
         Berington 623 (16)

Emmanuel

Right honourable, my humble duty to your good Lordship promised. Whereas it hath pleased God to call away out of this life Charles Russell, your Lordship's servant, my dear brother, by whose death there hath happened to us his poor friends a double grief: the one by the departure unexpected and untimely of the brother in whom we conceived a singular hope and comfort, the other by the low and shaken estate wherein he left his poor wife and little children by reason of some lately-entered actions and bargains, intended to his good and the bettering of his estate but falling out, by the prevention and suddenness of his death, unto the great hindrance, if not utter undoing, of his poor wife and the little infants, and withal to the hazarding of his credit and good name, whereof while he lived he took a special care to keep it unviolated: My humble suit is unto your good Lordship (whom he living served with faithful heart and all loyal duty) that, as he lived in good credit under the protection of your honourable countenance, so it would please your honour to continue your good favours towards his wife and the poor orphans his children, to defend them from injuries and oppression, and to maintain the credit of your late servant (if it may be) *uncracked*[?], which, except your Lordship stand our good lord and our sheet anchor, cannot choose but be greatly called into question and miserably be shaken, to the utter impoverishment of his poor children, by the great debts which he came into, specially by entering the bargain for the lease of the tithes of Dungarvan,[2] upon the value and speedy sale whereof the good estate of his poor wife and children shall stand or fall. If by your honourable means it may be sold unto any good and reasonable price which may amount unto the discharge either of all or of the greatest part of his debts, then there shall remain some good hope of the preservation of the dead's credit and of some reasonable provision for the better bringing-up of the little infants his children. If otherwise he were so far over-reached in his buying of the said lease that it should be nothing near worth his money to be sold, then do I no way see how by the residue of his goods his credit may be preserved and his poor children provided for. In this matter, resting thus difficult, we have no one to flee unto for succour, counsel and comfort but unto your honour, unto whose honourable direction and disposition both my sister his late wife and my brothers and I do refer the whole order of this cause and sale of the said lease and his other things in Ireland; and for that purpose we have requested my brother Rowland Russell to attend your Lordship's pleasure. What your lordship shall do therein, whether it shall be thought good to execute his last will or to administer his goods (which, by reason of his endangered estate, as yet we stand doubtful to ourselves), we promise, and by these our letters bind ourselves, to ratify and perform, acknowledging ourselves while we shall live, for your honourable care of his desolate infants, bound continually to pray for the long preservation and increase of your honourable and happy estate. Greenhill, the 2nd of April, Your lordship's in all duty most bounden, Henry Russell.

[1] Charles Russell, Henry's brother, died in 1588, leaving a widow, Eleanor (Davies), and two young children, Alderford and Elizabeth. By right of his wife he had an estate at Greenhill in Pwllcrochan, on the south side of Milford Haven four miles west of Pembroke; cf. nos. **76, 82, 91**. He also had a post in the household of Sir John Perrot (1528–1592) at Carew Castle, also on Milford Haven and eight miles east of Greenhill. Perrot was Lord Deputy of Ireland from 1584 to 1588, but incurred the enmity of Lord Burghley, was convicted of treason and died in the Tower, perhaps of poison, in November 1592. In August 1590 Perrot was also accused of hearing Mass and being absolved: *CSPD Elizabeth I, 1580–90*, 685 (SP 12/233/44–5).
[2] In Co. Waterford.

44. *John Halsey[1] to Elizabeth Pakington*
[before 1591]
Berington 565 (1)

Mistress Elizabeth, I have sent you a certain powder wrapped up in four several papers, and a syrup in a glass. If what time you look for your sickness, or, if you have them not, at the next change or the full of the moon, I would wish that four days together each morning early you did drink a draught made in this sort. Take two ounces of the best white wine, the fourth part of your syrup and so much powder as is in one of the papers. Mingle them perfectly well together, warm it at the fire and drink it off. Do this, as I said, four days together. It will be a means to bring down your sickness, the stay whereof is the cause of your infirmity. Your receipt of pills that I left with you, being first at divers times taken, will further the working of this medicine. If you send me word how you feel yourself upon the taking of them, you shall have my farther best advice. Commend me humbly to your good mother, to yourself, to your brothers and sisters.[2] And thus I refer us all to the tuition of Almighty God. Your worship's to command, John Haulsey.

[1] For John Halsey, see the Introduction, pp. xvii, xxiii above.
[2] For Elizabeth (Newport), Elizabeth Pakington's mother, see Michael Hodgetts, 'Origins of Recusancy: The Pakingtons', *Midland Catholic History* 4 (1995), 1–13. The brothers were Humphrey and John, the sisters Mary (Lutley; cf. no. **120**) and Margaret (Pen of Harborough Hall, Blakedown, about three miles from Harvington). The commendations suggest that the sisters were still living at Harvington, and therefore that the letter was written before Mary's marriage on 17 June 1589 and Margaret's on 9 July 1590 (Chaddesley Corbett register).

45. *John Halsey[1] to Elizabeth Pakington*
       [before 1591]
       Berington 565 (2)

My simple advice for Mistress Elizabeth Pagyngton for her rheum and other infirmities.[2]

Your rheum seeming to be cold and moist, distemperate and fluxive, your diet and medicine ought both to be hot and dry, temperate and strictive[3] or desiccative. Roasted meats better for you than boiled; white wine not good for you, nor raw herbs nor fruits, nor needeth porage specially made with yeast and onions and suchlike vaporous things. Sack or malmsey not wholesome for you; gross peppers with rare-roasted[4] eggs, new laid, is good for you, specially fasting; not drinking in an hour after them. Use to rub your head, fasting, with coarse cloths, and then with some nysing powder provoke nysing,[5] or with a bay-leaf. Use at night the fumes of old dried rosemary, and wink and take it in your mouth and nose, and in the morning the air or smoke of juniper or frankincense, and, to air your cap, and some brown paper and flax under it [*inserted*: with] the said perfumes, the one at night and the other in the morning. After you have nysed, it is very good for you to eat of the trochisks[6] of liquorice juice, and of that electuary[7] which I gave you of, which Mr Baylye Hosyer[8] of Worcester will make you for fivepence an ounce, good.

For your other infirmity. Use often to drink of the juices of balsam and the herb madder, with sack or white wine, fasting, with a little treacle, warm, two days before the full and change of the moon, and so likewise after both.

Another, if your stomach were able to bear it. I have holpen many of the like disease of long continuance with drinking of madder and making of pessaries or suppositories, and wet in the warm juice of herb-grace or rue [*inserted*: and put in the crotch];[9] and sitting in a close stool over the hot bath or fumes of gladdon,[10] hyssop, featherfew,[11] rue, thyme, sage and motherwort or mugwort and wormwood, carduus benedictus[12] and angelica. And sometimes use to stand in the warm bath of these herbs above the navel, at the time of the moon aforesaid. And use to drink ale, malmsey or white wine that carduus benedictus is sodden in, with liquorice, raisins and sugar or honey, after fasting. If you cannot get all the herbs, take them you can get.

[*Sideways in the left margin*] When you lay you down to sleep, eat a little of the trochisks of the juice of liquorice or of the electuary, and let it dissolve softly down with your spittle; lay your head high and lie on your right side with your left hand on the whole of your stomach. Anoint your stomach with oil of wormwood and your belly with oil of dill and of rue mingled together: warm the very bottom of your belly. And [*sha . . .*]

[1] The hand differs from that of the other prescriptions, and there is no (legible) signature.
[2] For the remedies (see also nos. **55, 57, 60**), see Nicholas Culpeper, *The English Physitian Enlarged* (London, 1653 and many reprints). In 2000–2001 the moatside herb garden at Harvington was replanted with herbs mentioned in Halsey's prescriptions. Elizabeth was apparently to take sack, white wine and malmsey for medicinal purposes only, and then with herbs.
[3] Astringent (*OED*).
[4] The MS spelling, 'Ryere Rostide', reflects the original pronunciation, 'rear'.
[5] Sneezing.
[6] Troches, round pills.
[7] A medicinal paste.
[8] Until 1621 Worcester had a High and a Low Bailiff, not a mayor. Berington 847 is a letter of 18 March 1588/9 (no address or endorsement) about a herbal recipe from Richard Nycolls of Worcester. On 19 September 1589 Richard Nyccols alias Hosyer took a lease of three shops in the High Street, which nine months later was transferred to Robert Steyner (see no. **71**): Worcester Corporation Archives, Order Book I (1540–1601), ff. 174, 175; cf. f. 159; typed transcript (1943) by Vivian Collett in Birmingham Central Library (574621), p. 108; cf. p. 101. In the Worcester Record Office are the will (1626/136) of Anne Nichols alias Hosier, widow, All Saints, Worcester, and the marriage-bond (1587/128b) of Elizabeth Nicolls alias Hosier, widow, of St Martin's, Worcester, and George Burkhill, clerk, of the city of Worcester.
[9] The word was in use in this sense by 1592: *OED*, 'crotch', 5.
[10] MS 'gladen' = stinking iris.
[11] Feverfew.
[12] 'Blessed thistle'; distilled, it was 'the only thing for a qualm': *Much Ado about Nothing*, III.iv.65–72. William Harrison, *The Description of England* [1577], ed. Georges Edelen (Ithaca, N.Y., 1968; repr. Washington, D.C., 1994), 266, refers to 'our common germander or thistle bennet'.

46.   *William Savage and others to John Russell II*
             June [1588?][1]
             Lechmere Box, 'Items Included' [2]

After our hearty commendations: whereas you have formerly been charged with one horse or gelding furnished as is underwritten for her Majesty's service: these are in her Majesty's name to will and require you that the horse and furniture, with a sufficient person mounted, be in a readiness and appear before us at [*deleted*: *illegible*; *inserted*: *illegible*] on Friday being the [*deleted*: xviij day of this instant June; *inserted*: second day of July next coming] by nine of the clock in the morning of the same day, there by us to be viewed, mustered and put in a readiness for the said service, as by letters from the Lords of her Majesty's most honourable Privy Council to us directed and signifying her Highness's commands. And hereof not to fail as you tender her Majesty's service and will for the [*same an*]swer at peril. From Wigorn this iiijth of June.

[   ]ry dwelling   Your loving friends
[   ]of wr   William Savage
                             Tho. Leighton
                             John Pakington
                             William Ligon

[1] This letter probably refers to defensive measures against the Spanish Armada, which was sighted off the Lizard on 19/29 July 1588. John Russell II died later that year.

47.   *Francis Willis to Henry Russell*[1]
             14 April 1595
             Lechmere Box B.10

Addressed: To the worshipful mine assured friend Mr Henry Russell at his house at Little Malvern.

. . . with your good liking. So, presuming you will not fail me herein, as you know you may use me in a far greater matter within the compass of my lot, with my heartiest commendations and my wife's to you and yours, I commend you to the grace of God. From Worcester this 14th of April 1595.

[1] This is a fragment, the rest of which has been used by John Russell IV for accounts, headed 'Thomas Greenwood's bill, 1687': see Introduction, p. xxxviii above. It is included as an illustration of how university friendships could cross the religious divide. Willis, the dean of Worcester, had been president of St John's College, Oxford, when Russell was a fellow there and principal of Gloucester Hall. When Willis died in 1596, although he was still dean of Worcester, his address was also given as 'Gloucester College': *Index of Wills*

Proved in the Prerogative Court of Canterbury, IV: 1584–1604, comp. S.A. Smith, Index Library 25 (London, 1901), 456 (77 Drake).

48.   *Katherine Willis to Henry Russell*[1]
          31 July [?1596]
          Berington 562 (23)

Brother Russell, After my most hearty commendations to you and your wife and the two young gentlemen your sons, not forgetting my sister Alice's her commendations unto you and your wife also: I know you know by this time of the death of your cousin James Mintridge of London: thus friends must part one from another. Good brother, you know always I make bold with you, as I hope you will with me in any affairs. You made me believe that you wished that I had continued by you: that I shall see now: I may come now, if I will, to be your near neighbour. Therefore, if I may have your good counsel and foresight in matters to my expectation and the counsel of my friend, then may it perhaps be a match if it please God to say Amen. I will show you the man and the matter; and when you have read my letter, let me hear from you again without any fail, as I would do by you in such a case. It falleth out at this time there was some friend made a motion unto me about a quarter of a year ago for one Mr Harforde your neighbour, who dwelleth at Bosbury by you,[2] and so hath written unto me ever since from time to time touching marriage. And now he himself hath been here at Oxford [he] with me, with his son and heir and his son-in-law Mr Scorye for to see me, and so entered into this matter. He offereth me seven score pounds in jointure of the best land he hath, and to deal with any of my friends how I shall think good. He seemeth to be a very mild gentleman; he hath nine children, as he telleth me: they shall all be provided for, that they shall no way be troublous unto me. His son and heir is to marry with a gentleman's daughter who was sometimes a merchant [*inserted*: in London] and dwelleth hard by you too. He hath but two daughters, and he shall have £500 with her and three hundred marks a year after the decease of her father, whereof she must have the one half of it, yet will not old Mr Harforde assure this young gentlewoman of a jointure, because he is now disposed to marry himself. His own wife shall make the first choice of any of his lands; he will bind out thereof his son's prentice, and they are very willing to be so; he saith he [*deleted*: h] is somewhat in debt but he will sell a piece of land to pay that and to maintain and place his children and that they shall have their portions. He will deal plainly and honestly in all these affairs, as he protesteth, and then the rest shall be to maintain him and whom he matcheth withal, which will be a sufficient living. These matters are too high for me to reach: I have no great heart-burning to marry but [?*it*] if

I might have that counsel and comfort of you as one of my best friends, as you know, then shall I be the willinger if everything be according to my desire and as I would have it. I pray you let me hear from you and your experience, and let your letters be conveyed so that they may come to my own hands; and so shall I think myself beholding unto you, as I have been ever.

[*Sideways in the left margin*] So I leave to trouble you, with my commendations to you and your wife once again from my house at Ruly[3] by Oxford this 31th [*sic*] of July, I bid you farewell. Your assured poor friend and sister to [*sic*] during life to command, Katherine Willis.

[1] This letter reveals the friendship, even affection, between Willis's widow and Henry Russell.

[2] Bosbury is five miles north-west of Little Malvern; on either side of the chancel there are superb monuments to John Harford (1559) and to Richard Harford (1578) and his wife Martha Fox (1601).

[3] Rewley was a quarter of a mile west of Gloucester Hall: fragments of the abbey there survive at the north end of the bus station, between Oxford railway station and the Said Business School.

49. *?[1] to [the dowager countess of Derby][2]*
        3 July 1596
        Lechmere Box, 'Items Included' [2]

After my humble [*commendations*] for your most honourable Ladyship's promise, with like humble thanks for your most honourable and courteous answer to my last letter returned by my servant, for which I shall ever think myself greatly bound unto you. And whereas I am to pay the Lady Arbella[3] on the 20th of this July, I have taken up the same here at London, not knowing your Ladyship's certain resolution and good pleasure (for that my son Percival refuseth to join with me in the administration), whether you will accept of the money or not. And for that the charge and trouble to carry down the money in vain would be great: therefore I am most humbly to beseech your Ladyship to signify unto me by letter your good pleasure in that behalf, and do most humbly take my leave, with my hearty prayers to the Lord Almighty for your Ladyship's good health and long life. London, this third of July 1596.

[1] There is no signature; the context might suggest that it was written by John Grove but it is not in his hand.

[2] Alice, Lady Derby (1559–1637), Edmund Spenser's 'Amaryllis', was the youngest daughter of Sir John Spencer of Althorp in Northamptonshire and Wormleighton in Warwickshire and of Katherine, daughter of Sir Thomas Kitson of Hengrave in Suffolk. She married (1) Ferdinando, 5th earl of Derby (d. 1594), previously the Lord Strange of Lord Strange's Men, and (2), in 1600, Sir Thomas Egerton, Lord Ellesmere, who appears in correspondence below. In 1634 John Milton wrote *Arcades* for her.

Of Lady Derby's seven sisters, Anne Spencer (Spenser's 'Phyllis') married (1) William Stanley, 3rd Lord Monteagle; (2), in 1581, Henry, 1st Lord Compton of Compton Wynyates in Warwickshire (d. 1589); (3), in 1592, Robert Sackville, 2nd earl of Dorset (1561–1608). Katherine Spencer married Sir Thomas Leigh of Stoneleigh Abbey in Warwickshire and became the mother of Alice Leigh, who married Sir Robert Dudley, son of the earl of Leicester, and of Catherine Leigh, who married Robert Catesby, the Gunpowder Plotter. Elizabeth Spencer (1552–1618), Spenser's 'Charyllis', married, in 1574, George Carey, 2nd Lord Hunsdon (1547–1603), who from 1597 onwards was Lord Chamberlain and patron of the Lord Chamberlain's Men. Cokayne, *Complete Peerage*; *Visitation of the County of Warwick, 1619*, 285. See also Mary E. Finch, *The Wealth of Five Northamptonshire Families, 1540–1640*, Publications of the Northamptonshire Record Society 19 (Oxford, 1956).

According to Nicholas Berden and Anthony Tyrrell, Lord Compton harboured priests and was a friend of the Jesuit William Weston: Morris, *Troubles*, II. 157, 379, 397, 408, 426–7, 479, 492; cf. Foley, II. 587. About 1586 Berden reported to the decipherer Thomas Phelippes that at the French ambassador's he had seen Francis Tresham and also Lady Compton (Anne Spencer) and Lady Strange (Alice Spencer), who were attended by Thomas Gerard (the elder brother of John Gerard the Jesuit): Morris, *Troubles*, II. 161 = *CSPD Elizabeth I, 1580–90*, 373. Harry Thorpe, 'The Lord and the Landscape', *Birmingham Archaeological Society: Transactions and Proceedings* 80 (1962), 38–77 at 56–7, notes that for a century the Spencers had been close friends of the Catesbys, from whom John Spencer I had bought Althorp in 1508. Cf. VCH *Northants.*, II. 293–9; George Baker, *The History and Antiquities of the County of Northampton* (London, 1822–41), I. 94–112.
[3] Probably Lady Arabella Stuart.

50. *John Halsey to Elizabeth Russell*
          17 October 1597
          Berington 565 (3)

Good Mistress Russell, Whereas I understand by your brother[1] that you are in some discomfort of yourself, I am sorry that the continuance of your pain doth breed that conceit in you. For, as for [*inserted*: any] further matter than the pain, I hope I may (by the grace of God) assure you. And, albeit that I know that long diseases are long in curing, and that these griefs are occasioned by reason of some vapours rising from the vessels about your womb, a part remote and not easily to be purged by any inward physic, yet I do remain assured [*inserted*: of] the good event, so you do for two or three weeks, once a week, continue the taking of your [*inserted*: former] described clyster. And then to use the ointment as I told you, but not to smell unto it, which may that way rather do you harm than good. If it do not take the success I expect, there remaineth one thing wherein I have singular confidence, which upon your letters I mind to send with a description for the use thereof. In the mean season, with my hearty commendations to your good husband and yourself, I recommend us all to the tuition of Almighty God, the 17th October 1597. John Halsey.

I have left order with your brother for further directions.

¹ Humphrey Pakington.

51. *John Halsey to Elizabeth Russell*
         25 January 1599/1600
         Berington 565 (4)

Mistress Russell, I understand by your brother that your health is not such as either he or I could wish it, and that for your part you have a great mind to a vomit, wherein my conceit cannot concur with yours. Not that a vomit in such a disease as yours is may not work a good effect, but that in yourself, being no stronger than you are, it is not your best course. The humour that offendeth is melancholy made of a burnt choler lying in your spleen and first veins. It is requisite that the party had great strength that should by vomit bring up so heavy an humour, and vomits are but churlish medicines: wherefore in others perhaps I might give my consent, but the care I have of you will not suffer me to put your estate in any untimely hazard, although [*deleted*: perchance; *inserted*: I will not say but] it might fall out well. In these things we are to follow the likelihood and never to use extreme remedies but in extreme diseases. Your sickness, I hope, is not such, but apter to breed fears than danger, more long and discomfortable than perilous. The boiling of melancholy breedeth abundance of wind, and wind partly occasions this way, partly the distillation from your head doth disquiet and offend your stomach. How these things may be respected you shall understand by my next letters, which, God willing, shall be very shortly, and before the time of the year most fit for any physic. Thus, thanking you greatly for many your courtesies, with my hearty commendations to Mr Russell and yourself, I commend you both to the protection of Almighty God, the 25th January 1599. Yours most assured, John Halsey.

52. *John Halsey to Henry Day*¹
         2 February 1599/1600
         Berington 617

Endorsed: To my loving friend Mr Henry Day give these.

Mr Day, I have not leisure at this time to discourse of the estate of Mistress Russell's body, but well assured I am that the whole habit of her body (*genus musculosum, venae, arteriae, cor, hepar*) *laborant in temperie calida et sicca*,² and such is her blood; and of this *cacochymia*³ cometh her biles, the chapping of the palms of her hands, the extreme heat she feeleth all over her flesh, the want of sleep; and truly she hath *melancholiam, atram bilem*,[4] which is of necessity (according to Galen in his second book *De Temperamentis*) to be expected *in declinante aetate* in all such *qui in aetate consistente habuerunt sanguinem calidiorem et sicciorem justo*.[5] This kind of melancholy he calleth μελαγχολίαν ἐκ τῆς μεταπτώσεως τῆς ἕξεως, *ex habitus mutatione*.[6] For the looseness of her body, it doth not proceed of any humour derived from her liver unto her gentles, but it is a diarrhoea caused by a distillation from her head into her stomach, which (according to Galen in the book before cited and the sixth book *De Sanitate Tuenda*) is a very usual thing. You may soon observe (if you converse with her) the co[*llater*]al falling of the rheum into her stomach, well agreeing with the extreme heat of her blood, from whence vapours do so abundantly ascend into her head. I have sent her down a magistral syrup against this humour. It is in all six. She may take four good spoonfuls with seven or eight spoonfuls of barley-water or whey clarified; and if you think it good after the first taking, being very gentle, you may mingle therewith three [*spoonfuls*] *confectionis hamec*,[7] or more, as you find it work. You shall the next week understand my mind farther. In the mean season, referring all to your discretion, I commend you to the tuition of Almighty God. The second of February 1599/1600. Your loving friend, John Halsey.

[1] Day seems to have been a physician or apothecary in Worcestershire who could supervise Elizabeth Russell's treatment while Halsey was in London. Her temperament, which ten years before (no. **45**) had been too cold and moist, was now, it seems, too hot and dry. Berington 562 (10) is a letter (with the date missing) from Henry Day to Henry Russell.

[2] '(Muscular structure, veins, arteries, heart, liver) suffer from a hot and dry temperament'.

[3] κακοχυμία: 'unhealthy state of the humours': Liddell, Scott and Jones, *A Greek–English Lexicon* (Oxford, 1940); *Dictionary of Medieval Latin from British Sources*; *OED* under 'cacochymy'.

[4] 'Black bile', a literal rendering of *melancholiam*.

[5] 'In their declining years [in all such] who in their maturity have had excessively dry and hot blood'.

[6] 'Melancholy arising from the change of life'.

[7] A common remedy including fumitory, which was then regarded as a cure-all. See Joan Lane, *John Hall and his Patients*, medical comm. by Melvin Earles (Stratford-upon-Avon, 1996), 83.

53.   *Humphrey Pakington to Henry Russell*
         23 February [1599/1600][1]
         Lechmere f.899:169(7)/C.7

My good brother, Mr Morton's[2] uncertainty driveth Mr Grove (as the case with him standeth for other things) into great perplexities, and would breed haply his greater inconvenience if he should rely only upon Mathington; so that I fear he will be forced to make his resolution, that if the bargain happen to be offered unto him in any beneficial sort, then to venture the taking up of money at interest (which is dreadful), if he proceed herein, until he may sell again that which haply about Easter he may bargain for in another place. For truly, Mr Grove would be glad of the neighbourhood as of the lands. Notwithstanding, upon the reasons by you alleged, I verily think that Mr Morton taketh the course [*inserted*: merely] to hinder himself [*inserted*: in his sale], and can no way prevail in [*deleted*: his] the indaginatory³ marriage of his son. Yet his price may be such, or his assurance so uncertain, that may hinder Mr Grove, who is loath to make a blind adventure of his whole estate. But if he give you meeting at our [*illegible*] (as I fear he will not), you haply may see further into the assurance than now you do. In the meanwhile, I cannot see but all must stand upon uncertainty of all hands, and therefore I forbear to write you more of the matter, when at our next meeting, which will be, I think, the week after Easter, we may perchance have longer discourse. I would advise my good sister to forbear the sending of anything to the good-natured gentleman you know of until you hear further from me, money being the only thing acceptable with such dispositions. At my coming down, I think I shall be able to advertise her of as much as he will ever do unto her, for I have employed all my endeavours to discover what may be for her good and avail. As yet, I hear nothing from Mr Body⁴ concerning your letter, but before he next return I will question him if he be oblivious in your cause.

I would advise my good sister [*inserted*: presently] to sell the nag I gave her, for I hold him fitter for her spurs than for her saddle. Let her rest assured that the nag and his value is merely her own; for, though I am poor, yet am I not so base either to recavil or to repine at my promise. If Mr Hall's⁵ nag be recovered, he will serve my turn, or if he be not, I hope I shall hear in what case he standeth by your next letter. If he be not sometimes travelled, he will take greater inconvenience by good keeping than I know he could do by the hardest travel you could give him. Wherefore I pray you, let him be used as your occasions require. By good fortune, I have found some means to stop in some sort Mr Felton's⁶ fury against me for the present, but how I shall presently speed resteth very doubtful. Yet I thought it my part to give you this intelligence [*con-form*]ably to my former letter in that point. The Duke of Burgundy's ambassory came to London on Monday last, but hath not yet been at the Court. Whether we shall have peace or war resteth so very doubtful that no man can tell what to think thereof. So in some haste, with all hearty commendations, I end [*this*] 23 February, Your poor brother, ever at your command, Humfrey Pakington

---

¹ This letter can be dated by the mention of the embassy from the 'Duke of Burgundy' (the Archduke Albert). In a letter to Dudley Carleton written the previous day (22 Febru-

ary), John Chamberlain reported: 'The Archduke's ambassador came hither on Monday accompanied only with eight or ten, whereof three be gentlemen, the rest servants; he is lodged at Alderman Bayning's and went yesterday to the court, being to have audience this afternoon': Norman Egbert McClure, ed., *The Letters of John Chamberlain* (Philadelphia, 1939), I. 87, from SP 12/274/48.

[2] See no. **59** below for Mistress Morton. They were probably Thomas and Anne Moreton, who had married by 1583 after the death of her first husband Simon Mucklow; she was still alive in 1603. VCH *Worcs.*, IV. 357n., 195, 293; *Visitation of the County of Worcester, 1569*, 98; *Visitation of Worcestershire, 1634*, 71–2.

[3] From the Latin *indago*, 'legacy-hunting'. as in Tacitus, *Annals* XIII.42. The word is not in *OED*, though seven cognate forms are, but the reading and the sense are clear.

[4] The context suggests a lawyer. A 'J. Bode of Herefordshire' was a suspected recusant at Gray's Inn in 1577: Ryan, 'Diocesan Returns of Recusants', in CRS 22, p. 103.

[5] A common name but one used among others by the Blessed Edward Oldcorne, who was then living at Hindlip (cf. nos. **103**, **153**–4). After Oldcorne's arrest he and his servant Ralph Ashley were questioned about a black gelding that Robert Wintour had given or sold him: Foley, IV. 224, 231, 269. See also no. **195** for a horse lent by Joan Russell to the Blessed Anthony Turner.

[6] Thomas Felton, a notorious exploiter of sequestrated recusants. *CSPD Elizabeth I, 1598–1601*, 253–4 etc.; Bowler, *Recusant Roll no. 2*, CRS 57, p. lxxvi; Talbot, *Recusant Records*, CRS 53, p. 177 (a petition about him to Sir Robert Cecil).

54. *John Halsey to Elizabeth Russell*[1]
   17 April 1601
   Berington 565 (5)

Mistress Russell, I give you most hearty thanks for the exceeding good bacon which I have received from you, and for the cheese, which I understand is already come up to London. And, upon advertisement given to me by your brother touching your estate at this present, I have imparted unto him what I would advise you to do, forbearing in these letters to descend to particulars because I know he will write unto you thereof at large. This only will I say unto you, that the very ground of your sickness is melancholy, which will make one think that a curable disease is incurable, which will mistrust more than there is cause, and construe all things unto much fear and to the worst. The sum of that I have appointed is to temper the heat of your liver, your spleen and your blood, partly by inward physic most gentle, partly by outward, which being effected, all these other accidents that you complain of I hope will take their leave of you. Thus, with my most hearty commendations to Mr Russell and yourself, I do commend you both to the protection of Almighty God, the 17th April 1601. Yours most assured to his power, John Halsey.

[1] This is the 'letter enclosed' of no. **55**, which in turn contains the 'particulars at large' referred to here. The identification fixes the date of no. **55** as 28 April 1601 and reveals that Humphrey Pakington was then in London.

55.   *Humphrey Pakington to Elizabeth Russell*
        28 April [1601][1]
        Berington 576 (13)

My most dearly beloved sister, I am sorry your pains continue, for your good health of me is more desired than mine own life; which I heartily wish (if God were so pleased) might take end to be so that very antidote, and pray the same; for then should I hold it very well spent, the spending whereof (as I fear it will be spent) will be unto me very loathsome and grievous. I have solicited Mr Halsey most earnestly to have care of you and to bend his best endeavours for your recovery. In accomplishment whereof, he hath sent you this letter enclosed and directed me to signify unto you his course of physic, which you are to use all this summer as occasion shall serve. Which is the best order, as he saith, he can possibly perceive; which that you may the better understand, I am to give you notice, that his very opinion is, your stomach is marred by the continual distillation from your head to that part, your head filled still by the vapour that ascendeth continually from your blood and other [*deleted*: parts] humours [*deleted*: of] in your body, the vapours raised by the overmuch heat in your body, and that heat most chiefly procured by the heat of your liver. So that he maketh your liver the root and first cause of all the inconveniencies; for the tempering and cooling whereof he hath set down the unguent in the gallipot, wherewith you are every day to anoint all [*deleted*: the] your right side, the place of your liver, which you know; and that you anoint also the other side, where your spleen lieth, it is not amiss; and, after those parts well anointed, to lay thereon a thin linen cloth for raying[2] the rest of your clothes, and so to dress you. He hath also set down a gentle potion for you, which once or twice a week you may still take as occasion shall serve. It will purge a little but with as little heating of your body as possibly may be. The [*omitted*: manner] of making and using of it is, viz. Take an ounce of French barley (I mean hulled barley) and after it [*inserted*: is] prepared by boiling in two or three waters [*inserted*: until it begins to break], as you well know how to do, put thereunto a pint of water and a few raisins of the sun strained, and seethe it to half. [*Marginal note*: If the decoction prove too little, then take two ounces of barley and a quart of water.] Then take off the thinnest of this decoction, about half a reasonable draught, and infuse therein three drachms of senna a [*inserted*: very] little bruised and one drachm of sweet fennel seeds also bruised [*inserted*: a little], which, standing all night in the embers in a counterfeit pewter dish, in the morning heat it in the dish a little until it begins to simper [*sic*], but let it not seethe. Then strain out all the liquor [*inserted*: as] hard as with your own hands you can wring the strainer, and to the same put two good spoonfuls of the syrup [*deleted*: of] in the glass and mix them well together, and with some more of the barley-water to make up a competent [*inserted*: draught] and the medicine more thin and apt to drink. Make the potion and take it in the morning, and (wherein I know you are not ignorant), though I write you two ounces of barley for a quart of water, yet an ounce and a half is sufficient, and that proportion you may [*inserted*: use] as the fitter.

The glass with the syrup, the gallipot of the ointment, together with senna and sweet fennel seeds, I have sent you in your basket by this carrier; in the which, I heartily thank you, I received your good puddings; also by the carrier your cheeses sent, being no way able to requite such your kindness. Mr Halsey taketh the cheeses very kindly at your hands. French barley I have not sent you, for I presume you have enough thereof or at least may quickly have from Worcester. When your unguents and syrup are spent, I will send you more. I presume you well know the weight of an ounce and drachm, for I have divers times written unto you. Though Mr Halsey set down three drachms of senna to be infused for one potion, yet if you begin with two drachms, it is not amiss, so that you see how it worketh, and it is more proper for you to purge often by little and little, this much at one time. You must leave the use of your *Diacidonium cum speciebus*[3] until your liver be well cooled. [*Deleted*: Thence] Then you may use that again, when your stomach is also corrected, for it will much help digestion. I have now detained you overlong and therefore must make an end. I shall be glad to see a letter from your hand to be truly advertised of the working of your physic, as also what other [*deleted*: troubles; *inserted*: griefs] you find that I may provide for you accordingly. So, leaving the event of physic to the goodness of Almighty God, our best physician, who I hope will grant my desired effect therein and send you your health with contentment, with my heartiest commendations I take my leave this 28 of April. Your poor worthless but true and faithful brother, Humfrey Pakington

You must use succory roots and other cooling herbs in your usual broths. Mrs Geffreyes[4] shall be advertised of your sending up the [?*pyrle*][5] the next week.

---

[1] See no. **54** above, and, for a similar prescription, no. **60** below.

[2] Dirtying, soiling. Cf. *The Taming of the Shrew*, III.ii.51, IV.i.3. On the second of these, the Arden edn (ed. Brian Morris (London, 1981), 239) quotes Nashe, *Summer's Last Will*: 'Let there be a fewe rushes laide in the place where *Back-winter* shall tumble, for fear of raying his cloathes.'

[3] 'Conserve of quinces [*cydoniae*] with spices'. These three words, unlike the rest of the letter, are in italic script.

[4] 'Mrs Geffryes' may have been one of the family at Earl's Croome; see nos. **39**, **101**.

[5] Possibly 'purl': twisted gold or silver wire for embroidery or edging.

56. *Humphrey Pakington to Henry Russell*
    17 October [1601]
       Lechmere f.899:169 (5)

Addressed: To the worshipful my approved good brother Henry Russell Esqre at Little Malvern.

Truly I hold Mrs Crewe the happier woman if the marriage be once ended which hath been so long in hand. I pray God send them both contentment, and then for my part I am well contented. You need not to doubt of all the assistance I can give you for the recovering of your bonds you intend to save, neither of my readiness to take all opportunities for your avail therein, but I greatly [*deleted*: feae] fear of the success. For my cousin Gilbert Lyttelton's debts far exceed his goods; besides, the cunning of him to whom the administration is divolted is great.[1] Whom I myself lately moved [*deleted*: in your behalf], offering him any composition in your behalf, but could find no comfort to do you good. If I forget not myself, the money for Woolepitts is by bonds due at Allhallantides. I pray you, good brother, get in the money at the day, which I hope will be truly paid, for I can assure you, the party hath need to use it to whom it is due. Our news, as they are great, so are they doubtful, and therefore I am loath to enter into any discourse herein. Almighty God turn all to the best, to whose merciful protection I commit you, and so with my heartiest commendations I take my leave. 17 October. Your poor brother ever at your command, Humfrey Pakington.

[1] 'My cousin' Gilbert Lyttelton was the son of Sir John Lyttelton and of Bridget Pakington, daughter of Humphrey's great-uncle. He and Humphrey were Sir John's executors: Nash, *Collections for the History of Worcestershire*, I. 493; cf. Birmingham Reference Library, Worcestershire Deeds, 357395 (1592–3) and 351663 (6 June 1596). On Gilbert's death in 1599, administration was granted first to his son, also John; then in July 1601 (after John's implication in the Essex Rising) to Humphrey Perrott; and finally in October 1601 to Gilbert's widow Elizabeth (Coningsby): *Index to Administrations in the Prerogative Court of Canterbury, IV: 1596–1608*, ed. Marc Fitch, Index Library 81 (London, 1964), 81; cf. nos. **106–7, 121–2**. So the 'cunning' administrator is Perrott and the year 1601. On the back of the sheet are some 'reckonings' and 'charges'.

57. *John Halsey to Henry Russell*
    2 January 1601/2
       Berington 565 (6)

Good worshipful sir, Your kindness towards me and great care for effecting things to my benefit is such that, do I what I can, I shall never be able to discharge the debt I owe you. Touching Mr Wrenford,[1] Mr Grove is content according to the former communication to let him have one hun-

dred marks upon mortgage [*inserted*: of the Gullers][2] for one year condi-
tionally that he take it of him back again by lease for one year, yielding
therefor £5 rent. You may signify unto him that he is drawn unto it by
your means. The payment shall be as soon as the assurance is perfected;
further, you may [*inserted*: say] as from yourself that it were better, for
saving of charges in making of the conveyance, that this were an absolute bargain passed between Mr Grove and him; for which purpose you
would labour to draw Mr Grove to £7, albeit that the next year it will be
little worth, and the next year after that much less, because almost all the
grounds will lie [*deleted*: lie] fallow. He shall also have present money
for the Pypers[2] if he mind to sell it reasonably. As for his oaths, Mr Grove
maketh little reckoning thereof, for he is thoroughly acquainted with his
manner [*inserted*: of dealing]. When he departed [*inserted*: out] of the
lands, he said that one Charles Trovell[3] did, one day or two before his
departure, offer him £100 for the Gullers. Of one thing I am sure: that
whosoever will give him most present money shall have it. And I see no
reason why any man that doth not dwell very near it should be desirous
of it; besides, I suppose that money is not so plentiful in the country as to
over-buy lands at this present.

If wishing or praying would restore Mistress Russell the clearness of
her sight, I would in my absence for my part effect what I could therein.
Touching the taking of her physic, I am sorry that I am not the overseer
myself. There is no reason that I would forget her who still doth remember me with one good thing or another, as now with two collars of brawn,
for which I give you and her most hearty thanks. Besides the instructions
that I sent in writing, it were good that she did boil in her broth a quantity
of eyebright, knit up in a bundle, and some fennel roots, the pith taken
forth, and moreover that divers times in the day somebody did chew fennel seeds in the mouth and presently breathe into her dimmed eye. Thus,
with my hearty commendations unto you both, and beseeching Almighty
God that we may all rest under his holy protection, I do for this time
cease to trouble you any longer. The 2nd of January 1601. Yours assured
to the uttermost of his power, John Halsey.

The basket and napkins are returned by the same carrier that brought
them.

---

[1] Thomas Wrenford of Longdon, five miles SE of Little Malvern: VCH *Worcs.*, IV. 114–15; *Visitation of Worcestershire, 1634*, 57; cf. nos. **58, 163** below. Both he and his wife Dorothy were recusants: C.D. Gilbert, 'Catholics in the Diocese of Worcester, 1580–1', *Midland Catholic History* 1 (1991), 21, 27 n. 28; British Library MS Lansdowne 53, f. 69; Hugh Bowler and Timothy J. McCann, eds., *Recusants in the Exchequer Pipe Rolls, 1581–1592*, CRS 71 (London, 1986), 187; M.M.C. Calthrop, ed., *Recusant Roll no. 1, 1592–3*, CRS 18 (London, 1916), 361; Bowler, *Recusant Roll no. 2*, CRS 57, p. 197; Talbot, *Recusant Records*, CRS 53, p. 129 ('Dorothie Ranckford'). In 1588 a priest, Paul Spence, was arrested in their house and sent to Worcester Castle, where he said Masses frequented by the

under-gaoler and his wife: Anstruther, I. 328; *Acts of the Privy Council of England*, n.s. XIX: *A.D. 1590*, ed. John Roche Dasent (London, 1899), 304.
[2] Probably Guller's End and Piper's End, two adjoining farms now immediately south of the M50 (SO 8435). Only neighbours would want them, since Longdon Marsh, a brackish backwater of the Severn, stretched for two miles beyond Longdon to Birtsmorton and Castlemorton. Cf. no. **64** below.
[3] Of 'Barton' (Court at Colwall, two miles west of Little Malvern). He married Alice Dyneley of Charlton, near Evesham: *Visitation of the County of Worcester, 1569*, 50; *Visitation of Herefordshire, 1634*, 17, 93, 165; cf. no. **129** below.

58. *John Halsey to Henry Russell*
     19 March 1601/2
       Berington 565 (7)

Good worshipful sir, Touching Bracie,[1] Mr Grove's tenant, I can say no more but that he expecteth to hear from you in what sort he would deal for the lease of Fulsthowse Farm,[2] for [*inserted*: how] many years he would have it, at what rent and what fine, and how it should be paid. As for the money that Mr Wrenford doth owe him, if he have not very good assurance for it, he shall hardly come by it. Upon his answer returned in your letters, he shall have resolutely put down whereunto he shall trust. And so much for him. Touching good Mistress Russell, in good faith I am heartily sorry that my business will not suffer me to be present at the taking of her physic. It seemeth by your letters that there is some superfluous moisture in the membrane of her brain by the shooting pain that she findeth in her head, which, stopping the sinew called *nervus opticus*, will not suffer the animal spirits to come from the ventricles of the brain into the eye. Whereupon (although I like well enough of the pills which Mr Cowarne[3] carried down from hence), I would think some stronger physic would be for that purpose more convenient. But the care that I have of her maketh me for doing anything in mine absence a coward; notwithstanding, I have enclosed in these letters such receipts as I think fittest for her. The one is a potion, the other certain bags to be applied very warm, one after another, to provoke her head to sweat. Thus, beseeching Almighty God to send her the clearness of her sight to her own desire, and promising her that, so soon as I may conveniently come into the country, I will without delay see her, with my hearty commendations unto you both, I do for this time forbear to trouble you longer, the 19th of March 1601. Yours most assured to his power, John Halsey.

[1] Edward Bracie; cf. no. **64**. For a Thomas Bracye at Upton-upon-Severn in 1594, see Bowler, *Recusant Roll no. 2*, CRS 57, p. 192. A Francis Brace(y) leased Rushock Court, two miles south of Harvington, from the Merchant Taylors' Company until his death in 1599, when it passed to Thomas Russell of Strensham: *Visitation of the County of Worcester, 1569*, 23–4; Aileen Hodgson, 'Rushock Manor', *Worcestershire Recusant* 3 (June

1964), 34–40; Michael Hodgetts, 'Rushock Court, 1595', *Midland Catholic History* 10 (2004), 1–8. But it is not clear that either was related to Grove's tenant.
[2] Also written as Fulshowse or Fulsthouse Farm (cf. nos. **71**, **107**). Apparently Filt House or Felt House Farm (now Veldt House or Velcourt), three miles south-west of Ledbury (SO 670345): A.H. Smith, *The Place-Names of Gloucestershire*, III: *The Lower Severn Valley; the Forest of Dean*, English Place-Name Society 40 (Cambridge, 1964), 184.
[3] Walter Cowarne, husband of Henry Russell's sister Joan, father of the Walter Cowarne of nos. **66–7** and tenant of The Darren, Garway, Herefs. During the riots of 1605 he resisted the bishop of Hereford and the sheriff with a javelin: Talbot, *Recusant Records*, CRS 53, pp. 138, 143.

59.   *John Grove to Henry Russell*[1]
      7 July 1602
      Berington 376 (2)

My humble duty to your worship with your good bedfellow and my worshipful friend remembered. On Midsummer last I received letters from my worshipful and dearest friend your brother-in-law, whereby I perceive he was the 13th of the last June in good health in Dublin, attended on with John Gressam, his honest and trusty servant, and meant on the morrow, upon some occasions signified to him from his lady,[2] to return for the province of Munster to despatch certain business there concerning them both for their profit, as I understand (yet I could have wished rather he had held his former determination of returning for England out of that barbarous and rebellious nation), further signifying his happy and fortunate success hitherto in all things in those parts according to his expectation.

It seemeth he understandeth, by my lady's own letters to him sent, of her delivery of child, and taketh the same very gladly, as by his own letters to her directed and by her to me since showed appeareth. He further certifieth me of the particulars of his good success in Ireland, whereof I do rejoice and would impart the same to you if leisure permitted. I have not been often with the lady since Mr Pakington's departure, and not at all unless she sent for me or that I was urged to convey letters to her out of Ireland once or twice. And on Tuesday last she told me that she presently, on the next morning at the furthest, meant to depart hence to my Lady Kingsmill, her mother, in Hampshire, where she would stay until she had sent to Chaddesley[3] to Mr John Pakington[4] to entreat him to come to her thither, if he could, to accompany her into Worcestershire, and to cause her husband's own coach mares to be conveyed to her. For that, as she told me, Mr Pakington had written to her that Mr John Pakington would accompany her home if she sent for him. The which I verily suppose to be so indeed. I demanded of her to know what provision she would have sent from London into Worcestershire if she meant to go thither, and she answered, nothing but a couple of trunks to be safely conveyed to Chaddesley against her coming (the which I sent from hence on Saturday last by one Lorimer, a wainman of Wychbold[5]). She said that she would remain at Chaddesley House as privately as she could till her husband's coming thither, and would not come at Harvington at all for fear of forfeiture of the new lease granted by the Queen to one Mr Verney[6] at her suit. The which she needeth not to doubt of if persuasion could prevail, as I told her, alleging many reasons. Whereunto she replied with fear and will, whereon I was constrained to leave her.

No doubt you shall hear variable reports and censures of her marriage with my most worshipful and worthy friend, the which, I pray you, for his sake, and till he may be present, take in the best part, according to his own will and direction, who is the chief party and director of his friends in the same, unless you shall perceive any danger may thereby happen to him. The which to prevent, for so much as in me lieth, I will use all my fidelity and power towards him whilst I live, as in duty I am bounden.

One thing, without commission but of mere duty and goodwill, I am bound to put you in mind of once again: that you use such means that the lady whom I lately wrote to you of may be by your means prevented if she should endeavour to possess herself of the writings and evidence of her husband's lands before his return, as formerly I wrote to you I thought, or leastwise feared, she was too much, I know not for what good cause, desirous. And therefore, if you omit this to be done, as I think I could scarcely do if I were there present, offensively to none, I suppose you omit a matter of no small moment, to be regarded if any ill intention should possess her in her husband's absence. Wherein I need neither to dilate nor persuade you further, but as one chiefly bound to regard the good of my dearest absent friend and of all them who truly love him. And so during life will remain your worship's at command to his poor power for ever, John Grove

London 7 Julii 1602

PS.

[1] Mistress Morton hath been with me lately and offereth me land, as she says, worth above £2,000 to be mortgaged for £1,000, which land is known to your worship, as she saith. Upon which offer I would help her to money, so I might have good assurance of the land if default of repayment should happen. I told her, if I should come into that country this August I would confer with your worship about it and send her word how I like the same offer. She standeth much upon the advance of her son's marriage to receive money for redemption of the land, whereof I thought good to advertise you, praying your favourable advice as occasion shall require.

[2] I pray you send me word so soon as you hear of Mr Pakington

his coming in those parts, for it will hasten my coming to his worship, if leisure permit me.

[3] Howsoever this bearer do report touching the marriage, I take him a true-hearted and well-affected friend. Yet I could wish a temperate and pleasing course in all things, so far for that may stand with credit and without damage may be held, for divers special causes, till Mr Pakington his presence, which God grant in safety for his mercy's sake, wherein I repose all my trust.

---

[1] The first half of this letter was printed with the original spelling in Hodgetts, 'Elizabethan Priest-Holes, IV: Harvington', 27–8.

[2] For Humphrey's wife Bridget Kingsmill, see the Introduction, pp. xxi–xxii above.

[3] Chaddesley House was probably what is now known as Lodge Farmhouse, a much-altered building of about 1500 near Chaddesley Corbett church.

[4] John Pakington was Humphrey's younger brother (see nos. **93–6**); he was not the (Sir) John Pakington of Westwood, near Droitwich, who signed no. **46**.

[5] Wychbold is a village about seven miles south-east of Harvington, near Droitwich.

[6] Sir Richard Verney of Compton Verney in Warwickshire, sheriff in 1605, was a connexion of Bridget Kingsmill through her mother's family, the Raleighs of Farnborough on the borders of Warwickshire and Oxfordshire. Through her influence he had recently become Crown tenant of Humphrey's sequestrated lands, including Harvington Hall: Anderton Webster and Anderton Webster, 'The Pakingtons of Harvington', 208–9.

60. *John Halsey to Henry Russell*
    22 October 1602
    Berington 565 (7.1)

Addressed: To my worshipful friend Mr Henry Russell at Little Malvern give these.

Upon the three receipts that are sent to you in gallipots is written what they are, and according to your directions you are to use them. The purging electuary is to be used in clysters[1] in this sort: first, take one ounce of French barley, boil it in water until it break and become as though it were fermented; then, being strained from the liquor, put it in three pints of whey and let it simmer upon the fire with fennel roots and polypody roots of the oak, of each one ounce; of mercury, of mallow, of violet leaves, of the flowers of camomile and melilot, of each one handful; of the four great cold seeds bruised, of each to the weight of twelve penny-weights. Here let them boil softly till half the liquor be spent. Take of this liquor strained one pint and, by the means of a spoon, by little and little perfectly well mingle them with one ounce of your purging electuary, and so without more ado let it be given blood-warm, either about eight o'clock in the evening or about four o'clock in the afternoon. Within three hours after you may eat broth or meat, or both as your stomach shall serve you. This clyster is to be used once or twice a week as you see occasion, or as the shooting in your head shall be more or less. Sometimes, when your stomach shall be full of wind and water and can hardly digest your meat, you may take of your stomach-pills to the weight of seven pennyweights or eight pennyweights, made up in five little pills to be covered in the pap of a roasted apple and to be swallowed down about seven of the clock in the morning, after which you are to fast two or three hours. Lastly, when your stomach is cleansed, you are to take of the comfortable confection every morning on the point of a knife to the quantity of a chestnut. Of all other things that are not in the gallipots there is sent sufficient for to be put in the decoctions of four clysters, so that of all such things, barley-roots, herbs, seeds and flowers, you are for one clyster to take the fourth part, and how much for the first, so much for each of the rest. Thus, beseeching God to send good success, I do for this time take my leave, the 22nd of October 1602. Your most assured to his power, John Halsey.

[1] A clyster was an enema or suppository and an electuary a medicinal paste.

61. *Alderford Russell's battels*
     December 1602
     Berington 609

A note of money received and laid out for Alderford Russell, first term, *finito ad Festum Nativitatis Domini* 1602

Imprimis, received of Mr Henry Russell	£3

Laid out thus:

For his caution to our College	11s 0d
To the Dean of Divinity	5s 0d
Among the College servants	5s 0d
For Aristotle's *Organon*	2s 0d
For Case and Sanderson's *Logic*[1]	2s 6d
For a prayer-book	18d
For a Horace	12d
For the facing his hat with taffeta	3d

       Summa £3

Laid out since for him:

Imprimis, for two paper books	12d
Item, for four pounds of candles	16d
Item, for a bedstead, mat and cord	9s 2d
Item, for a candle-box	6d

Item, for a steel for his tinder-box	4*d*
Item, for a pair of slippers	2*s* 0*d*
Item, for a standish and points	14*d*
Item, for a chair, a candlestick and snuffers	5*d*
Item, footing two pair of stockings and mending his hose and doublet	6*d*
Item, for a load of wood for the winter, carriage and cleaning thereof	9*s* 6*d*
Item, soleing and mending two pair of shoes	16*d*
Item, a chamberpot	18*d*
Item, carriage of his bedding	12*d*
Item, a penknife, ink and paper	12*d*
Item, tuition and reading to him	13*s* 4*d*
Item, for repairing his study and making a new window	4*s*
Item, for the boy that maketh his bed	2*s*
Item, for to buy papers and other furniture for his study	5*s*
Item, for soleing a pair of shoes	10*d*
Item, for chamber rent and study	4*s* 8*d*
Item, for his commons and battels	42*s* 4*d*
Item, for decrements and fees	3*s*

Summa £5 11*s* 11*d*

Item, hereof £5 of Walter Cowarne, and so remaineth since last quarter	11*s* 11*d*
Item, for a pair of shoes and mending his shoes	2*s* 6*d*
Item, for buttons and setting them on and edging his gown	9*d*
Item, for a table in his study	3*s* 6*d*
Item, for a desk and green cloth	12*d*
Item, for two pounds of candles	8*d*
Item, for a new joined stool	18*d*
Item, for Aphthonius and Quintus Curtius	16*d*
Item, for polling of his hair	3*d*
Item, for mending two pair of breeches, footing two pair of stockings, mending jerkin and hose and two dozen buttons	2*s* 6*d*
Item, for a Greek grammar 12*d*, and *Apophthegms* 8*d*, a psalter 12*d*, and Isocrates 3*s*, and Thomas Thomasius' *Dictionary* 4*s* 6*d*	10*s* 2*d*
Item, for Kykerman his *Logic*[2]	3*s*
Item, for a quire of paper	4*d*
Item, lent him to entertain his kinsman	2*s* 6*d*
Item, for carriage of his cheese	6*d*
Item, for the boy that made his bed	2*s*
Item, for his laundress for two quarters	5*s*
Item, for his study	3*s* 4*d*

Item, for his tuition	13*s* 4*d*
Item, for his commons and battels	£3 12*s* 3*d*
Item, for his decrements, chamber and fees	4*s* 4*d*

Summa £7 2*s* 10*d*

---

¹ John Case (*c.*1546–1600) was a fellow of St John's; his 'logic', the *Summa Veterum Interpretum*, was first published in 1584.
² Bartholomew Keckermann (1571–1609) was a German Lutheran; see Brian P. Copenhaver and Charles B. Schmitt, *Renaissance Philosophy* (Oxford, 1992), 122–6, 73–4.

62. *Alderford Russell to Henry Russell*¹
   27 March 1603
   Berington 562 (31)

Endorsed: To the worshipful his loving uncle Mr Henry Russell Esquire at his house at Little Malvern give this.

Literae ultimo ad te missae, patrue dignissime, in memoriam mihi revocant ac etiam renovant promissum istud quod tibi feci, scilicet ut inter breve quoddam temporis intervallum te latinis literis salutarem, quod nunc (Deo volente) exegi. Ad te enim (Patrue ornatissime) scribo partim ut me, qui totus, quantus quantus [*sic*] sim tuus sum, tibi aliquantulum gratum faciam ac officium efficiam, partim ut tibi in memoriam revocem de iis rebus adprime necessariis de quibus tibi scripsi in postremis literis, partim ut te certiorem faciam de iis sumptibus, tum ad victum, tum ad vitam necessariis [*q*]uos ego a festo Divi Thomae Apostoli usque ad Annunciationem beatae Martiae virginis consumpsi, licet non otiose; qui quidem sumptus, licet maiores et plures mehercule quam velim, spero tamen te velle ecqui [*sic, for* aequi] bonique consulere, quippe quod Nativitas servatoris nostri Jesu Christi, tum etiam hoc ipsum tempus ieiunandi plures quam solitos sumptus requirat. Te igitur (Patrue liberalissime) oro ut quam primum poteris hos meo procuratori, seu ut vulgo locuntur tutori, mittas, ita ut illius expectationi satisfacies [*sic*] et mihi gratissimus efficies [*sic*]. Vale. Oxonii, decimo Nonarum Aprilis, anno salutis humanae 1603. Tuae dignitatis studiosissimus, Alderford Russell

I pray you above all things remember my shirts, for those I have will scarce hang on my back. Furthermore, I pray you send me word how I should scape receiving the Communion now at Easter,² since I did not take it at Christmas.

[*Translation*:] Letters sent to you lately, most worthy uncle, recall to my mind and also renew the promise I made to you, namely that within a brief interval I would greet you with a Latin letter, which now, God willing, I have carried out. I write to you, most illustrious uncle, partly that I, who, whatever I am, am wholly yours, may be pleasing to you and do my duty to you; partly that I may recall those things of which I wrote to you in my last letter; partly that I may inform you about those expenses, both for food and the necessities of life, which I have incurred from the feast of St Thomas the Apostle to the Annunciation of the blessed Virgin Mary, yet not idly; which expenses, though, indeed, more than I would wish, I hope nevertheless that you will consider right and fair, especially as the Birthday of our Saviour Jesus Christ, and also this present time of fasting, requires more than usual expenses. And so, most generous uncle, I pray you to send them as soon as possible to my procurator, or, as they say in the vernacular, 'tutor' so that his expectation may be satisfied and you most pleasing to me. Farewell. At Oxford, the tenth of the Nones of April in the year of salvation 1603, Your worship's most dutiful, Alderford Russell.

¹ The endorsement and postscript are in English, the body of the letter in Latin. It seems to have accompanied a statement of Alderford's battels for the quarter after the previous item. John Russell I's grandfather, also John, married Joan Alderford (Grazebrook, *Heraldry of Worcestershire*, II. 484–6), which accounts for the unusual Christian name.
² Easter Sunday 1603 was on 24 April in England and on 30 March abroad.

63.	*Henry Russell to [Humphrey Pakington]*
		*25 April [1603?]*¹
		Berington 570 (1)²

[. . .]ty and weighty occasions drawing you speedily out [*of our country, and n*]ot suffering you to make any stay or repose y[*ourself a*]mong your poor Worcestershire friends: depriveth [. . .]f of your company, counsel and comfort, by us (myself [*and your sister my*] wife) desired, hoped and looked after. We are glad [*of*. . .] and take no small comfort to be advertised thereof, and do and will continually pray to God to bless you with all happiness, to preserve your health and prosper all your actions.

My wife (God help her) hath evil health, great pains in her head and stomach; and, as she hath utterly lost the sight of one of her eyes, so the fear of loss of the other doth greatly dismay and discomfort her. A surgeon, one Eager, who had laid a cataract in Captain Lister his wife's eyes, the Captain dwelling by Smithfield, was requested by Mr Pigott,³ a friend of mine in Oxford, that, coming down into Worcestershire upon other occasions, he should see my wife and do his best to cure her cataract. He, upon trial and view of her sight utterly failing by a candle, affirmed that her sight on that eye is irrecoverable as deprived according to the rule in logic, *a privatione ad habitum non est regressio*;⁴ which was an hard judgement and no small grief to the poor woman. Yet, to recover her spirits and to recomfort her, he said he could warrant to preserve the sight of the better eye by taking up with needle and thread an artery, and so by cutting it asunder in time to divert the course of any hot blood or humour that by that passage were likely to annoy the eye. Mr Stubbs and my brother John Pakington being there by chance, it was thought it could do no harm and might do her good, and so he was yielded unto. But, being a sevennight since, she hath had very great pain therewith night and day, where he promised the contrary. I pray God upon the end she may be freed of fear of danger in her better, according to his promise. For my part, I hope better than that. She hath lost utterly the sight of her other eye, saying that there is an apparent cataract covering the sight. This Eager is much about London: it may be you have heard of him, what skill he hath; *magna pollicetur*.[5] This, God help her, is your sister's case: *inter spem metumque haeret*.[6] So, thanking you for all your brotherly kind cares, which maketh us bold to impart unto you, as our chief comforter, our griefs, with our hearty commendations I commit you to God. From Worcester this 25th of April, Yours to command during life, Henry Russell.

[1] This letter is hard to place. It seems that Elizabeth's eyesight was worse than it was in nos. **57–8** (January and March 1601/2) but that Henry Russell was still not used to Humphrey's prolonged absences at Ashridge and Harefield. So I have provisionally assigned it to 1603. But since Henry died on 4 March 1607/8, it could be as late as 1607, and on 6 June 1607 Humphrey sent Elizabeth a pair of spectacles: see no. **80**.

[2] About two inches are missing from the left-hand side of each of the first six lines.

[3] Ralph Pigot of Oriel College, Oxford. The Collection includes at least eleven letters from him to Henry and Elizabeth Russell, mostly dated 'from [my] chamber in Oriel College' (Berington 573 (1–6); Lechmere Box, B.6, C.6, C.24, C.27, C.35). C.27, of 31 March [1608], refers to Henry Russell's death since 'my last departure from Little Malvern', which implies that he was a regular visitor there. Richard Yate, third son of James Yate, married a Jane Pygott of Beachampton, which is five miles north-east of Buckingham, off the A422 to Old Stratford: *The Four Visitations of Berkshire, 1532, 1566, 1623, 1665–6*, ed. W. Harry Rylands, Harleian Society 56–7 (London, 1907–8), I. 61; VCH *Bucks.*, IV. 150–51. Eager and Capt. Lister have not been identified.

[4] 'There is no way back from privation to possession'.

[5] 'He makes great promises'.

[6] 'She is stuck between hope and fear'.

64. *John Halsey to Henry Russell*
3 February 1603/4
Berington 565 (8)

Good Mr Russell, The continual kindness which I receive from you and Mrs Russell will not suffer me to forget how much I am beholding unto you both. Your brawn shall be eaten between your friends and mine, and you (God willing) remembered among us at that time. Mr Grove denieth either grant [*deleted*: or] of his farm to [*inserted*: any of] the parties mentioned in your letters or any [?*speech*] at all to any of them. Wherefore, for aught he yet intendeth, Rowland Turner your servant shall be his servant also. Would you would give Edward Bracie to understand that, if he perform not the articles whereunto he is bound, he shall farther hear of it than will be to his ease. As for the buying of Guller's [?*crofts*],[1] assure yourself Mr Grove is willing to buy them at any reasonable reckoning. He knoweth that Mr Wrenford hath offered [*inserted*: them] to divers, and if he could by chaffering with any other man make a greater benefit unto himself, I do not doubt but they had been sold before this time. [*Deleted*: If; *inserted*: Had] Mr Wrenford [*deleted*: were; *inserted*: been] some other man than he is, that bargain were not now to be made. *Flos unguentorum*[2] applied to your son's temples is to little purpose: I could advise him to drop now and then two or three drops of *mel rosarum*[3] into the ear that runneth. Thus, with my hearty commendations to Mrs Russell, yourself, your sons [*and*] Mr Coworne,[4] whom I hear I shall shortly see in London, I do for this time take my leave, the 3rd day of February 1603. Yours ever most assured, John Halsey.

[1] See no. **57**.
[2] 'Flower of ointments'.
[3] 'Honey of roses'.
[4] For Walter Cowarne, see nos. **58**, **66**.

65. *John Grove to Henry Russell*
  5 February 1603/4
  Lechmere f.899:169 (6)[1]

My humble duty to your worship, with good Mrs Russell remembered. I am glad to hear of both your healths. I have received your letter dated the [*illegible*] of January last with a basket wherein were three lamprey[2] pies [*illegible*] for my master and the other for my worshipful dear friend Mr Pakington, and a round of brawn for your physician.[3] All which I have delivered according to your direction, and they yield you and Mrs Russell hearty thanks for the same. Wherein I pray you note Mr Pakington went on Candlemas day to Ashridge[4] and cannot return hither before Sunday or Monday night next, and therefore I have reserved one of your lamprey pies for him. Touching the bond, you shall have the same sent down when Mr Pakington returneth unto these parts, and then you may seal anew for the time you require to have for repayment of the money herein mentioned. The which bond I would have sent to you sooner if I could have safe conveyance. The matters in variance between Mr Pakington and the lewd madam are likely to come to some end this term, which if it take effect, Mr Pakington is to allow her yearly £120 during her life, which God amend or cut off, if it be his divine pleasure I may so pray for her without offence; and she is to surrender to him all things whatsoever she, or any for her, hold from Mr Pakington by any pretended grants from him, and to discharge him for all future debts concerning her any way, and [?*presently*] thereupon if she can give content for [? *the same*], Mr Pakington to release to her use all dem[*ands*] that he hath, or may have, touching her debts. Wherein I heartily pray God [? *we may*] by his wise and learned counsel avoid [? *both these*] and future snares and dangers. Touching [?*your*] terms or wardships,[5] I cannot yet [?*hear*] any [?*further*] of the King in his [?*royal*] resolution therein [?*than*] formerly I have done. London[*, the*] 5th Feb. 1603.

[1] The letter is badly torn at the bottom right-hand corner.
[2] Of the rivers in Worcestershire, the lamprey is found only in the Severn.
[3] John Halsey; see no. **64**.
[4] The reference to Ashridge in Herefordshire shows that by now Humphrey Pakington was in the service of Sir Thomas Egerton (1540–1617), who in July 1603 had become Baron Ellesmere and Lord Chancellor.
[5] See no. **67**.

66.   *Walter Cowarne*[1] *to Henry and Elizabeth Russell*
          25 February 1603–4
          Berington 562 (36)

Most loving uncle and dear aunt, I thank God I write now to you in be[*tter fig*]ure than on Tuesday last when on a sudden at four hours' warning I was like to have been sent to my master; when, if I had gone, I had never seen London again, having taken that day a surfeit which at night wrought unto miserable sickness with me. I thank God and Mr Halsey's marvellous kindness I am now reasonably well and am now like to go either tomorrow or one of the two next days, in more care of you and your health than of mine own; but Almighty God, I trust, of whom I have often and shall with tears desire it, will grant me continua[*nce*?] of your welfare. All that ever I have, I have conveyed upon you absolutely, as may appear in the lesser box that hath 'Marcle'[2] written upon it. I pray you, when you receive it, devise and execute some means to manifest and testify the trust *in omnem eventum*. I have sent my most beloved aunt her trunk again, and in it some of my, or rather her, clothes, to dispose of at her pleasure, and my cloak to you, but you must pay eleven shillings for it, which is too dear, seeing that you shall discharge that and ten shillings more which I think to borrow of good Mr Halsey out of your Marcle's rent at midsummer. I have also sent therein for my aunt and you each a pair of slippers, and for her a pair of shoes. For my sweet cousins, though I remember them with all love, as reason good I have, yet, having been sick of late and my money ebbing, I can return them nor my sister nothing. But Almighty God bless them, make them good learned men and her his obedient servant and yours. Now, good uncle, I have no more (you shall hear from Mr Pakington himself) but this: for God's sake make much of yourself and my aunt and pretty cousins: continue you your goodness to my poor sister in her well-doing. Pray for me, and God send us a merry meeting. Yours ever to command during life, W. Acutto [Hackett], London, February the 15th 1604.

Commend me, I pray you, to my cousin Alderford and all friends, and all your house. No news but that some young gentlemen that were going beyond sea (amongst whom is Mr George Berington[3]) have and do lie in prison [*deleted*: unto] here, unless they be, as the speech was they should be, delivered today upon bail. I pray you send for your evidences to Mr Guillim presently: the note of his hand you shall find in one of the boxes left at home. I should be glad if perhaps I should stay to hear from you [*the*] next week.

[1] Walter Hackett ('Acutto') *vere* Cowarne (1579/80–1607) was born at Ross-on-Wye and educated at Worcester and Oxford. In 1604 he went to St Omer's, *ab archipresbytero missus*, and then on to Valladolid, where he was admitted on 30 May 1604: Henson, *Registers of the English College at Valladolid*, CRS 30, p. 83. Another letter from him to the Russells is Berington 562 (46). On 29 September 1604, Halsey wrote to Henry Russell, 'Your letters to William Acuto, Mr Carie hath undertaken to convey unto him within this se'nnight': Berington 565 (10). But on 5 January 1605/6 he wrote, 'For the letters sent to William Acuto, I am sure that Mr Carie did his best for the conveying of them. Yet I must confess, when he first received them, he misliked the endorsement, which he said might be a means that they were not delivered, as he hath known it happen in the like case before': Berington 565 (12). For Carey, Carye or Carie, see also nos. **71, 75, 79, 84, 89**.
[2] Much and Little Marcle are villages in Herefordshire; cf. no. **113**.
[3] He had been at Valladolid from 1596 to 1600: Henson, *Registers of the English College at Valladolid*, CRS 30, p. 43. His brother John had reconciled Cowarne in 1601: ibid., 83; see Anstruther, I. 34.

67.   *Humphrey Pakington to Elizabeth Russell*
           27 October [1604][1]
           Berington 576 (18)

Most dearly beloved sister, My Lord of Cranborne hath granted to my most honourable good lady the Countess of Derby that you shall have a wardship of your son if my brother Russell chance to die before he come to age and you live; and that no man shall prevent you therein; and also at as reasonable rate as he granteth any of such nature, so that your expectation therein may be satisfied. But for the contenting of your mind, I would not have made the suit before there had been more likelihood of the fall of the ward than I hope I shall ever see. For my Lord Cranborne passeth none absolutely before they fall, which I hope my good brother will prevent by his life, which Almighty God long continue to his pleasure and my hearty desire. If either my Lady of Derby or my poor self chance to live and the ward fall, my Lord of Cranborne holding the office, make no doubt of the matter, I pray you, and let it not so much as come into your mind, for I hope you shall have no cause. When I can hear of Sir Edward Blount coming to London, I will do my best to move him concerning my good brother his Privy Seal.[2] My Lady of Derby determineth to take Davie his son for a footman,[3] if he can get himself to that profession, and therefore I would wish his father to provide him a convenient suit of apparel of some fustian or suchlike, and if his deserts prove good he is like never further to be charged with him. It were good also he practise to run until John Gresham[4] come into the country, which will be shortly, and then he shall know the time of his coming up—all which I forgot to write in my last letter. So in great haste, with my heartiest commendations to my good brother and you, I take leave, Your poor faithful brother, ever at your command, Humfrey Pakington. Harefield, 27th October

[1] Sir Robert Cecil became Viscount Cranborne on 20 August 1604 and earl of Salisbury on 4 May 1605.
[2] A demand for a forced loan of £30 to the King, sent to Henry Russell by Sir Edward Blount on 31 July 1604 (Berington 574 (24)) and mentioned again in no. **71** below.
[3] See no. **68**.
[4] Humphrey Pakington's secretary, who appears as a signatory to some of his deeds; see also no. **59**.

68.   *The dowager countess of Derby to Humphrey Pakington*
         [November 1604]
         Berington 815 (23)

Addressed: To my very loving cousin Mr Pagington give these at Ashridge.

Good cousin Pagington, For your care and pains to come to Harefield I must needs give you many thanks, and desire that when you see fit time and [*when*] my business there require your [*coming*] that you will not be wanting. For the footman you provide for me, if you and he be ready, I wish you would let him come before Christmas, at which time I would willingly have him. And so, leaving you in your best conceits, I rest, as I will ever, Your assured loving friend and cousin, A. Derby.

69.   *Henry Russell's will*[1]
         29 November 1604
         Lechmere Box, 'Items Included' [3]

In Dei nomine Amen. I, Henry Russell of Little Malvern in the county of Wigorn., gentleman, sick in body but whole in mind (thanks be given to Almighty God), do make and ordain this my last will and testament in manner and form following. First, I bequeath my soul unto Almighty God, trusting to be saved by the merits of the Passion of our Saviour Jesu Christ as a member of his mystical Body the Catholic Church, whereof he is the Head, and my body to be buried at the discretion of mine executors in Christian burial where I shall fortune to die; but if it shall please God to call me out of this life near or within Little Malvern, then my desire is that I may be buried in the upper end of the chancel in the church there on the north side opposite to my good parents. Item, I give [*erased*: to the — of that parish £40] to be bestowed on the reparation of the church there twenty shillings. Item, whereas I purchased of Mr Thomas Nash and Marget his wife certain free land in Coddington[2] in the county of Hereford, I do give the said lands, with all profits and appurtenances to them or any part of them belonging, unto Edmund Russell my younger son and to his heirs for ever. Item, I give unto the said Edmund all my cattles, household stuff and implements of husbandry remaining at Ismayes[3] in Coddington in the said county of Hereford. Item, in token of my love toward him and of my desire that he shall always have in mind his duty, fear and love toward God above all things and embrace virtue and learning and never decline or step aside from virtue but contain himself within the bounds and compass of God his holy will and law, I give unto him my ring of gold wherein is set a precious stone, an emerald, which was the gift of my father to me. [*Inserted*: Item, upon like considerations I give to my son John my signet of gold which was also my father's.] Item, I give unto my eldest son John all my lands and tenements in [*deleted*: the county of Wigorn.] Little Malvern in the county of Wigorn., to have and to hold to him and his heirs for ever. Item, whereas I stand indebted to divers persons in great sums, as may appear by a schedule [*deleted*: hereunto annexed; *inserted*: under mine own hand], my will is that, by the consent of mine overseers, mine executors shall sell toward the paying of my debts any quillets and parcels of land lying in any other parish or hamlet, parishes or hamlets within the county of Wigorn., if my corn and cattles there which I shall leave at the time of my death shall not be sufficient to pay debts which for the discharge of my conscience I desire to be fully discharged, contented and paid.

Item, my little plate and household stuff in Little Malvern I give unto my son John, so as Elizabeth my dearly beloved wife may have and enjoy the use and occupation thereof during her natural life. And so likewise my will is that she, my said wife, shall have the use of all stocks of cattle which (my debts paid) shall be left unsold (at Little Malvern), if any such shall be, during her natural life, and the remainder and property thereof I give to my said son John. Item, I give unto Frances Cowarne[4] either a ring of gold worth twenty shillings or the value at my wife's pleasure. Item, I give to her sister Margery a ring of gold worth twenty shillings or the reasonable value, and to either of them, a bed (bedstead with furniture) which was their father's, and betwixt them the silver salt and twelve silver spoons which were their father's [*and*] the linens, brass and pewter which were their father's. [*Deleted*: Also I give unto either of them twenty shillings to make them and every of them a ring of gold.] Item, I give unto my cousin Alderford, in token of my love toward him and in hope that he will be kind toward my wife and children, twenty shillings to make him a ring. Item, I give to every of my sisters Anne Chelmyck and Margery Berrow twenty shillings apiece to make each of them a ring. Item, I give unto St John's College in Oxford, where I was brought up in learning, either the Course of Civil Law with the gloss in great books and Bartol his commentaries thereupon[5] or £6 13s 4d, desiring God to bless that College and company and them to pardon all my defects. If my poor ability would have extended further, I would have dealt with them more liberally. My books I give to my two sons to be divided [*and*] delivered to them by my overseers as they in their discretion shall find them most apt for their studies.

The rest of my goods and chattels, my debts and legacies being discharged, I give and bequeath unto my well-beloved wife and unto my two sons, whom I make, constitute and appoint executors of this my last will and testament. And I desire my dear brothers-in-law Humphrey Pakington esq., John Pakington and Richard Hayward gentleman to be overseers of this my last will and testament and by their discreet counsels to advise and direct mine executors in the execution thereof, and for their pains I desire them to accept ten shillings apiece in gold, which I give unto them. And, for that I am deeply indebted and my estate low, I require my executors to bury me [*inserted*: secretly and privately] without pomp or solemnity, giving to the poor of Coddington 6s 8d, of Moreton 6s 8d, of Welland 6s 8d and of Little Malvern twenty shillings, to be sent to their houses. In witness whereof I have written, sealed and delivered this my last will and testament this 29th of November in the second year of the reign of our sovereign lord James by the grace of God King of England, France and Ireland and of his reign in Scotland the 38th. My will is that my evidences in the study and desks be preserved to the use of my children carefully, and that all evidences concerning lands in Pembrokeshire lying on an upper shelf in the study or elsewhere be safely delivered to my nephew Alderford Russell. By me Henry Russell

Signed and sealed in the presence of Alderford Russell, Charles Burford his mark, John Suffild[6] his mark.

---

[1] Although Henry did not die until 4 March 1607/8, his will, like the arrangement made for the wardship of his son (no. **67**), was a necessary precaution and was not changed during

the remaining three years of his life. Probate was granted to Elizabeth Russell on 16 March 'Anno Domini Stylo Anglie 1608'.

[2] Four miles from Little Malvern, just into Herefordshire.

[3] Possibly the present Mayfields Farm, half a mile north-east of the church.

[4] Cf. no. **66**. In an undated letter to Elizabeth Russell, her nephew John Mintridge (cf. nos. **97–8**) understood 'by Walter Cowarne and Mr Bland [cf. nos. **109, 119**] that the marriage for my cousin Frances is to be solemnised this next morning and that she is to go to Worcester presently': Berington 615 (4).

[5] The commentary on the Code of Justinian by Bartolus of Sassoferrato, a fourteenth-century law professor at the University of Bologna.

[6] John Suffield. See also nos. **78, 85, 105**, and Appendix III, no. **[5]**.

70.   *Sir Edward Blount[1] to Henry Russell*
        22 December 1604
        Berington 562 (34)

Sir, You may discern by the letters which I lately received from the lords of the most high Privy Council, the copy whereof I have sent you to peruse, that their lordships are not satisfied with your answers for the none payment of the money required by the Privy Seal which I friendly sent to you. And therefore for mine own discharge, who undeservedly, as you know, have incurred some suspicion of negligence, as also to hasten this payment according to my duty and the trust reposed in me, I have thought it my part once more to require you that the same may be paid to my hands at the house of one Mr East without Aldersgate, when, upon receipt thereof, I will be ready to subscribe your Privy Seal. Which, for the avoiding of blame to me and haply your own further vexation, I pray you take order so to do before the first day of the next term at my lodging aforesaid, that I be not forced to return your recusancy,[2] whereof I presume you will have due consideration. And so I commit you to God, the 22 of December 1604. Your loving friend, Edward Blunt.

If otherwise you cannot convey your money to my hands, then if it please you to deliver the same to my servant Nicholas Bowyer the younger, who is always abiding at Kidderminster, he will by way of exchange make it up to me. And upon a note of his hand for the receipt of your sum, I will subscribe your Privy Seal, which will be a good course for your case and for the safety of the money.

[1] Sir Edward Blount (*c.*1555–1630) was the brother of Sir Christopher Blount, who married Lettice Knollys, widow of the earl of Leicester and mother of the earl of Essex, and was executed for his part in the Essex Rising (*ODNB*). In St Mary and All Saints, Kidderminster, is an imposing alabaster monument to Sir Edward and his two wives.

[2] Although Henry Russell was apparently never convicted, it is clear that he was a known recusant—which calls into doubt statistics of recusancy based only on Exchequer records. Cf. nos. **67, 71**.

71. *John Grove to Henry Russell*
   6 April 1605
   Berington 376 (4)

Right worshipful, My humble duty to you and good Mistress Russell remembered; to whom in sorrow of my heart I am to impart the death of our true ancient friend, Mr John Halsey, which happened on Easter Day last[1] in the morning at the inn called The Angel without Temple Bar; where he was, through earnest entreaty, moved to visit a patient. And, as he was holding the urinal of his patient to the fire, to turn the water, which was settled by long standing thereof, he being discontented with the maid in the room, who did not go about the same according to his mind, he suddenly fell down with the urinal in his hand, and with his fall burst the same, and was taken up by the patient, leaping out of his bed, and the woman there present, but never spake word after nor could be revived by any means. The death was not to him sudden, for he many times, and lately before it happened, prognosticated and foretold the manner thereof and doubted the same, and therefore most devoutly prepared himself this Lent to that end, in such sort as I assuredly hope his soul is in joy amongst the saints of Almighty God: more comfortable than a number of us poor creatures who are left behind him. Mr Carey and the rest of his friends here present have caused him on Monday last in the afternoon to be in decent manner buried in St Sepulchre's church. My special request is that you would vouchsafe me so much favour as [*to*] give order to my tenants of Fulshurst Farm and of other lands in those parts, which he in his lifetime caused me to purchase and take, as you know, to pay their several rents to your worship for me, and not to pay the same to any other without my special order.[2] And that you would likewise cause one Mr Steyner of Worcester,[3] in whose hands he left divers goods and chattels as wool, hops, and had other reckonings with him, as by notes and inventories thereof and other means shall appear, that he do not dispossess himself thereof by colour of any administration of his goods, which some go about to procure that have nothing to do therewith, without special order of Mr Richard Cox of London, merchant, and myself.[4] And you shall make us beholding to you for the same, and shall perceive your endeavours in that case will be to commendable purpose. So in haste, leaving you and yours to Almighty God's merciful protection, I remain, Your worship's at command to my power for ever, J. Grove. London, 6 April 1605.

I imparted to Mr Pakington at Ashridge how much you were beholden to Sir Edward Blount; who sayeth he hath and ever will endeavour to clear you of that and like charges, and otherwise stead you wherein he may.

---

[1] Easter Day 1605 was 31 March.

2 Halsey owned or rented lands close to Little Malvern, at Colwall, Eastnor and Ledbury, including Fulsthouse or Fulshowse Farm. Cf. nos. **58, 72, 75, 107**, and LaRocca, *Jacobean Recusant Rolls for Middlesex*, CRS 76, pp. 39, 40, 41, 42, 47, 111, 112, 123.

3 For John Steyner (1560–*c*.1634), see Diarmaid MacCullough and Pat Hughes, 'A Bailiff's List and Chronicle from Worcester', *Antiquaries' Journal* 75 (1955), 235–53, esp. 238–9. On 21 March 1610 the benefit of his recusancy was assigned to Thomas Gurlyn, together with that of Francis Moore (no. **112**) and of Sir Thomas Russell (no. **101**): *CSPD, 1603–10*, p. 593.

4 Halsey also owed debts for recusancy, payable through Grove and Richard Cocks, who was a London Mercer and alderman.

72. *John Grove to Henry Russell*
      13 April 1605
      Berington 376 (5)

Addressed: To Henry Russell

Worshipful, My humble duty to you and good Mrs Russell remembered with like thanks. I doubt not but the ill news of the departure of our true friend Mr Halsey out of this life is come to your ears before this time. Which happened Easter Day in the morning last so suddenly that he fell down in a knight's chamber at the inn called The Angel without Temple Bar, to whom he was then sent for to minister physic; that he was taken up and in his own judgment not many hours before his death by reason of an infirmity he had increasing all this [*inserted*: last] Lent, which caused him the more devoutly to prepare himself to take that journey in hand which he is now gone [*inserted*: before] (as I hope) to the eternal joys of heaven. To which place I humbly beseech his divine Maker to grant us access and everlasting dwelling there. I am now, for the love you bear to us both, to pray you to assist me that I be not defrauded of such things in your country of Herefordshire which I lately purchased and got by that means, and to advise the tenants there, which you know better than I, that they pay their rents and duties to none other than yourself only without my order; whom I do hereby humbly entreat to reserve some of them to my use, which use I hope you will commend, upon hearing of me at next meeting, to be laudable and to your good liking. Touching Mr Clinton's[1] motion for me to furnish him upon a mortgage, I cannot by any means deal with him herein because I am in hand with another bargain with Mr Coles; which if we agree, as I think we shall upon my worshipful friend Mr Pakington's liking, I shall [*be*] constrained to borrow money for myself. Notwithstanding, for the money of mine in your hands use your discretion. And so in post haste I humbly commend your worship and all yours to the protection of the Almighty God. London, this 13th of April 1605. Your worship's to command for ever, John Grove

Mr Halsey left certain corn and other goods of mine at Donnington,[2] the certain particular quantity whereof I am ignorant and doubt that I shall be therein most deceived. I pray you certify me, if you can, what you have heard him say was there, and in whose hands the same was.

[1] Ivo Clinton (b. 1575) owned Eastnor on the Herefordshire side of the Malverns: Charles J. Robinson, *A History of the Mansions and Manors of Herefordshire* (London, 1873), 109–11; cf. nos. **73, 107**. He married Maud Nanfan of Birtsmoreton, four miles from Little Malvern (see nos. **131, 196**): *Visitation of the County of Worcester, 1569*, 99.
[2] For Halsey's lands at Donnington, near Stow-on-the-Wold, see no. **73** and LaRocca, *Jacobean Recusant Rolls for Middlesex*, CRS 76, pp. 40, 111.

73.   *John Grove to Henry Russell*
   4 May 1605
   Berington 376 (6)

Right worshipful, My humble duty remembered. Your letter of the 27th of April I received this 3rd of May, together with another letter of yours enclosed in Mr John Bache's[1] letter directed to Mr Pakington at Ashridge; which shall be delivered with all convenient expedition. It seemeth that you wrote former letters to me concerning the death of Mr Halsey, but none of them came to my hands. Wherefore I pray God they be not intercepted by Zachary Field, who rangeth about the country and gathereth unto his own hands as well the rents as goods of other men's, supposing the same to be of Mr Halsey's. Wherein he is so far deceived that he will be urged to make restitution and pay damages at a dear rate. Touching my corn and other goods and chattels at Donnington, I have taken such order with one Mr Chadwell, my tenant, in whose charge and custody the same were left by Mr Halsey, that I doubt nothing of my friend Zachary's rapine or any other practice to dispossess him thereof without my special order. It may fortune I may be there the next Whitsun week, but thereof I am yet uncertain. Wherefore I have thought good hereby to advertise you that, if by that time Mr H. Pakington your brother (to whom I have already written) or yourself can help me to such a sufficient honest man that may lie at Stow or Donnington to see the threshing out, measuring and sale of the corn at Donnington for me, I will content him in your own judgement for his pains. And that in the mean time you need not greatly to employ anybody specially about that business, for one Mr Thomas Tyrer, the schoolm[*aster*] of Stowe, who is brother to my brother-in-law Tyrer, hath certified me of his doings therein by my directions formerly to that effect you write. Touching the rent by you received for me, I pray you keep the same in your safe custod[*y*] till you hear further from me. On Sunday last [. . .] Hill of Worcester, being a clothier,[2] received a l[*etter from*] me for you. I humbly thank you for your care an[*d . . .*]

to pleasure me in all things, especially in these causes happening upon Mr Halsey's death, whose good work and will in this last time deserve in mine opinion a reverent remembrance, whereof I perceive you not to be forgetful any way. Touching Mr Clinton, for your sake I have taken pains with him, but his haste is such that it exceedeth a convenient time of consideration to be had, so far that none of my friends dare deal with him as yet. And so, with daily prayers to God for preservation of you and yours, I cease further to trouble you more at this time. London, this 4th of May 1605, Your worship's for ever at co[*mmand*], John Grove.

¹ One of Humphrey Pakington's servants: see no. **78** below. At Warwick Record Office is a letter from him to Humphrey and a rental of 1597 marked 'John Bache his book' on the back flap: Throckmorton MSS (CR 1992), Box 52, stitched set [e]; 'Tribune Carved Chest 44'. For 'Box 52, stitched set [e]' see also p. 223, n. 18. Cf. no. **101**.
² The cloth trade was the most important in Worcester. Clearly Hill and other clothiers acted as bankers; cf. nos. **79, 83, 110**.

74.   *John Grove to Henry Russell*
         16 November 1605
         Berington 376 (7)

Right worshipful, I received not your letter till last night late of Mr Pakington. For an answer thereunto I can write no more to you than I have formerly done. That is, I do refer myself wholly to perform such bargain as you shall conclude for me with Mr Hartland,¹ with hearty thanks for your most friendly care for my good, signifying further that I shall be always ready to accomplish your requests for your kinsman Mr Alderford Russell if he shall need. [*Inserted*: I have] not seen him since he delivered your letter to me. My brother Tyrer² telleth me he doth sometimes see him, but what success he hath in his business I am ignorant. So, with my humble and hearty commendations to you, together with good Mrs Russell, I cease your further trouble at this time, committing you and yours to God's tuition. London, this 16th of November 1605.³ Your worship's at command most bounden, John Grove.

Mr Pakington himself, being in town, caused your business with my Lady Derby to be despatched and meaneth shortly to see you.

¹ For John Hartland of Colwall, see nos. **75, 77, 79, 80, 105, 107, 108, 111, 124** and Berington 562 (1).
² For Tyrer see also nos. **101, 110, 116**.
³ Despite the date, Grove says nothing about the Gunpowder Plot.

75.   *John Grove to Henry Russell*
          21 March 1605/6
          Berington 376 (9)

Right worshipful sir, Your letter of the 15th of March I received this day, giving you most hearty thanks for your kind advertisements of good counsel and many other benefits received from you. So it is, that upon some occasions concerning both Mr Pakington and myself I repaired on Wednesday last[1] to Harefield, where I saw him with his noble Countess in good health; and amongst other good news he signified to me that his own lady was like to die of a consumption, for whose amendment I did ever pray to God, and still will till she may be a saint in heaven, and that is the worst I wish her.[2] I think Mr Pakington will visit you at your next Assizes (all his business here set apart),[3] but my Lord Chancellor must not know so much if it may be concealed from his lordship. You made an answer to him who would have bought my lease of Hartland's lands according to my mind; and where you did say then that you thought it to be my mind, you may answer him resolutely that I intend rather to buy more lands in those parts, if I can, than to sell that, for aught I do yet know. Mr Carey is somewhat amended, and I think that in the cause in Chancery between Mr Halsey's kindred and myself, we shall go to commission presently for examination of witnesses. Wherein I must rely upon you and Mistress Russell in that country for two of my chief witnesses to be examined at Worcester if we proceed. I will trouble you but with two or three interrogatories at the most, hoping you will add so much pains, if need be, to all your former favours, especially in so true and honest a cause, that, for want of testimony of the truth, the true meaning of our deceased friend may not be wickedly and most untruly perverted in this case; wherein, besides your doing me a work of charity, you shall not find me unthankful. And so, commending your worship, with good Mistress Russell, to the Almighty God's preservation, I remain, London 1605, 21 March, Your worship's at command for ever, John Grove

---

[1] 19 March 1605/6.

[2] Bridget Pakington did die: she was buried at Chaddesley Corbett on 14 April.

[3] Edward Oldcorne, Ralph Ashley, Humphrey Lyttelton and Thomas Habington were tried at Worcester at the Lent Assizes in the first week of April 1606; the first three and John Wintour were executed there on 7 April before a huge crowd: John Gerard, 'A Narrative of the Gunpowder Plot', ed. John Morris as *The Condition of Catholics under James I*, 2nd edn (London, 1872), 264–77; Richard Challoner, *Memoirs of Missionary Priests*, ed. John Hungerford Pollen (London, 1924), 291. Humphrey Pakington and his brother John were convicted of recusancy at the same Assizes on 3 April: E.377/14, *Item Wigorn*. Altogether, an eventful fortnight.

76. *Acquittance by Alderford Russell to Richard Middleton,
       archdeacon of Cardigan*
   27 March 1606[1]
   Lechmere Box ('Items Included' 5)

To all Christian people to whom this present writing shall come Alderford Russell of Greenhill in the parish of Polchroningham alias Porter-
chrongham in the county of Pembroke,[2] gentleman, sendeth greeting.
Know you that, whereas Henry Russell of Little Malvern in the county
of Wigorn., esq., as my guardian hath received of Richard Middleton,
clerk, Archdeacon of Cardiganshire, late farmer of Greenhill aforesaid
with other my lands adjoining by him occupied, for me, to my use and
in my behalf divers sums of money for rents and parcels of rents due to
him my said guardian to my use, as by several acquittances thereof made
by the said Henry Russell unto the said Mr Richard Middleton dated in
divers years doth and may appear; all which sums the said Henry hath
bound himself in an obligation of £200 that I, the said Alderford, after
the accomplishment of the full age of twenty and one years, should acknowledge received, and thereof and [*of*] every part and parcel thereof
discharge and acquit the said Richard Middleton, his executors and
administrators for ever and ever: in performance of that condition, I, the
above-named Alderford Russell do by these presents remit [*and*] release
unto the said Richard Middleton all such sums of money as shall or may
appear to be received of him by the said Henry for rents and parcels of
rents due out of Greenhill and other lands and tenements demised unto
the said Richard by the said Henry as my guardian, and of every part and
parcel thereof I do for ever by these presents clearly acquit, release and
discharge the said Richard Middleton, his deputies and administrators.
In witness whereof I have sealed and subscribed this acquittance the 27th
day of March in the fourth year of the reign of our sovereign lord James
by the grace of God King of England, France and Ireland, Defender of
the Faith, and of his reign in Scotland the 39th. Alderford Russell.

Sealed and delivered to the use of the above-named Richard Middleton
in the presence of Henry Russell, Charles Burstow, John Suffilde and
Margery Berrow

---

[1] This acquittance indicates that Alderford Russell was born at the end of 1584 or early
in 1585, and so was about seventeen when he went to Oxford (nos. **61–2**). Since 1604 his
inheritance at Greenhill, Pembrokeshire, had been let to Richard Middleton, the archdeacon of Cardigan. Although their arms do not match, Richard 'may have been' a son of
Marmaduke Middleton, who was bishop of St David's from 1581 until 1592 (when he
was deprived for forging a will): *ODNB*; Glanmor Williams, *Wales and the Reformation*
(Cardiff, 1997), 376. Berington 288 is a bond from Middleton to Henry Russell, dated 13
November 1601.
[2] Greenhill is in Pwllcrochan, three miles west of Pembroke Dock; cf. nos. **85–7**.

77. *John Grove to Henry Russell*
  22 November 1606
  Berington 376 (10)

Right worshipful sir, I wrote to you the last week a letter which I hope you have received before now. If not, I pray let my grounds, late in Hartland's possession, to such tenants as you think best for this year, taking such assurance for my rent to be paid half-yearly as you shall think good. And to that effect I formerly wrote. Touching Mr Alderford Russell's debts to Mr Harvye, I have talked with his creditor and told him what you writ, which being performed I hope will give him partly satisfaction for the time you writ of. Mr Pakington, God be praised, is in health and merry. My master[1] his nephew, Mr Edward Sebright,[2] both without my master his privity or consent, on Monday last came to London and married Mr Gerard Whorwood's eldest daughter, who attended on her aunt, the Lady Leighton, at Highgate. Wherein he hath made a great adventure of loss of my master his favour &c., although he has matched with an honest young gentlewoman (as is said). I would gladly entreat you to send me the remainder of that money of mine in your hands towards Christmas or against Wednesday next after Twelfth Day next at furthest, if it may be, for that then I am specially to use some money. But I do not mean the £100 owing by bond, unless you please so to do. And so, with hearty commendations and like thanks both to you and good Mistress Russell, I commit you and yours to God's preservation, and rest, in London, this 22d of November 1606, your worship's at command for ever, John Grove.

If I had Hartland's bond here, I would put it in suit presently, and not lose the benefit of this term.[3]

[1] William Sebright of Wolverley, near Kidderminster; see no. **91**. He was Town Clerk of London, MP for Droitwich, founder of the Sebright School at Wolverley and from 1591 to 1602 lessee of Humphrey Pakington's sequestrated estates (including Harvington Hall). See also the Introduction, p. xix above.
[2] (Sir) Edward Sebright (1585–1657) married Theodosia Whorwood, daughter of Gerard Whorwood (1564–1627) and Dorothy Barbour of Compton Park and Stourton Castle in Kinver, Staffordshire. Anne Whorwood had married Ambrose Dudley, earl of Warwick, whose brother, Robert, earl of Leicester, married Lettice Knollys, whose sister Cecilia married Sir Thomas Leighton (*c*.1530–1610) of Watttlesborough in Shropshire. So Lady Leighton and Theodosia Whorwood, though not 'aunt' and 'niece', *were* related. William Sebright had no children and Edward's father had died in 1592, so Edward was William's heir. Stebbing Shaw, *The History and Antiquities of Staffordshire* (London, 1801; facs. repr. Wakefield, 1976), II/1. 129, 264, 266; VCH *Staffs.*, XX. 131; *ODNB* s.v. 'Leighton, Sir Thomas'; *Visitation of Shropshire, 1623*, II. 324–5; VCH *Worcs.*, IV. 21.
[3] Berington 562 (1) is a letter from John Hartland at Colwall dated 'Palmeson' (no year). The point of the postscript is that the Michaelmas law-term ended on 28 November and Hilary term did not begin until 23 January.

78.   *John Bache to Henry Russell*
    7 December 1606
    Berington 562 (39)

May it please you: concerning the greening trees my master left no direction with me, but if any be left with Mr John Pakington or my fellow Suffill, it shall be fulfilled. Otherwise, they shall be safe set and kept till we can give him intelligence or receive directions from him. John Suffill demanded to know of me whether my master came into country before or in Christmas, wherein I could not then answer him; but since a letter came from my master dated the last of November, whereby I understand [*deleted*: whe] we shall not see him before Christmas be [*p*]ast, for the morrow after New Year's Day he is to attend my Lord Chancellor's coming to Ashridge. Thus, praying God to bless and [*inserted*: ever] keep both you and yours, with my most humble duty take [*sic*] my leave this 7 of December 1606. Your worship's ever to command to my power, John Bache junior.

79.   *John Grove to Henry Russell*
    10 January 1606/7
    Berington 376 (11)

Right worshipful sir, I have received of Mr George Stynton of Worcester,[1] clothier, the bearer hereof, the £20 mentioned in your last letter dated 4th of this January. The which I doubt not but you will make him satisfaction of upon receipt of this my letter. I have also received of the carrier of Worcester a basket of good puddings and birds, the which I have distributed amongst my friends, saving a share of puddings, whereof this bearer, Mr Stynton, can testify the goodness by his taste, The birds were a dainty dish for weak and infirm friends, who had the same wholly amongst them. I pray you spare your further charge till God make me a householder for myself. In the mean time, I do most heartily thank both you and Mistress Russell for your continual goodness to me, and hope, when God shall better enable me, to show myself more thankful to you than I have done. I thank God for the goodness of my late cause in controversy and fidelity of my good friends therein, which hath so far prevailed against the lewd attempts of my adversaries that now both myself and others in like case with me have just cause to say with the holy Psalmist, *Beati quorum inimici convertuntur ad eos.*[2] For all our adversaries, save one, have most willingly submitted themselves to accept thankfully whatsoever should please Mr Carye[3] to give them, disclaiming any right to the same or anything else which was our deceased friend's at the time of his death. Touching the disposing of my lands, late in Mr Hartland's occupation, I have and do hereby give you all the power I have to let the same from year to year, or longer, to whomsoever you please that will assure me of such yearly rent and such days of payment as you shall agree, and I will warrant and defend them in the lawful enjoying thereof against all men, and will perform any other lawful act as you shall in your wisdom think reasonable to me to do, with many thanks; and will assuredly save both you and all others who you shall appoint to follow your directions harmless in preserving my right therein. And with my hearty prayers to the Almighty God for the health and happiness both of your worship and Mistress Russell and all your friends, I end to trouble you further at this time and will remain during life, Your worship's in duty most bounden at your command, John Grove. London 10 January 1606

Mr Pakington told me it might happen he would be in Worcestershire about this time, if my Lord Chancellor came to Ashridge, but his Lordship hath not been there since Christmas. If you chance to see Mr Pakington, I pray you certify him I will be mindful to follow his directions in speaking to his Lordship only if he return and bring not the books he wotteth of with him, and not otherwise to trouble my Lord.

¹ George Stinton the elder and younger were both counsellors at Worcester in 1621: Valentine Green, *The History and Antiquities of the City and Suburbs of Worcester* (London, 1796), II, pp. lxxviii–lxxix.
² 'Blessed are those whose enemies flinch and blush': cf. Vg Ps. 69:3–4.
³ Carey seems to have acted as Humphrey Pakington's attorney in London: cf. nos. **71**, **75**, **84**, **89**. Was he the recusant Richard Carey, 'late of St Andrew's Holborn, esquire' (LaRocca, *Jacobean Recusant Rolls for Middlesex*, CRS 76, pp. 19, 41, 66, 80)? Cf. no. **66**.

80.   *John Grove to Henry Russell*
     6 June 1607
     Lechmere f.899:169 (12)¹

Worshipful sir, My humble duty to you and good Mistress Russell with like thanks remembered. I have not yet answered your two last letters because I was at the time of the receipt thereof both busied specially and also was to take advice what was best to do against Hartland. Since which time I have determined as it may be to expulse him sooner than he shall think of by lawful means and meet with his devices, whereof I shall certify you more at large hereafter, praying the continuance of your friendship herein. I hear it said by some to whom Mr Alderford Russell is indebted here in London further than I knew of before that he is in London, but I have neither seen him nor heard of him otherwise than by your late letters and the reports of his creditors, who lie in wait for to take him, being outlawed for debt, as I hear. Good Mr Russell, let not me stand long in doubt for [?*hearing*] that you can devise how I may be hereby satisfied, [*for if it*] had not been for yourself and his security [*nothing*] will have moved me to [*deal*] with him in that case. . . . Your good brother Mr Pakington, with his kind commendations to you and Mrs Russell, hath sent her here enclosed a pair of spectacles, which he, being lately in town, prayed me to cause conveyed to her. He is in as good health as ever I knew him and merry withal, although very busy and much employed by his most honourable friend,[2] who respecteth him his private affairs above all men's expectations. I am greatly busied to defend a just cause in the Exchequer,[3] where I hope well because the cause is good. And so in haste I rest, London, this 6th of June 1607, Your worship's at command to my power for ever, John Grove.

[1] Most of this letter is now illegible. Aileen Hodgson's transcript omitted a sentence in the middle (four and a half lines in the MS), only part of which can be recovered.
[2] Lord Ellesmere.
[3] See no. **81**.

81. *The earl of Derby[1] to Sir Julius Caesar[2]*
12 July 1607
British Library, MS Lansdowne 153, f. 241

Addressed: To the right honourable Sir Julius Caesar, knight, Chancellor of his Majesty's Court of Exchequer and one of his Majesty's most honourable Privy Council.

Good Sir Julius Caesar, The bearer, Mr Grove, being a man whom I well know and respect, is (after long suit in the Chancery) unjustly molested in the Exchequer by certain informers supposing that some lands and leases in his possession are liable for payment of a debt to his Majesty intended to be begged, in respect of the recusancy of one John Halsey, physician, long since deceased (as he can inform you); and, for that the defence of the suit may hardly countervail the benefit that may be to him thereby saved, is now advised, for his speedy avoiding of future vexations, to be an humble suitor to his Majesty for his Highness' grant of all such debts, penalties and forfeitures that may happen to his Majesty by conviction of the same recusant. Wherein I am very heartily to pray your honour, the rather for my sake, that you will be pleased by the best means you can devise to take upon the effecting thereof, the suit being very honest and this party well deserving his gracious favour in respect of many services without recompense by him done of long time, as well to our late Queen as also to his Majesty. And so doing, I shall think myself beholding unto you as for a special favour done to me, and he shall yield you so liberal a gratification as the benefit to him hereby arising will bear. And so, with my hearty commendations, I rest this 12th of July 1607. Your very loving friend [*flourish*] Derby.

¹ William Stanley, 6th earl of Derby (*c*.1561–1642) was the brother of Ferdinand, 5th earl, who died in 1594 a few months after inheriting the title and whose widow Alice (Spencer) had married Lord Chancellor Ellesmere (see nos. **67–8**). William and his two brothers had been at St John's College, Oxford, in 1572, when Henry Russell was a don there. On 26 July 1594 he married Elizabeth, half-sister and coheir to Henry de Vere, 18th earl of Oxford, and eldest daughter of Edward, the 17th earl, by his wife Anna, daughter of William Cecil, Lord Burghley.
² Lechmere Box C.28 is a letter from Grove to Henry Russell dated two days after this one.

82.   *Henry Russell to [?] Bowen*¹
        [? September 1607]
        Berington 570 (2)

Good Mr Bowen, I have much to thank you for many kindnesses towards myself and my nephew, your godson. I am to pray the like continuance of your good will, countenance and counsel towards him, whereof his young, unskilful and inexperienced years hath much need of. I hope yet he will prove an honest man and comfort to his friends, and be not carried away with the vanities of youth, and be not wedded to his own will overmuch, weening of his own wit as young men of this age unduly do, thinking themselves wiser than their elders and able to teach them, of whom, God knoweth, both they may and ought to learn. He hath concluded with Mr Middleton to depart from Greenhill now at this Michaelmas, but how and to whom he shall let it he as yet knoweth not. Some do advise him to let his tillage to thirds and his kine to a dairyman, either for rent or cheese and butter, and I know not what order to take with sheep. He hath no provision for winter in oats, for cattle but a little hay. Mr Middleton carrieth away corn and straw. I know not what counsel to give my nephew, being so far off: let me entreat your best direction. Mr Middleton hath sold him for £40 a pig of his own sow—I mean the right in Wade's land, which Mr Henry White standeth bound in £200 to assure unto him by virtue of an award made by Mr Revill and Mr Canon,² which I left with you and you have delivered to my nephew; so as upon the point he hath bought nothing for his money. I make bold with you, as you may command me in anything I can stead you. So, with my hearty commendations, together with my wife's, to yourself and your good children, Mistress Joyce and Master Charles, I permit you to go, hoping that you will afford your best direction to your godson in disposing of his poor living and of himself. Yours faithfully to be used, Henry Russell.

Mr Morgan Powell³ questioneth certain land at Greenhill as bought of Sir Griffith Markham,⁴ whereas we acknowledge only a rent which we have ever paid as a quit-rent issuing out of the land. We neither took—Sir W. Davis[5] nor my brother Charles nor any since—ever took lease or grant from Sir Griffith or his ancestors, but in all descents have held it in their own right and paid fine and recoveries thereof to greater numbers of acres than are in the whole of Greenhill, and without claim, so for many years have enjoyed it, as it may appear. Mr Powell is content to reserve the matter to your ordering, and so are we, if it will please you to take pains therein.

[1] The Bowens (from the Welsh 'ab Owen') lived at Upton Castle, a minor stronghold two miles west-north-west of Carew Castle (nos. **43, 91**) and eight miles east of Greenhill.
[2] For 'Mr Canon' and perhaps for Henry White, see no. **40**.
[3] Powell (cf. no. **85**) has not been identified.
[4] Sir Griffin Markham. Named after his mother Mary Griffin of Dingley in Northamptonshire, he was keeper of Bestwood Park, near Nottingham. About 1602 a spy reported that the Jesuits John Gerard, John Percy and Thomas Lister were to be at a hunt there, with 'Francis Tresham, young [Lord] Vaux and Mr Griffin's son and heir'. If the Bye Plot had succeeded, Sir Griffin would have been Earl Marshal, and in August 1605 he was banished. In November, his wife offered to betray Gerard and told Salisbury, 'If the watch had continued but two days longer, Mr Gerard had been pined out at Harrowden.' On 22 July 1606 Sir Griffin saw Gerard and Fr William Baldwin in a church in Brussels, but Gerard understandably 'did shun him'. Anstruther, *Vaux of Harrowden*, 248, 261, 298, 318, 328, 390.
[5] Sir William Davis. Like 'Sir' Hugh Evans in *The Merry Wives of Windsor*, not a knight but a Welsh parson. He was Charles Russell's father-in-law and so Alderford Russell's maternal grandfather; cf. nos. **43, 76, 91**.

83.   *John Grove to Henry Russell*
          17 October 1607
          Berington 376 (15)

Worshipful sir, I have received your letters to Mr Pakington and me. But, by reason of Mr Pakington's absence from London and employment in my Lord's business, I cannot speak with him or hear of him within so short time as you have limited. And, as I heard say, he hath been the last week in Worcestershire and is not yet returned to Ashridge. When he cometh hither or thither, you shall know his mind. In the mean time, the matter lieth in your hands who are arbitrators for proceeding or staying the suit. I think no advantage of costs or other matters will be stood upon by any party if you stay proceeding till further consideration may be had of the cause. Let Mr Newport,[1] if he be not contented so to do, let him use his discretion, and I suppose it will fall out worse for him. There is nothing intended against Mr Newport for aught I know but more good than he deserveth unless more reason rule him now than of late hath done. And so in great haste I humbly commend both you and Mrs Russell to God's merciful preservation and rest, London, the 17th of October 1607, Your worship's ever at command, John Grove.

I have received the cloak-bag and all other things therein, and pray you would be pleased, if you can, conveniently cause some Worcester clothier or other to make payment of the £15 in your hands at your convenient pleasure.

¹ See no. **84** and Appendix IV.

84. *John Grove to Henry Russell*
15 November 1607
Berington 376 (17)

Addressed: To the right worshipful Henry Russell esquire at Little Malvern give these.

My hearty commendations, with the like thanks to you and to good Mrs Russell remembered. I have received from Greenbank, the carrier of Worcester, £15 which he left with his porter named Parsons (as is alleged, for me), together with your letter, at his departure hence; which came not to my hands till this day morning, after his departure [*deleted*: hence]. Whereby I perceive you sent the same, although you had since occasion to use [*?it*], whereof I would you had advertised me and kept [*the mon*]ey in your hand longer if it had [*p*]leased [. . .]e thing. Touching Mr Walter and Mr [*Coven*]try's¹ resolution of Mr Newport's ambig[*uities*]: here was present the last week Zachary Field in the behalf of Mr Newport and himself, and at his charge caused both Mr Walter and Mr Coventry to have special meetings and deliberate consideration of the cause in question. W[*hereupon*] they have both delivered their resolute [*opinions*] and Mr Walter (as I am informed) hath [*written*] to Mr Newport that the land being never in the supposed recusant's hands can no way by law be subject to the payment of any his debts or forfeitures by reason of his recusancy, and that the King's supposed title in law for the same need not to be feared. But what censure the same may be subject to in the Exchequer Chamber he knoweth not, although he is inclined to think the same cannot be [*deleted*: *illegible*] prejudicial. All which being now made known to your brother Mr Pakington, now in London, he sayeth that he will be shortly in that country and speak with you himself concerning the same. Yesterday Mr Newport and his kinsman [*?Lee*] had not exhibited any bill in Chancery. But if he had, Mr John Pakington cannot answer this term, because my Lord hath granted that he shall answer by commission of *dedimus potestatem* in the country, by reason of his inability to travel this winter. I verily suppose that he meaneth not to put in any bill, and so it is best for him.² If he do, let him assure himself he shall be answered little pleasing him to peruse if he take that course. The matter will only *consist*[?] what the arbitrator or umpire will award.

This title being now cleared to Mr Newport's satisfaction, you remember what Sir Edward Blount said: that was, he would tax what should [*be*] paid. And so, [*comme*]nding you, with good Mrs Russell, [*to God's tui*] tion, I take my leave. London, this [. . .] November 1607. In haste. Your worship's to command, John Grove.

¹ For 'Mr Coventry', see the notes to no. **101**.
² On 11 January 1607/8 Grove wrote to Russell that 'Mr Carey and I have given joint answers to a bill in Chancery and Mr John Pakington's answers drawn by Mr Coventry at Harvington' (Berington 376 (19)); cf. nos. **89–90** below.

85. *Humphrey Pakington to Henry Russell*
*[November 1607]*¹
Lechmere f.899:169 (10)

My good brother, I must ever acknowledge your love and fidelity towards me, as also in this your particular desire that I should have Mr Alderford Russell's land at Greenhill. But, seeing it appeareth not that Mr Alderford hath made any value or certain price of the same, as I expected and as I understand by conference with John Suffield you directed he should do at his last going into the country, I may almost certainly resolve that it will not come into my hands. For I dare not in any degree deal with the young gentleman upon any uncertain mortgage in respect of my certain apprehension of his nature and disposition. Morever, mine estate is not, being now a married man, to adventure the indebting myself upon certain loss, except I would stand upon the taking of advantage upon a young man's negligence, as I think another [*inserted*: man] will that loveth Mr Alderford no more than he loveth you or me. I presume Mr Grove could furnish Mr Alderford with the £300 required if I durst give my word for Mr Alderford's true meaning, or the certain value of the thing, neither of which I can or dare do. So that I think Mr Powell or some cheating fellow will have the thing, unto whom Mr Alderford will afford the best pennyworth. For which I am sorry in respect of your love to the young gentleman and hate to Mr Powell, but such is the world. I shall be very shortly in London, but I presume it will be little to the purpose, notwithstanding I would either give or pray Mr Grove to give the true and right value of the thing for the same, if it might so be had, as I know Mr Powell will not. And this is all I can answer, except I know Mr Alderford's selling price. I presume Mr Newport is before this time advertised from Zachary Field that Mr Walter hath delivered his resolute opinion, that the King by law can have no title to the Lea Farm, so that Mr Newport may well give £100 for my title, except he stand too much in his own lights, which I refer to himself. He hath yet put no bill into the Chancery, so that no answer can be made according to your promise, neither can I say how he can frame any bill there to do himself any stead. And of this much I thought good to advertise you, that you might, if you see cause, return answer unto them. And I verily think Mr Newport would not have forborne his bill so long if he meant to commence any at all. So, with my heartiest commendations unto you and my good sister, together with the like from my wife, I take leave, ever remaining, Your poor brother, most faithful at your command, Humfrey Pakington.

¹ This letter refers to the legal opinion mentioned in no. **84** and must be a week or so later, about 20 November. It seems that it was written from Ashridge and that Humphrey proposed to visit London to see Grove before returning to Harvington for Christmas (nos. **86–9**).

86. *Humphrey Pakington to Henry Russell*
    *[December 1607]*¹
    Lechmere f.899:169 (13)

My good brother, If I were of myself to determine with Mr Newport, then would I take the £50, both in respect of the time wherein we are and the danger that may follow. And yet Mr Newport's most advantageous mind deserveth not the favour; but, depending on Mr Grove, I can make no definitive answer but this: that if Mr Grove return no resolution, my brother, in discharge of our word, shall speedily answer [*inserted*: upon the first part], but yet by *Dedimus potestatem* in respect of his inability to travel; and I hope Mr Grove will have the like in respect of your credit; whose pains also in this cause deserveth further recompense. Tomorrow I depart for Ashridge and therefore would wish that no notice were taken of my receipt of this your letter, if it may be, but answer made in this sort: that if Mr Newport durst trust [*deleted*: your] my words, he need not fear the King's title if he had mine, as he should plainly see and find if I were called as a witness for the King, as I must be; and that the difficulty is no other than that is in Mr Newport's own power to avoid, which is to cause a Herefordshire jury [*deleted*: in] but ordinarily indifferent, and not to be *moved*[?] or palpably forsworn; for, one jury once passing against the King, I would not give sixpence for all the informers hereafter; and this Mr Newport knoweth better than I can tell him. If he were not over-covetous with desire, for good luck and conscience sake I could wish he would bridle a little in himself. For Mr Alderford his lands at Greenhill, I can say no more but this: that if I might have a pennyworth for a penny I would strain myself and for the thing, in respect [*deleted*: in respect] of the causes foreknown unto you, and the rather if I might pay interest unto him till I might be able to get money. For I protest unto you in conscience, in respect of taking my lease of Warwick² and other charges, my estate is yet weak; but I despair of his indifferency, and therefore say no more but that, when he hath tried all his chapmen, if I may have it for as much as the best will give him *bona fide*, I shall account myself much beholding unto him and be ready to requite the same in all faithful respects. For your own purchase, if you find it profitable (wherein, knowing nothing, I can say nothing), my credit shall be yours to procure you money in the best sort I can, and when I have any myself, you shall command it. So, ever resting yours and my good sister's, whose griefs and pains are also grievous unto me, I take leave and remain during life, Your poor brother at command, Humfrey Pakington

Harvington, this Monday morning

Time will shortly come in for my sister to send her greenings.[3]

[1] This letter seems to come after no. **85** and before no. **87**. If so, the possible 'Monday mornings' are 30 November and 7 and 14 December 1607. Humphrey was in Worcestershire in the second week of October (no. **83**), probably at Ashridge in mid-November and in London 'very shortly' afterwards (no. **85**), and certainly back at Harvington by 20 December (no. **88**).
[2] The Corporation of Warwick had leased the rectory and other lands in Chaddesley Corbett to Humphrey's great-uncle Sir John Pakington (d. 1551). In 1578 Humphrey's father, another John, had 'one lease of the parsonage of Chaddesley Corbett for certain years yet enduring, £60': Worcs. Record Office, 008.7 (1578), 35c, published in Michael Hodgetts, 'The Priest-Holes at Harvington Hall', *Transactions of the Worcestershire Archaeological Society* n.s. 39 (1962), 10. In 1583 it was said that Sir John's lease still had 'many years' to run and that it had been inherited by Humphrey: Worcs. Record Office, 899:115/7, published in Michael Hodgetts, 'Two Harvington Letters', *Worcestershire Recusant* 9 (June 1967), 19–21. It appears that in 1607 it had recently expired and been renewed.
[3] A kind of apple, green when ripe; cf. nos. **78, 89**.

87. *John Grove to Henry Russell*
        19 December 1607
        Berington 376 (17)

Right worshipful, My humble duty, with like thanks, to you and to good Mistress Russell remembered. The whole discourse concerning your cousin Alderford I leave to the relation of Mr H. Pakington and your loving good kinsman Mr Chelmyck.[1] Only I thought good to signify this much to you: that for me to accomplish your request can neither pleasure Mr Alderford Russell nor stand with my safety nor yet save him from ruining his estate. I have no mind to have any dealings with him for his lands. Assure yourself he should not want £500 to do him good. But I hear of his estate against both our wills. I have caused the Grocer[s][2] to convey to one of the carriers of Worcester a sugar-loaf for yourself and good Mistress Russell to mollify your wines if they prove hard in that country this Christmas. And I intend to deliver this letter to the same carrier if I can, for my leisure doth not permit me to send both together.

Therefore you must cause enquiry if I miss of the same carrier. The sugar-loaf is directed to you and containeth ten pounds ten pennyweight in weight and is of the best sugar.

I hope before Mr Pakington's return the variance between Mr Pakington and Mr Newport will be finally ended, either by the arbitrators or umpire, Mr Newport having Mr Walter's opinion for the law as amply as he required it at our last being together. So that now, as Zachary Field thinketh, nothing resteth but time and place of meeting and growing to a final resolution only for price and such assurance as Mr Pakington hath in the land to be made with warrants only against himself and all others claiming under him. Your Camden[3] I cannot send by this carrier because the same is locked amongst other things that I cannot come by yet. In haste, with hearty prayers to God for your health, I leave you and all yours to his most holy tuition, and remain, London, this 19th of December 1607, Your worship's for ever at command, John Grove.

I shall tell you more concerning Mr Alderford Russell ruinating his estate than I would willingly write, because I do understand the same but by report.

[1] William Chelmych had married Henry's sister Anne.
[2] John Grove belonged to the Grocers' Company.
[3] The Little Malvern library, now in Birmingham University Library, contains copies of Sir William Camden's *Magna Britannia* and *Briefe Description of England and Wales*.

88. *Humphrey Pakington to Henry Russell*
        20 December 1607
        Lechmere f.899:169 (4)

My good brother, By a letter I did yesterday receive from Mr Grove I understand that you are much blamed by Mr Salwaye and Mr Newport for that you refuse to give meeting for ending the controversy between me and Mr Newport according to order and promise on all sides.[1] And I myself am deeply taxed by Mr Newport of fraudulent intention, notwithstanding I outwardly submitted me to arbitrament, to get the lands to myself when opportunity may best serve me, and so to have combined with you to delay and hold off from any agreement. But how true it is, God and you know better than he knoweth either sincerity or goodness. But to avoid clamour and suspicion, I heartily pray you to enlarge your pains so far in behalf of good Mr Grove and my poor self as, when your leisure may best serve, to send word to Mr Salwaye or Mr Newport that you will give meeting unto them for full conclusion in the matter, if they so determine, and that you marvel that, upon the resolution brought down by Zachary Field that the counsel on both parts resolved that [*deleted*: you;

inserted: Field's] title in law was good against the King, if I confirmed the same, they did not send to you about the matter, as was convenient; whereby the suspicion of ill dealing is returned upon them and I purged of the accusation. Zachary Field gave Mr Grove the intelligence which he sent me and I have here related unto you. I shall stay in the country until the end of Christmas, so that, if Mr Newport would anything with me, it might be signified before that time. But that I presume that you and my good sister would be loath to be from your own house this Christmas, I should be very glad of your good company. I never could hear of Mr Alderford Russell at my being in London, neither did he ever reply unto Mr Grove but once, which was before my coming, at which time Mr Grove, upon your request retained the statute. But if he should be hardly pressed here, and his money tendered, he knoweth not how to deny the can[*celling*] of the statute. So, with my best salutations unto you and my best sister for this time, I take leave, ever remaining most faithfully, Your poor brother at your command, Humfrey Pakington.

Harvington 20 December 1607

I am sorry for poor John Hill[2] his hard chance, who troubleth you greatly. But his charge of surgery shall be truly repaid and God will requite your other liberality towards him.

[1] In December 1607 Humphrey Salway complained to Henry Russell that 'there was not an answer put in . . . , although I make no doubt but the bill was put in at the day agreed': Berington 562 (40). See further Appendix IV.
[2] A yeoman named John Hill was a recusant at Castlemorton from 1581 onwards: Gilbert, 'Catholics in the Diocese of Worcester, 1580–1', 11; Bowler and McCann, *Recusants in the Exchequer Pipe Rolls*, CRS 71, p. 83; Calthrop, *Recusant Roll no. 1*, CRS 18, pp. 362, 364, 369; Bowler, *Recusant Roll no. 2*, CRS 57, p. 197.

89.　*Humphrey Pakington to Henry Russell*
　　　22 December 1607
　　　　Lechmere f.899:169 (3)

My good brother, Upon perusal of your letter now received, I am to add to that I [*deleted*: received] had written unto you before, which also by this bearer I do send. Mr Newport's bill came not in according to his own appointment, neither many days before the end of the term; to which Mr Grove and Mr Carye have already answered, as Mr Grove hath assured me, and my brother will do at the beginning of the next term [*inserted and deleted*: with] by *Dedimus potestatem* [*inserted and partly illegible*: with . . . process] if no end be made, and more was never promised. So that, if you please, you have means to return an answer upon my cousin Sallawaye to your good liking. For I hope Mr Grove hath advertised me truly; but upon mine own knowledge I can say no more but that my brother shall have answered the bill, the copy whereof I have brought down with me; in which there is no matter of moment to be [*inserted*: or that can be] answered for Mr Newport's advantage, as I also dare affirm unto you. For Mr Grove and Mr Carie, as Mr Grove telleth me, have answered by absolute disclaimer, and my brother's answer must be *near*[?] in the same nature. So that it appeareth nothing is aimed at by this bill but to make a preparation to commence a suit against me. That which I have signified of the resolution from Mr Walter and Mr Coventree is upon the report of good Mr Grove, who I presume will report sincerely. So that upon the whole matter I know not what to say but leave to your own wisdom whether it be convenient to request any further meeting at their hands. Of this I am sure: that if Mr Newport had my letter he would not give ten shillings for the King's release, neither need he to do it, for he well knoweth where I promise fidelity I will not fail. Because my brother goeth himself unto you, which when I [*deleted*: writ] began to write this letter I did not know, I will leave the rest to his narration; and with mine and my wife's heartiest commendations to you and my good sister, with many thanks for your good blackbirds, wardens and greenings,[1] I take leave, ever remaining, Your poor brother, ever at your command, Humfrey Pakington

Harvington 22° Decembr. 1607

[1] For 'greenings', see nos. **78**, **86**; wardens are a kind of pear: cf. *A Winter's Tale* IV.iii.44.

90. *John Grove to Henry Russell*
    26 January 1607/8
    Berington 376 (20)

Worshipful sir, It may please you to be advertised that this 16th of this January I received your letter dated the 9th of the same, together with a letter enclosed to Mr Henry Bartlett,[1] the which I cannot deliver till tomorrow some time, because the same, by reason of foul weather hindering the poor carrier's passage, came not to my hands until this evening late. I did understand of Sir John Hungerford's purpose [*inserted*: to receive the rents], as I have formerly written to Mr Pakington and you; but it seemeth those letters came not to your hands. But all is one in effect, for you could not prevent the injurious practices against me there that I cannot remedy myself here; which I determine to do by the best advice I can get, and am put in good hope that the King's title cannot prevail against me. The only consideration to be used is whether a peaceable composition upon reasonable conditions, if it may be, or a defence by course of law will be least chargeable for me; and in this case I stand, having [*spent*] most part of this day in attending arbitrators, Mr Spiller[2] for me and my Lord Secretary for worshipful Sir John, the base instrument of a Scottish beggarly gentleman. But the Secretary, having urgent business to dispatch, could not this day be at leisure to hear is, and there[*fore*] the time of hearing is deferred till after our next gaol delivery, which shall be on Tuesday next.

I thought you had known by Mr Chelmyck's report at his return homewards, as by my former wri[*ting*], that your cousin Mr Alderford Russell hath satisfied Mr Harvye [*and*] procured me my bond, and redelivered to him his statute, or else he would have been half-mad ere this time. Mr Chelmych can tell you of Mr Harvye's endeavour and mine— only for your sake, not his—to have stayed his intent and saved his land for [*as*] long and in such sort as your cousin Chelmyck thought good. And then, seeing that course work no effect for his good, but would have rather prejudiced him, both Mr Harvye and I, after sundry admonitions to him for his good, did by Mr Chelmyck's advice yield to accept the money. Otherwise, it would have been tendered and we should have been compelled in Court of Equity, after costs and charge of suit, to have done the same he required. I cannot say any more of him but pray God turn his heart and make him no less comfortable than thankful to such an uncle who wished him so well as you have done.

I will do my best endeavour for effecting your desire with Mr Bartlett according to your instructions, and certify thereof the next week. In the mean time, I do humbly and heartily commend you, with good Mistress Russell and all yours, to the preservation of Almighty God, and for ever remain your worship's to be commanded to my power, London, 16 January 1607/8, John Grove.

The commission was this [*day sealed*] for taking Mr John Pakington's answer in the country and shall be sent down to him tomorrow.

---

[1] See no. **91**.

[2] For Sir Henry Spiller of Eldersfield, near Little Malvern see the Introduction, pp. xxix–xxx above. On 11 January Grove had told Russell that he had approached Lord Treasurer Buckhurst and that Spiller was to be arbitrator: Berington 376 (19); cf. notes to no. **84**.

91. *Henry Russell to Humphrey Pakington*
  24 January [1607/8]
  Berington 570 (3)

Addressed: To the right worshipful his singular good brother Humphrey Pakington esquire at Mr William Sebright's house in Lumbard Street in London give these with speed.

Good brother, Your departure out of the country was so sudden that I could not, as I would, impart unto you my mind in divers things whereof I had given you some taste and had received from you brotherly comfort. Mr John White and I have gone through with a bargain for his lease, either for three lives or fifty years, of certain arable land in Castlemorton,[1] good for wheat and pease or barley, lying within one little mile of my house, most necessary for my possession of any land in England and the nearest to me, as I am environed with the Chase; and the lease is holden of Mr Henry Bartlett and Sir Thomas Bartlett his son, lying without Temple Bar near the sign of The Plough. The land is holden *in capite*, the rent reserved upon long leases granted of that and other lands; there is about fifty shillings by year without any expectation of further profit during long time. I understand by Mr White that Mr Bartlett will sell it, and, as he saith, that he hath a price thereof and offereth me to buy it at his hands, but then I should dearly buy. I would gladly have it from Mr Bartlett at first hand, and to this purpose I made bold to trouble Mr Grove with a letter unto Mr Bartlett from myself and another from Mr Bartlett's brother, a good friend of mine, desiring Mr Grove to send his price, and if he can conclude with him before Mr White's coming up, lest he prevent me. I must pay for the lease and wood on the ground. The leases are large, the rent small, granted without impeachment or clause of re-entry. I say I must pay to Mr White for his terms by lease £270. I shall be driven to pray aid of you for payment, if you can help me without your hindrance, and, God willing, I will take care, whether I live or die, that you shall be repaid, and thankfully, at your time appointed; and myself will be always at your commandment, as acknowledging myself bound unto you as the pillar of my poor house and estate.

Seeing that my nephew Alderford forgetteth himself and forsaketh his friends and their loving counsels and admonitions tending to his good, and will needs ruinate his estate and run downhill the hasty course to perdition, I will look to myself and preservation of my wife and children, whom I hope to live in obedience and in the fear of God. He shall not live in hope and expectation of their deaths, nor be encouraged to practise wickedly their destruction. I will, and he shall know that I will, alter the state of my lands by other remainder after my children, that the bankrupt may not live in hope thereof. And for my lease of the Forde in Pembrokeshire,[2] I will surrender and take it again for other lives. He shall never have that which I took with mine own money that so unthriftily wasteth and misspendeth his own. I fear not any hurt that he, in desire of revenge in his mad mood or desperate beggary, can practise against me so much as I fear the spoil of my children in hope of the reversion in my lands. The Forde is a [?*pretty*] entire thing. It will keep fourteen kine, two hundred sheep and a [*illegible*] in good land. The rent is £6 yearly. It is worth £20 *de claro* and lieth in Carew parish over against the Castle, on the other side of the Haven and very near the Haven, but farther in the land and not so near the mouth of the Haven by five miles as Greenhill. If it will pleasure you as an introduction into that country, I promise you it shall be at your command and disposition. I have sent up the lease unto Mr Grove that you may see it; and if you please to take a course for the renewing thereof for other three lives, without clause of forfeiture but rather somewhat *nomine poenae* (as I hear new grants be made), what the charge shall be I will thankfully repay and the thing shall be yours to command. Mr Hanbury,[3] that was my cousin Edmund Broad[4] his master, is Auditor in that shire: perhaps by his means the lease may be altered in names. Methinketh the changing of names should be no great charge: this lease cost me but £26 13s 4d. His sister now dwelleth on it and payeth me nothing and so is content: I thank her so to do. Alderford, her brother, brought me a letter from Mr Auditor [*inserted*: sent herewith], requiring me to enrol the lease, which Mr Edmund Broad telleth me will be satisfied by 2s 6d given to his master. I durst not trust Alderford to carry my lease lest I should never see it again and he being in reversion joining with his sister's husband, by not paying the King's rent may now, when they will, forfeit my estate. As the case is now, I dare not trust them, but I have need to shift for myself. Thus far I have presumed to make bold on your courteous pains, being encouraged thereunto by your friendly and brotherly offers. I can return no other recompense but myself wholly to be at your command.

Mr Salway failed his meeting at the Quarter Sessions, where I was for that purpose, but sent his letter of excuse.[5] Now he desireth that we should meet at the Assizes, when Mr Walter and Mr Coventry may satisfy such questions as may be objected, and would know whether you did continue in us authority to order the matter. I have answered that I know nothing to the contrary. He requireth my brother John Pakington's answer to Mr Newport's bill; they do not seem to be satisfied with the counsellors' resolutions. Gladly would they avoid the payment of an £100, which I see no reason to the contrary but that he must pay. So, with mine and my wife's most hearty commendations, and like thanks for all your brotherly favours, I commit you to the protection of Almighty God, this 14th of January, Your ever bounden, Henry Russell.

Mr Salway's last letter I have herewith sent to Mr Grove.

---

[1] Castlemorton is three miles south-east of Little Malvern, across Castlemorton Common; the Bartletts owned Hillend Court there: see nos. **90, 139**. In 1692 Ralph Clayton (Anstruther, III. 35–6) 'live[d] sometimes with Mr John Russell of Little Malvern and sometimes with Mr Bartlett of Hill End' (Stanfield, 'Particulars of Priests in England and Wales', in CRS 9, p. 113). In the eighteenth century Little Malvern and its neighbourhood were served by Felix Bartlett, SJ (1708–1777). Until 1632 Malvern Chase was a royal forest, and land within it could not be used for farming. Since Little Malvern was 'environed with the Chase', Henry Russell was eager to lease this land close by.

[2] As the seagull flies, Ford Farm (SS 0403) is a mile west-south-west of Carew Castle (cf. no. **43** above), at the head of Ford Pill, a creek of the Carew River.

[5] See note to no. **88**; cf. Appendix IV.

[3] Perhaps John Hanbury of Feckenham or his father Richard of Elmley Lovett: VCH *Worcs.*, III. 117, 380; *Visitation of the County of Worcester, 1569*, 68.

[4] Edmund Broad of Dunclent, a mile from Harvington, was one of the appraisers who had made the probate inventory of Humphrey's father John Pakington in 1578 (Worcs. Record Office 008.7 (1578), 35.c) and chaired the commission which valued Humphrey's property when it was sequestrated for recusancy in 1591 (Anderton Webster and Anderton Webster, 'The Pakingtons of Harvington', 207). In 1778 a John Broad of Chaddesley Corbett published at Birmingham *The Worcestershire Farmer, or The Young Farmer's Guide*.

92.   *John Russell III (1594–1641), Vivat Rex!*[1]
     [before 1610?][2]
     Berington 620

Cum pater omnipotens crines canescere vidit,
Elizabetha, tuos et lassa senescere membra,
haec secum: Multos tulerit per regna labores
pro patria, nunquamne suae quae debita vitae
praemia sunt capiat? Nunquam superis requiescat
sedibus? Haud aequum est caelo fraudarier illam
quae meruit caelum tantos subeundo labores.
Haec fatus Mortem compellat talibus atram:
Pelle moras, sumptisque celer delabere pennis
ad Britonum gentem, quam claram rupibus albis   10
turbida caeruleo circumdant aequora fluctu!
Hoc regnat regina loco cui nomen Elisa est.
Hanc pete, et humano caelestem ex carcere mentem
solve, suae ut capiat faelicia praemia vitae.
Neve perire suo timeat cum corpore gentem
quam sua florentem fecit sapientia, regem
e summo dabimus caelo, qui sceptra tenebit
caelesti sacrata manu, multosque per annos
felices faciet tranquilla pace Britannos.
Sic ait, et Mortem caelo demittit ab alto,   20
nec mora: Mors atras liquido movet aere pennas,
et tandem ad claras sedes accessit Elisae,
perque fores clausas ad clara cubilia venit
reginae, quae sola pios studiosa libellos
volvebat, placido studio minuente laborem.
Et stetit ante oculos deformi pallida vultu,
nam macie consumpta caro est et in ossibus ossa
nodata aspicias. Quam cum regina videbat

92.   *Translation by Michael Hodgetts*

When *JOVE* (*Eliza*!) saw thy Locks turn grey,
And thy exhausted Members waste away,
So much (He mused) she for her Realm has borne,
And shall she never have her just Return?
Shall she not take her Ease in Seats on high; ⎫
Is't lawful to defraud her of the Sky, ⎬
For which her Labours surely qualify? ⎭
Whereat he summon'd dusky-visag'd *DEATH*.
There is a *Queen*, by name *Elizabeth*,
To whom (said He) my Message thou must bear.   10
Straight take thy Wings, and swiftly cut the Air,
To where white Cliffs, round which blue Surges fret,
Mark where the glorious *BRITISH* Race are set!
Her Soul celestial from its human Cell
Do thou release, that she in Bliss may dwell!
Nor should she fear the *Nation* she has left
Shall perish too, of Wisdom thus bereft:
From highest Heav'n a *King* shall we bestow
Upon the lucky People there below,
To grasp the Sceptre in anointed Palm,   20
And rule the *BRITISH* long in Peace and Calm!
Straight on her Errand *DEATH* departs from there:
Her dusky Pinions cleave the liquid Air,
Until (at last) she reach'd the Halls of Fame,
And thro' clos'd Doors into the *Chamber* came
Wherein *Eliza* burn'd the Midnight Oil
(Her *Piety* diminishing the *Toil*).
Before her Eyes the horrid *Vision* stood,

palluit, vel gelido riguerunt membra timore,
cum sic orsa loqui Mors est: Ne nescia nostros   30
extimeas vultus (populi regina Britanni):
non ego sum monstrum Stygiarumve una sororum,
sed ea qua superis est nulla potentior oris.
Nam quodcumque oritur mortali ex semine corpus
falce velut segetem reseco, nec munere flector
nec prece, sed cunctos vel ad astra vel ad Styga mitto.
Tu mihi causa viae es, nam me tibi misit Olympi
rector, ut eductam mortali ex corpore mentem
ad summos super astra feram radiantia caelos.
Neve perire tuo timeas cum corpore gentem   40
quam tua florentem fecit sapientia, regem
e caelo dabit ipse [*omitted*: pater], qui sceptra tenebit
caelesti sacrata manu, multosque per annos
felices faciet tranquilla pace Britannos.
Sic ait, et jaculum reginae in pectora mittit,
quod simul ac venas rupit fibrasque calentes,
mens volat ad superas moribundo ex corpore sedes.
Et postquam caeli valvas intravit eburnas
constitit ante Jovem supplex precibusque rogavit
ut velit e caelo promissum mittere regem.   50
Tum pater omnipotens caelesti voce profatur:
Pone metum, regina, tuam. Rex clarus habebit
imperium gentis qualis nec floruit inter
Romanos proceres nec reges inter Achaios.
Sic fatus, caeli demittit ab arce Jacobum;
cumque tua, regina, dolet Brittannia morte,
nescia quis tantae gentis moderetur habenis,
ecce venit caelo felix Jacobus ab alto,
egregius forma, magis egregius virtute.
Quem laeto excipiunt animo pro rege Britanni,   60
felicemque jubent felicia sceptra tenere.
Hic multos vertit jucunda in gaudia luctus,
tristibus hic fecit pro planctibus edere plausus:
si norunt omnes talem succedere regem,
nemo Caledoniae mortem plorasset Elisae,
nam quantum praestas pallenti, Phoebe, sorori,
tantum laude praeit magnam Jacobus Elisam.
Clara quidem fuit illa, sed illa clarior ille,
cara suis fuit illa, sed illa carior ille.
Entheus est illi vigor atque calescit origo,   70
qualis erat prisco validis heroibus aevo,
et qualem Iapeto satus altis clepsit ab aulis.

Wither'd, arthritic, Features drain'd of Blood;
Whereat the *Queen* turn'd stiff and pale for Fright, 30
And *DEATH* began to speak to her aright:
Fear not, *Eliza* (*BRITAIN'S* noble *Queen*),
Because thou dost not recognise my Mien:
No *Monster* I, no *Sister* sent from *HADES*:
I am the first of all *Heaven's* noble *Ladies.*
Whatever Bodies grow from mortal Seed
Like Grain before my Sickle must recede;
Nor Prayers nor Bribes turn me from my Intent,
But all by me or Up or Down are sent.
The Cause of this my Journey here is — *Thou*! 40
For *JOVE* himself has sent me hither now,
To bear thy Spirit from its mortal Corse
Above the radiant Stars unto its Source.
Nor shouldst thou fear the *Nation* thou hast left
Shall perish too, of Wisdom thus bereft:
From highest Heav'n a *King* shall *JOVE* bestow
Upon the lucky People here below,
To grasp the Sceptre in anointed Palm
And rule the *British* long in Peace and Calm!
She spoke; and thrust her Dart athwart the *Queen*, 50
That burst the Veins and smoking Nerves within.
Up from the dying Corse her Spirit flies,
And pass'd the *Ivory Gates*, and reach'd the Skies;
Before great *JOVE* she stood, petitioning
That he would send from Heav'n the Promis'd *King*.
Whereto in solemn Tones the *god* reply'd:
O *Queen* of *BRITAIN*, lay thy Fears aside!
An *Empire* shall this glorious *King* enjoy
Surpassing *Rome's*, or theirs who fought at *Troy*.
Whereat, from *Heav'n's* high Tower, he sent down — *JAMES*! 60
While *BRITAIN* mourn'd the greatest among Dames,
Uncertain, who should drive the *Nation's* Steeds, ⎫
From highest Heav'n the *Lucky JAMES* proceeds, ⎬
Unique in Form, and more unique in Deeds! ⎭
As *BRITAIN's King*, they gladly greet him there,
And call the Blest, the Sceptre blest to bear.
The *Nation* he from Grief to Gladness draws,
Their plangent Sadness turning to *Applause*.
If all had known, that such would be their Lord,
Eliza's Death no *Scot* would have deplor'd. 70
For, as the *Moon* must yield to *PHOEBUS'* Flames,
So great *Elizabeth* must yield to James.

Anglia nec magnum collaudat sola Jacobum,
verum aliae gentes immensis laudibus illum
extollunt, optantque sibi contingere talem
qualis [is] est, Phoebumque putant regnare, nec ipse
si regnet Phoebus melius sua sceptra gubernet.
Quas igitur grates summo reddamus Olympi
rectori, qui nos tam claro rege beavit.
Ipsa mihi tellus et pascua laeta videntur   80
et placidi flores, volucresque per aera vectae
dulcisonum tenui modulantes gutture cantum,
adventu gaudere tuo, clarissime Princeps.
Nec mirum est quod te tua gaudeat Anglia rege,
nam tu sola salus populique columna Britanni.
Tu vitiis poenam, virtuti praemia reddis,
Brutigenasque tuos tanta gravitate gubernas
Ut vere lapsus caelo videaris ab alto.
Ergo sonet 'vivat' resonetque Britannia 'vivat',
sitque precor sero caelum rediturus in altum,   90
ex quo proveniens nostras accessit ad oras.
    Vivat rex!

[1] In a later letter (**130**), referring to one of his compositions in Greek which has not survived, Russell professed to be 'much sorry and ashamed that my choleric Muse hath not altogether withheld her quill from the least touch of satirical vinegar'. It is doubtful if he was sorry or ashamed of this magnificent take-off. While on the surface it is a conventional tribute to the new king, Russell shows considerable skill in making his compliments double-edged; when, for instance, he says that 'no Scot' (*nemo Caledoniae*, l. 65) would have deplored the death of Elizabeth, or when he describes James as 'unique in form and more unique in deeds' (*egregius forma, magis egregius virtute*, l. 59). The language and idiom reveal an easy familiarity with classical Latin poetry, as well as echoing the Hail Mary (*Ne . . . extimeas vultus*, ll. 30–31) and the *Dies irae* (*Tu mihi causa viae es*, l. 37).

[2] The date of the poem is difficult to fix. John Russell was nine when James I came to the throne and can hardly have written it then, but by the second decade of the seventeenth century the jokes would no longer be so topical. Here it is placed immediately after the death of his father Henry in 1608, by way of an introduction to this John Russell, who came of age in 1615 and owned Little Malvern until his death in 1641.

Clear as she was, yet he is clearer still!
Dear as she was, yet he is dearer still!
His Vigour is *divine*, his *Birth* a Blaze,
Like the great *Heroes* of the golden Days;
Or like *Promethean* Fire (obtain'd in *devious* Ways)!
Not only *ENGLAND* praises *James the Great*,
But, other Lands extol his high Estate:
'With such a *PHOEBUS* would that we were blest   80
(Tho' truly, *PHOEBUS* would be Second-Best).'
Thanks be to *JOVE*, whose Mercies are so *rare*;
Who gives us here a Prince beyond Compare!
The Earth, and smiling Pastures, seem to sing
For Joy at thy Arrival, gracious *King*!
The Flowers, the Birds that on the Breezes float
Warble sweet Ditties in their little Throat!
What wonder, then, that we should celebrate
The *Pillar* and the *Saviour* of the *State*?
Thy Pains, and Prizes, are so gravely giv'n   90
That thou seemst truly fallen down, from *Heav'n*.
Then let the Sons of *Brutus* gladly sing,
And shout, and shout again, Long live the *King*!
And may his Passage back to *Heav'n* be late,
The *Heav'n* which now he leaves, to *emigrate*!
   Long live the King!

93. *John Pakington to Henry Russell*
        27 July [?1607][1]
        Berington 569 (2)

Good brother, We look for my brother's coming home every hour and
have done this two days, so that before we hear some more certainty
from him I cannot devise how to cause your letter to be delivered unto
him. Therefore I fear ([u]nless he do now [*come*] home) it will come too
late unto his hands to give him knowledge for prevention of anything
which may chance prejudicial, either to yourself or any of his friends,

by this commission, the time being so soon for the execution thereof; and if any prevention be to be had for it, it is likely (as I conjecture) to come by means of your letter, which is already sent to Mr Grove, who will not fail, as I verily believe, presently to advertise my brother of their proceedings. My man, who should have been at home on Friday last by my appointment, is not yet returned, whereby I surely [?*presume*] my brother stayeth him to attend him down; and this is as much as I know or can tell (without further instruction) what to do in this business. God send it at [*sic*] a good end and grant that Mr Haulsey[2] prove not to have a profit in that behalf. My sister[3] hath her heartily commended unto you and my sister Russell, with many thanks to you both for your great kindnesses, which she knoweth not how to requite. So with my heartiest commendations unto you, my good sister and my two cousins, with thanks likewise for my cheeses, I leave you all to God Almighty's keeping, this 27th of July. Your true and assured brother ever, John Pakington

[1] None of the eight surviving letters of John Pakington, Humphrey's brother, or of the four surviving letters of John Mintridge, Henry Russell's nephew, include the year in the date. There is not enough internal evidence to supply the omissions, except that those written to Henry must be before 1608. Since, however, four of the six printed here show Elizabeth Russell's relatives advising and supporting her after Henry's death (cf. no. **99**), they have been placed here as a group in numerical order.

[2] John Halsey. Since the Exchequer went on pursuing his recusancy debts until 1620/21 (LaRocca, *Jacobean Recusant Rolls for Middlesex*, CRS 76, p. 123), the letter could have been written after his death in 1605, so this reference offers no help in restricting its date.

[3] Sister-in-law, Humphrey's wife. If she was his second wife, Abigail Sacheverell, the date is 1607. If she was his first wife, Bridget Norreys, the date is between 1602 and 1605.

94.   *John Pakington to Henry Russell*
      8 March [before 1608]
      Berington 569 (4)

Good brother, I make myself over-bold with you, both to detain your own mare and trouble you with the keeping of my lame *trudge*[?];[1] but I will be ever ready to perform like kindness unto you and yours if it lie within my poor fortune at any time to do. If you stand any way needful of your mare, let me know by this bearer and I will presently send her over unto you, for I can well and sufficiently provide me of a nag until Easter to perform those journeys which I should undertake. I have received two comfortable and most kind letters from my brother (concerning my money which was in young Mr Talbott's hands), the one by the carrier, written before my man came to him, the other this last night by my man, wherein he signifieth unto me that, though with great pains, by such friends which he hath made he well hopeth it shall be no great loss unto me in the end, though it be like to be some hindrance unto me in the meanwhile—the particulars to write unto you would be over-long. My Lord of Shrewsbury hath gotten the wardship of the heir, and my Lord Chancellor hath moved him in my behalf by the procurance of my loving and kind brother. This I thought requisite to impart unto you and my good sister, for that I know your friendly care likewise over my estate doth desire to hear of good success in this matter. My brother thanketh my sister and you for his lamprey pie,[2] which he hath received. This [*sic*] in some haste at this time, with my hearty commendations unto you both and my little cousins, I leave you to Almighty God's keeping and remain ever, Your faithful brother, John Pakington

March 8

[1] The noun, 'slow or heavy walker', gives excellent sense but is not recorded in *OED* until 1748 (Smollett). The verb was in use by this time, as in *The Merry Wives of Windsor*, III. iii.11.
[2] See also no. **65**.

95. *John Pakington to Elizabeth Russell*
  23 November [?]
  Berington 569 (7)

My good sister, With many thanks for your pains and kind care bestowed upon me when I was last with you, which I will be always (God willing) ready to requite towards you and yours as far as my ability should any way serve. You shall know that I have spoken with Mr William Lutley about the keeping of your court, as you wished me to do. His answer is that he hath never [*taken*] part of himself as yet, and therefore doubteth of the well performing thereof. Notwithstanding, if my brother and you do think that by your instructions he can execute it according to your liking, he will be ready at any time, either in this or any other thing he can do, to do you any stead or courtesy that lieth in his power to do. I am sorry Mr Alderfoord left his hawk so soon, for I bestowed that trifle upon him in hope it might have detained him from worse company, as by experience I have found it to do in myself. This [*sic*] with my very true and hearty commendations unto you and my brother, with the two little boys, not forgetting Mr Heyward, I end the 23rd of November. Your faithful brother to his uttermost power, John Pakington

All here commends them very heartily unto you and my brother. My sister yet *troubleth*[?] about the house. God send a good *time*[?], which draweth on apace.

96. *John Pakington to Elizabeth Russell*
3 September [?]
Berington 569 (8)[1]

Addressed: To my very loving and approved good sister Mrs Elizabeth
Russell give these.

Good sister, At [*my*] cousin John Russell's being at Harvington, he told
my sister[2] that he thought you would help her to a good servant-maid,
which now she standeth in need of,[3] for Catherine, who supplied the
place (as you know) for the making of white m[*eats?*] and malt, departed
hence yesterday. My sister heareth of a servant about Witche,[4] but delay-
eth time with her until she hear from you. Therefore she would request
you to let her know, as soon as conveniently you could, whether she
should rely upon one from you or enquire further after this at Witche. *S*
. . . *e* the foot-boy's father passeth this way many Thursdays; by whom
(if you have no other messenger) you may send two or three words if
you light of anyone to serve the turn. We would have you to agree with
her before she come hither what ways she is to come. And so my sister
commendeth her kindest love unto you, and I my best wishes and commendations to you and my cousins, with all other good friends, remaining ever Your faithful loving broth[*er*] to my power, John Pakingto[*n*]

September the 3

[1] The bottom right-hand corner is missing.
[2] For the identification of Humphrey's wife, John Pakington's 'sister', see no. **93**.
[3] In a letter dated 'Harvington, 17 of August' (no year), Humphrey Pakington wrote to
Elizabeth: 'My wife, presuming still of your love towards here, desireth now the laundry-
maid you promised her, for her other bad servant is gone' (Berington 576 (14)). But this
may refer to another appointment.
[4] Droitwich, seven miles south of Harvington.

97. *John Mintridge to Elizabeth Russell*
[1608]
Berington 615 (2)

Addressed: To the worshipful my very good aunt[1] Mrs Elizabeth Russell
be these [*delivered*].

Good aunt, I sent unto Mr *Gunlm*[?][2] according to your appointment,
who promiseth to come over this week. His desire is to know the time
and place of [*deleted*: met] meeting: wherefore I thought good to send
unto you, whereby he may have a present answer. I could wish you
would procure some friend to give meeting for it. As far as I can gather

by my cousin Berington[3] letters, he will not be with you until Thursday, which day if you please to appoint, I will, God willing, see you; and for the meeting of Mr *Gulln*[?] I pray you set down where you think best, either at Ledbury, Colwall or at your house. Thus, desiring your present answer, I leave you to the protection of the Almighty, not forgetting my commendations unto you and all others our friends. The Hall,[3] this prese[*nt*] morning, Your ever loving cousin to command, John Mintrich.

[1] John Mintridge's father James had married Henry Russell's sister Maud, after whose death he married Elizabeth Walwyn: see nos. **35, 113** and the reference to 'my cousin Walweyne' in the next letter.

[2] There were several families of Gwillims: *Visitation of Herefordshire, 1634*, 34, 53, 101. In 1605 John Gwillim of 'Dower' Frome was a recusant (Matthews, 'Records Relating to Catholicism in the South Wales Marches', in CRS 2, pp. 290–92), but this place-name has not been recorded elsewhere: A.T. Bannister, *The Place-Names of Herefordshire* (Cambridge, 1916), 78. Bishop's Frome, Canon Frome, Prior's Frome, Castle Frome and Halmond Frome are all in the valley of the River Frome, between Bromyard and Ledbury.

[3] Anne Blount married Richard Berington of Stoke Lacy; her sister Elizabeth married a Mintridge of Bosbury; their nephew Roger Blount of Monkland married Mary Berington of Winsley House, Hope-under-Dinmore: *Visitation of Herefordshire, 1634*, 32. It is not clear which cousin Berington is meant here, nor which Hall.

98.   *John Mintridge to Elizabeth Russell*
     2 January [?]
      Berington 615 (3)

Addressed: To the worshipful my very good aunt Mrs Elizabeth Russell be these d[*elivere*]d.

Good Aunt Russell, I have had conference with William Winsmore concerning his title to your lands at Coddington, who hath showed me his deeds: first, a feoffment made by Richard Nashe, of the which you have the counterpart, in the eighteenth year of Queen Elizabeth unto Francis Unet and others, where is reserved a power in himself, by will or otherwise, to alter anything in the said deed; and also one indenture of covenant tripartite between Richard Nash, Dr Thirkill and Peter Elton for the assuring of all his lands in Coddington to Anthony Nash [*deleted*: and] Mr Elton and their heirs, made about the twentieth year of the said Queen, with a deed and fine upon the same. Which deed, being made by the old rates,[1] I fear will be good unless there may some defect found in the covenants. Winsmore said it was reserved to my cousin Walweyne and Mr Coventry, but not effected by means that God took my uncle. But he is yet content to do the same, if it may stand with your liking. I have promised to return him an answer after my next meeting with you. Winsmore put me in mind of some speeches I used unto him the last year concerning your departing with the copyhold lands, and saith he will give for the same as good lands in fee simple, or to the like value by the year. Which being performed, I do think it very well worth £600. This I thought good to signify unto you, whereby you may be the better advised in this business. With my humble salutations to yourself and the rest of my worshipful good friends, I leave you to the protection of the Almighty. The Hall, the second day of this present January. Your ever loving cousin, John Muntrich

[1] Manner, fashion; cf. *The Merchant of Venice* I.i.127.

99.   *Justinian Stubbs to Elizabeth Russell*
     5 March [1607/8][1]
     Berington 616 (2)

Good Mistress Russell, In all love I commend myself to you. I have dealt with Mr Howeford,[2] and I promised his uncle Mr Bramedg[3] to speak unto him in the cause, but the answer was flatly that he would not appear at the Assizes in Worcester. The cause by me demanded, his reply was that he was never yet of any jury, neither would he ever be if he could by any means keep himself out of it. He was so peremptory in his resolution. I have written to Mr John Pakington for his abiding with you. At my departure from you, methought you were greatly oppressed with grief, and none in my judgement so fit to continue with you for your comfort, in my return thinking upon your woeful case, and that I did think it the best for you to entreat his continuance with you. I will see you as shortly as I can possibly. I have sent to my old chamber-fellows[4] two dozen points, all of one colour. Wishing unto you and them all happiness, I commit you with them to the tuition of the Almighty, whom I beseech to be your protector and defender. Gloucester, 5th March, Your loving friend, for ever assured, Justinian Stubbs

[1] Although the date does not include the year, this letter seems to have been written the day after Henry Russell's death. If so, it implies that Stubbs attended him in his last illness. For his association with Russell and Campion at Oxford see the Introduction, pp. xv–xvi above. Like Russell, he took a degree in law (1589) and so deferred the requirement to be ordained within three years of taking his MA in 1577/8: Foster, *Alumni Oxonienses*, IV. 1439.
[2] Not identified.
[3] There were several Bromwich families in Worcestershire, Gloucestershire and Herefordshire: *Visitation of the County of Worcester, 1569*, 24, 99, 109; *Visitation of Worcestershire, 1634*, 74; VCH *Worcs.*, III. 25, 70; *Visitation of the County of Gloucester, 1623*, 29; VCH *Glos.*, X. 146–7. Berington 859 is a counterpart of a lease dated 1 January [*c*.1600] by Roger Bromewyche of Taddington, four miles south of Broadway.
[4] The Russells' sons, John and Edmund: cf. nos. **100, 114, 118.**

100. *Justinian Stubbs to Elizabeth Russell*
   21 April [1608][1]
   Berington 616 (1)

Mistress Russell, In all love I commend myself to you in good faith. Now Mistress Cassey[2] is in physic, one Mistress Gootheridge her daughter very sick; upon Monday next I am to ride to my Lady Verney[3] in Warwickshire: she hath sent to me twice. Upon my return I will come over to Little Malvern without fail, which will be within eight or ten days, I hope: I will not fail you. And now the full moon will be better for the gouttes for the first part of next week, and the time will be better. Wishing unto you as to one that I most esteem, I commit you to the tuition of the Almighty, Deerhurst, 21 of April. Commend me to Mr John Pakington and to my two chamber-fellows, God bless them. Yours for ever or never his own, Justinian Stubbs.

[1] The mention of John Pakington suggests that this letter also was written in 1608, seven weeks after the previous one.
[2] Thomas Cassey (1558–1634) of Deerhurst in Gloucestershire married Cassandra Gifford, daughter of John and Jocosa Gifford of Chillington in Staffordshire. 'Mistress Gootheridge her daughter' means 'a daughter of Mrs Gootheridge', not that Mrs Gootheridge *was* Cassandra Cassey's daughter: J.M. Langston, 'Old Catholic Families of Gloucestershire: The Casseys of Wightfield in Deerhurst', *Transactions of the Bristol and Gloucestershire Archaeological Society* 74 (1955), 128–52, esp. 140–43 and pedigree facing p. 152; VCH *Glos.*, VIII. 36.
[3] Sir Richard Verney of Compton Verney in Warwickshire was Crown tenant of Humphrey Pakington's sequestrated estates from 1602 to 1605: see above, no. **59**. In 1610 he was also one of the Crown tenants of the confiscated estates of Sir Robert Dudley, son of the earl of Leicester, which included Kenilworth Castle (*CSPD James I, 1603–10*, 628). Lady Verney was a sister of Sir Fulke Greville, who had been at Shrewsbury School with Humphrey Pakington and to whom James I granted Warwick Castle in 1604, despite Dudley's claim to it as heir to his uncle Ambrose Dudley, earl of Warwick. Sir Richard's son, Greville Verney, married a Southwell of Woodrising (Catherine), like Dudley. See Michael Hodgetts, 'Coughton and the Gunpowder Plot', in Peter Marshall and Geoffrey Scott, eds., *Catholic Gentry in English Society: The Throckmortons of Coughton from Reformation to Emancipation* (Farnham, 2009), 93–121.

101. *John Grove to Elizabeth Russell*
   27 June 1608
   Berington 376 (23)

Good Mistress Russell, It may please you to be advertised that, according to your directions signified in John Bache's[1] letters, I have sundry times conferred with Mr Henry Bartlett and in the end of the last term fully concluded with him for the things which my late worshipful friend, now at rest with Christ Jesus, was desirous to buy of him for his hopeful posterity to your good comfort. Which was in this manner: that I was content to give him £30 in hand and £10 more upon survey, if I liked it at my next coming into that country, for all the things he had in Cas-tlemorton. And afterwards, when he came to pass the assurance to your eldest son, by advice of Mr Coventry,[2] my brother Tyrer and Mr White, Mr Bartlett, most honestly showing himself to be the very same honest gentleman which your late deceased husband wrote to me formerly of, confessed that the same land and rents, which he intended to convey to your said son, were subject both to statute and judgments. Which encumbrance I of myself, as dealer for you and your son, knowing by long experience may happen more troublesome than profitable, utterly disliked, and told Mr Bartlett that of myself, without further advice from you and your other friends, for whom only I dealed, I would no further proceed therein without your good liking and other of your friends. But such then was the present occasions of Mr Bartlett to use money and Mr White the bearer's willingness to furnish him, the rather thereby to free himself of some danger he standeth in by his means, that he hath taken assurance thereof to himself, meaning you will have it at his hands when he cometh into that country for £30, which he hath taken up here for it (as he saith), if you please to accept thereof by advice of your friends. The which I pray you duly consider of, for in mine opinion he did best to take it out of Mr Bartlett's hands this term, for that it may be worse than it is if it had remained in his hands till the next term. All which is referred to you and your friends' best consideration and pleasure. Your cousin Coventry will be shortly in that country and faithfully assist you with his best counsel in anything. I dare assure you, you may boldly use him, who will most willingly pleasure you in anything he can.

Here is a secret attempt to indict your loving good neighbour and vir-tuous, Lady Russell,[3] whom I have heard you much commend; and pray for me against my continual adversaries, not only to me but to God and the commonwealth. What I can do to prevent it, I will, and write to you more hereafter. The evidences which you sent for your cousin Alderford are by his own consent delivered to an honest man to be delivered to him upon his giving you discharge thereof under his hand and seal. But his price and charge is at such a height that I doubt it will shortly surmount the worth of his lands, which is all gone. I hope to see you this August. In the mean time, and ever after, I humbly commend you and your comforts to God's preservation and rest, London, this 27th of June 1608, Your worship's at command for ever, John Grove.

How the proceeding for the wardship of your son[4] and all other things are, I pray you think that there is as much done as is possible may be [sic]; whereof you shall hear shortly the effect.

---

[1] See no. **78** above.
[2] Thomas Coventry (1578–1640), subsequently Lord Keeper and first Lord Coventry, was

the eldest son of Sir Thomas Coventry and Margaret Jefferies, both of Croome d'Abitot near Upton-upon-Severn. 'Mr Jeffrey of Ercombe' (Earl's Croome) harboured a Marian priest, John Felton, about 1580 (no. **39** above), and in 1596 'Frances, wife of John Jeffrys, gent.,' was a recusant (Talbot, *Recusant Records*, CRS 53, p. 129). For Coventry's career, see *ODNB*. By 1606 he had married Sarah Sebright, niece of William Sebright, which is why Grove calls him 'your cousin Coventry' (cf. no. **113**). She died in 1609 (no. **110** below) and in 1610 Coventry married Elizabeth Pi[t]chford neé Aldersey (1583–1653), the widow of a Grocer named William Pi[t]chford.

³ The wife of Sir Thomas Russell (d. 1637) of Strensham, near Tewkesbury. In 1582 John Felton admitted saying Mass there, 'finding at Strensham such vestments and other furniture as is usually occupied in the celebrating of Mass': no. **39** above. On 21 March 1610 a grant was made to Thomas Gurlyn of the benefit of twenty recusants, eleven of them, including Sir Thomas Russell, from Worcestershire: *CSPD James I, 1603–10*, 593 (SP 14/103/28). Sir Thomas was overseer of Shakespeare's will and acquired the lease of Rushock Court, near Harvington, where St John Wall was arrested in 1678. See note on no. **58** above; J.D. Crichton, 'Rushock, the Russells and the Moores of Ripple', *Worcestershire Recusant* 4 (December 1964), 34–7; Hodgetts, 'Rushock Court, 1596', 1–8.

⁴ The wardship of John Russell III had in fact been granted to Thomas Marbury a fortnight before, on 11 June (Berington 101; cf. Berington 293).

102.   *J[ames] Yate¹ to Elizabeth Russell*
      11 July 1608
      Lechmere Box C.8

Good Mrs Russell, These are to advertise you that I am requested by one Mr Browne out of Buckinghamshire,² who had good acquaintance with your old friend Mr Foxe³ before he died, that I should let you understand that Mr Foxe left unto your husband a hat in sign of their old friendship, and unto your sons some books of Aristotle's works, all of which are yet in Buckinghamshire,⁴ which he is willing to send into this country when he hath convenient messenger. But for the hat, he thinketh [*it*] cannot be better bestowed than on someone whom you will appoint to pray for your husband his soul. He desireth to hear from you who you will make choice of, and it shall be delivered according to your will. If you send your mind to Mrs Throckmorton's at Moor's Hall⁴ any time before St James tide, your answer shall be sent unto him. Mrs Throckmorton doth very kindly commend her unto you. Thus, with my hearty commendations committing you to God's protection, I end this 11th day of July 1608. Alcester.⁴ Your very loving friend, J. Yate

¹ J[ames] Yate may be the don of that surname who was at Lyford with Henry Russell and Justinian Stubbs when Campion was arrested there on 17 July 1581: no. **4380**; see Introduction, p. xv above.

² Was he the Anthony Browne (1579–1637), brother of the 2nd Lord Montague, who became a Jesuit brother at Liège in 1614? His mother was Mary Dormer of Wing in Buckinghamshire; one of his uncles was Sir George Browne of Great Shefford in Berkshire; in 1590 Sir Robert Dormer of Wing, later the first Lord Dormer, had married Elizabeth

Browne, daughter of the first Lord Montague. Foley, II. 428–41, VII. 95; T.B. Trappes-Lomax, 'Some Homes of the Dormer Family', *Recusant History* 8 (1965–6), 175–87; cf. Michael Hodgetts, 'Campion in the Thames Valley, 1580', *Recusant History* 30 (2010–11), 32–4.

[3] The context suggests that Mr Foxe was also a priest who had been at Oxford with Henry Russell. But the only man of that name in Anstruther or Bellenger is Nicholas Foxe, who was arrested in 1591 and had died in the Tower in 1592 (Anstruther, I. 123–4). He cannot have left books to Henry Russell's sons, the elder of whom was not born until 1594. The hat may have been a keepsake of a priest who had died in prison: Campion and Persons had exchanged hats when they parted on 11 July 1581. Richard Simpson, *Edmund Campion: A Biography*, 2nd edn (London, 1896), 310; Evelyn Waugh, *Edmund Campion*, 3rd edn (London, 1961), 141.

[4] Alcester is in Warwickshire, two miles south of Coughton Court; Moor Hall is a Throckmorton dower house near by; the reference to Buckinghamshire may point to the Throckmortons' house at Weston Underwood, near Olney.

103.   *Mary Habington[1] to Elizabeth Russell*
30 August [?1608]
Berington 614

Good Mrs Russell, These be to request you to let unto me some rooms in your house, which at this time of my stay in Worcester I should be very glad to take, which will be until a fortnight Michaelmas or thereabouts; which would be unto me a very great pleasure and a thing Mr Abington and I shall take very kindly and seek by all means we may to requite. And lest any scruple or doubt may arise in your mind of damage or prejudice which may seem [*deleted*: ar] to arise toward you by reason of the late statute, I can assure you upon diligent view and consideration which hath been had thereof that there cannot be any danger toward you for the same, for that sojourning indeed is forbidden thereby, but not the letting or demising of any house or rooms, which thing I request to have at your hands. And if I did but think that any the least damage or danger might grow toward you for this my request, I would not for a world make the least motion thereof. And thus, resting thankful to you for your kindness showed unto Mr Abington and myself, I commend and commit you to God this 30th of August. Your loving friend, Mary Abington.

[1] Mary Habington was the sister of Lord Monteagle and the wife of Thomas Habington of Hindlip, where Garnet, Oldcorne, Nicholas Owen and Ralph Ashley were arrested in January 1605/6 (see no. **75**). An Act of 1606 required recusants not to travel more than five miles from home and to return home each night. Nevertheless, from about 1608 to 1617 Habington was almost continuously in London prosecuting an Exchequer case, 'exceeding in length the siege of Troy', for the recovery of his forfeited estates. See C.D. Gilbert, 'Thomas Habington after the Gunpowder Plot', *Midland Catholic History* 2 (1992), 37–41; Gilbert, 'The Composition of Habington's "Survey of Worcestershire"'; Gilbert, 'A Thomas Habington Manuscript in the Shropshire Archives', *Transactions of the Worcestershire Archaeological Society* 3rd ser. 20 (2006), 129–38. After its ransacking in

1606 and Habington's subsequent absence, Hindlip may have required more work to make
it habitable than a brief visit would justify.

104.   *Humphrey Pakington to Elizabeth Russell*
         24 September [1608][1]
         Lechmere f.899:169 (8)

My good sister, I have, as I promised, enquired the opinion of lawyers
concerning the danger of statutes to be laid of Mr Barckley's[2] land;
and they tell me that your case is not so dangerous altogether as I took
it. For if your lease of fifty years yet to come be before any statute acknowledged, as you say it is, they think it very hard for any, after that
time expired, to levy execution upon that land by any statute, except
he should be exceeding cunning in the knowledge of all the lands that
ever Mr Barckley had at the time of the acknowledging of such statute.
For, if he miss but in one acre, his suit is void. So that if such execution
should happen, it will either be avoided or else may be compounded for
a little after so long time. Of which I thought to advertise you, and so
I leave you to your own discretion to deal or not deal with Mr Whit as
you please. But it is not good to tell Mr Whit or any of this I have written
but make the matter as dangerous to him as formerly you have done. So,
with my wife's and my heartiest salutations unto you and unto my two
nephews, for this time I leave and ever remain Your faithful brother to
his uttermost power, Humfrey Pakington.

[1] Humphrey seems to have misread his sister's letter and writes about 'Mr Barckley' (of
Spetchley near Worcester) rather than 'Mr Bartlett' (of Hill End in Castlemorton near Malvern). But the mention of 'Mr White' makes it clear that this letter belongs with nos. **90–91,
101, 105, 108**, and therefore that the year is 1608.
[2] For the Berkeleys of Spetchley, see Aileen Hodgson, 'The Berkeley Family of Spetchley
Park, Worcestershire', *Worcestershire Recusant* 14 (December 1969), 22–33; 16 (December 1970), 22–34.

105.   *John Grove to Elizabeth Russell*
         4 November 1608
         Berington 376 (25)

Good Mistress Russell, It may please you to be advertised that this fourth
of November I received your letter without date. But because the carriers
depart hence tomorrow in the forenoon, I cannot confer with Mr White
to send you any direct notice what he will do, further than I wrote by
your man John Suffeild. There is no need to search a statute confessed
by the gentleman who made sale to Mr White. I told you all I know, at

my late being at Little Malvern, touching that bargain, which is a mere adventure to lose both money and labour about the same. Nevertheless, all things considered, if you please to proceed by advice of your cousin Coventry, and my brother desire to pass the same, I will at your request disburse the money. But Mr Pakington yesterday departed hence towards Harefield with the honourable countess, and after to Ashridge, and then to Harvington very shortly (as he says): therefore you may have that counsel of him, if you please, which I cannot have. One material matter not yet agreed on will be whether the conveyance shall be to you or your eldest son, or to both of you, or to me or those or any of those paying the money and charge sustained for and about the same; whereof I cannot advertise you the best till I have asked Mr Coventry or some other friend's advice. Yet I think good that you write unto me by the next carrier your mind, for Mr White his estate will be void if he proceed not in such time to take further assurance; which if he do, and you have it (as aforesaid), then that charge disbursed by him will be lost. By the next carrier or messenger I will advertise you more, and in the meanwhile and ever after remain, London, 4 November 1608, Your worship's assured at commandment, John Grove.

Postscriptum. Mr Jermayne, your curate,[1] certifieth me that Hartland would speak with me if I will promise not to arrest or molest him in his going and coming to me. The which I do hereby promise to perform for myself and all others for me, if he will, [*deleted*: whereof I] during one month's space from this day; whereof I have certified Mr Jermayne. I pray you let the goodmen Turner and Daneford know that Sir John Hungerford and I are both in bonds of a new submission to abide a short censure; wherein I hope he will not much boast of his getting. I will [? *omitted*: not] Turner in any case pay the rent to him or any for him, but rather so much as is due to the sheriff; and I doubt not but [*I shall*] get my rent again from the court.

[1] William Jermayne was presented to Great Malvern by Lord Lumley in 1575 and was still there in 1597: Nott, *Some of the Antiquities of 'Moche Malverne'*, 140, 175. The references to him as 'your curate' here and in nos. **107–8, 111** suggest that he also served, or drew the stipend of, Little Malvern.

106. *John Grove to Elizabeth Russell*
        14 November 1608
        Berington 376 (27)

My humble duty remembered. It may please you to be advertised that I have yesterday night received your letter and lease touching your son's wardship;[1] and if I can see Mr Child,[2] being now in London, before his departure, he shall be paid. So shall Mr Coningsby,[2] the Feodary of Herefordshire, be presently; and touching all other business mentioned in your letters about the wardship, it shall be effected according to your require[*ment*] without any doubt or care to you for the same. I do not understand by Mr Freeston's[3] man of Kidderminster that he hath any order from his master to pay me any money, but if he fail, I will lay down the same for you till it may be sent up. And so, heartily commending your worship and all yours to Almighty God's preservation, I rest, London, the 14th day of November 1608, Your worship's at command to his power, John Grove.

[1] In 1609 John Russell's wardship and marriage and forty shillings a year out of property in Little Malvern etc. were granted to Thomas Marbury, who was described as of St Martin's-in-the-Fields, London: Birmingham Archdiocesan Archives C.7. Cf. nos. **107, 121–2** below.

[2] Henry Russell's lands in Herefordshire were surveyed by Thomas Coningesby on 10 April, and his lands in Worcestershire by Walter Child on 17 April 1608: The National Archives, Wards 5/47. For the Coningsbys, see also Robinson, *History of the Mansions and Manors of Herefordshire*, 148–9.

[3] Freestones are recorded in Kidderminster parish registers from 1559 onwards; this one may have been John or Nicholas. In 1636 a John Freestone was the first Bailiff of Kidderminster under the new charter. John Richard Burton, *A History of Kidderminster* (London, 1890), 73, 205, 209, 211, 213, 222.

107.   *John Grove to Elizabeth Russell*
      26 November 1608
      Berington 376 (28)

Good Mistress Russell, My hearty commendations and like thanks to you remembered. The lease for your son's wardship is enrolled, the Feodary of Herefordshire paid, and some tender of like duty were [*sic*] [*deleted*: made; *inserted and deleted*: tendered; *inserted*: made] to Mr William [*sic*] Child, Feodary of Worcestershire. But he would not accept thereof here but said he would take it of yourself in the country, for that he had made up his account and paid in the money for this term, and the not paying of it should not be prejudicial to you. I delivered to Mr Jermayne, your curate, his son here in London, in the beginning of the term, two several letters, whereof one was directed to yourself and the other to Mr Jerman. But I heard not of your receipt of them, nor of Mr Jerman's son since that time, which maketh me believe that your curate his son came to me of purpose to search what mind I did bear touching Mr Hartland, whom I heard since then was in London and conversed with the good knight who is hungry for my lands. But I am in good hope, although to my great charge, otherwise to help him to pass without it like a base promoter or relator. The law is resolved against him, so that he flyeth to the Court of Conscience for his relief. Mr White will attend you this vacation about the old field, wherein you may assure yourself nobody but yourself desireth to have it with such assurance as he offereth to you of it; neither can I advise you to meddle with it unless the assurance were better than it is. As the title now is, I think Mr White will take what you will give. So, leaving this matter to your best consideration, I rest, London, this 16th day of November 1608, Your worship's at command to my power, John Grove.

Postscriptum. [1] I do not hear that your money is returned hither yet, neither is the same yet due in the Court of Wards. [2] If you see goodman Turner and the goodman Danford,[1] I pray you tell them they will lose all that they pay to Sir John Hungerford for rent at Loweshurst [*sic*, for Fulshurst][2] unless they take security of him for repayment thereof if it be required of them; or else that they pay the same into the court to be disposed of according as in right it ought to be upon ending of the suit there. And so doing, they may have an order in court for their discharge and for their quiet occupying of the farm. The sheriff hath returned nothing against them. [3] Mr Coxe[3] is now at Castleditch and will return hither shortly, by whom you may safely write if you please.

---

[1] A James Danford was a papist and nonjuror at Castlemorton in 1715: W.E. English, 'Worcestershire Nonjurors in 1715', *Midland Catholic History* 4 (1995), 31.
[2] See no. **58** above.
[3] Richard Cocks (no. **71**) had bought Eastnor from Ivo Clinton (nos. **72–3**). Between 1810 and 1820, John Somers Cocks, 1st Earl Somers, replaced Castleditch, the manor-house there, by the Regency Eastnor Castle: Robinson, *History of the Mansions and Manors of Herefordshire*, 109–11.

108.   *John Grove to Elizabeth Russell*
        10 December 1608
        Berington 376 (29)

Addressed: To the right worshipful Mrs Elizabeth Russell at her house in Little Malvern.

It may please you to be advertised that yesterday I received a letter of your own hand, whereby I perceive you do by the advice of your worship's brother apprehend the best course to be taken touching Mr White and Mr Bartlett about sale of the lands. And for your further advertisement, so it is that tender was here made to Mr William Child, the Feodary, of the duties by him to have been received the last term; but he, in presence of sundry witnesses, would not receive it here, but in the country, and for avoiding of peril says he would give acquittance for receipt thereof, bearing date when you would have it, with further protestations that you should be free from all damage thereby, more than is needful to write of at this time. I have within this hour received the threescore and three pounds sixteen shillings and eightpence to be paid into the Court of Wards. Your lease is enrolled, the money now received: if it had not come, other money of mine had been paid in by me for you in due time for avoiding of forfeiture; but now this shall be in season as, my leisure serving within the time limited for discharge of you, assure yourself. I pray you tell Mr Jermayne, your curate, I received his letter but do not yet hear of Hartland; neither shall I unless he perforce hear of me, as is [*thought*], and especially I beseech you to cause goodmen Turner and Danford not to fear the Hungerford knight, for I doubt not but his fury is abated with the false pretence of his title. It may be I shall see you before Twelvetide; in the mean time I humbly recommend you and yours to God's merciful protection, and rest, London, this 10th day of December 1608, in post haste, Yours to command, John Grove.

109.   *John Grove to Elizabeth Russell*
          [January 1608/9]
          Berington 376 (22)

Addressed: To the worshipful Mrs Elizabeth Russell at her house in Little Malvern give these.

Good Mistress Russell, I give you mine hearty thanks for your letters, advertisement and other things therein [*deleted*: therein] mentioned, being many ways much bounden to you. I am glad to hear of your health and that you were in so good company at Christmas, where I wished myself some part at that time. I hope both the young gentlemen your sons are well. I pray you, when you see my tenants Danford and Turnor, let them know from me that, if they deny the Hungerford knight rent, they do him no wrong and do themselves and me great right; and that in so doing and paying me the rent, being by law due to me, I will defend them against him, whatsoever it cost me. Otherwise they will be surely compelled to pay me. But I hope before the end of this term to prevail more clearly against all his false [*deleted*: pra] and most dishonest and unlawful practices against me, to his perpetual infamy and shame. Yet he seemeth to be shameless, and also void of truth and grace: God amend him or confound him in his devices according to his holy will and pleasure. So soon as the ways be somewhat fairer, if my leisure serve, I will be in that country one day about some business, but no longer. In the mean time, if Mr Hartland mean to talk with me, your letter and Mr Forman's, or one of your letters, shall free him from all molestation at my suit and by my means in coming and going to talk with me. And so I pray you tell them if you see them, and that I will not be found in such a case contrary to my word. And so, commending you to the protection of the Almighty God, I remain, London 1608, Your worship's at command to my power, John Grove.

Postscriptum. The sessions before Christmas, two of the Pewtresses and one Dorothy Elton of Ledbury[1] were indicted of recusancy amongst seventy and more of that country. It were good they knew of it, that they might prevent further trouble. If they be none, it were good they came hither and brought certificates of their conformity presently; otherwise they will be extracted [*sic*]. The Lady Russell[2] had been indicted above two months past, had not a friend you know, being now nameless, prevented the same. It is flatly purposed the 16th of February that she shall be here indicted of recusancy at the suit of Lord Kynknavell [*sic*], who married the late Lady Southwell[3] who is the Lord Admiral's daughter. The Lord told me that it was to be done by her own consent, but he did not otherwise make it appear.

[1] She and Thomas and Joanna Pewters, all described as of St Andrew's Holborn, were convicted in London on 11 January 1608/9. Dorothy did produce a certificate of conformity, signed by Archbishop Bancroft, and was quit. LaRocca, *Jacobean Recusant Rolls for Middlesex*, CRS 76, pp. 26–27. 'That country' was Herefordshire, in which Ledbury is.

[2] See no. **101**. The anonymous 'friend' was probably Sir Henry Spiller; cf. nos. **137–8**.

[3] Frances Howard, daughter of Lord Admiral Howard, earl of Nottingham (1536–1624) and Katherine, daughter of Henry, 1st Lord Carey. She married Sir Robert Southwell of Woodrising (d. 1598) and was the mother of Elizabeth Southwell, the second wife of Sir Robert Dudley, son of the Elizabethan earl of Leicester (*ODNB*; *The Visitacion of Norffolk, Made and Taken . . . Anno 1563 . . . and also . . . Anno 1613*, ed. Walter Rye, Harleian Society 32 (London, 1891), 260–61; cf. no. **100** above). On 26 October 1604 Frances married a second husband, John Stewart, a Scottish courtier who in 1607 was created Lord Kinclaven. Bernard Burke, *A Genealogical Account of the Dormant, Abeyant, Forfeited and Extinct Peerages of the British Empire*, new edn (London, 1866), 287; James Balfour Paul, *The Scots Peerage* (Edinburgh, 1904–14), II. 441–2.

110. *John Grove to Elizabeth Russell*
    20 February 1608/9
    Berington 376 (31)

Good Mrs Russell, I have received of Mr John Bland, clothier of Worcester, the £10 for use of the £100 by me lately lent to Mr Russell, your late husband and my worshipful good friend, the which £10 upon equal reckoning was due to me in or about November last past, as by the bond of your late husband may appear. I have now very urgent cause to use the principal debt owing me as ever I had, for that I have made a bargain for my brother his beginning to take a shop and wares of his master and for the dwelling-house for myself, which will cost me more money than

I have or can hastily get of mine own into mine hands. So that I shall be in the mean time constrained to try my credit for more money than ever I did at one time. But hereof I will acquaint you with more after conference had with Mr Pakington or yourself touching mine occasions to use money in performance of our agreement in the bargain hereafter. I have paid my brother Tyrer all the money disbursed out of his purse for enrolling your lease of your son's wardship, as may appear by his bill of charges; and I have also paid 5s 8d more for charge of taking up the bond of Mr Marbury and myself upon payment of the moneys before Christmas left in the Court of Wards. A copy of which charge I will hereafter send you, for that that bearer standeth upon his hasty departure. Your good brother Mr Pakington is in health and departed to Ashridge; and your unknown honest kinswoman, being the very best and happiest of her father's children, [*deleted*: did on Sun] I mean Mr Thomas Coventry his wife, on Sunday last is departed this mortal life and hath, I hope, in God changed [*it*] for everlasting joy and rest, and hath left many sorrowful friends for her death so suddenly, especially her good husband, who meant shortly to settle himself with her amongst you, and whose counsel and company I know you and your children and friends would have much delighted in. She hath left two comfortable branches, a son and daughter, living, the son with his grandmother Walsh and the daughter with my master, of her own body; and her loving husband, although now sorrowful, will bear a true love to all her friends. I fear nothing more than the sudden hearing of the news will hurt Mrs Walsh, Mrs Coventry's mother, unless the same be made known to her by degrees. And so in haste I humbly commend your worship to God's preservation and rest, London, this 20th of February 1608, Your worship's at command, John Grove.

Sir John Hungrifort [*sic*] is turbulent but he cannot prevail against me, whereof I will certify at more leisure.

111. *John Grove to Elizabeth Russell*
    25 February 1608/9[1]
    Berington 376 (32)

Good Mistress Russell, Your basket and all things therein mentioned in your letters I have received of this carrier Greenbank. For the which, as for many other friendships and gifts, I heartily thank you and rest ready to do you or yours the best service I can for requital. Earle the carrier his son deceived me of a good basket of puddings which you lately sent to me; whereof I told him, but he made me a remedyless answer that he had left the same behind him in Oxfordshire, and what he did with the same returning homewards I know not. It may please you to tell Mr Jermyn your curate, when you see him, that his friend Mr Hartland never came to me, as he wrote he would. But no marvel if he break the promise or play other as honest parts with me, for thereunto he seemeth addicted wholly, like a man desperately disposed in the course of his lies. He deserveth no favour at my hands, and therefore I will from henceforth proceed against him as law permitteth me. If your health and ability to travel will permit you in the Easter week to testify your knowledge upon two or three questions before my Lord Chief Baron, [*it*] shall do me more good, in respect of your credit, than may other witnesses. Therefore I pray you let me at your leisure hear how you find yourself disposed to travel to Burford, either by coach or horseback. The charge shall be mine and will by no means [*e*]ntreat your trouble to endanger your health. And so I pray you note that my spe[*ci*]al meaning is: I will treat with the executor of[2] [. . .] do her all the stead that I lawfully may, as [. . .] a man or friend of hers, being with me at the end. I [. . .] and so in haste I commend your worship and [*your com*]fortable branches to God's merciful protection and yo[. . .] this 25th day of February 1608, Yours ever at command, John Grove.

[1] There is a hole at the beginning of the last four lines.
[2] Henry Russell had provided for his wife and sons to be executors of his will (no. **69** above), but the boys were too young to act.

112. *Lord Chancellor Ellesmere to [Francis Moore]*[1]
       4 April 1611
       Berington 378

After my very hearty commendations. Whereas, upon information given unto me in the behalf of Mrs Russell, a widow and your neighbour, and her son, his Majesty's ward, that some disordered persons who dwell near unto some of the ward's woods had openly given out many threatening speeches and menaces that they would assemble multitudes of like unruly persons, and with force and strong hand cut down and destroy the woods growing upon the lands of the said ward, specially if the committee of the ward should attempt the felling or selling any of the ward's woods upon the same lands, although the same should be felled or sold for the ward's use and by his own privity and consent: I did, for prevention of any such disorders and offence, heretofore write my letters to Sir Thomas Russell and other his Majesty's justices of peace the nearest adjoining to the said lands, as I was then informed, thereby requiring them, that if any such riotous or unlawful course as was threatened should be at any time attempted, either against the ward or his committee, that then

they should take special notice of it and use the[*ir*] best means to prevent it, or at least to see his Majesty's peace preserved and the offenders
punished. Since the writing of which my letters, being willing to inform
myself whether that country hath since continued in that quiet state and
government as is fit it should, among other things whereof I have thence
received advertisements, I understand that your convenience and near-
ness of dwelling to the ward's lands is such that not only in that respect
I hold you very fit to join with these gentlemen in this business, but
also sithence your fitness otherwise and sufficiency to be employed in
a matter of this nature for the quiet and service of your country is better
known unto me, I have thought good, so soon as I had notice that you
were so near a neighbour to the said lands, to address these my letters
unto you, hereby praying and authorising you to take consideration of
my former letters to Sir Thomas Russell &c., and to join with and assist
these gentlemen in the due execution and performance thereof; that nothing be hereafter done by any violent and disorderly course which may
tend to the breach of the peace or disturbance of the quiet of the country.
Whereof nothing doubting but you will have that due regard as appertaineth to the duty of your place, I bid you heartily farewell, at my house
in Ashridge, 4 April 1611, Your very loving friend, Thomas Ellesmere,
Cancellarius.

[1] This letter was enclosed in Berington 576 (20), which is dated from Ashridge on 8 April
1611 and gives the name of the local justice, which is not in Ellesmere's letter. For Francis
Moore of Hanley Castle and his recusancy, see *CSPD James I, 1603–10*, 593; Willis Bund,
Calendar of the Quarter Sessions Papers, pt 2, pp. xxii, ccxv, 145. For Humphrey Pakington's post in Ellesmere's household and its implications, see the Introduction, pp. xix–xx
above, and nos. **65, 67, 68, 71, 73, 75, 79, 83, 85, 86, 113, 126**.

113.   *Humphrey Pakington to Elizabeth Russell*
            28 August [1608–15]
            Berington 576 (21)

My good sister, My businesses were such that I had no time to answer
your letter at my last being in the country, neither could I tell what to say
concerning Mr Walwinn's demand of a heriot for Marcle[1] because I am
no way instructed in the matter; but in my conceit you did well to detain
the ox, for, seeing it is in the right of the King's ward, I presume Mr
Wallwine will not be too imperious, For if he should, that would be good
remedy against him, but if he will friendly and honestly reserve the consideration of his right to lawyers chosen on both parts, it were well, and
I would wish you deal neighbourly with him, and do make choice of my
cousin Coventrye for you to have the matter debated, either at London in
the term or in the country; and if I have warning of the time, I will do my

best to be there myself to do you the stead I may. I see not how you can sell that land or any other until your son come to full age, so that I conceive other means must be made for money than by sale if you stand in so extreme danger. Therefore I would not wish you in any case to deject your own mind, for that would but hurt yourself and all your worldly occasions. You shall be seen to find a poor faithful friend of me during my life; moreover, you must think that Almighty God never forgetteth his servants in their tribulation. So, with my heartiest commendations unto you, I leave you for this time and ever to his blessed protection, and remain Your faithful brother during life, Humfrey Pakington

Ashridge 28 Augusti:

[1] Much and Little Marcle are in Herefordshire, about halfway between Little Malvern and Ross-on-Wye; Hellens, a Jacobean manor-house at Much Marcle, was owned by the Walwyns, who had also held land from the bishops of Hereford at Coddington (see no. **69**). Elizabeth Walwyn had married James Mintridge (see no. **35**): Morgan G. Watkins, *Collections towards the History and Antiquities of the County of Hereford*, V/2: *Hundred of Radlow* (Hereford, 1902), 50–52, with pedigree on p. 51. In 1612 Humphrey Walwyn founded a school at Colwall, near Little Malvern, to which seven children from Little Malvern were entitled to go: VCH *Worcs.*, III. 453.

114. *Justinian Stubbs to Elizabeth Russell*
    10 July [1608–15]
      Berington /616 (3)

My most dear and loving friend Mistress Russell, I commend me to you most kindly. I have sent to you a bottle of Bristol water for your sister Mistress Pakington.[1] Let me entreat you to get it sent with as much speed as you may. I have been at Lydney[2] ever since Whitsuntide, and I am to return upon Thursday next, God willing. I am to trouble you again—I presume upon your love. I have sent my mare unto you by this bearer or messenger, and I pray you send my little mare by him. I would request John Saracin to get her shod, and at my coming to Malvern I will repay him with thanks. You told me that you thought you could get me a chapman for my great mare that is with you—I should be glad: I pray you let me know. If I can sell her, I will make away with my little mare and this other mare that I now send—if she do not prove with foal: she was covered with a very fine horse of Sir Edward Winter's. I rest yours for ever, and I beseech God to bless you and my chamber-fellows, your sons. Commend me to your own good self and to my chamber-fellows, and to Mistress More[3] when you see her. Gloucester, the 10th of July, Your loving friend for ever, or never his own, Justinian Stubbs.

[1] Humphrey Pakington's second wife Abigail (Sacheverell), whom he married in 1607: see Introduction, pp. xxi–xxii above.

[2] In the Forest of Dean; the home of Sir Edward Winter, who had married Anne Somerset, third daughter of Edward Somerset, fourth earl of Worcester (*c.*1550–1628), and Elizabeth Hastings. Altogether, the earl and countess had seven sons and seven daughters. The sons were: (1) William (*o.s.p.*); (2) Henry, 5th earl; (3) Thomas (= Eleanor Buttevant/Ormond); (4) Charles (*ob. juv.*); (5) Francis (*ob. juv.*); (6) Charles (= Elizabeth Powell); (7) Francis II (*ob. juv.*). The daughters were: (1) Elizabeth (Guildford); (2) Catherine I (Petre); (3) Anne (Winter); (4) Frances (Morgan); (5) Mary (*ob. inf.*); (6) Blanche (Arundel of Wardour); (7) Catherine II (Windsor). See Bradney, *A History of Monmouthshire*, II/1: *The Hundred of Raglan*, 26–7 (genealogical table). One of the chaplains at Raglan Castle was Sir Tobie Mathew (p. 15). See also nos. **118–19** below.

[3] Not identified. There is a monument of 1613 in Worcester Cathedral to six Mores, who were prosperous city merchants: Ralph Richardson, 'The Effigy Tombs of the Gentry of Worcestershire, 1500–1700', *Transactions of the Worcestershire Archaeological Society* 3rd ser. 19 (2004), 149, 162–3, 166, 172.

115.   *Humphrey Pakington to Elizabeth Russell*
      21 January 1614–15
      Berington 576 (22)

My good sister, By your Worcester carrier there came at this return a letter from you to my nephew John Russell, together with a basket. Which basket I made bold to open for fear anything therein might be spoiled or lost before my said nephew his return, and I found apples therein, together with some money, as I conjecture, safe lapped in a leather purse, which shall be safely retained until either my nephew himself or some other letter from you shall direct the delivery [*inserted*: or employment] thereof, which shall be performed accordingly. We here are now in very good hope that you have either recovered your health, or that your sickness is not dangerous, because we can hear nothing from the carrier to the contrary, so that the fear we conceived by my nephew Edmund his letter is now somewhat lessened; which upon my nephew John his return will, I hope, be turned into perfect joy. In the mean time, my dame and I do heartily thank you for your apples, which we take are sent hither to be eaten; and so for this time, with both our heartiest salutations remembered unto you, and likewise to [*inserted*: both] my nephews if my cousin John be not departed before the letter shall come unto you [*deleted*: ? first], I take leave, ever resting Your assured faithful brother during life, Humfrey Pakington

Little St Helen's London 21 Januar. 1614

116.   *Humphrey Pakington to Elizabeth Russell*
          2 January [1609–15]
          Berington 576 (2)[1]

My good sister, Sending for Mr Tyrer[2] to know of the causes which the
last term I committed to his care, amongst which Thomas Nash[3] his
suit against Turner, your tenant, was one, he signifieth that Nash hath
declared against Turner in an action of trespass, the copy of which declaration he hath brought down unto me, giving further to understand
that he verily thinketh, upon probable conjecture, that Mr White your
neighbour followeth the cause for Nashe, but, you understand, using
the name of one Harbert and Atkins. But, touching the matter, Mr Tyrer
and I have conferred thereof, diligently perusing your writings; and he
holdeth your cause to be so good in law that he doth not advise to draw it
into the Court of Wards, which will be chargeable, but to answer plainly
at the Common Law to this action, whereby Nash cannot resolve the possession but very small damage if he should prevail, as I hope he cannot.
Yet, for better instruction and security therein, Mr Tyrer desireth to be
resolved in the question contained in this enclosed note; for if Thomas
Nash, now plaintiff, be the son of Thoma[s or] Samuel Nashe he is
flatly concluded, or if h[*is father d*]id live five y[*ear*]s after my brother
Russell did pur[*chase*] the [*la*]nd, and if old Richard Nashe lived five
years a[*fter my*] brother [*his*] said purchase it is the [*l*]ong[*er*] for [. . .].
But herein, I pray you, return ce[*rtain*]word within six or seven days,
for you may easily learn so much of some that do know that unthrifty
generation. I desire to receive this intelligence from you the sooner, for
that I am uncertain of my departure to London and some course must
needs be taken at the beginning of the term for answering of Nashe. My
dame commendeth her right heartily unto you, and from me I hope you
conceive no less; and so for this time I take leave, ever remaining Your
faithful brother to his best power, Humfrey Pakington

Harvington 2° Januarii.

Our little one is sometimes sick and sometimes reasonable well, so that
we stand between hope and fear for her. But the most certain imputation
that we can perceive is that it doth scour but seldom, viz. about once in
24 hours.

---

[1] About half way down, the MS is badly torn, with bits missing.
[2] John Grove's brother-in-law: see nos. **73**, **101**, **110**.
[3] For Thomas Nash, from whom Henry Russell had bought Coddington, see no. **69** above.

117. *Benedict Hall¹ to Justinian Stubbs*
          16 August [1615]²
          Berington 621

Kind Mr Stubbes, Thanks be to God, by your assistance I am, as it were, well recovered of my ague, but since my first beginning of amendment I have been troubled with a continual rheum, which hath perplexed me very much, that I have thought twice or thrice to have sent unto you to have had your advice concerning it. Therefore let me now entreat you, with thankful overtures for my former benefits, [*omitted*: that I may] at your best leisure and opportunity receive some recomfort, or at least your counsel, to remove this rheum from me.

Now, good sir, let me give you to understand that I have received your loving and kind letter, by which you [*deleted*: declare] certify me of a certain match for one of my sisters, which should be to the son and heir of one Mistress Russell. Also you writ of his estate and the honesty of the young gentleman, which honesty, amongst honest men, is to be preferred before riches. Many other praises you writ of the gentleman, which, my head being addled, I cannot answer in particulars. Sir, concerning this matter you desire an answer whether I like or dislike of it. Dislike I cannot, therefore like unto my power. But I doubt not but that either you know or have heard, or at leastwise let me give you to understand, that I have an uncle whose name is Winchcombe,³ who hath a hand over me and [*that*] so much that I dare do nothing without his consent and knowledge herein; by reason whereof I can send you no direct answer before I speak with him. Willingly I would speak with you first, that we might confer concerning it. Until that time, I let you fare well, wishing you all happiness [*and*] entreating you to accept of my true love, which proceeds from sincere amity and not from a temporising flattery. Vale. Yours to his power, Benedict Hall

High Meadow, the 16 of August.

If God send me [*pe*]rfectly well, I mean to be with my uncle in Oxford-shire before Bartholomewtide: therefore, if you can, let me speak with you first.

---

¹ Benedict Hall was the son of William Hall of Highmeadow, a mile west of Coleford in Gloucestershire, and of Mary, daughter of Thomas Winchcombe of Chalgrove in Oxford-shire. He married Anne, daughter of Sir William Winter of Lydney in Gloucestershire (cf. no. **114**). His sisters were Cecily (born in 1597), who later married Edward Morgan of Pencoyd, and Mary (born in 1592–3), who later married Sir Henry Jerningham (*Visitation of the County of Gloucester, 1623*, 74). On 9 July 1646 two-thirds of Benedict's lands in Oxfordshire (see n. 3 below) were sequestrated for his recusancy (The National Archives, C.203/4), and by 1650 those in Gloucestershire had been also (VCH *Glos.*, V. 277). Part of the gatehouse range of the late-fifteenth-century house at Highmeadow survives as a barn: Verey and Brooks, *The Buildings of England: The Vale and the Forest of Dean*, 321–2.

² The dating of this letter and of those that follow depends on nos. **118–19**, where Stubbs says that he is to travel to Hereford 'tomorrow', 31 August, and later that he went there 'on Thursday'. Thursday 31 August means that the year is either 1615 or 1620. It seems more likely that Elizabeth Russell would attempt to make a match for her son without his consent when he was twenty, rather than twenty-five (cf. no. **123**), and that he would experience the scruples described in no. **127** at the age of twenty-one, rather than twenty-six. John Russell III's son Thomas was 'twenty-two and above' when John died in February 1640–41 (inquisition post mortem quoted in *Dominicana*, CRS 25, pedigree opp. p. 172), which means he was born about 1618. Benedict Hall did not become head of the family until his father William died on 6 February 1615–16 (*Visitation of the County of Gloucester, 1623*, 74), but William may already have been too frail to deal with such business.

³ Benet Winchcombe of Noke, a descendant of 'Jack of Newbury', the famous clothier; in 1623 Benedict inherited his estate there: Stapleton, *Post-Reformation Catholic Missions in Oxfordshire*, 114–15, 270–71.

118.   *Justinian Stubbs to Elizabeth Russell*
        *30 August [1615]*¹
        Berington 616 (5)

Mistress Russell, On my first coming to Raglan I could not get from thence. I am to go with my Lady Petre² and Mr Crowper one day's journey—I think to Hereford—tomorrow, God willing. And so to New Grange³ too, for me to speak with my brother that came out of Lincolnshire above three months since,⁴ and from thence to my Lady Winter;² and in my way I will go by High Mead, [*as*] this is my purpose. Commend me to my chamber-fellows and, afore and above all, to your own good self. So in haste I take my leave the 30th of August, Yours for ever or never his own, Justinian Stubbs.

¹ For the dating, see the notes to no. **117**.
² Lady Petre and Lady Winter were both daughters of the fourth Earl of Worcester at Raglan Castle: see notes to no. **114**; Benedict Hall married the Winters' daughter Anne.
³ For New Grange, see no. **119** below.
⁴ Stubbs's brother from Lincolnshire may be Joseph Stubbs of Stamford, who married Mary Gulston of Hertfordshire and died about 1630; their eldest son, another Justinian, became vicar of Ryhall in Rutland in 1670. *Lincolnshire Pedigrees III: P–Z*, ed. A.R. Maddison, Harleian Society 70 (London, 1904), 933.

119.   *Justinian Stubbs to Elizabeth Russell*
        4 September [1615]
        Berington 616 (4)

Mistress Russell, My kind love remembered. I left a letter upon Saturday last at Mr Haslocke's of Worcester to be sent to you (and also at my coming out of town I signified as much to Francis Bland),¹ that was for the staying of John Saracin's² coming to New Grange.³ Mr Morgan of

Llantarnam[4] sent for me in my way to Hereford upon Thursday to come to him. I could not get away at that time from my Lady Petre: I promised to be there with him this night at the furthest. From thence I do ride to my Lady Winter, and my journey I will make by High Mead. Thus in haste I commit you to God. New Grange, 4th September, Your loving friend for ever, Justinian Stubbs.

[1] See Berington 562 (4).

[2] See no. **114**.

[3] New Grange is six miles north-east of Ross-on-Wye and 1½ miles south-west of Dymock. The name is first recorded in 1589 (Smith, *Place-Names of Gloucestershire*, III. 170); Old Grange is 1½ miles further north.

[4] Llantarnam Abbey, a former Cistercian house, was four miles north of Newport in Monmouthshire. After the Dissolution it was acquired by William Morgan of Pentre Bach. His grandson Edward Morgan married Lady Frances Somerset, fourth daughter of the 4th earl of Worcester, and was therefore brother-in-law to Lady Petre and Lady Winter, for whom see also no. **114**. According to a report of 1607, Robert Jones, later the Jesuit superior, was often there: 'Robert Holland, alias Powell, alias Morgan, which is thought to be his truest name; of the age of fifty-four or fifty-five years . . . ; of stature tall, broad-faced, high-foreheaded, great-eyed, his hair then turning from Abram colour. He is to be known by a sword-blade put in a rapier hilt. He frequenteth the house of Edward Morgan of Llantarnam in Monmouthshire, whose wife is a recusant and whose eldest son married the Earl of Worcester's daughter; likewise the house of John Aubrey of Monkland in Herefordshire, tenant to Mr Blunt the Councillor, and the house of Richard Clarke of Wellington in Herefordshire': SP 14/28/122/1, printed in Michael Hodgetts, 'Shropshire Priests in 1605', *Worcestershire Recusant* 47 (June 1986), 31–2.

120. *Humphrey Pakington to Elizabeth Russell*
  28 October 1615
    Berington 576 (4)

Good sister, I have safely received the money you sent up in the basket, together with your very good apples and fat hen, for which my dame and I do give you hearty thanks. And I will not fail to pay the money to both the feodaries and take their acquittances for the receipt thereof according as you required,[1] which as carefully and faithfully I would have performed if your letter had comen unto me without either apples or hen. For neither that unfortunate accident[2] that happened nor any other that may fall out shall cause me neglect the office of an honest brother towards you in anything that may further the good or prevent the harm which may [*deleted*: happen; *inserted*: fall] unto you. And yet I must say (my condition being all to speak what I think without dissimulation), it was my fortune, without any fault, to be suspected, where I dealt most honestly and no less carefully to prevent the inconvenience, nay the fault, that I was committed without my privity or possible knowledge thereof. But I leave the matter to God his mercy and to such worldly fortune [*inserted*: that may fall out], being more desirous to forget than either to think or write thereof, and do further signify unto you concerning the former business that as yet, having some other earnest employments, I could not pay in the money, but by the next carrier I hope my advertisement unto you shall be that it is despatched and the same confirmed by two acquittances from them, which you shall receive enclosed in my letter. And so for this time, with my heartiest salutation remembered, I rest and will ever remain, Your faithful brother, Humfrey Pakington

From the Strand in London near the New Burse,[3] 28° Octobr: 1615

[1] For the payments to the feodaries for the wardship of John Russell, see nos. **101**, **107–8**, **121** and the receipts in no. **122**.
[2] Despite the negotiations with Benedict Hall, John Russell made a runaway match with his cousin Mary Lutley; see the Introduction, pp. xxvi–xxvii above. If that was the 'unfortunate accident' for which Elizabeth blamed Humphrey, this letter gives an approximate date for it. For Humphrey's efforts to reconcile his sister to her niece (and daughter-in-law) see no. **123**.
[3] The New Burse or Exchange was a shopping precinct, built in 1608–9, on the river side of the Strand, about a quarter of a mile north-east of Charing Cross.

121.   *Humphrey Pakington to Elizabeth Russell*
[November 1615][1]
Berington 576 (11)

My good sister, I have paid in your whole year's rent to the Feodary of Worcestershire, according as you require, and have here enclosed sent you his acquittance. But Mr Conisbye, the feodary of Herefordshire, is not yet comen up to London, whereby I cannot yet despatch that business; so that I am therein to expect his coming, at which time I will not fail to despatch that business also, if Mr Conisbye absolutely refuse not to receive the same rent, which I trust he will not, or if he do, that I shall be able to entreat him thereunto, either by myself or some friend. In the mean time, with my heartiest salutations remembered, I cease your further trouble and at all times do wish your good health and felicity, ever remaining, Your assured faithful brother, Humfrey Pakington.

[1] Berington 377 consists of twenty-eight acquittances for payments to the Crown by Thomas Marbury and Elizabeth Russell during the minority of John Russell III (1608–1615). Four are printed below as no. **122**. Although Marbury owed £1 13s 4d a year for the Herefordshire lands and Elizabeth £5 6s 8d a year for those in Worcestershire, this letter shows that, at least sometimes, Humphrey Pakington dealt with the feodaries for both. Payments were due at Lady Day and Michaelmas, but no. **122**(*d*) (the last) was for the Worcestershire lands for a whole year, and must have been the one enclosed with this letter, which can therefore be dated from it.

122. *Four receipts for John Russell III's wardship*
1614–15
Berington 377

(*a*) *10 April 1614, Worcestershire*

Decimo die Aprilis 1614. Received the day and year above written of Elizabeth Russell for the rent of the lands of John Russell, his Majesty's ward, and for one half year ended at the Feast of the Annunciation of the Blessed Virgin Mary last past, the sum of fifty three shillings four pence: I say received by me, Walter Childe, gent., his Majestie's Feodary of the County of Wigorn., to the use of the King's majesty that now is, the sum of fifty-three shillings and four pence. Per me, Walterum Childe Feodarium.

(*b*) *5 October 1614, Worcestershire*

Wigorn. Quinto Octobris die anno Regni Domini nostri Regis Jacobi dei gracia Rege Anglie, Francie et Hibernie xiimo et Scotie xlvimo. Received the said day and year of Elizabeth Russell, widowe, Lessee to his Majestie, for the lands and tenements aforesaid [*sic*] during the minority of John Russell, gent., son and heir of the said [*sic*] Henry Russell, his Highness's ward, for one half year's rent due to his Majesty at the feast of St Michael the Archangel last past, the sum of fifty-three shillings and four pence of lawful English money. Walter Childe, Feodar. Comitatus predicti.

(*c*) *21 May 1615, Herefordshire*

Vicesimo primo die Maii Regni Regis Jacobi dei gracia Anglie Francie et Hibernie xiimo et Scotie xlviimo. Received the day and year above written by me Thomas Conyngesbye, his Majesty's Feodary for the county of Hereford, of Thomas Malberry [*sic*], the committee of the body and lands of John Russell, his Majesty's ward, for one half year's rent due to his Majesty at the feast of the Annunciation of the blessed Virgin St Mary last past, the sum of sixteen shillings and eight pence. Per me, Tho. Conyngesby, Feodary.

(*d*) *24 October 1615, Worcestershire*[1]

Vicesimo quarto die Octobris 1615. Received the day and year above written to the King's Majesty's use by Walter Childe, gent., his Majesty's Feodary [*for*] the county of Wigorn., the sum of five pounds six shillings and eight pence of [*Elizabeth*] Russell, widow, committee of the body and lands of [*John*] Russell, gent., his Majesty's ward, being due for one whole year ended at the Feast of St Michael the Archangel last past before the date hereof: I say, received the sum of £5 6*s* 8*d*. Per me, Walterum Childe, Feod.

---

[1] The last item is damaged, but the missing words are obvious.

123.   *Humphrey Pakington to Elizabeth Russell*
       12 January [1615/16]
       Berington 576 (8)

My good sister, I delivered some short spee[*ches to my*] nephew John
Russell, your son, about the £10 wh[*ich he told*] me you did owe Mr
John Grove, but, for your further direction and satisfaction therein,
I thought good to let you understand that you may well forbear the payment of any consideration money therefor until you hear further from
me about the same, f[*or*] it may so fall out that I may obtain you either
reasonable days for the payment of the principal without consideration
or procure you some abatement, so that you pay in the rest within half
a year. Wherein you shall shortly hear further from me and, I hope, to
such purpose that you shall well perceive I do not forget either yourself
or your estate, which in common judgment is impaired by the marriage
of your son, though, if he had married to your desire and choosing, yet is
it uncertain whether the effect thereof would have been more profitable
or not, or better for your quietness, so inscrutable are the designments of
Almighty God, and so chargeable are the maintenances of gentlewomen
that bring great portions.

   I am glad to hear that you use your son so kindly, which, to his great
comfort and my contentment, he hath related unto me. Let me, good
sister, without offence, say this unto you: in my poor judgement, I hold
it not only requisite but necessary that you should call his wife home
unto you, if it be for no other respect but to acquaint and enable her by
your good instructions to keep and uphold, as far as concerneth her part,
your son's estate hereafter, which you so carefully and discreetly, to
your commendation, have hitherto preserved and, I pray God, long may
do. Pardon me, my good sister, that [*omitted*: I] make bold to write this
much unto you in a matter that concerneth you and not myself, as haply
you may think; and pardon me further still that, being led by an honest
conscience (as I protest), without the motion or knowledge of your son
or any other, [*omitted*: I] make bold to say more: if you suffer the young
woman to get a habit of idleness at Bromcroft, having there nothing to
do, you do not well; for, the longer she runneth on in such a fashion, the
unapter she will be both to apprehend and obey good instruction: which
in the opinion of the wisest will be [*word deleted*] accounted your error
and the hurt of your son. So, praying and hoping here[*in you*] will not
blame me for my plainness, which you cannot justly do, except you
blame me for the true affection I bear you, which causeth the same, I take
leave, ever remaining, Your loving and ready brother to do you what
stead he may, Humfrey Pakington

Harvington, 12° Januar:

124. *John Grove to Elizabeth Russell*
   2 March 1615/16
   Hodgson Transcripts; source unidentified[1]

Worshipful Mrs Russell, My humble duty and like thanks to you remembered. I have received your last letters at Shrovetide with the abundance of good poultry, and also another letter therein mentioned before, and also in the [*same time*] the bounty of provisions for my household to spare my purse in London markets. The cause why I did not write thanks to you for the same was for that mine intent hath been, and yet is, to see you myself and answer your two letters viva voce, I mean by word of mouth. But now, by these [*designs of*] Mr Hartland and his knight,[2] being occasions of travel into your parts, I thought before my coming to present to you a little roundlet of four gallons of sherris sack, free of carriage to Worcester, which you shall receive of Earle the carrier there, as this bearer, Mr Hartland [*sic*], who saw the filling thereof and had then a taste of it, can certify you. Touching my tenants William Daneford and Rowland Turner, I have not of long time received any rent of them for my land at Eastnor.[3] Whom I pray you certify that I mean to be in that country at or before Our Lady Day night, and then I will talk with them concerning all things fit to be considered touching the farm, and that they would provide my rent against that time, whereof they shall have entry before my departure hence. And so, in some haste at this time, I heartily commend you and yours to God's most merciful protection, ever as in duty bound remaining, Your worship's poor friend at command, John Grove.

London 2 March 1615

[1] Apparently the item listed by Lechmere as 'C.43. John Grove to Mrs Elizabeth Russell, 1625 [*sic*]' but not now in the Lechmere Box.
[2] Sir John Hungerford: cf. nos. **105**, **107–8**. The reference to 'this bearer, Mr *Hartland*,' seems to be a slip of the pen.
[3] See above, nos. **71**, **72**, **107**.

125. *Humphrey Pakington to Elizabeth Russell*
   22 November [1615–22]
   Lechmere Box C.32

Good sister, At my last being in the country, my nephew John Russell, your son, told me of his intention to sell his cloak lined with velvet for relief of his present wants, unto which I advised him to acquaint you. But, little expecting, the last week I received his letter, together with two cloaks, signifying your privity to his intention and requiring speedy sale of the cloaks and return of the money. But I know not what to say, and as little what to do, in this business so unproper for me, having thought good to let you know that I fear in this town the cloaks will not be sold for half the worth, though they be little to the worse for wearing. For old apparel flieth daily to the brokers so fast, where there is such change, that it yieldeth little, and I would be loath to make such a bargain for him that he and you should both dislike. But if I might know the certain price under which the cloaks should not be sold, I would with more content-ment or, more truly said, with less discontentment, undergo the effecting of your son's desire, and use the help of others here that have more skill in broking than myself and whom I may trust. I therefore pray that I may speedily hear from you and my nephew herein, for I hold it not requisite to go through with any bargain before I have some further knowledge of your minds. For, having the last week the advice and help of Mr Couden, my honest tailor, to get sale for the cloaks, he cannot be offered above £7 for the cloak lined with velvet and verily thinketh it will never yield much more or reach to £8. Wherefore, presuming that such a rate will be disliked of you both, my best endeavours will be but repaid with discon-tenting my good sister and nephew if I make such a sale, and yet by the little trial I have now made in such business, wherein I little expected any experience, I think I can buy a better cloak for £7. So, having detained you long in this occasion, with my heartiest commendations to you and your sons remembered, I wish you all good health and all other happi-ness, remaining, Your faithful and loving brother to his power, Humfrey Pakington

The Strand, London
22° November

126. *Humphrey Pakington to Elizabeth Russell*
           3 February [1614–17][1]
           Berington 576 (5)

Addressed: To my approved good and loving sister Mrs Elizabeth Rus-sell at Little Malvern give these.

M[y good] sister, My dame and I, together with our two lit[tle] ones, are in reasonable good health, saving for this general cold, which here with us possesseth and troubleth almost everybody. But I think God will have it in such a mediocrity and remissness that we respect it not much. The thing that most doth grieve us, and many others, is that my lord the Lord Chancellor hath it at this instant extremely, whereby since yesterday was sevennight he could not come to Westminster Hall; but if this bitter cold weather would amend and turn warmer, we hope his amendment would also follow. In the mean time, I pray Almighty God send him health. My dame and I have received your two fat pullets, together with your two fair birds, somewhat strange in our city, especially in our poor kitchen; and, seeing you speak nothing of the the [*sic*] little bird with the long bill, I may suspect that the great ones, being male and female, might hatch it by the way, if the length of the bill did not prove the contrary. I have returned you your basket again by the carrier that brought it, and therein a few figs, which I think are such of that kind that seldom have been seen in Worcestershire. Thus in [*some*] haste, being forced to continual attendance on my Lord in his sickness, with my heartiest salutations remembered, for this time I end, ever resting, Your assured faithful brother, Humfrey Pakington.

London 3º Februar:

I hope you all at Little Malvern are also in good health, to whom my dame also returneth her kindest remembrance.

¹ The mention of the 'two little ones' shows that the year was after 1613, when Anne Pakington was born. Lord Chancellor Ellesmere died in March 1617.

127.   *? to John Russell III*¹
         [?1616]
         Berington 623 (1)

As touching your prayers, I have turned and do turn all the obligation you have to say them under mortal sin into fasting of Saturdays and giving 30s yearly in alms. And I allow you but one hour in the forenoon and one other in the afternoon to attend to devotion, not meaning that you should spend a whole hour together but forbidding you to spend above an hour, though you take the same by pieces. And commonly say with your wife or with your brother: especially answer the Litanies at night,² or say them your brother or wife answering you, your mother being present if conveniently she can. And that shall satisfy for all the defects and omissions which you made in the daytime. But if you be not present at the Litanies, then say three Ave Marias and *Laudate Dominum omnes gentes*³ before you go to bed, and that shall satisfy for all omissions of prayers, so that you shall not sin so much as venially for omitting them. Vex not yourself, trouble not yourself, examine not yourself about your resolution to serve God, but, rejecting all such cogitations, in your daily practice and carriage perform the part of an honest man in loving God with your heart so near as you can, in being dutiful and kind towards your mo[*ther*] and just and charitable towards others [*hole in MS*] in all things; and upon all occasions confidently use your rule, *Quidquid &c.*,⁴ unless in matters of justice touching others; and do not think anything to be a sin unless you be certain that it is against the express commandments of God, or that learned men have told you that it is sin. And [*read*] this pa[*per*] often and follow it boldly [*notw*]ithstanding [*your dou*]btes about it. As touching your marriage, rest absolutely secure till you and I meet again, and use your wife as your wife in all respects; for there is far greater danger of sin *in abstinendo* than *in reddendo debitum matrimoniale*.⁵ For unless Mr Clendock, your cousin,⁶ Mr Martin, myself or Mr Walpoole be and were extremely wicked or extremely ignorant, you are most secure—and so secure that in conscience you are bound to prefer their and my authority before your own scrupulous or otherways conceited doubts. And therefore in this business use the rule I have given you: *Quidquid non est evidens, rejiciatur*.⁴ As touching vows, I have dispensed with all past (saving those of religion and chastity), whether they were expressed well by you to me or not, whether they were certainly made by you or not; and therefore about all these use your rule, *Quidquid &c*.⁴ And in dispensing with you in these and turning them into the fasting of Saturday and giving 30s yearly in alms, I relied not at all upon your informations but upon my own proper knowledge and judgement. And I forbid you seriously to make any vows hereafter and disenable you to make them without the consent of a learned ghost[*ly*] f[*ather*]; and if you make any, they shall [*be*] void and of no effect. For I turn all [*that you*] shall make any day or night into the saying of one Ave Maria once in two days. As touching the vows of religion and chastity, those which you made since your marriage are not valid; those which you made before were sudden and imprudent and not accepted of by Almighty God. And therefore in this respect also, upon my peril, use your rule, *Quidquid non est evid*[*ens reji*]*ciatur*,⁴ and rest quiet. . . .

¹ John Russell's runaway marriage was followed by an attack of scruples, which were sensitively and practically dealt with in this letter. For identifications of the writer and of the other priests mentioned see the Introduction, pp. xxvi–xxvii above.
² A copy of the *Manual* of 1614, including the Litany of the Saints and the Golden Litany, is still in the Little Malvern library at Birmingham University Library: see J.D. Crichton, 'The *Manual* of 1614', *Recusant History* 17 (1984–5), 158–72.
³ 'Praise the Lord, all you nations' (Ps. 116/117: the shortest psalm).
⁴ 'Reject whatever is not clear.'
⁵ 'In abstaining from', 'in performing the marital duty'.
⁶ It is not clear whether Clendock or Martyn was Russell's 'cousin'.

128. *Humphrey Pakington to [John] Russell*
     *[before 1623]*¹
     Berington 576 (16)

I have send [*sic*] down to my good sister by the Worcester carrier of this week's return her basket, and in the same three of your books which were with Mr Hoult,[2] retaining the Dictionary for a time until I hear further from you, because it would not go into her basket, and also two papers of raisins of the sun, which are for your mother. So, with my very hearty commendations remembered to my good sister and your [*inserted*: self], not forgetting my nephew and brother,[3] I wish unto you all good health and happiness and so will ever remain Your faithful uncle and assured friend to his power, Humfrey Pakington.

London 23 November

[1] The mention of 'my good sister' shows that this letter was written before Elizabeth's death in 1623. Since there is no other evidence for the date and this is Humphrey's only surviving letter to his nephew, it has been placed here, as about 1620.
[2] Francis Holte, younger brother of Sir Thomas Holte, the builder of Aston Hall in Birmingham. A recusant and benefactor of religious houses on the continent, he is mentioned as 'my cousin Francis Holte' in a letter of the 1630s from Humphrey's younger daughter, Anne Audley, to her mother, Abigail; the connection was through Abigail's mother, Joan Bradbourne. Hodgetts, 'The Yates of Harvington, 1631–1696', 152–81, esp. 157; Michael Hodgetts, 'The Holtes of Aston Hall, Birmingham', *Midland Catholic History* 9 (2002–3), 13–26; and see the index to LaRocca, *Jacobean Recusant Rolls for Middlesex*, CRS 76. The Grace Holte mentioned there was Sir Thomas's first wife.
[3] Edmund Russell and John Pakington.

129. *Licence for Humphrey Pakington to travel*[1]
        22 April 1622
        Acts of the Privy Council of England, n.s. XXXVIII:
            July 1621 – May 1623 (London, 1932), 199

A licence for Humphrey Packington of Chaddesley in the county of Worcester, esquire, a recusant convict, to repair to the cities of London and Westminster and the counties of Worcester, Warwick, Salop, Nottingham, Kent, Hereford, Flint and Hertford for the following of his business during the space of six months ending the 22th [*sic*] of October next following the date hereof. Lord Archbishop of Canterbury, Lord Keeper, Earl Marshal, Lord Viscount Falkland, Lord Digby, Mr Secretary Calvert.

[1] None of Humphrey Pakington's surviving letters were written after the death of his sister in 1623. But his movements can still be traced through the licences to travel which were granted to him regularly from 1613 to 1629. This is the only one of the series to mention Flintshire, and may suggest a visit to St Winifred's Well. The indexes to the printed *Acts of the Privy Council* (under 'Licences') show that, thirty years after the Act of 1593, few recusants now applied for such permission. On 13 March 1621, the Justices of Westminster had informed the Privy Council that of the recusants there none were confined and only Humphrey Pakington was licensed: *CSPD James I, 1619–23*, 234 (SP 14/120/19).

130.   *?¹ to John Russell III*
            30 May [? after 1622]²
            Berington 648 (2)

Most loving and dear cousin John, Time permitteth me not to write unto
you in that manner as I would, for this very morning the King's Messenger, who is to see me transported on the great river, hath been here with
me at my chamber and hath appointed to fetch me away in the afternoon.
By reason whereof, businesses of divers sorts have and do press me not
a little. When I shall come, if it please God, to my journey's end and be
settled and at rest, I will not fail, God willing, to write more at large. In
the mean time, I have sent you back your books; for the which, as also
for all your singular love and charity towards me, I give you a thousand
heartiest thanks and shall ever esteem myself obliged to [*be*] mindful of
you. I pray you remember my most loving and respective commendations to your bedfellow, and to your brother and his wife,³ and to signify
unto him that I earnestly entreat him, if some course be not already taken
for the satisfying of Mr Pater's legacy,⁴ that the stuff which he had may
be prized and the value of it, at the least, if no other thing can be had from
Mr Badger,⁵ be sent to the Coll[ege] of D[ouay] so soon as with any convenience may be. Thus, commending myself to your prayers, as I forget
you not any one day in mine, I commit you [*to*] the sacred tuition of our
sweet Saviour and rest

May 30   [*The signature has been cut away.*]

¹ The writer may have been Ralph Stamford alias Palmer, a cousin of John Russell through
the Alderfords of Abbots Salford, near Evesham, who on 5 June 1618 was ordered to
be moved from the Clink to go into exile with the Spanish Ambassador (Anstruther, I.
330–31).
² The letter was written after no. **127**, since John's brother Edmund is now married. But
there is no mention of their mother, who did not die until 1622, and priests were deported
after 1618.
³ Edmund Russell's wife was Elizabeth Mintridge; see the Introduction, p. xxxiv n. 94
above.
⁴ 'Mr Pater' may be one of the Petres (see nos. **114**, **119**) or one of the Pewters (see
nos. **109**, **197**). There is no reference to the legacy in the *The Douay College Diaries,
1598–1654*, ed. Edwin H. Burton and Thomas L. Williams, CRS 10–11 (London, 1911).
⁵ For the Badgers, see Jennings Walker, 'Elizabethan Recusancy in Hanley Castle', esp.
12–13.

131.   *Giles Nanfan II¹ to John Russell III*
            [?1628]
            Lechmere Box B.8

Sir, This morning I have received letters from London from a kinsman of mine wherein you are mentioned. My cousin Trovile² of the White Friars, out of his respect to you, wished me speedily to let you know that you are informed against for [*deleted: illegible*] depopulations³ and not ploughing, and to that purpose comes down one Smith suddenly. Divers others are questioned, but because you should be prepared for his coming with good advice for prevention, I thought fit to let you know all this morning. So in haste, being glad of your recovery, I rest, At your service, Giles Nanfan.

I am in great distress for christening my children⁴ and have sent divers ways and can light of none. If you can help me I shall be much bounden to you. I have [*deleted: illegible*] sent you the news of the overthrow of the French.⁵

¹ Giles Nanfan II of Birtsmorton Court, four miles south of Little Malvern, was the elder son of Giles I (1548–1614) by his second marriage to Elizabeth Southwell, a sister of the martyr: *Visitation of the County of Worcester, 1569*, 99; *Visitation of Worcestershire, 1634*, 73; VCH *Worcs.*, IV. 31. In 1614 both Giles II and Elizabeth submitted certificates of conformity (The National Archives, KB 145/14/12), though perhaps merely as a matter of form; cf. no. **109** above.
² Giles was married to Anne Troville.
³ This may refer to the sale by the Crown in 1632 of Malvern Chase, in which John Russell had an 'assart': Aileen Hodgson, 'The History of Little Malvern Court: III', *Worcestershire Recusant* 40 (December 1982), 30. See also no. **196** below.
⁴ These may be the two sons, Thomas and John, of Giles and Anne.
⁵ Possibly the siege of La Rochelle in 1628.

132. *John Russell III to ?*¹
[?1630s]
Berington 619 (4)²

Madame, You see by these enclosed that Mr Coks³ hath delivered your message, and that your poor servant (though distracted with many businesses) hath not been altogether unmindful of your command. The paper that hath the most verses is written unto yourself (although toward the end of it I tune my speech to him that hath so blasphemed our English endeavours in the Greek tongue),⁴ as it will appear to you in the English translation, which I have placed on the other side of the leaf, that you may have a shadow at least of what is said in the Greek. For I presume you conceive it impossible [*inserted*: to] transfuse anything out of a language more copious and elegant into a barbarous and penurious [*sic*] without much loss of its native grace, especially in verse, the phrase and foot being so far different. I understand since that the gentleman hath so much worth and true desert in him that I am sorry and ashamed that my choleric Muse hath not altogether withheld her quill from the least touch of satyrical vinegar. But truly, upon those provocations by which she found herself charged with the long washing of an Aethiop, it was hard to make the ink run without some small mixture of that liquor. Yet I am glad to hear that he is learned and versed in this kind, for, being so, he will without doubt judge the better and with more candour, whereas a smatterer would have soonest disliked what was least faulty. I hear by my brother Humphrey Lutley[5] that he was pleased to send by him some verses of his own in Greek to me; for which I readily acknowledge myself his most humble servant, although (being unfortunately and to my great grief lost by my brother) I had not the happiness to see and admire them. But howsoever, I am by my brother's relation so enamoured on the man and his virtues that truly I long for nothing more [*than the*] opportunity to testify unto him my great desire to kn[*ow*] him and to deserve his acquaintance. W[*it my u*]ttermost service, I humbly beseech you to please to signify unto him that if he have occasion to come into this country and shall please to vouchsafe me that great favour as to see poor Little Malvern, he will find in my poor closet store of books not everywhere obvious, although nothing in myself worthy of his learning but a [*man truly*] and wholly at his command and service. For the rest, I presume of your ladyship's leave to [*remain*] your most [*humble servant*], John [*Russell*].

---

[1] 'Madame', 'your ladyship', may have been a daughter of the 4th Earl of Worcester: cf. the Introduction, pp. xxvii–xxviii above, and nos. **114, 117–19**.
[2] The bottom right-hand corner is missing.
[3] Unidentified.
[4] It is not possible to identify the rival Greek poet, but cf. nos. **154, 92**.
[5] Humphrey Lutley (*c.*1599–1653). Third son of John Lutley (d. 1646) of Broncroft Castle in Shropshire and Mary Pakington, Elizabeth Russell's sister: *Visitation of Shropshire, 1623*, II. 345. He was in Worcestershire or Shropshire as a priest by 1631 and at Harvington by 1642: Anstruther, II. 205–6; Hodgetts, 'The Yates of Harvington, 1631–1696', 159, 161. No. **165** below is one of his letters. For his brother Philip (1601–1684), see Anstruther, II. 206.

---

133. *Edmund Russell to John Russell III*
         [?1630s][1]
         Berington 623 (3)

Jesus

Worthy and dear brother, I trust in God that there is not any least cause of fear on your part, for Mr Hough assured me as faithfully as I could desire that he would search the Sheriff his books on Tuesday last, and, if there were aught against you, that he would instant[*ly*] give you to understand at large all the particulars, what and how; and if that at any time hereafter he could learn anything to your purpose you should have present notice thereof, you paying the messenger, which I undertook you should. So that I conceive you need not doubt. Nevertheless, for as much as some buzzing of mischief hath been abroad, I will talk with the Sheriff myself and search his books at his next coming to Worcester, which I fear will not be before Saturday, for he seldom cometh Wednesdays. But howsoever I will [*put*] all other business aside and attend to his coming on Wednesday next, for otherwise this harvest-time I should not be in Worcester in the middle of the week, nor constantly on Saturdays. But for this business I will [*go*] there both Wednesday and Saturday, for be [*inserted*: you] assured that *neque istic neque alibi tibi unquam erit in me mora.*[2] It would be vain for me to attempt to render you thanks answerable to so many brotherly courtesies as I have formerly received, and you have now feasted me and mine with a dainty tid,[3] which maketh it more impossible. Wherefore, instead of thanks I will humbly beseech the Supreme Majesty to be your daily reward and retributor for all your goodness towards me. And so in extreme haste I take leave but will ever rest, Your brother and servant, Edmund Russell.

[1] This letter may or may not refer to the prosecutions mentioned in the next five items: it does not seem possible to date it.
[2] 'Neither there nor anywhere else will I ever delay for you.'
[3] The form 'tidbit' for 'titbit' is still in use in North America.

134. *Abigail Pakington to John Russell III*[1]
   July [1632]
   Berington 623 (19)

Worthy dear nephew, At my coming out of town, June the 25th, you were free of troubles, although threatened by Bee,[2] for the preventing of whose designs a vigilant care is promised to be taken by a friend of ours[3] this Sessions; and if nothing happen more than an ordinary course, I have left 3*s* 4*d* to be paid for you. But in case of greater danger you are not to pay that but shall have present intelligence (as formerly) for the procuring of a *scire facias.*[4] My son Awdley his solicitor stays in town to wait the business,[5] and I will be ready upon the least occasion to give you present notice of anything I shall hear may be prejudicial unto you. The underwritten is the money laid out for you, and the particular reasons of disbursing it shall be yiel[*ded*] you more at large when I have the happiness to see you. According as you gave order, I took up for you [*from*] Mr Edward Burford[6] £6, which is no more (you see) than the charges that will serve you to bestow in [*ord*]inary charity. So, with my kind remembrance to you and my dear niece, I rest, Your very loving Aunt Pakington.

July the [ ]th

	£	s	d
After Ca[*nd*]lemas Term paid	£0	4*s*	5*d*
For a *scire facias*		8	0
Before Easter Term		13	4
After Easter Term		4	5
Before Midsummer Term		4	5
For [. . .] James or Jones	3	0	0
his charge	1	2	0
After Midsummer Term left		3	4
Sum	£5	[*19*	*11*]

[1] Humphrey Pakington died on 6 August 1631; for his monument at Chaddesley Corbett see C.D. Gilbert, 'Humphrey Pakington's Monument at Chaddesley Corbett', *Midland Catholic History* 13 (2006), 20–25. But Abigail was still visiting London, where she obstructed prosecutions of Worcestershire recusants who included her nephew John Russell III, her sons-in-law Sir John Yate and Sir Henry Audley, and John Russell. This and the next eight letters give a picture of their subsequent legal manoeuvres to avoid conviction, culminating in a draft petition to the King (no. **142**).

[2] Possibly the Edward Bee, 'his Majesty's servant' or 'the King's servant', mentioned in *CSPD Charles II, 1635*, 571, and *CSPD Charles II, 1635–6*, 258; see no. **137**.

[3] Probably Sir Henry Spiller; cf. no. **137** and the Introduction, pp. xxix–xxx above.

[4] A writ ordering a matter to be brought to someone's notice, so that he could appear and defend his case; cf. nos. **137–8, 142** below.

[5] Sir Henry Audley had first been indicted in Middlesex on 29 August 1632, when his addresses were given as St Giles-in-the-Fields and 'Harrington [*sic*] in Chadgley Corbett': Jeaffreson, *Middlesex County Records*, III. 43.

[6] For the Burfords, see also nos. **69, 179, 185**.

135.   *Abigail Pakington to John Russell III*
       20 March [1632/3]
       Lechmere Box C.44

Worthy dear nephew, Excuse my no sooner answering of yours (staying the better to answer you) and know that, notwithstanding Pollard his exhibiting of an information to precede and include that of Grimston against you, thereby to stop his further information, such is this age that neither you nor we are hereby (although it be accordingly done) freed from being indicted by Bee;[1] who with much earnestness laboured to indict us all this last Sessions and, being prevented by way of the jury (although with some charge to us), who pleaded we stood already indicted and they had no reason to indict us again: whereupon he went to the Under-Sheriff's office of Middlesex and took up all the exigents there, purposing to indict us all anew the next Sessions. These he took up cunningly by way of one of the Under-Sheriff's men, unknown to the Under-Sheriff himself, who told a friend of yours and mine that went to his office (to put in two *supersedeas*'s[2] to secure you and me in the country) [*in margin*: thereof], and promised him that since Bee had so dealt without his knowledge he should no more put those into his office. So that we at this present stand unindicted, and all in Worcestershire, and are to endeavour to prevent this his design of new indicting us. To which purpose we are advised to deal underhand with Bee his two creatures, Avery and Hayton[3] (by whom he first indicted us), to take them off; who, having so long been in agitation with him and gained nothing, will the sooner fall from him. Which if we can effect (as I hope we shall), I doubt not but Bee will be tired. This will be somewhat chareable but (upon deliberate counsel had) the securest way we four, I mean my two near friends, with you and myself, have to go; wherein I will as for myself tender your readiness and, as occasion shall be offered, certify you of our success herein. With my kind love to your worthy self and my good niece remembered, I remain your true loving aunt, A. Pakington.

March the 30.

If others in the shire would (whom it as much concerns as us) join with us, we should all receive equal benefit and the burden would be the easier.

[1] For the background to this letter and for Bee, see no. **134**.
[2] 'A writ commanding the stay of legal proceedings which ought otherwise to have proceeded, or suspending the powers of an officer' (*OED*).
[3] Avery and Hayton have not been identified; see further no. **142**.

136. *Abigail Pakington to John Russell III*
      [February–March 1633/4][1]
      Berington 648 (9)

My son Audeley pleaded a foreign plea[2] the last term unto the indictment, saying that his chief residence was at Berechurch in the county of Essex, and that sometimes he did repair to that parish church and sometimes to others in the same county. Whereupon Bee forbore further to trouble the King's Bench Court to get that plea overruled and to try it in Middlesex, so that as yet it is at a stop. There was a treaty held with Bee at the beginning of the last term to this purpose: that if he would warrant that such inquisitions as should issue out for the finding of their estates whom he hath indicted (viz. Sir Charles Smyth, Mr Morgan of Weston, Mr Middlemoor, yourself, my two sons, Mr Dormer, myself etc) should stand good and valid without cavil at such indifferent easy value as good neighbours would find them, and that the Commissioners, allowing of those rates, should grant leases accordingly: that then Bee should have a good sum for his labour. But in fine he could give no assurance of more than ordinary usage by the Commissioners in this behalf, for that every man is left to his own fortune, the Commissioners going on very slowly in the affair, and with those few that they compound use little favour and pass of late very few leases or none. The exigent against you is not returnable until Easter term, and then will he expect that you should appear and plead. But by the course of the Court he is to make two [*inserted*: several] motions in a week's distance before the judges will grant a peremptory rule; and by that time I shall be better instructed how to do as well for you as for myself. In the mean time, I will give order that by putting in a *supersedeas* the first day of the term he shall not return [*deleted*: outlaw you] the writ outlawed. And [*deleted*: upon] when he hath had a trial and recovery against you for three months, the better opinion is that it is a conviction whereupon you may have your land found and go to a composition if it shall be hereafter thought best so to do. As soon as I can find the safest and best way [*deleted*: for myself] I shall desire my friends to walk with me and omit no opportunity to acquaint you therewith. But by paying in the £60[3] you have no benefit [*deleted*: or] but [*deleted*: that] are still subject to be indicted again [*deleted*: whensoever the malice of man shall induce or provoke].

[1] On 20 February 1632/3, five Warwickshire recusants had also been indicted in Middlesex, as of St Andrew's Holborn: Thomas Morgan of Weston-under-Weatherley; Richard Middlemore of Edgbaston; Anthony Dormer of Budbrook (Grove Park); Sir Charles Smyth of Wootton Wawen; and Anthony Sheldon of Temple Grafton: Jeaffreson, *Middlesex County Records*, III. 45. They were indicted again on 1 September 1634: ibid., 54, 134. The names mentioned in this letter show that it was written after 20 February 1632/3. But since then, there has been a 'treaty' at the beginning of last term, the Commissioners have been going on very slowly, and the exigent against Russell is not returnable until Easter term. So this letter is likely to have been written nearly a year after the last one.
[2] 'A refusal of the Judge as incompetent because the matter in hand was not within his precincts': definition of 1607 quoted in *OED*, 'Foreign', 11.
[3] The £60 was for three months' recusancy: payment did not exempt the offender from repeated subsequent convictions.

137. *Sir Henry Spiller[1] to John Russell III[2]*
       10 September 1634
          Berington 623 (21)

Addressed: To my very worthy good friend and loving neighbour John Russell Esq. at his house at Little Malvern d.d.

Good Mr Russell, Some extraordinary occasions calling me lately to London (sithence the Assizes at Worcester) and the Sessions of Gaol Delivery happening in the time of my stay there, at the very ending of the Sessions it was observed by Mr Recorder and myself that divers gentlemen of name and quality dwelling in foreign counties were then proclaimed upon indictments for recusancy; amongst whom I was very sensible of what thereby concerned yourself and some other gentlemen of this county of Worcester whom in my true well-wishing I have particular reason to respect. That which was for the present in my power I then did, which was to require the Clerk of the Peace to deliver me an abstract of the names of the persons so indicted, the counties of their residence and the names of the persons prosecuting, who I find (upon examination) to be mean and base fellows hired or set on by one Bee, sometimes the King's servant. The note enclosed is the same I received from the Clerk of the Peace of Middlesex, whereof when you have taken notice in what concerneth yourself and other the gentlemen your neighbours and mine in this county, please you to return the same unto me, I having promised to redeliver it at my return to London. Before which time (if I may certainly know of your being at home) I shall be willing to come unto you and to second the testimony of my well-wishes both to you and the other gentlemen by any further good office resting in my power as, Your faithful friend and affectionate neighbour to serve you, Henry Spiller.

Eldersfield[3] 10 Sept. 1634

[1] For Spiller see the Introduction, pp. xxix–xxx above; Brian Magee, *The English Recusants* (London, 1938), 65, 66, 70, 71, 101, 110, 214–15; Notestein, Relf and Simpson, *Commons Debates, 1621*, IV. 102; British Library, Lansdowne MS 153, f. 1578; Hodgson, 'Sir Henry Spiller of Eldersfield', *Worcestershire Recusant* 1 (April 1963), 25–9.
[2] On 1 September 1634 six Worcestershire recusants were indicted for recusancy at the Middlesex sessions. Of these, John Weedon, Francis Hanford and John Russell had previously been indicted in February 1633/4; Francis Acton, Rowland Bartlett and John Hornyold had not. The next six items deal with the consequences of this indictment and show how Sir Henry Spiller, the Receiver of Recusant Revenue at the Exchequer, used his position and contacts to help his Worcestershire neighbours.
[3] Eldersfield is about six miles south-south-east of Little Malvern; the Russells owned land there.

138. *Notes on indictments of recusants*[1]
[September 1634]
Berington 871

King James, his Majesty's father of most famous memory, vouchsafeth in a printed declaration of his royal pleasure etc to use these words—fol. 27 and 28.

'Whereas we have been contented heretofore (and so are still determined) to bestow upon divers persons, according to their merit, some portion of benefit which the laws have given us upon conviction of recusants, we do first expressly signify our great dislike of such as, out of desire of their own private profit, have taken or shall take undue and extreme courses against any our subjects, as well by indicting them in places where they have no residence as otherwise'. Hitherto King James *lib*[*ro*] *citato.*

It is presumed that his blessed majesty that now is approveth not the course which his most royal father, by so plain and public expression of his sacred will and pleasure, so much disliked and endeavoured to abolish. We are [*deleted*: able to prove; *inserted*: credibly informed] also that there was an especial order made at the Council Table that none should be indicted where they were not resident, and proceedings in this kind stayed upon that order.

---

[1] These notes are the enclosure mentioned in the previous item: they formed the basis of a petition to the king on behalf of the six Worcestershire recusants indicted on 1 September 1634 (no. **142** below).

139.   *Rowland Bartlett to John Russell III*
         [? October 1634]
         Berington 623 (6)

Sir, The contents of Mr Brand's letter concerning B.[1] verbatim is, viz.— 'The Clerk of the Peace[2] hath given me, Mr Weedon and others of judgement and power their satisfaction that the indictment is void of itself.' But it is not so certain and undoubtedly to be allowed of as that I would have you to rely so much upon it as not to come, for that otherwise you forfeit your recognizance, and thereupon we stay the petition till we see the event of the indictment. We shall not plead till the next Sessions. My Lord Keeper, the barons and judges of the King's Bench had directed Mr Morgan's and Mr Middlemore's[3] convictions to be certified into the Exchequer, and yet they are stayed, which comforteth me much. Thus, with my best service to you and good Mrs Russell, do rest, Your loving friend and well-wisher, Rowland Bartlett.

---

[1] Presumably the informer.
[2] Presumably the one for Middlesex (no. **137**).
[3] Rowland Bartlett of Castlemorton (three miles south-east of Little Malvern), Thomas Morgan of Weston-in-Weatherley (in Warwickshire) and Richard Middlemore of Edgbaston (in Warwickshire) were among recusants indicted on 20 February 1632/3 and 1 September 1634: Jeaffreson, *Middlesex County Records*, III. 45, 54.

140.   *John Hornyold to John Russell III*
         [? October 1634]
         Berington 623 (13)

Sir, By this enclosed you may see that I performed your command in sending your unwelcome news to our friends, and, had the weather suffered me, I would have come to you myself. The mistake of my name (God grant it a mistake)[1] will absolutely discharge me from all danger, but I have taken order to have search made lest the mistake should be in Bettham[2] that sent this copy, and again, I am not a little perplexed lest the ill-managing of the business may make the mistake (if it be a mistake) to appear too soon before the tempest be o'erblown. Yours ever, John Hornyold.

This instant Wednesday.

[1] John Russell had clearly informed his neighbour John Hornyold of his indictment on 1 September, but the indictment might be void, as the name had been spelt 'Hornyfold' (Jeaffreson, *Middlesex County Records*, III. 54).
[2] The Bethams were a Warwickshire recusant family, but was this Betham the Clerk of the Peace for Middlesex (see no. **137**)?

141. *John Hornyold to John Russell III*
 [? October–November 1634]
 Berington 623 (8)

Sir, The continuation of your far more than friendly courtesies towards me I confess must be most burdensome to you; whereof I know not as yet how to unload you, so hardly can I spare the comfortable assistance I daily receive from you. I wish I were able therein to keep a proportionable correspondence with you, the want whereof, as I ingenuously confess, so you cannot but sensibly perceive, although your more than brotherly affection to me gives you no leave to take notice of it. But I stand upon my watch to attend all occasions to express a grateful mind, and[1] a wished-for opportunity be offered, whereby I may be able to put something in action that may give you argument what I would do if I could.

I have not heard anything of comfort concerning our common affairs but what your pen saluted me with; but that, I confess, was a good cordial. If you have received any news beside, I should be glad to be partaker of it. I understand of your going to London a week beforehand, because I intend, for aught I know, to ride up with you. As you are with a cough, so have I been much perplexed with a pain in my ear, the fear of an eruption doubling the trouble of it; but, I thank God, the fear is past, and so I compass the pain much better.

I doubt not that your letter to Mr Maskely will effect what I desire,[2] and as soon as you hear from London, acquaint your truly affectionate friend, John Hornyold.

This instant Tuesday.

[1] In the sense of 'if'.

[2] No. **143** suggests that what Hornyold desired here was a priest for Blackmore Park. In that case, 'Mr Maskely' may be George Fisher alias Muscott, who, having been sentenced to death and reprieved in 1629, was running an active apostolate from the Clink and writing lengthy letters about to it Cardinal Barberini. In 1641 he was appointed president of Douai and released to take up this post. Anstruther, II. 102–9.

142. *Draft petition to the king*
   [1634–5]
   Lechmere Box [E.12][1]

To the King's most excellent Majesty. The humble petition of A.B. and C.D.,[2] your Majesty's subjects, for and on behalf of John Russell, Francis Hanford, John Weedon, Francis Acton, Rowland Bartlett and John Horniold, gents., also your Majesty's subjects.

SHOWETH

That all the said gentlemen are, and for divers years together last past have continually been, inhabiting in the county of Worcester, near eighty miles from London, and not any of them in the parish of St Giles in the county of Middlesex or elsewhere within the jurisdiction of the Sessions held for London and the county of Middlesex;

That, nevertheless, the said gentlemen and oth[ers] living in several counties remote from London and Middlesex were all [indicted at the] last Assessions held for London and Middlesex by the irregular prosecution of one Bee upon the evidence of one Avery, an alehouse-keeper in London, who confesseth he had not been in these counties of twelve months before the said indictments preferred, and one Haines, an informer, who your petitioners conceive knew not the said gentlemen indicted as recusants living in the said parish of St Giles, where they were never resident; neither have they any notice given them thereof, contrary to the usual proceedings in the like cases, being usually and of right had in the counties where the parties presented do live. So that, whether they be recusants or Protestants, they (though never admitted to make their defence) will at the next Assessions at Newgate, being monthly, be convict and put to excessive troubles and charges, as your petitioners conceive: a course which your Majesty's most royal father declared himself utterly to dislike,[3] and contrary unto your Majesty's royal intentions heretofore in the like cases declared and thereupon redressed, unless your royal Majesty be pleased to favour them herein.

Therefore, to avoid all such irregular proceedings of such prosecutors in your Majesty's courts, and in continuance of your Majesty's justice and mercy, that your subjects may not, contrary to the usual prosecution

of your Majesty's laws, be prosecuted out of their own countries where
they abide, but there, when the cause require it, take notice of the prosecutions against them, and be legally admitted unto their defence before
they be condemned: May it therefore please your royal Majesty either to
give warrant and directions unto your Majesty's justices of London and
Middlesex to withdraw all such indictments so as aforesaid presented, or
that several *certiorari*'s may be awarded to remove all such indictments
into your Majesty's court of King's Bench and to be proceeded upon
here according to the usual course of that court. And your petitioners and
subjects shall daily pray etc.

[1] There is another copy in Berington 624.
[2] It is not clear who would have presented the petition—or whether it ever was presented.
[3] The draft cites the precedent quoted in no. **138**; cf. nos. **134**ff.

143. *John Hornyold to John Russell III*
           [?1630s]
           Berington 633 (9)

Good Mr Russell, I wish I were so happy at this time as to be of power to
accept of my cousin Read's[1] choice, to whose worth every way I am no
stranger, though not so happy as to have acquaintance with him. I have
disposed of the place two or three years since, and to one who I fear will
not prove so well as I expected.[2] But now there is no remedy, otherwise
I should have been very glad to have been advised by my cousin Reade;
to whom I pray you, when you next see him, convey my kind salutations.
So in haste I commend unto you the good wishes and neighbourly affection of him who will ever remain yours in all assurance of love, John
Hornyold.

B.L.[3] this instant Thursday.

[1] For the Reads of Gubbershill at Ripple (a Jesuit house) see the Introduction, pp. xxxvi–
xxxvii above and no. **147** below.
[2] Does this letter (with no. **141**) refer to the placing of a priest?
[3] Blackmore Park.

144. *Thomas Rea to John Russell III*
           28 January 1636/7
           Berington 633 (22)

Worthy Sir, I have caused Moris Hughes to surcease his prosecution
against you, and I have promised him that you will send him £20 speedily, which you may do by my son Morgan from Powick Mills.[1] He will be

careful for the good of your brother Mr Giles Nanfan and yourself, and I will be yours at command, Thomas Rea.

January 28th 1636, Old Radnor

[1] Powick is three miles below Worcester, at the confluence of the Teme and the Severn.

145. *Acquittance from Maurice Hughes to John Russell III*
     12 July 1637
     Lechmere Box B.38

12 July Anno Domini 1637.

I, Maurice Hughes of Old Radnor in the county of Radnor, gentleman, do by these presents fully acquit and discharge John Russell of Little Malvern in the county of Worcester Esq. of all debts, charges, suits and demands from the beginning of the world to this day and do hereby covenant to and with the said John Russell to relinquish all suits and proceedings in law [*whatsoever*] against him the said John Russell or Mary his wife or Thomas Russell his son and Elizabeth his daughter,[1] so that such suits etc shall not any way, either now or hereafter, damage, molest or proceed against any of the above-named, either on my part or on his Majesty's part on my information. By me Maurice Hughes.

[1] By 1637 John and Mary Russell had six children (see Introduction, p. xxviii] above), but only Thomas and Elizabeth would be old enough to be prosecuted for recusancy.

146. *Charles Stanford[1] to John Russell III*
     30 [?] 1640
     Lechmere Box B.1

Right worthy sir, I having safely come unto Oxford cannot but let you understand thereof, since by your most kind assistance it hath been most conveniently effected and I do persist to go sell my mare as I signified unto you. Concerning my nag, if Sir William doth not accept of him I shall not be discouraged, believing that your horseman, by your encouragement will so much help his pace that I would not leave him for £12, although I have been offered upon the way in one day three several bargains that might have won me to deal for another horse: all three very able and easy goers, especially a mare much like your bay nag, being thorough-paced and trotting like yours but her pace is singularly easy. The which, if it were convenient, I might have a week or two hence for under £7. Yet I am persuaded that you may more surely stead me if my nag be sold. Thus, with my many thanks for your manifold favours to me, most unworthy, as also to my cousin your wife and the rest of my cousins with you, I rest, craving your best wishes, and commit you to God. Oxford, the 30th [sic] 1640, your most unworthy kinsman and servant, Charles Stanforde.

If you please to write unto me, the direction may be to Charles Green of the Mitre,[2] and within unto me at Mr William Reynolds his house at Cassington.[3]

[1] Charles Stanford was related by marriage to John Russell, whose cousin Richard Berington of Cowarne in Herefordshire had married Ann, daughter of Robert Stanford.
[2] The Mitre is the inn still on the corner of High Street and Turl Street in Oxford.
[3] For William Reynolds of Cassington, see Stapleton, *Post-Reformation Catholic Missions in Oxfordshire*, 188–94. In 1568 his uncle Edmund Reynolds was ejected from his fellowship at Corpus Christi College, Oxford, and moved to Gloucester Hall, where he remained until his death in 1630. He was therefore a contemporary there of Henry Russell. The former manor-house at Cassington, now Reynolds Farm, still had its attic chapel when Stapleton wrote; cf. VCH *Oxon.*, XIII. 39, 46, 52.

147. *Charles Stanford to John Russell III*
       16 September 1640
       Berington 623 (27)

Most honoured cousin, My desire hath been to satisfy these good people with whom I live in attending until that she be brought to bed, which may cause that it be at least a fortnight, it may be a month, before that I may conveniently come into your parts; which I did not believe would so come to pass when I writ you an answer to your kind letter dated the 16th of August last. And therefore I beseech you to have patience with me and I will make all convenient speed to bring you back your mare you lent me, and make use of my nag, unless by your (undeserved) care I be furnished of a fitter horse for my use. For other ways I am not minded to take £8 for him, having been bade £10 for him of one in these parts, that now, I believe, would give it me, were my nag here. When I come unto you, you shall see my mare, for I have not sold her but she is now with Mr Richard Read[1] in your parts and, as he judgeth, not to be sold for less, although there is some danger to be feared that she may give me a fall if she be not more thoroughly mastered than hitherto she hath been.

Concerning news, the last is that of very good intelligence from London of the 10th of this present, that all the nobility were called by the King to York, except the Lord Arundel who is Lord Marshal, the Lord Cottington and Secretary Windebank, who are to assist the Queen. Many already are on the way—all are to be there by the 24th of this present; which hath been caused by the two petitions, one made by the Scots from Newcastle to the King, the other by twelve lords. All do urge for a Parliament, but it is believed that with the Lords only the King will conclude much better. Thus, with my humble respects to my cousin Mistress Russell, your beloved wife, and all my good friends about you, in haste I humbly take my leave and crave your good prayers, this 16th of September from Cassington, 1640, Your unworthy and troublesome cousin, Charles Stanford.

[1] For Richard Read of Gubbershill in Ripple, see the Introduction, p. xxxvi, with no. **102** above.

148.   *Sir William Russell[1] to John Russell III*
       26 October 1640
       Berington 623 (30)

Sir, I am to thank you for your favour in sending your son[2] with your tenants to the election of knights for this Parliament. When I saw the business would not be decided without going to the polls, I thought it best to dispatch those of our side first in whom I had least interest, for fear they should slip away from us, reserving my dearest friends for the last, when others should grow weary of attending.[3] So I put your son to a double journey and greater expense because I did build more on him (at a time of need) than many others.

Mr Palmer hath surveyed the ground that this bearer, Gardner, desires to take, and, as appears by this enclosed note, it is 75 acres, so Gardner desires to have but 40 acres of it and some timber to build and that (for you had written it) I allowed him when he pays his first rent. I have sent him unto you, and when you have agreed what part of the ground he will resolve to have, then I pray you draw a note in writing to express the bargain. Mr Palmer mentions the measuring of nine acres of the hill ground for Mr Willett. I conceive he hath mistaken himself in that, for, as I remember, Mr Willett is tied to have as many acres on this hill as Abbott's Meadow containeth. When I was last at Worcester, Ambrose Cooke was importunate to have [. . .] the odd £6 per acre for the assart and told me he [. . .] would not ever deal for it. Therefore if [. . .] will yet give £10 an acre, I pray you let me know as soon as you can, that I may put Mr Cook better to it. I hope about a week hence to be at my brother Hornyhold's,[4] and then I desire you would please to meet me to settle all business. With my due respects and your most assured to command, Wil. Russell.

26th October 1640

[1] Sir William Russell of Strensham (1602–69) was the son of Sir Thomas Russell (d.

1632) and of Elizabeth Spencer of Yarnton, Oxfordshire. In 1627 he was created a baronet and in 1660 he was nominated for the proposed Order of the Royal Oak: *Visitation of Worcestershire, 1634*, 84; *The Visitation of the County of Worcester, begun in 1682 and finished in 1683*, ed. W.C. Metcalfe (Exeter, 1883), 84; Nash, *Collections for the History of Worcestershire*, II. 482–4. In the 1660s he was received into the Church by the Carmelite Bede Travers and set up a chapel in his house in London, where Travers said Mass twice a week. The furnishings there included a medieval chalice and paten and a crucifix by the Genoese silversmith Francisco Fanelli: Benedict Zimmermann, *Carmel in England* (London, 1899), 203, 209–11.

2 Thomas Russell I.

3 The Long Parliament met on 3 November 1640. For Worcestershire two strong Parliamentarians were elected: John Wylde, serjeant-at-law, and Humphrey Salway (see Appendix IV). Sir William, as a Royalist, would have preferred the unsuccessful candidate, Sir Thomas Lyttelton. *Diary of Henry Townshend*, II. 6.

4 Russell's sister Elizabeth married John Hornyold.

149. *Order from the Long Parliament to the Worcestershire justices*
   2 December 1640
   Diary of Henry Townshend, II. 22

Die Lunae[1] 2nd December 1640.

Upon an order made this day by the House of Commons now assembled in Parliament that all the Justices of Peace within the several counties of England and Wales be from this House required and enjoined to command the churchwardens and other officers of the said counties within their precincts to present unto them the [*names*] of all the several recusants within [*their*] parishes to the end they may be pro[*ceed*]ed against with effect according to the law at [*the*] next Sessions, notwithstanding any inhibition or restraint: These are by virtue of the said order to require and enjoin you, the Justices of Peace within the county of Worcester and the liberties thereof, to command all the churchwardens and other officers within the said county and the liberties thereof to present unto you the names of all the several recusants within their parishes and precincts, to the end they may be proceeded against with effect according to law and according to the full intent, purpose and true meaning of this order.

1 Monday.

150. *John Russell III to [? John Hornyold]*
   [?1634][1]
   Berington 619 (3)

Honoured Sir, I received yesternight, after my return from you, these enclosed in the same manner as you received them here. You guess (I presume) by the enclosing the author of the enclosed (though shadowed in a different hand) and give d[ese]rved credit unto them. I doubt [*inserted*: not] but you will [*be re*]adily silen[*t*] of the contents of the up[*p*]er and of the conjectured author of the inner; and humbly pray to return the*m* both (but sealed) by this bearer to your poor servant, John Russell.

I pray you, forget not to use your interest with Mr Kinge about the tree. I conceive 40*s* may satisfy him, but if not, rather try him with more than fail. I know you have much power with him, and I none.

[1] This letter may refer to the prosecutions instigated by Bee (nos. **134–42**) or by Maurice Hughes (**144–5**) or to some other threat. Since there is no means of dating, it has been placed last of John Russell's letters. It has survived because the recipient did return it as requested.

151.　*Lord Keeper Littleton*[1] *to the sheriff etc. of Worcestershire*
　　　　8 November 1641
　　　　Diary of Henry Townshend, II. 44

To his loving friends the Sheriff, Deputy Lieutenants and Justices of the Peace within the county of Wigorn. Whereas there hath been notice given to the Parliament that the Popish recusants have appointed a day to assemble themselves, being the 18th day of this instant November, within certain counties of this kingdom, whereof your county is one, which may tend to the great disturbance of the peace of this kingdom: These are therefore, in his Majesty's name and by the authority of the Parliament, to will and require you, the then Sheriff and Deputy Lieutenants, Justices of the Peace and all other officers of the several counties, to look carefully that no such unlawful assemblies shall be; and to require you to suppress such assemblies or meetings by the force of the county or otherwise, as you will answer to the contrary. London, this 8th November 1641. Edw[ard] Littleton.

[1] Edward Littleton (1589–1645) was briefly Lord Keeper from January 1641 to May 1642. He came from North Wales and was not related to the Lytteltons of Hagley (nos. **56, 148**).

152.　*Certificate of search at Little Malvern*
　　　　28 February 1641/2
　　　　Berington 631

These are to give notice to all those whom it may or shall concern that

I, Charles Wright, Messenger and Servant to the Commons House of Parliament, have made diligent search in the house of Thomas Russell of Mawborn Parva in the county of Worcester, Esq., for Jesuits, Romish priests, all Massing stuff, Popish relics, Popish books and warlike ammunition, but did not find any such in the house, as John Bayle of Worcester, who was with me at the searching of the house, doth witness; as also that the said Thomas Russell is and will be ready at all times to attend the pleasure of the honourable House. Given under my hand the 28th of February 1641/2. Charles Wright, Messenger. John Bayle, Apparitor of the Deanery of Powick.

153. *Sir Simon Archer*[1] *to Thomas Habington*
      23 April 1642
      Berington 632

Addressed: To his much honoured friend Thomas Habington Esq. of Henlip these present.

Sir, I have sent you herewith those parcels of manuscripts I lately received from you, for which I render you many thanks. I have also sent you a kind of rent-roll concerning the Priory of Worcester: I found it amongst some papers of Mr Russells of Little Malvern.[2] When you have done with it, I pray you return it to him again with my thanks for the use of it. I should be much beholding unto you if I might see his ancient deeds or ledger-books, if he hath any concerning that Priory. There was land in Warwickshire given to it: I would very willingly know who were the donors thereof; I hope by your good means to procure such a favour. I shall be very glad to hear that your labours were at the press. So, presenting mine and my wife's kind respects to you and your lady and all yours, I rest, Your affectionate friend to serve you, J. Symon Archer.

Tanworth, the 23 of April 1642.

[1] Sir Simon Archer (1581–1662) of Umberslade Park in Tanworth-in-Arden, Warks., was a pioneer in county history and a friend of William Burton, Spelman, Cotton, Dodsworth and Sir William Dugdale. In his 'Epistle Dedicatory' to the first edition of *The Antiquities of Warwickshire* (London, 1656), Dugdale acknowledges 'the signal furtherance which this work hath received' from Archer, 'a person indeed naturally qualified with a great affection unto antiquities and, with no small pain and charge, a diligent gatherer and preserver of very many choice manuscripts and other rarities, whereof I have made special use'.
[2] This letter shows that Habington was thinking of publishing the *Survey of Worcestershire* on which he had been working since about 1634. The Civil War made that impossible, and the *Survey* was not in fact printed until 1895–9, when it was edited by John Amphlett in two volumes for the Worcestershire Historical Society. On Thomas Habington see C.D. Gilbert in *Midlands Catholic History* 2 (1992), 37–41; *Recusant History* 26 (2002–3), 415–25; *Worcs. Arch. Soc. Trans.*, 3rd ser. 20 (2006), 129–38.

154.   *Thomas Habington to [John] Cox*[1]
      19 May 1642
      Lechmere Box, 'Items Included', 4 [no. on back: 5]

Endorsed: To my worthy approved good friend Mr Cox at Cokesey.

Sir, I beseech you to [*inserted*: see this] paperbook safely conveyed to Mr Russell of Little Malvern.[2] It is an excellent rental of all the lands belonging to the Dean and Chapter of Worcester[3] and may perhaps greatly pleasure them. I kept it over-long with me because I desired to know somewhat in it. I send you withal Sir Simon Archer's letter which I received from him with this book, whereby you may know his earnest suit to Mr Russell, which I greatly desire you to further, for the knight is my most dear friend and in many things much pleasured me. I entreat you also to let me have Mr Russell's answer to Sir Simon Archer's request, that I may certify Sir Simon of it. And resting ever much beholding, I rest, Ever assuredly yours, Thomas Habington.

19 Maii 1642

[1] John Cox of Crowle, five miles east of Worcester and three miles south-east of Hindlip, was a recusant in 1646: cf. nos. **184**, **132**.
[2] In 1642 Habington was eighty-two and perhaps willing that Cox should save him the ride to Little Malvern.
[3] The Dean and Chapter were successors to the cathedral priory of St Mary, which since the tenth century had owned the great triple Hundred of Oswaldslow, containing a quarter of Worcestershire. The rental is not now in the Collection.

155.   *Order for arraying of soldiers for the king*
      8 August 1642
      Berington 873

[To] the Constables of Welland, Malvern Parva, Holdfast, Berrow and [P]endock.[1]

By virtue of a warrant to me directed from the Right Honourable Thomas, Lord Coventry,[2] Sir Thomas Littelton, knight and baronet,[3] Sir William Russell, baronet, and others, that, whereas they have received a Commission of Array for this county of Worcester under the Great Seal of England, bearing date the 14th day of July last past in the 18th year of the reign of his Majesty, concerning the arraying, training and mustering of the inhabitants of this our said county for the necessary defence of the King and country in these times of distractions, according to the tenor of the said command and instructions under his Majesty's hand: These are therefore to will and require you to give summons and warning unto all the trained Freehold and Clergy Bands within your constablewicks, both horse and foot that are charged with arms, to come and appear before the said Commissioners, or any three or more of them, upon the 12th day of this instant August, being Friday, in the morning by nine of the clock in the morning, at and in the great meadow called Pitchcroft[4] near the city of Worcester, completely armed and arrayed. And you are to take notice and warning that neither you or they nor any of them [*fa*]il of their appearance upon pain of such penalties a[*s sha*]ll fall thereon. And further I require you to signify unto all such as are well affected to this service that so many as will voluntary come in at the day and place appointed with their arms or otherwise shall be well received and perform an acceptable service to their King and country. Dated at Kempsey[5] the 8th day of August 1642. By me, Richard Winslowe, High Constable.

[1] The parishes mentioned are all between the Severn and the Malvern Hills, in the south-west corner of Worcestershire.
[2] The second Lord Coventry (*c*.1606–1661) was the son of Thomas, 1st Lord Coventry (1578–1639/40) and Sarah Sebright (1583–1609): Cokayne, *Complete Peerage*, s.v. 'Coventry of Aylesborough'; see also nos. **84**, **101**, **110** above.
[3] Sir Thomas Lyttelton (1595/6–1650), governor of Bewdley in 1643–4, was the eldest son of Sir John Lyttelton and Meriel Bromley, sister of the Sir Henry Bromley who searched Hindlip in 1606. He lived at Hagley, near Stourbridge, where Robert Wintour and Stephen Lyttelton had been arrested on 9 January 1606. (The Sir Gilbert Lyttelton mentioned in no. **56** was his grandfather.) His son Henry (1623/4–1693) was also a Royalist but was sheriff of Worcestershire in 1654–5 (*ODNB*).
[4] Pitchcroft, now Worcester racecourse, was where the Royalist army mustered before the Battle of Worcester in 1651. When Charles II dictated to Pepys his account of his escape after the battle, he confused it with the name of his host at Moseley, referring to him as 'Mr Pitchcroft'.
[5] Kempsey is four miles downstream from Worcester.

156. *The setting forth of a soldier*
[August 1642]
Berington 630

A note of such money laid out by me, Peter Tiler,[1] Constable of Little Malvern, for and towards the setting forth of a soldier.

Item, for four yards of cloth	13*s*	4*d*
Item, for canvas	1*s*	2*d*
Item, for buttons and silk	1*s*	0*d*
Item, for linen cloth to line his doublet	2*s*	0*d*
Item, for calico to line the skirts	1*s*	9*d*
Item, for pasteboard and loop lace		2*d*
Item, for linen of his hose	2*s*	0*d*
Item, for pockets		6*d*
Item, for hooks and eyes and tape		4*d*

Item, for making of the apparel	4s 0d
Item, for two shirts	7s 10d
Item, for two bands	2s 0d
Item, for one pair of shoes and tyings	3s 0d
Item, for one pair of stockings	2s 6d
Item, for favour	7d
Item, for tyings at the knees	6d
Item, for a cap	2s 6d
[*Item*], for a snapsack	2s 0d
Item, for charges from Thursday night till Sunday 2 o'clock[2] for diet and lodging, for press money	23s 10d
The sum comes to	£3 11s 0d
Whereof received of Welland[3] towards part of payment	40s 0d
Item, for charges at Hugh Shuter's when I took him	6d
Item, for charges from Monday morning until Wednesday morning,[2] and one to look to him	3s 8d
Item, for charges in Worcester for our dinner and other expenses for drinks	3s 0d
Item, for Welland[3] soldiers: they were at the like charges for these expenses, wherefore for this they will pay nothing, for they were at the like charges for their two soldiers	
Item, for expenses with Hugh Shuters	4d
Item, for making my books	6d
The sum is	8s 0d

[1] An undated fragment in the Collection (Berington 633 (1)) runs: 'Peter Tiler desires to be remembered unto his wife and his daughter and desires to hear the next return how all things goeth with her.'
[2] The days of the week suggest that the uniform was made on Monday–Wednesday 8–10 August, after which the constable and the soldiers stayed in Worcester from the night of Thursday 11th until dinner on Sunday 14th. They were to muster on Pitchcroft by nine on the Friday morning (no. **155** above).
[3] Welland is two miles east of Little Malvern, on the road to Upton-upon-Severn and Worcester, so that it was sensible for the two parishes to share the costs.

157. *Robert Cruse[1] To Thomas Russell*
         3 November 1642
         Berington 633 (21)

Mr Russell, I am sorry, not that you sent for your jack, but that you prevented me in sending you word, or those other gentlemen about you that were plundered, that I had such a thing; for I protest (as my brother can tell you at large), I knew not for certain whose it was. For when Dudley[2] saw I refused books which he would have given me out of your study (as the curate can justly testify, if he doth me right, that I told him I would have none of them, nor anything that was yours), he desired me to buy the jack, and said he hid it from another soldier out of another place. For it was in the alehouse, and the maid would fain have bought it also.

There was with me a man of Sir John Somerset's whose horse was like to be taken, and my man's sword was taken away, and we came hither by chance and were glad to comply with them (as your neighbours did too much). He offered to sell me sheep. I would have none, nor anything else, but Sir John Somerset's man was desirous to have one book that he saw, which I persuaded him by no means to take. Yet Dudley would needs make an offer for five shillings apiece to sell the jack and the book which he had, and Sir John's man had the book and I carried home the jack. But as soon as I came home, I told my brother how I came by it and wished him, when he rode that way, to enquire of you or others whose it was, that they might have it again upon the same terms I bought it. And so you shall have it, and should have heard of it if you had not sent first unto me, as I have acquainted divers with it and of my honest intentions therein.

It seems your man or his mate have reported that I bought many things of yours, but I protest upon the word of an honest man I neither have nor ever meddled with anything else, nor would not with this, had it not been in the alehouse and that others were a-buying of it and I wanted a strong one for the present. So that if you knew my intentions towards you and all men else, I was far from wronging you, but only to serve my own turn for the present and to preserve it for you at so small a price, lest Dudley should have sent it away (as he did a great pot and other things he also offered me) to Worcester, so that you should never have heard of it again.

And I doubt not but you will deal as fairly with me that I shall have the money again I laid out. I have also spoke to Sir John Somerset's man for the book, and he is very ready to send it. When my man carrieth the jack, or that yours calleth for it, he will deliver it. It was Gerard[*s*] *Herbal*,[3] which is of a good value, and I wished him to be careful not to do it away, neither hath he; they both cost but ten shillings.

You were much beholding to some of your neighbours to show him your cattle and goods etc. I was sorry, being a stranger unto you, to see you so abused. But for any action concerning myself (coming accidentally thither for my sword and sitting up with Dudley, having no lodging, and so complying with him for company's sake), I have given you a true account. If it had not rained, I had been gone before I ever saw the jack. If you have any other information concerning me, or any other part of your goods, they do me much wrong and I shall be glad to give you any meeting, either at your town or you should be welcome hither, or I will meet you at Redmarley at any time. So, with my respects unto you, [*deleted*: being a stranger] being very glad you are in a way of recovery of your goods and future safety, I rest, Your loving friend and well-wisher, Robert Cruys.

Pauntley, 3 of November 1642

[1] The Cruses lived at Pauntley Court, seven miles south of Little Malvern and near Redmarley d'Abitot, where they have monuments in the church.

[2] 'Dud Dudley', a son of Edward, Lord Dudley, was a Royalist colonel and General of the Ordnance to Prince Maurice. He is famous for discovering how to smelt iron with coal instead of charcoal. During the Civil War he raised men in Staffordshire and Worcestershire at his own cost—and maintained them, at least in part and to begin with, by pillaging, as this letter records. Among others who were plundered was Rowland Bartlett of Castlemorton, who had been indicted for recusancy in 1634 with John Russell III; see nos. **139**, **184**. Dudley died in 1684 and was buried in St Helen's, Worcester, which during the second half of the twentieth century was used for storing county and diocesan records, including the Berington Collection.

[3] A copy of John Gerard, *The Herball, or Generall Historie of Plants* (London, 1636), is still among the books from Little Malvern in Birmingham University Library.

158. *Three letters on one sheet*
[? October–November 1642][1]
Berington 633 (31)

(*a*) *William Prym to Thomas Russell*

Sir, My master[2] is now going forth and wished me to write unto you that he cannot have leisure to keep your court before his going to London, for he goeth towards London this day sevennight and is engaged every day before his going. And so with my service I rest, Yours to be commanded, William Prym.

Poole Court[3]

(*b*) *Thomas Russell to Edmund Russell*

Dear Uncle, Here you may see what I have from Mr Dowdswell: therefore we must go unto him with all convenient speed. The party went yesterday from me towards Worcester. Thereof is the best wishes of Your nephew and servant, Thomas Russell.

Tuesday instant.

(*c*) *Edmund Russell to Thomas Russell*

Worthy and dear nephew, I find there is a great necessity of a timely haste, but what day will best suit with our journey I cannot at this time express but, referring it to God, consider the best we can of it. If you send to me before I come to you, upon your notice given [*I will*] instantly come [*to you*]. If I come to you before you send, I beseech you resolve to go along immediately with me. So, praying God above to bless and direct us in this and all our other actions, I take leave and will remain your unc[*le and servant*],[4] Edmund Russell.

[1] Aileen Hodgson identified 'the party' that had gone towards Worcester (in **158**(*b*)) as Dudley's plundering party (cf. **157**), and therefore dated these letters to the end of October or the beginning of November 1642. The phrase is as likely to mean 'the party that brought this letter', but since there is no other clue to the date, I have left them here. Cf. nos. **161–2**.
[2] Richard Dowdeswell. After the Restoration, he was MP for Tewkesbury.
[3] Pull Court was at Queenhill, six miles east-south-east of Little Malvern and halfway between Tewkesbury and Upton-upon-Severn. It was rebuilt by the Dowdeswells in 1838 and is now part of Bredon School and separated from Queenhill church by the M50.
[4] Cf. nos **175**, **178**, **187**, **193**.

159. *Sir Rowland Berkeley*[1] *to Thomas Russell*
18 December 1643
Lechmere Box C.2

Sir, I having received a commission from his Majesty for the trained band horse of this county to be under my command, together with a letter for the speedy calling in of the said horse for the defence of the county, and you being charged with a man and horse, these are, in his Majesty's name and by virtue of the authority aforesaid, to require you to send in to me to the College Green[2] in Worcester by eleven of the clock in the morning of the 30th day of this month a man and horse armed for present service in the war.[3] Your punctual service hereof will be a special testimony of your good affection to his Majesty's cause and service, I having command to return the names of all those who shall refuse and to take sure course with them as I shall think fit for the fetching in of a horse and man. But I doubt not of performance in you herein: I only add this to give you the like notice as to all others, and rest, Your assured friend to serve you, Rowland Berkeley.

Cotheridge[4] the 18th of December 1643.

[1] Sir Rowland Berkeley (1613–1698) was MP for Worcester and later one of the intended Knights of the Royal Oak. Sir Rowland's first cousin, Thomas Berkeley of Spetchley, became a Catholic about 1649, but the Cotheridge line remained Protestants. See T.B. Trappes-Lomax, 'The Berkeleys of Spetchley and their Contribution to the Survival of the Faith in Worcestershire', *Biographical Studies* [*Recusant History*] 1 (1951–2), 45–58; Hodgson, 'The Berkeley Family of Spetchley Park, Worcestershire: I', *Worcestershire Recusant* 14 (December 1969).
[2] College Green is the large open space to the south of Worcester Cathedral.

[3] On 22 June 1642 the King had instructed commissioners of array 'to take notice that recusants, being disabled in law to bear arms, are to be assessed to find arms for other men, and if their tenants that are Protestants bear arms, you are to receive them': John Noake, *Worcestershire Relics* (London, 1877), 248–9. But many recusants did bear arms, and a list 'of the gentlemen that find horse for the county of Worcester' about 1643 includes 'Mr Russell de Malvern', as well as Abigail Pakington, Thomas Hornyold, John Nanfan, Francis Finch (of Rushock), Sir George Wintour (of Huddington) and Francis Hanford: *Diary of Henry Townshend*, II. 77–8. But Thomas Russell later claimed ' that your petitioner was never in arms against the Parliament' (no. **173** below).

[4] Cotheridge Court is four miles west of Worcester. Part of the Elizabethan black-and-white house survives, and in the church there are monuments to the Berkeleys.

160. *Proclamation by Prince Rupert*[1]
10 February 1643/4
Berington 876

At the Town Hall of the city of Worcester.

It is ordered by his Highness Prince Rupert, with the consent of the Commissioners and the Council, that the contribution money of this county should be raised to £4,000 *per mensem*, to continue only for the 10th, 11th and 12th months and after to return to the former rates of £3,000 per month, and, if occasion be, an abatement whereof; half to be paid in money and the other half in provisions at the county's choice. It is further ordered by his Highness, with the consent of the Commissioners, that with this contribution two thousand foot and five hundred horse shall be maintained for the better safety of the county and city.

That the county and city shall be no longer subject to any free quarter or billet free for any horse or foot soldiers, otherwise than for a night as his Majesty's forces shall pass through, without present payment for the same in money, nor any soldier whatsoever quarter without an express order from his officer in chief, who shall be answerable for the damage sustained by his soldiers to the party suffering; and in case any soldier shall attempt to force his quarter without order, they shall be brought before the Governor of Worcester or the next garrison and there be liable to a Council of War.

That no officer shall press or take any horses by his own power, and that hereafter there shall be no plundering of horses, cattle or goods, nor violence offered by any of the King's soldiers to men's persons for defending their own; and if any soldier shall presume to commit any such violence, that restitution shall be made to the owners out of the weekly pay, and martial law executed upon the offenders according to the qualities of the offence, for which purpose a Council of War shall sit weekly at Worcester; and that it shall be lawful for all his Majesty's loyal subjects to assist one another for the suppressing of such forces and the apprehending of the persons to bring them to punishment.

That the Petty Constables shall pay in weekly the monthly contribution of the 10th, 11th and 12th months according to the assessment of the Treasurer of the County; and if any captain, officer or soldier shall fail to pay his billet, then the Treasurer of the County shall default out of his pay so much money as may satisfy his quarters by the knowledge and consent of the Commissioners.

That all those who shall voluntarily arm themselves for his Majesty's service and the defence of the county and city shall have liberty so to do, and shall be assured their arms shall not be taken from them, giving in a list of their names and arms.

That no parishes which are allotted to any garrison shall be chargeable to send labourers to make fortifications of another garrison, unless by special order from myself.

That, for the ease and security of all the inhabitants of this county, the rates of provisions for this county which are or shall be from time to time sent in, for and in lieu of one half of the contribution money, shall be according to these rates following: hay per tod, 4*d*; oats by strike, 18*d*; pease and beans by strike, 2*s*; straw per load, 6*s*; grass per week for a horse, 2*s* 6*d*; cheese per centum after 2*d* ob. the best, the other for 2*d* per pound; butter per pound, 4*d* ob.; bacon per pound, 4*d*; beef per pound, 2*d*; the horseman and his horse to be billeted for 18*s* by the week, and 5*s* to have a peck of provender by day for his horse. The foot-soldier is to be billeted for 2*s* 6*d* by the week. That no free quarter or billet shall be taken by or for any horse- or foot-soldiers in any garrison, town or parish or house within the county, except house-room and such fire, candle and salt as them of the family use for themselves, with payment for the same in ready money according to the rates.

That no more soldiers be billeted in a house than the said house will conveniently receive. No quartermaster shall quarter any person without the assistance of the officer of that place. Nor that no women, boys or children be allowed to quarter without the consent of the master of the family.

That all those parishes, villages and houses within this county who have quartered any soldiers of the Lord Chandyes[2] and Sir William Vavassor, or any under their command, or have sent in any oats or other provisions to their several quarters, shall draw up their particular bills of quarter and damage, and restitution shall be made by Sir William Vavassor.

That, if any parish or person shall default of payment weekly, either in money or provisions according to their tax, that such parish or person, upon return of their names by the constables to the officer-in-chief of that garrison to whom such contributions shall belong and to the Treasurer,

are desired to have liberty to send forth parties of horse and foot to distrain and collect the same, provided that no person be liable to quarter
any such party sent out unto any parish or to any persons, but only such
persons as make default and are delinquents therein.

That all such provisions to be delivered in by this order and agreeement shall be delivered at the city of Worcester on every Saturday, and
town of Evesham and garrison of Hartlebury every Monday, to the Commissioners to that purpose appointed by the Governor thereof, who shall
keep books wherein shall be set down what is paid in money, what in
provisions.

That this be published in all parish churches within your [*parish*] cum
membris with all speed. Dated the 16th of February 1643. Your loving
friend, William Nicholls.

¹ Clearly the plundering activities of Dudley (and perhaps others) had aroused great
resentment against the Royalists, which this proclamation was intended to counter. But
there is no record that Thomas Russell received compensation for his losses a few months
before, and Richard Dowdeswell's letter to him (no. **162**) suggests that he was not alone.
² Grey Bridges, 5th Lord Chandos of Sudeley Castle, near Winchcombe in Gloucestershire. He commanded a force quartered in Worcestershire: *Diary of Henry Townshend*,
I. 51. His daughter, 'frances shandus of Shoodle Castle', married the recusant Edmund
Fortescue of Cookhill, near Coughton, where Dom Augustine Baker had been living in
1606. Their daughter Elizabeth Fortescue (1645–1675) was clothed as a Franciscan at Princenhoff in 1663: Richard Trappes-Lomax, ed., *The English Franciscan Nuns, 1619–1821,
and the Friars Minor of the Same Province, 1618–1761*, CRS 24 (London, 1922), 36;
Frances Agnes Onslow, '"Born in Wooster": A Second Instalment', *Worcestershire Recusant* 21 (June 1973), 20–21. Sudeley Castle was slighted by order of Parliament in 1649
and rebuilt in the nineteenth century.

161. *Richard Hopton to Thomas Russell*
          19 February 1643/4
          Berington 633 (24)

Good cousin Russell and much esteemed, I am much rejoiced to hear of
your well-being with your new spouse, wishing you both all health and
happiness, with all joy to your own heart contentment. It was no want of
goodwill but merely mine own want and necessities which hath hindered
me all this while in giving you content for my [*deleted: illegible*] oxen's
keeping and with my man [*sic*]. And, though I cannot satisfy you at this
present, yet (God willing) I will do it some time the next week, with
many thanks. The mean time and ever, I shall rest, Your most assured
loving kinsman and friend to serve you, Richard Hopton.

Canon Froome, 19 February 1643/4

162. *Richard Dowdeswell to Thomas Russell*
   28 May [1644?][1]
   Berington 633 (17)

Good sir, As the present occasions stand, it seems no former contributions are to give any ease. It is not your case alone. Voluntary acts take great impression for future beings, but what help to propose in this particular I no ways know. The God of heaven and earth send us the blessing of peace and enable us to bear what happens. So I am, Your most faithful friend and servant, Richard Dowdeswell.

Poole Court, 28th May.

Plunders and losses are accounted only misfortunes to the sufferers.

[1] The context seems to be that of nos. **157**, **160**, which suggests that the year is 1644.

163. *Receipt for monthly contribution to the king's army*
   7 August 1644
   Hodgson Transcripts; source unidentified

August 7th 1644. Received of Thomas Russell Esqr of Malvern Parva the sum of three pounds fourteen shillings and fourpence for the 14th monthly contribution.[1] I said, received by me. Thomas Wrenford.[2]

[1] For the way in which such assessments were apportioned among the tenants on the estate, see no. **179**. At the end of August Thomas Russell's assessment was raised to £4 11*s* 0*d*: *Diary of Henry Townshend*, II. 177.
[2] For the Wrenfords, see no. **57** above, though there is no Wrenford pedigree in *Visitation of the County of Worcester, 1569*, or *Visitation of Worcestershire, 1634*.

164. *Demand and receipt for contribution in kind*[1]
   6 March 1644/5
   Berington 877

To the Constables or tithing-man of Little Malvern.

These are to will and require you upon sight hereof to bring in this present day to The Talbot at Upton-upon-Severn four quarter of oats for Captain Brewerton, whereof fail not at your uttermost peril. M. Stampe, Quartermaster.

March 6th 1644

March. Received in full of this warrant of Mr Thomas Russell four quarter of oats for Captain Brewerton. I say, received. p.c. M. Stampe, Quartermaster.

¹ The warrant is addressed to the constables as officers of the parish, the receipt to Russell, who clearly had to supply the oats himself.

165. *Humphrey Lutley¹ to Thomas Russell²*
      17 January [1642–53]
      Berington 633 (12)

Cousin, If you please to send your Commissioner to Harvington betwixt this and Friday come sevennight, he shall be very welcome, and if Sir John Yate³ and he can end the business I shall be very glad. If not, I must be forward to take that course I will think fit, for to refer it to ump[*ires or*] any else, I will not, nor delay it any longer. And whereas you desire my bond for standing to the Commissioner's agreement, I will not give it, but my word passed shall by the grace of God serve you as well as any bond I can make. And if you will not stand to the Commissioner's award, I shall try what I can do upon the security I have. I[*n*] case your Commissioner come not within the time prefixed, I shall presume you allow this way of proceeding, and rest, and shall be ready to serve you what else you please to command your poor servant and kinsman, H. Lutley. January 17

¹ For Humphrey Lutley (d. 1653), see no. **132**. Lutley seems to have acted as agent to Sir John Yate and Abigail Pakington, like the Jesuit William Appleby, who was then employed by Elizabeth Darell at Scotney in Kent 'only to buy and sell for her and to manage her estate': Michael Hodgetts, 'A Topographical Index of Hiding-Places: III', *Recusant History* 27 (2004–5), 489. The Collection includes two other letters from Lutley to Russell (Berington 633 (16); Lechmere Box, C.38) and, according to Sir Edmund Lechmere's notebook (see Introduction, p. xliv above), a summons to Russell to appear before the Prerogative Court at St Paul's Wharf in London (Lechmere Box, [B.43]; not found). All these items suggest an illicit bequest, of which Russell was administrator but which he would not or could not pay.
² A copy of this letter is now on display in the Priest's Room at Harvington, where it was perhaps written. In December 1994 a rosary of about 1600 was found under the floor of this room; it had perhaps been hidden there in June 1644, when the Hall was pillaged by Parliamentary troops: British Library, Thomason Tracts, E 2.20 (ref. from Prof. Malcolm Wanklyn).
³ Sir John Yate (1605–1659), was often at Harvington after his marriage to Mary Pakington in 1630: see nos. **134–7** and Michael Hodgetts, 'The Yates of Harvington, 1631–1696', esp. 154–63.

166.   *John Unett[1] to Thomas Russell*
        19 [October 1644?][2]
        Berington 633 (9)

Noble sir, The perfection and real worth of a true friend being never thoroughly known but by separation and banishment from each other; who, walk[*ing*] in valleys and mounting hills and sitting down, did there revolve of fish and fowl, of man and beast, of fire, water, air, earth, heaven and hell and what else our wandering thoughts did fix upon. Thus necessity fronts us all and for the present doth me exile.[3] But, to replenish you with most absolute company, I have directed unto you a Prince endowed with all the ornaments of a complete gentleman,[4] whose wisdom and valour, policy and religion, are so perfectly mixed that hardly it is discernable whether doth ponderate each other; to whose company and to whose gallant parts I leave you; not forgetting to remember my humble service unto yourself and your courteous lady. With my thankfulness for my free welcome, remaining your devoted servant, John Unett.

Castle Frome, the 19 Saturday.

Forget not to run over your notes before you practise any tune.[5] I will wait upon you very shortly. Brown the glazier will be with you upon Thursday next.

[1] There is no John Unett in the pedigree printed in *Visitation of Herefordshire, 1634*, 147. The then head of the family, Francis Unett, whose monument (1656) is in Castle Frome church, married Sarah Nicholetts, sister of Gilbert Nicholetts of Hopton Sollers in Herefordshire: ibid.; *Visitation of Worcestershire, 1634*, 76. A Gilbert Nicholetts was the Under-Sheriff at the execution of St John Wall. A Richard Unett or Unitt was a tenant at Little Malvern in 1653: see no. **179** below.
[2] The mention of Russell's wife dates this letter to 1644 or later: cf. no. **161**. It is assigned here to the first possible Saturday 19th after the marriage. It could have been written in April or July 1645, September or December 1646, June 1647, February or August 1648, May 1649, January or October 1650 and April or July 1651.
[3] Despite the sentimental style, Unett's 'exile' was hardly severe: as the crow flies, Castle Frome is only seven miles north-west of Little Malvern, though the ride across the Hills would be further.
[4] This may have been a copy of Henry Peacham's *The Compleat Gentleman* (1634).
[5] This advice suggests that Unett may have been Russell's tutor.

167.   *Thomas Hornyold[1] to Thomas Russell*
        18 [August 1646?][2]
        Berington 633 (4)

Addressed: To his honoured friend Thomas Russell Esq. these present at Little Malvern.

Your news does much comfort me, and I am no less engaged to you for it. I am very glad your business is so well, but for my own part I shall be forced this term to go to London to prevent my conviction from being recorded. I know no better course, if you will send to Sir William Russell,[3] than to deliver your letter to Abraham his man, who lieth in Worcester on any Friday night or Saturday very gerdly [sic][4] in the morn; and if you know not where to direct it (as I have forgot), he will make William wrote the superscription, so it will be sure to come safe to his hands together with my lady's. Sir, I should have a tender of my services to you in proof, were I able, but I am still, as I ever must be, Your most faithful servant, Thomas Hornyold.

Tuesday the 18th.

[1] Thomas Hornyold (1628–1691) was the son of John Hornyold II, who was killed at Worcester in 1643. In 1646 two-thirds of his estates were sequestrated for 'Popish recusancy'.
[2] On the assumption that this letter refers to the sequestration, 'Tuesday the 18th' has been taken to be 18 August 1646. But, as with no. **166**, other dates are possible: May 1647, January or October 1648, September 1649, June 1650 and February or March 1651.
[3] Sir William Russell of Strensham (1602–69) was Sheriff in 1642 and Royalist Governor of Worcester. A portrait of him in armour is reproduced in M. Wight, 'Sir William Russell of Strensham', *Transactions of the Worcestershire Archaeological Society* 3rd ser. 1 (1965–7), 79, illus. on 98.
[4] 'Gerdly' seems to be a form of 'yarely', which is cognate with the Dutch *gaar* (*OED*); cf. *The Tempest* I.i.3; *Antony and Cleopatra* II.ii.216, III.iii.131, V.ii.282.

168.   *William Dingley[1] to Thomas Russell*
           26 July 1647
           Berington 633 (29)

Good sir, I was lately with my Lady Russell, and should have come over unto you but that I have strained my leg, so that I cannot well wear boot or shoe. But her request to you is that, when the neighbours in the parishes about you give in to the Committee (which will be suddenly) a note of their payments and losses, you would (if it be possible) procure them to mention Sir William Russell's[2] losses in their several parishes; and if they will not be drawn to particular the sum of his losses, yet that they will mention near after the enclosed note, which Strensham men will do upon Friday next. She knoweth not who to presume of in your parts but yourself. My most humble service to yourself and good Mrs Russell remembered. I am, sir, at command, Your servant, Will. Dingley

26 July 1647

[1] In 1638 William Dingley was indicted for recusancy in London as of Strensham (Jeaf-

freson, *Middlesex County Records*, III. 142), but was probably one of the Dingleys or Dineleys of Charlton, which is between Pershore and Evesham, seven miles upstream from Strensham as the crow flies (though considerably further as the Avon meanders). According to *Visitation of Worcestershire, 1634*, 31–2, William Dingley of Naunton Beauchamp, four miles north of Pershore, was a brother of Edward Dingley (1601–1647). The Dingley monuments are in the church at Cropthorne, a mile from Charlton. Henry Dineley of Charlton was the only Elizabethan pupil for whom there is documentary evidence that he was at Stratford-upon-Avon Grammar School: Philip Styles, 'The Commonwealth', in *Shakespeare in his Own Age*, ed. Allardyce Nicoll, Shakespeare Survey 17 (Cambridge, 1964), 118 with n. 2 (256–7).

² For Sir William Russell of Strensham, see no. **148**.

169. *Demise to Thomas Russell by the Worcestershire*
         Committee for Sequestration
         1 April 1648
         Berington 107

These presents witness that the Committee for Sequestration of Papists' and Delinquents' estates within the county and city of Worcester have and do by these presents demise and set unto Thomas Russell of Little Malvern, gent., two parts in three to be divided of all the messuages, lands and tenements of him the said Thomas Russell, being a Papist, within this county, valued at £141 according to the particulars thereof brought in by the Solicitor and recorded before this Committee: To have and to hold the same from the first day of November last for one whole year, yielding and paying therefor unto the said Committee or their Treasurer the rent or sum of fourscore pounds in manner following: viz. £20 thereof in hand, £20 more on the 24th day of June, £20 more on the 24th day of August, and £20 residue on the first day of November next; and also paying all payments whatsoever payable for the premises for and during the said term. In witness whereof the said Committee have hereunto put their hands this first day of April 1648.

B. Lechmere, Daniel Dobyns, Will. Moore, Wm Collins, Thos. Yonge¹

¹ The signatories were Sir Berwick Lechmere of Severn End, Hanley Castle; Daniel Dobyns of Kidderminster; William Moore; William Collins, who was the Treasurer; and Thomas Yonge, a draper of Evesham. Dobyns was a London merchant and a connexion by marriage of the poet Edmund Waller, from whom he bought a house in Kidderminster which had formerly belonged to the Blounts: VCH *Worcs.*, III. 169.

170.   *Edward Berkeley to Thomas Russell*
       1 May 1648
       Berington 633 (32)[1]

Sir, For want of healthe I could [*not come unto you*]
on Saturdaye laste, though I did verey [*much feare y^t I must*]
stilbee importunate with you for [*dischargeing of a debte*]
whereunto you and your uncle are [*severally engaged,*][2]
as appeareth under both your handes [*by two bonds taken*]
from you in y^t serious manner purposely y^t you [*should*]
bee careful to performe the tenour of that same agree[*ment.*]
I can noe longer forbeare my journey to London, so praye
you at your first leasure repayre to my cosen Richardson, of
whom you shall heare most market dayes at Mr Marshalles in
the highe streete, and geve him satisfaction in my own and your
executors behalfe. Were I assured of your lifes, having such
an extraordinary good opinion of you both, I should howld
my selfe well satisfied, but fearing y^t mortality maye befall
you, which is dayely incedent to every one, I dare not longer
insist upon y^r thendur[*an*]ce of your lifes. It is [*inserted*: to] noe purpose to [*illegible*: ?awayt] further; I refer you to my former expressions,
not forgetting my thankfulness to you and Mrs Russell
for my late and kind entertaynment with you. With my
kind respects to you both and also to your good uncle I
rest,
       Your friend and servant
          Ed. Berkeley

Worc. y^s i of Maye 1648
Y^r bond for payment of £200 is dewe ye 29th January 1639
Y^r bond for £150 is dewe ye 2 of March i640

[1] Since this letter is more damaged than most, the original spelling and lineation have been
kept, so that readers can judge the likelihood of the restoration.
[2] See no. **171**, which shows that the debt had still not been repaid two months later.

171.   *Edward Berkeley to Thomas Russell*
       1 July 1648
       Lechmere Box C.19

Good Mr Russell, When I went last out of your country, I writ you and
desired you to take some course in settling your business, and passing
further assurance in my behalf to your liking of my cousin Richardson.
What hath since passed therein I do not know, but (if it please God) I will

shortly be with you and will not leave you till your own and your uncle's faithful engagement be performed. For furtherance whereof in the mean space, if you two are not agreed already (as I hope you are) in the tender of satisfaction, I pray you fail not to agree upon it between this and my being with you; which I purpose, if it please God, by or about the end of this present July. Let it not be then to do, but speedily be dispatched, for I doubt not but you will make a fair tender which will be to liking. Desiring you not to fail herein, with my service to you and Mr Edmund Russell, I rest, Your servant, Edw[ard] Berkeley.

London, the 1 of July 1648.

172.   *Assessments of papists' estates, 1648*
          14 November 1648
          British Library, Add. MS 5508, f. 191[1]

The real and personal estate of Mr Thomas Russell,			
demised and sold to him, in the year 1646, rent	£73	6	8
The same demised to him for the year 1647, rent	66	13	4
The same to him for the year 1648, rent	80	00	00

[1] Add. MS 5508, f. 181v, is a letter dated 14 November 1648 from William Stephens (see no. **174**), solicitor to the Committee for the County and City of Worcester, to the Treasurer for Sequestrations at Guildhall, London. The following folios are his enclosed returns of sequestrated estates, which include Thomas Russell's as here.

173.   *Petition of Thomas Russell to the Worcestershire*
          Committee for Sequestration
          [December 1649?]
          Berington 108

To the Hon[*orable Committee*] for the city and county of Worcester. The humble petition of Thomas Russell of Little Malvern in the said county, gent.

SHOWETH

That, whereas your petitioner was tenant to this Committee for his lands this last year at a very dear rate and compounded as a Papist for two parts thereof, notwithstanding, the officers of the sequestrators took the issues and profits of your petitioner's whole lands for the said year: Your petitioner humbly prayeth that your honours will be pleased to allow him in his composition (for this year) for his said third part, your petitioner having nothing else to maintain himself, his wife, two children[1] and eight brothers and sisters, and being very far in debt. And the rather also for that your petitioner was never in arms against the Parliament.[2] And your petitioner shall ever pray etc.

[1] John Russell IV was born in 1647. Thomas Russell and Joan Smith had two other sons, Thomas (1655–1724) and Francis, and five daughters: Mary, Katherine, Milburgha, Anastasia and Anne. The second child mentioned here was probably Mary. For Thomas's eight brothers and sisters, see the Introduction, pp. xxviii, xxxiii above.

[2] In view of no. **159**, Russell's claim never to have been in arms against Parliament must be understood as 'in person, as opposed to paying for someone else to be'. Nevertheless, no. **174** shows that his claim was accepted. See also nos. **169–70** above.

174. *Certificate of the Worcestershire Committee to Thomas Russell*
          3 January 1649/50
          Lechmere Box E.11[1]

Upon the request of Thomas Russell of Little Malvern in the county of Worcester, Esqr., we do hereby certify all whom it doth or may concern that there is not any charge of Delinquency against the said Mr Russell taken before the Committee for the county and city of Worcester, and that two parts only of the said Mr Russell's estate, valued according to the particulars hereunto annexed, are under sequestra[*tion*] for the recusancy only of the said Mr Russe[*ll*], as by a lease thereof made by the said Committee doth and may plainly appear. In witness whereof we have hereunto put our hands this 3rd of January 1649/50.

> William Stephens, Solicitor
> Dan. Greeves, Clerk to the said Committee

[1] This item is numbered E.11 in Sir Edmund Lechmere's notebook but is numbered '6', also by him, on the back.

175. *Edmund Russell to Thomas Russell*
          17 March 1649/50
          Berington 633 (35)

Worshipful nephew, Whatsoever Mr Lingin[1] hath informed you, I am able to make it appear that the matter was fully composed. Notwithstanding, I find by his enclosed that he would willingly wafe[2] the same, although I am certain I have done nothing since our last conference to distaste him. I beseech you fear nothing, for, by the assistance of God, I doubt [*not*] but that I shall give him honest and fair content. I do daily expect, not needing to be remembered, when ourselves may have some fitting conference. So, praying God for his daily blessings upon us all, I remain, Your uncle and servant, Edmund Russell.

Coddington,[3] this 17 March 1649.

I returned Mr Lingine an answer, which, if you cannot with convenience send from home, you may on Tuesday next cause to be conveyed to him from Ledbury, which shall be soon enough.

[1] The Lingens of Stoke Edith, six miles west of Ledbury, were a well-known recusant family; one of them married a sister of the martyr John Ingram: Anstruther, I. 182–4; John Hungerford Pollen, ed., *Unpublished Documents Relating to the English Martyrs*, I: *1584–1603*, CRS 5 (London, 1908), 243. In 1586 a report on Ufton Court, Berkshire, mentioned one George or James Lingen, who 'under colour of teaching on the virginals goeth from Papist to Papist: is thought also to be a priest, so made in Queen Mary's time, and like to be the man that was kept in the top of the said Perkins' house [Ufton] at a time when her Majesty was but ill served by her officers in a search there made': Michael Hodgetts, 'Elizabethan Priest-Holes, II: Ufton, Mapledurham, Compton Wynyates', *Recusant History* 12 (1973–4), 102. Sir Henry Lingen of Freen's Court at Sutton St Nicholas, four miles north-east of Hereford, was Royalist commander of Goodrich Castle, near Ross-on-Wye, during the Civil War; his brother-in-law was Fulke Walwyn of Much Marcle (nos. **66**, **113**): Hodgetts, 'A Topographical Index of Hiding-Places', *Recusant History* 16 (1982–3), 165–6. But there is not enough evidence for a firm identification of this 'Mr Lingin'.
[2] A variant form of 'waive': see *OED*.
[3] In accordance with his father's will (no. **69** above), Edmund Russell, the younger son of Henry Russell and Elizabeth Pakington, had inherited the estate at Coddington, which is just across the Hills into Herefordshire, four miles west-north-west of Little Malvern and three miles north of the little market town of Ledbury.

176.   *John Lingen to Thomas Russell*
        [?] April [1650][1]
        Berington 633 (5)

[Ho]noured sir, [In] case I do not come at the time prefixed when I last saw you, to wit some time the next month, these are to let you know that I will not fail, God willing, to be in those parts soon after Whitsuntide at the furthest. I desire, therefore, that you will acquaint your uncle with the same, and withal to let him know that I expect to receive from him either the principal in whole, or at least the one half thereof, together with the arrears behind: otherwise I shall not be able to make any commodity of it, and consequently be destitute of a considerable part of my present maintenance and livelihood. Thus, with the tender of my best respects to your wife and the rest of your good company, I am, sir, yours ever to command, John Lingham.

[*Ap*]ril

¹ This letter seems to follow from Edmund Russell's answer to Lingen, mentioned in the last item; cf. nos. **170–71**.

177.   *Francis Ash to Richard Dowdeswell*¹
3 May 1650
Berington 633 (36)

Addressed: To the worshipful Richard Dowdeswell Esq. present these. To the worshipful Thomas Russell Esq. these be delivered.

Sir, There is no certain news. The York army, we hear, is to quarter about Newark, and that Montrose his army is landed in Scotland and the rest are in a readiness. All things, we hear, is agreed between the K. and the Scots, but very secretly carried as yet. I cannot as yet furnis[*h*] that sum you desired: I find very great difficulty to get in debts. When it is in my power, I shall very willingly serve you. With the remembrance of my due respects to you, I rest, Your faithful friend, Francis Ash.

May 3   There is
[*16*]50.   there is [*sic*] little news.

¹ This letter was written to Richard Dowdeswell of Pull Court, Queenhill (cf. nos. **158**, **162**), and forwarded to Thomas Russell.

178.   *Edmund Russell to Thomas Russell*
20 December 1650
Berington 633 (39)

Worshipful and dear nephew, I understand that Dannett¹ his steward hath found some of his master's cattle in Little Malvern, delivered to you by one [?K]ies.² This gentleman's before-mentioned steward is an honest and a near kinsman of yours and mine: you need not to fear but that his master or himself will sufficiently prosecute the offenders, which I myself will also undertake; as also that you shall be satisfied for your keeping. I pray you therefore, let there be no delay on your part in delivering the beasts, for that standeth our kinsman much upon to have that done. Now, in the absence of his master, I [*deleted*: trouble] will trouble you no further at the present but I will remain, Your uncle and servant, Edmund Russell.

Codington, this 20th December 1650

I will by the grace of God wait upon you on Sunday next³ by one of the clock or thereabouts [*three words unintelligible*], in the afternoon.

¹ This would be John Dannett of Bosbury, five miles north-west of Little Malvern and two miles north-west of Coddington; cf. Anstruther, II. 32. But there is also a fragmentary monument (1615) to a Gerard Dannett of Elmbridge in the church at Dodderhill, near Droitwich: Brooks and Pevsner, *The Buildings of England: Worcestershire*, 255. On 27 October 1624 Dorothy Lady Pakington wrote from Westwood Park, also near Droitwich, to Mrs Sarah Dannett of Elmbridge about a water-channel passing through the land of a Dannett tenant: Humphrey and Richard Pakington, *The Pakingtons of Westwood* (privately printed, 1975), 16.
² [K]eyes has not been identified.
³ 22 December.

179. *Assessment of Little Malvern*¹
       1653
       Lechmere Box A.24

The assessment for Little Malvern for the r[*aising*] of £18 11*s* 2*d* for six months' contributions from the 24th June until the 25th of December 1653. Assessed by us, George Hawkins and William Lane.

Henry Burford	14*s*	3*d*
Charles Burford	5	6
John Wrine[?]	2	10
Richard Wager	3	0
Richard Trahearne	1	6
Richard Unitt	1	6
John Howman	1	6
William Lane	2	11
Peter Tiler	4	2
John Cornewell	1	6
George Hawkins	5	6
Francis Burford, elder	1	4
Thomas Burford	1	4
Francis Burford	1	4
John Howman the younger	7	9
William Hope	4	2²

¹ This assessment shows how demands from the County Committee were passed on to tenants on the estate. For similar assessments by the same officers, see also nos. **185**, **194**.
² These figures add up to £3 0*s* 1*d* a month, so that over the six months there would be a shortfall of 10*s* 8*d*. Berington 381, an account-book, gives rents paid by some of the tenants in 1658: Hawkins £5 for the year, 'Widow Hope' £1 5*s* 0*d* for the half-year and Richard Unett 'all the rent [unspecified] due from him to me from the 19th of September last past'. See also nos. **196–7**.

180.   *Petition of Thomas Russell to the Committee for*
           Compounding[1]
           19 January 1653/4
           The National Archives, SP 23/115/1

1741 Russell.   To the Honourable Committee for Compounding.   The
humble petition of Thomas Russell of Little Malvern in the county of
Worcester, Esqr.

SHOWETH

That two third-parts of your petitioner's estate in the county, mentioned in the particulars annexed, are sequestered for his recusancy only.
Wherefore he humbly prays to contract for the same at such rates and
values as shall in your wisdom (upon consideration of his particulars)
be thought reasonable. And that he may have the benefit of such further
rules and abatement as shall be made concerning estates so to be contracted for. And your petitioner shall pray. Thomas Russell.

Jan. 19 1653

Referred to Mr Reading to report

R.W.   R.M.   (not drawn)

[1] By an Act passed on 21 October 1653, recusants and delinquents could contract for life
for their sequestrated estates, though if they failed to pay they would then lose even the
right to rent them. This application is recorded also in the *Calendar of the Proceedings of
the Committee for Compounding*, V. 3197.

181.   *John Weedon*[1] *to Thomas Russell*
           [1655]
           Berington 633 (48)

Sir, Mr Standish[2] returning on Thursday, and I not being at home, he left
word that you desired to know to whom you should pay in the money for
your brother.[3] To which I answer that it must be paid in London to Mr
Halsey the goldsmith,[4] the same to whom you paid the money for your
sisters, or else to Mr Perrcee,[5] or to whom you please who will deliver it
to Mr Perrcee, for he will not be satisfied to have it paid in the country.
Thus, with my respects, I rest, to serve you, John Weedon.

[1] A John Weedon of Feckenham was one of the Worcestershire recusants indicted with
John Russell at Middlesex Quarter Sessions in 1632/3 and 1634: see nos. **137**, **139**, **183**,
192. Arrangements for the younger Thomas's journey to Saint-Omer (no. **192**) were made
through Thomas Weedon alias Williamson (1637–1719), who was born at Hanley Castle,
the son of Thomas Weedon and Elizabeth Collins: Anstruther, III. 245. A John Weedon
who may have been Thomas's brother was ordained at Seville about 1668 and died in Kent
in 1694: ibid.

² Mr Standish cannot be identified.

³ Thomas Russell's brother Martin (see note to no. **182**). Their sisters Margaret and Helen entered the English Benedictine convent at Brussels on 24 June 1655 (cf. no. **186**), but Martin had been 'sent away' by August (no. **183**).

⁴ It is not clear whether Mr Halsey the goldsmith was a connexion of John Halsey, the physician to Elizabeth Russell. But a generation earlier a Margaret Halsey, daughter of William Halsey, married John Feake, the second son of a London Goldsmith: *The Visitation of London, anno Domini 1633, 1634, and 1635*, ed. Joseph Jackson Howard and Joseph Lemuel Chester, Harleian Society 15, 17 (London, 1880–83), I. 268.

⁵ Mr Perrcee may be the Thomas Pearce or Percy who was procurator at Ghent in 1648: McCoog, *English and Welsh Jesuits*, CRS 74–5, II. 263; cf. Anstruther, II. 239.

182. *Landing pass for Martin Russell*[1]
12 June 1655
Berington 641

Dover. Landed at this port from Dunkirk Martin Russell, Englishman, who hath been examined by us Commissioners for passage and is discharged and free to travel to London about his necessary occasions. Given under our hands this 12th of June 1655.

      Nath. Smith   Tho. White

¹ Martin Russell was born in 1632 or 1633 and entered the Jesuit school at Saint-Omer about 1640: Geoffrey Holt, *St Omers and Bruges Colleges, 1593–1773*, CRS 69 (London, 1979), 227. He was back at Little Malvern by February 1647, when he signed Berington 236, and on his own statement he fought at the Battle of Worcester in 1651, when he would have been about nineteen. It appears from no. **183** that he had subsequently tried his vocation with the Jesuits and was now returning to England, not having persevered or having been dismissed; cf. no. **186** below. He died in 1711.

183. *John Weedon*[1] *to Thomas Russell*
22 August 1655
Berington 633 (51)

Addressed: To my much honoured friend Mr Russell these present with my service at Little Malvern.

Worthy sir, This enclosed letter I received yesterday from Mr Edward Bedingfield,² to be sent to you with all speed and likewise to desire a speedy answer. Be pleased then to write by this messenger (whom I hired expressly for the purpose), and when I return from Boston, which will be on Friday next about one or two o'clock in the afternoon, I will call on Mr Tom the junior³ to receive it. I writ a complaint to Mr Knott⁴ that Mr Darcy⁵ sent away your brother in the manner he did, and I am told it was by his own desire. His return is very much desired, and he will be heartily welcome to the place and company he came from. Be pleased to assure him as far as you are able, so he will. Your faithful friend, John Weedon.

From Mr Tom's shop,[3] 22 August 55.

[1] See no. **181**.

[2] Edward Bedingfeld alias Silesdon (1595–1659) was superior of the Jesuit Residence of St George (Worcestershire and Warwickshire).

[3] 'Mr Tom's shop' must be a Jesuit chaplaincy in or near Worcester, but the residences of the Worcestershire Jesuits at this period are not fully documented: T.G. Holt, 'The Residence of St George: Jesuits in Warwickshire and Worcestershire in Penal Times', *Worcestershire Recusant* 20 (December 1972), 45–78. It seems possible, however, that 'Mr Tom the junior' was Thomas Berkeley of Spetchley, who had become a Catholic at Brussels about 1649: cf. nos. **159**, **170–71**. He was disinherited by his father, Judge Robert Berkeley, who died in 1656 leaving the estate to Thomas's son, Robert II, on condition that he was brought up as a Protestant. But Robert II was then only six, and until he came of age the trustees allowed Thomas and his wife, Anne Darell of Scotney in Kent, to live at Spetchley. Hodgson, 'The Berkeley Family of Spetchley Park, Worcestershire: I', *Worcestershire Recusant* 14 (December 1969).

[4] Edward or Matthew Wilson alias Knott (1582–1656) was Jesuit Provincial from 1639 to 1646 and from 1653 to 1656; see McCoog in n. 5 below.

[5] Charles Thompson alias Darcy (1607–1673) was rector of Saint-Omer from 1650 to 1655 and subsequently superior of the London district. Foley, VII/1. 45; VII/2. 769, 850–51; McCoog, *English and Welsh Jesuits*, CRS 74–5, II. 224, 294, 331–2.

184. *Return by the Worcestershire Committee for Sequestration*[1]
May 1656
National Archives, C.203/4

The names of all such persons whatsoever, two third-parts of whose estates in the county of Worcester the day of the said writ were under sequestration for Popish recusancy, and the times when such persons were sequestered in the said county of Worcester by the respective Committee or Commissioners for sequestration in the said county of Worcester thereunto authorised by Parliament, as followeth, that is to say—

Richard **Almond** of Redditch in the said county of Worcestershire, gent., sequestered for Popish recusancy 24 March 1646 and so remaineth.[2]

John **Almond** of Redditch, gent. 23 March 1649

Edward **Barrett** of Droitwich, esq.

Dame Mary **Blunt** of Penross in Co. Monmouth, widow, sequestered in co. Worcestershire

Mary **Batch** of Chaddesley Corbett, widow

William **Blunt** of Sodington in co. Salop, esq., sequestered in co. Worcs. 25 March 1653

William **Barnes** of Wolton, gent. 28 March 1645

Rowland **Badger** of Hanley Castle, gent.

Rowland **Bartlett** of Castlemorton, gent.

Jane **Bodenham** of Redmarley [d'Abitot], widow.

Stephen **Birch** of Oddingley, gent. 24 March 1645

Thomas **Barrett** of Droitwich, gent. 24 March 1645

Walter **Blunt** of Soddington in co. Salop, esq.

John **Cox** of Crowle, gent.

Catherine **Giffard** of Wolverhampton in co. Staffs, widow. 24 March 1645

Thomas **Hornyhold** of Blackmore Park, esq.

Mary **Habbington** of Hanley, widow. 24 March 1647

Walter **Handford** of Wolastone [Wollas Hall], esq. 24 March 1647

Mary **Kempson** of Weston, co. Warwick, spinster.

Walter **Luddington** of the city of Worcester, gent.

Theophilus **Mascall** of Tardebigge, gent.

Alice **Nash** of Elmbridge, widow.

William **Nash** of Selby, co. Essex, gent.

Abigail **Packington** of Chaddesley Corbett, widow.

Humphrey **Perrott** of Belbroughton, gent.

Amphilia **Roane** of Upton Warren, widow.

Thomas **Russell** of Little Malvern, gent. 24 March 1647

Richard **Reade** of Witton, gent. 24 March 1647

William **Sheldon** of Weston, co. Warwickshire, esq.

Thomas **Smith** of Somerton, co. Oxon, gent. 24 March 1651

Mary **Talbott** of Upton Warren, spinster

Mary **Wheeler** of Chaddesley Corbett, widow

John **Walstead** of the city of Worcester, gent.

Frederick **Winsor** of Claines, esq.

Edward **Wakeman** of Beckford, co. Gloucester, esq.

John **Williamson** of King's Norton, gent.

James **Yateman** of Redmarley [d'Abitot], gent.

John **Yate** of Chaddesley Corbett, knight.

Richard [   ] of Beoley, yeoman

Ann **Barber** of Redditch. 20 March 1643

William **Court** of Beoley. 23 March 1643

[   ] **Jacob** of Beoley, widow. 23 March 1649

William **Jacob** of Beoley. 23 March 1649

John [   ] of Beoley. 24 March 1650

Peter **Morgan** of Beoley. 23 March 1649

George **Maunder** of Beoley. 23 March 1649

William **Wagstaffe** of Redditch. 23 March 1649

---

[1] This return is included for the light that it throws on Worcestershire recusants who are mentioned in the letters. Of the forty-seven sequestrations, twenty-eight had been on 24

March 1646. Two had been in 1643, three in 1645, four (including Thomas Russell's) in 1647, seven in 1649, one in 1650, one in 1651, and one in 1653—all on or about 24 March. There had been none in 1644, 1648, 1652 or 1654–6. So most of these recusants had been under sequestration for ten years or more, and only three of them for less than seven years.
2 The words 'in the said county of Worcestershire', 'sequestered for Popish recusancy' and 'and so remaineth' are repeated in each entry (except where another county is given). These phrases are omitted here, as is the date, except in the nineteen entries where it is *not* 24 March 1646.

185. *Order to the assessors and collectors for Little Malvern*
    October 1656
    Berington 891 (2)

Endorsed: Malvern Parva

Wigorn. To Charles Burford, William Lane and George Hawkins,[1] Assessors and Collectors for Malvern Parva, and to the Constables thereof.

By virtue of an Order and Declaration of his Highness and the Council dated the 24th day of July 1656 for an assessment of £60,000 per mensem for six months more from the 25th of December next to the 24th June 1657 towards the maintenance of the armies and navies of this Commonwealth: These are to require you to assess at once within the parish by an equal pound rate the sum of £9 2*s* 4*d*, being your proportionable part of the said six months' assessment, and to collect the same, by distress and sale of goods if need require, in such convenient time so as the one moiety of the said sum be paid to Mr Ambrose Barker, our High Collector, on or before the 7th day of November next, and the other moiety thereof on or before the 7th day of February next following; whereof you are not to fail under the penalties in the said Order and Declaration recited. Given under our hands and seals this 8th day of October 1656.

           Gervase Burke   Thomas Bound   Henry Hill

[1] For Burford, Lane and Hawkins see also nos. **134, 179, 194.**

186. *Religious professions of Martin, Helen and Margaret*
    Russell
    11 June, 26 August 1657
    Dominicana, CRS 25, p. 173; 'The English Benedictine Nuns of Brussels and Winchester', in CRS 14, p. 187

Anno Domini 1657 11a Junii professus est frater Martinus Russel, Anglus, pro Conventu Bornhemiensi[1] sub Reverendissimo Patre Joanne Baptista de Marinis, Magistro Generali et Adm. Reverendo et Eximio Patre Fratre Jacobo van den Heede priore. Cedat ei in salutem.

[*Translation*:] On 11 June 1657 was professed Bro. Martin Russell, an Englishman, for the convent at Bornhem, under the Very Rev. Father John Baptist de Marini, Master General, and Prior Jakob van den Heede. May it bring him to salvation.

Dame Hilda Russell, daughter of John Russell of Little Malvern in the county of Worcester, Esq., was received into the monastery the 24 of June Anno 1655. Invested with the holy habit of St Benedict the 11 of July 1656, and made her profession the 26 of August Anno 1657 at the age of 25. Died 1700.

Dame Mildred Russell, daughter of John Russell of Little Malvern in the county of Worcester, Esq., was received into the monastery the 24 of June Anno 1655. Invested with the holy habit of St Benedict the 11 of July 1656, and made her profession the 26 of August Anno 1657 at the age of 19. Died 1712.

[1] Martin Russell was sent to the Dominican house in Ghent in May 1656 by Philip (Thomas) Howard (1629–1694), afterwards cardinal, and clothed there on 18 June 1656. According to Palmer, *Life of Philip Thomas Howard*, 97, 105, Russell's profession a year later (at which Howard was present) was for 'the convent of London' since it was not until April 1658 that Howard obtained the property at Bornhem, of which he became the first prior and Russell the first subject. Nevertheless, the entry in the Ghent register records that Russell was professed for Bornhem.

Russell was ordained fifteen months later, in September 1658, and sent to Brussels at the beginning of 1659 to study philosophy. In 1660 he was sent to Rome by Howard on business with the master general, after which he studied theology at Milan and taught philosophy in the Dominican house at Rimini, where he stayed until 1664: Palmer, *Life of Howard*, 118; Aileen Hodgson, 'A Worcestershire Dominican', *Worcestershire Recusant* 32 (December 1978), 24–9. This sequence of events and no. **183** suggest that he had already done part of his ecclesiastical course with the Jesuits before returning to England in 1655, when he was about twenty-two.

187. *Edmund Russell to Thomas Russell*
       13 September [1657?][1]
       Berington 633 (13)

J.

Worshipful and dear nephew, I have been enforced to travel upon a bruised sore foot all this week, till Thursday night I came home very late indeed. The morning, before I arose, there came an officer to bring me to Hereford before the Commissioner. I having no horse was forced to travel again upon my sore foot, yet, I thank God, I returned yesterday in the beginning of the night, my foot so sore that I was unwilling to rise this morning. Nevertheless, God willing, [*deleted*: I willingly] once this day [*is over*], if it be possible, I will wait upon you. I do continually pray for you and so remain, Your uncle and servant, Edmund Russell.

Coddington 13 September

¹ Edmund Russell was summoned to Hereford on a Friday. Despite his bruised foot, it is
likely that he walked the sixteen miles there the same day, returned on Saturday ('yesterday') and wrote the letter on Sunday, as otherwise the previous Monday to Thursday would
be 'last week', rather than 'this week'. If the day was Sunday the 13th, the year was either
1646 (cf. no. **184**) or 1657. Here the letter has been placed under 1657, but this dating
cannot be certain.

188. *John Nicholas, receiver general for Worcestershire, to*
Thomas Russell
3 April 1658
Berington 633 (52)

These are, in the name of his Highness, Oliver, Lord Protector of the
Commonwealth of England, Scotland and Ireland and the dominions and
territories thereunto belonging, to will and require you to appear before
me, his Highness's Receiver General of the county of Worcester, upon
Wednesday, being the fifth day of May next, by eight of the clock in the
morning at the sign of the Talbot in Sidbury¹ in Worcester, then and there
to make payment of all such funds of money, duties, annual rents and arrears thereof as is due and payable by you into his Highness [*or to any*]
person or persons for his Highness's use, by [*virtue of*] grants, letters,
patents, orders, contracts, indentures, releases or assignments thereof, or
otherwise owed. Hereof fail you not at your peril. Dated the third day of
April 1658, Your loving friend, Jo. Nicholas, Receiver.

¹ Sidbury is the street which runs south-east from the Cathedral end of High Street towards
Sidbury Gate and the roads to Evesham and London. It was the scene of heavy fighting
during the Battle of Worcester, when the King led a charge on that side but was forced back
into the city. The Talbot inn (named after the badge of the earls of Shrewsbury) has been
rebuilt on the same site.

189. *Thomas Russell's Discharge by the Exchequer*
11 July 1660
Berington 111

The County of Worcester. In the Charge of the Receiver General of his
Majesty's Revenues in the said county for the half-year ended the 25th
day of March 1660 (among other things) is contained as followeth, that
is to say:

Parcel of the possessions of Thomas Russell, recusant

Rents and Farms. Two third-parts of certain lands with their appurtenances lying and being in Little Malvern in the said county of Worcester, now or late in the tenure or occupation of the said Thomas Russell or his assigns, so to him let from year to year under the yearly rent of £70, which for the half year aforesaid is ——————— £30.

Ex per [*sic*] Wm. Chislett Dept. Auditor

Trinity Term in the 12th year of the reign of King Charles the Second.

Unto which charge (amongst others) the said Thomas Russell came here into court the 11th day of July this term and demurred. And Sir Geoffrey Palmer, Kt and Baronet, Attorney General of our said lord the King, allowing the said demurrer, judgement of the Court of Exchequer was entered: That the hands of our said lord the King shall be amoved from the possession of the said two third-parts of the par[*cels*] in the aforesaid charge and inquisition mentioned: And that the said Thomas shall be restored to the possession thereof, together with the issues and profits thereof whereof our lord the King is not yet answered: And that as well he the said Thomas Russell, as all other the farmers, tenants and occupiers of the said premises of the said yearly rent mentioned in the said charge and also of the said value found of the said premises by the said inquisition; and arrearages thereof not yet answered as aforesaid against our said lord the King and his heirs and successors shall be discharged: And that for the present he may depart this Court without day[1] by virtue of the premisses, saving the right and accompt of our said lord the King.

If gr[anted]
Exd by Tho. Hodgson abs recd thus [*sic*]

[1] *Sine die*, indefinitely.

190. *Philip (Cardinal) Howard*[1] *to Thomas Russell*
    22 September 1660
    Lechmere Box C.17

Addressed: These for Mr Thomas Russell at his house in Little Malvern—Recommended to Mr Francis Rea,[2] bookseller, in High Street, Worcester.

Sir, The enclosed will give you an account of your brother's[3] welfare. I hope he will be no discomfort to yourself nor me but daily improve himself in those talents God hath given him, for I am certain he wanteth nothing towards his encouragement or conveniency of improving himself therein. If you please to return him any answer, I shall as willingly serve you therein as in anything else of your commands. Your humble servant, Phillippe Howard.

London, 7ber the 22nd 1660

Your letters may be directed to me at Arundel House.

Howard seal

¹ Philip (Thomas) Howard (1629–1694) was a brother of Thomas, 5th duke of Norfolk (1627–1677) and of Henry, 6th duke (1628–1684); a nephew of the Blessed William Howard, Viscount Stafford (1611–1680); and a great-grandson of St Philip Howard, 23rd earl of Arundel (1557–1595). He studied at Rennes in France and was professed as a Dominican in 1646, ordained in 1652 and created a cardinal in 1675. In 1684 he was appointed cardinal protector of England and Scotland, and during the 1680s he rebuilt the English College in Rome.
² In the Worcester Record Office are wills of a Francis Rea of Worcester (30 May 1690) and a Francis Rea of Warndon, two miles north-east of Worcester (30 October 1695).
³ For Martin Russell, see the Introduction, pp. xxxiv–xxxvi above, and nos. **181, 183, 186**.

191. *John Greene¹ to Thomas Russell*
      30 April 1662
      Berington 633 (54)

Sir, I have sent the cloth but could not have so much as you desired, for Birmingham² market would not afford so much of this sort, neither could I have it in the country, otherwise I had sent it before this time. It is in all eight-and-twenty ells: it cost elevenpence the ell, and piece cost a groat over: the remainder of your money I sent by this bearer. Sir, I humbly desire, if you can, to procure me £5 or £6 for a little time, but if you cannot do it with convenience, I pray you send me word and I will make some other shift. Your sister is very well and doth present her best service to you and my mistress. I shall ever pray for both your health and happiness, and shall ever be, Your faithful servant to my poor power, John Greene.

This last of April 62

¹ A John Joseph Greene was confirmed by Bishop Leyburn at Edgbaston, near Birmingham, in 1687, and a John Greene and his wife were papists at Knowle near Solihull (cf. no. **197**) in 1691: J.A. Hilton et al., eds., *Bishop Leyburn's Confirmation Register of 1687* (Wigan, 1997), 234; Monica Ory and Kevin Down, 'A List of Warwickshire Papists, 1691: II', *Worcestershire Recusant* 34 (December 1979), 11. The sister may have been Elizabeth, Mary, Anne or Susan: *Visitation of Worcestershire, 1634*, 85; none of them are in *The Visitation of the County of Warwick, begun . . . 1682 . . . and finished . . . 1683*, ed. W. Harry Rylands, Harleian Society 62 (London, 1911).
² Birmingham, at this time a small market-town, is fifty miles NNE of Little Malvern, and for purchases there it would be convenient for Russell to use an agent.

192.   *Thomas Weedon¹ to Thomas Russell*
[1663–7]
Berington 633 (6)²

Dear Sir, I am safely arrived to London, and no sooner arrived to it than ready to depart from it for the Low Countries. I desire you to send up your son³ with all speed, for my stay hereafter in Town will be for him only. I have spoken with them that have care of the place concerning him, and they tell me it is necessary for you that you depose one half year's pay beforehand in the hands of one Mr Peaseley for his maintenance there. The negligence in paying of several gentlemen that have their sons thither hath been experienced to be so great that they have suffered no little damage for it; wherefore their custom is to demand security for the payment of the moneys for his maintenance. Mr Standish's word will be sufficient, and I question not his good will in doing you such a courtesy; wherefore, upon presumption of it, I have writ unto him in this behalf, and you may intimate unto him as much either by paper or word of mouth, for I saw him but once in my life and by consequence am of mean authority with him. It is required of you likewise to be one half year's pay aforehand with them, for woeful experience of many gentlemen's negligence in paying enforceth them to that what in courtesy they perchance would not do. I believe you will make little difference in paying before⁴ what justice expecteth to be paid once.

Wherefore, if you send up your son you must send up £12 10s for his first half year's pay, and besides as much as is necessarily required for the journey over, concerning which we have had some discourse formerly when we were together. Touching the sum of what it will be out of my own way, I think it will be thirty shillings out of my own way, and more if his arrival to the city be delayed and prolonged.

For matter of news, here is some good and some bad. The Bill against Catholics is passed the Lower House. Jamaica and Tangiers are like to be sold for £200,000 to the Spaniard. The Earl of Southampton's brother-in-law, a Frenchman and Huguenot,⁵ is arrived hither from France to treat with the King and Parliament concerning them of our judgement, for the French King protesteth to proceed with the Huguenots there as they proceed here with us. Moreover, London ringeth again with the fame, sanctity and miracles (and doubtless the country will be filled with it suddenly) of an Irish priest now resident in London by the Queen's authority.⁶ His works, or rather God's in him, are wonderful and strange. He healeth the diseased, cureth the lame, restoreth sight to the blind, and the cripples to the use of their limbs, as I could rehearse in particulars if it were not too long. Protestants and other sectaries are amazed, though not convinced, by evident testimonies, not of words but of deeds. The Bishop and ministers [*deleted*: are like the Jews in that] they attribute his

works to Beelzebub; but a Parliament man, convinced by the evidence
of facts, disputing with a minister about it, told him he would give him
half his estate if either he or any other of his cloth could do the like by
what means soever. God Almighty surely hath some particular intent or
other best known to himself in it: let us not be so curious in searching
what it is, but let us serve him and praise him. In the meanwhile I rest,
remembering my kind respects to your love and children; and remember
in your best thoughts a poor sinner but a well-wisher to your noble self
and yours, Thomas Weedon.

My lodging for the present is with one Mr Cooke in Duke Street, hard
by Lincoln's Inn Field, at the next door to the Sign of the Duke of Lor-
raine. There your son will find me if he come: if not, acquaint me with it,
I beseech you, for my only stay is for him.

[1] Thomas Weedon (1637–1719) was born at Hanley Castle, ordained in Rome in January
1661 and sent to England in January 1663: Anstruther, III. 245; cf. nos. **181**, **183**.
[2] The bottom of the sheet is torn and the date is missing, but the letter retains its seal with
the Weedon arms: Azure, two bars gules, in chief three martlets sable.
[3] Thomas Russell's second son, also Thomas (1655–1724), was educated at Saint-Omer
until 1676 (Holt, *St Omers and Bruges Colleges*, CRS 69, p. 227) and then joined the Jesuits at Watten, was ordained in 1685 and worked in England from 1690 onwards.
[4] 'in making one payment in advance, after which payments would fall due anyhow'.
[5] Thomas Wriothesley (d. 1667), 4th earl of Southampton and Lord Treasurer, married
Rachel Ravigny, a French Huguenot.
[6] The Irish priest has not been identified.

193. *Edmund Russell to Thomas Russell*
      2 June 1665
      Berington 633 (56)

Jesus

Worthy nephew, I was in good hope to have received some lines of
comfort in answer to my last, but, receiving neither lines nor message
to that purpose, in the sorrow of my heart I do present unto you the
words of Holy Job uttered in his misery,which are these: 'Take pity on
me, take pity on me, at least you, my friends'. Take pity on me; to use
many reasons or motives I esteem is to [*no*] end: you know enough, and
formerly I have expressed, I think, sufficiently. It now remaineth that
godly compassion do now put things in speedy execution. I present my
service to yourself and my sweet and gracious niece. I do and will pray
for the blessings of God upon you both, myself thirsting to see ye. And
so, praying God to bless and keep us all from all evil, I am, Your uncle
and servant, Edmund Russell.

From the prison[1]
June 2, 1665

[1] Probably Hereford Castle. An extensive Marcher stronghold, it was held by the Royalists during the Civil War, taken by the Roundheads in 1646 and mostly demolished in 1660. But the water-gate, now known as Castle Cliffe, was kept as the county gaol or Bridewell.

194. *Order to the assessors and collectors for Little Malvern*[1]
14 December 1667
Berington 892

Endorsed: Malvern Parva

Wigorn ff.   To Charles Burford and George Hawkins, Assessors and Collectors for Malvern Parva, to the Constables thereof, and to every of them.

By virtue of an Act of Parliament made the 9th day of February in the 17th year of the reign of our sovereign lord Charles the Second for the granting of a royal aid unto his Majesty of twenty-four hundred, three score and seventeen thousand and five pounds, to be raised, levied and paid by twelve quarterly payments in the space of three years commencing from the 25th December in the 16th year of his Majesty's reign: These are to will and require you forthwith to assess the sum of £4 15s 4d equally by a pound rate upon all lands, tenements, hereditaments, annuities, rents, parks, warrens, goods, chattels, stock, merchandise, offices (other than judicial and military offices and offices relating to the Navy and his Majesty's Household), tolls, profits and all other estates, both real and personal, within your parish, being the proportion charged on the said parish for the last of the said quarterly payments, commencing from the 29th day of September; AND also by virtue of an Act of the same Parliament, holden by prorogation at Oxford the 9th of October in the 17th year of his said Majesty's reign, for the granting of the sum of twelve hundred and fifty thousand pounds to his Majesty for his present further supply, to be assessed, levied and paid by eight quarterly payments beginning from the 29th December 1665: These are also to will and require you forthwith to assess the sum of £3 12s 7d equally by a pound rate upon all estates chargeable by the first recited Act within your said parish for the last of the said quarterly payments, commencing from the 29th day of September; and that you make several and distinct assessments of the said several sums, and that you pay in the said several sums of four pounds, fifteen shillings, fourpence and three pounds, twelve shillings, sevenpence unto Richard Hodgkins of the city of Worcester, High Collector, on or before the seventh day of January next.

And that you also return in a duplicate of the said several assessments to us or to any one of us on or before the said <u>7th day of January</u>, and if any person shall refuse or neglect to pay any sum of money whereat he shall be rated and assessed by you as aforesaid, then you or either of you are hereby authorised and required to levy the sum so assessed by distress and sale of the goods of such person or persons so refusing or neglecting to pay, restoring the overplus to the owner thereof, reasonable charges of distraining being first deducted. And hereof you are not to fail upon the penalties comprised within the said Act.

Given under our hand and seals the <u>14th day</u> of <u>December</u> in the <u>19th</u> year of the reign of our sovereign lord Charles the Second, King of England, Scotland, France and Ireland etc. Annoque Domini 1667.

Tho. Wylde   T. Streete   Tho. Symondes[2]

[1] This is a printed form with the variable details (here underlined) filled in by a clerk. Little Malvern was to pay £4 15s 4d of the £2,477,005 and £3 12s 7d of the £1,250,000. For an example of how these sums were apportioned, see no. **179**. For a similar Cromwellian order to the same assessors, see no. **185**.

[2] Appended are the seals of Wylde, Streete and Symonds. Thomas Wylde owned The Commandery, a former medieval hospital in Worcester which was the Royalist headquarters in 1651. Cf. Hal Dalwood, 'The Commandery Excavation, Worcester: Second Interim Report', *Worcestershire Recorder* 75 (Spring 2007), 5. Wylde's wife was Dorothy Berkeley, sister of Sir Robert (1584–1656); cf. no. **183** above.

195.   *Blessed Anthony Turner[1] to Joan Russell[2]*
         17 March 1672/3
         Berington 643

Honoured Madam, I return you many thanks for your horse.[3] I rode him on Saturday to Worcester, and yesterday back again. I find him not for my turn: he trots so hard that I cannot endure to ride him. News still continueth very ill, God Almighty help us. The proclamation for banishment of priests is come down: the time given them to be gone in is till the 13th of the next month. I beg your prayers and rest, Honoured Madam, Your faithful servant, Anthony Turner. From Gobberhill,[4] March 17. 1672/73.

Mrs Brent[5] presents her services, and I desire mine may be presented to your good company.

[1] Anthony Turner, superior of the Residence of St George, was one of the 'Five Jesuits' executed at Tyburn on 3 June 1679. His brother Edward, also a Jesuit, died in the Gatehouse in 1681. This letter was written immediately after the passing of the Test Act in February 1673 and shows that Turner was on familiar terms with the Russells, possibly that he had said Mass at the Court.
[2] Thomas Russell had died in 1670: Joan (Smith) was his widow.
[3] Cf. no. **53**.
[4] For Gubbershill see the Introduction, p. xxxvi above. The house is next to Ripple church,

which is famous for its misericords representing the Labours of the Twelve Months. It is close to the Gloucestershire boundary and the Severn. By 1582 'many Papists' were resorting to the house of Thomas and Rhys More at Ripple 'to hear Mass and to have other conference'. The Mores were watermen, but Thomas had also been Bishop Bonner's porter under Queen Mary; James More of Ripple was still a recusant in 1637. Halstead, 'Worcestershire Recusants from the Quarter Sessions Papers', *Worcestershire Recusant* 3 (July 1964), 13; Crichton, 'Rushock, the Russells and the Moores of Ripple', 36–7.
⁵ The Brents lived at Lark Stoke in Ilmington, seven miles south of Stratford-upon-Avon; their connexion with Little Malvern was that Catherine Brent married Thomas Bartlett of Hill End: Stapleton, *Post-Reformation Catholic Missions in Oxfordshire*, 45–9; Estcourt and Payne, *English Catholic Nonjurors*, 67–8.

196. *Will of John Russell IV*
16 *July 1676*
Hodgson Transcripts; source unidentified¹

In the name of God Am[*en*]. I Jhon Russell of [*Little Malve*]rne in the County of [*Worc*]ester, though infirme in [*body*] yet in perfect memory and understanding make my last will and testament as followeth in writing.

As for my soul I bequeathe [it] into the hands of God my Creator and my body to be buried in Christiane bur[*ia*]ll according to the direction of my exe[*cu*]trice.

As to [*my*] worldly estate, I dispose of it in man[*ner fol*]lowing.

It being my intention to keepe my estate in my name and family, I do give and bequeath [*all*] my reall estate to my dear Brother Thomas Russell for [*life*] and his heires male for ever, provided that he the said Thomas shall reside in England and live a secular life: and shall well and duely perfor[*m*] these following particulars in my will heare mention[*ed*]. That is to say that he pay six hundred pounds of lawfull money of E[*ngland*] for portion to m*y* [*sister*] Anastasia upon reasonable demand. And three [*h*]und[*red*] pounds a peece to my sisters Mary and Catherine [*un*]to both at one and twenty yeares of age with lawful oute[*goings*² *in*] the meane tyme for [*their fi*]tting maintenance. And to my brother Francis thirty pounds per annum during his natureall life³ to be payd without defalcation [*deleted*: with] by two equall proportions at the feast of St Michael the [*Arch*]angell and the Feast of the Annunciation of Our Lady [*But*] in case my brother Thomas shall dispose of himselfe [*to the*] church⁴ or should dye without issue male of [*his body law*] fully begot, that then my will is that my b[*rother*] Francis shall inherit my estate provided that he [*shall perform the con*]ditions [*aforesaid. And if my*]⁵
brother Thomas [*shall dispose of himselfe to the ser*]vice of the Church then [*I*] do give and bequea[*the to him 30 pounds per annum*] for the term of his natural life [to *be paid*] out of my lands with out any def[*alcatio*]n

provided [*li*]kewise [*that if*] my brother Thomas shall not dispose of himselfe to the [*Ch*]urch and yet neglect or shall refuse to performe the particulars of this my will that then it shall be lawfull for the Fefees in trust hereafter men[*tioned*] to enter upon and dispose of my estate by such lawfull [*actions*] and meanes as to them shall seeme best for the use and only behoofe of my brothers and sisters, until theise legacies of my brothers and sisters shall be duly payd and my [*wi*]ll duly performed.

And in case my brother Thomas shall dye beyond seas before his returne into England, and so my estate fall to my brother Fran[*ci*]s (to whom I do give and bequeath it in case my brother Thomas dye without issue male), then my will is that duringe the minority of my said brother Francis my Fefees in trust hereafter mentioned shall and may lawfully enter upon the estate and dispose of the whole revenue towards the raising of the portions of my sisters and other legacies in this will mentioned, and make lease or leases of the estate or any parte or parcell thereof not exceeding the term of [*?twenty-one*][6] years fully from the date thereof to be compleated and ended. Also I do give and bequeath to my uncle Martin Russell[7] ten pound [*per annum*] during his na[*tur*]all life to be payd by equall propo[*rtions at*] the Feast of the Annunciation of Our Lady and the Fe[*ast of St*] Michael the Archangel without any defalcati[*on. Item, I*] give unto Richard Wajer[8] and Marjery his prese[*nt wife the*] hous wherein he lives together with out-hous[*es thereunto*] belonging, garden, orchards and backside [*and plots*] of ground which he hath out of the Common in my [*liberty paying therefor* [*illegible*]] per annum if demanded, to have and to hold for [*their*] naturall l[*i*]ves, that is the house and outhouses etc [*aforesaid* . . .]

[John] Russell[9]

Item, I give to Sammuel N[*a*]sh my servant after the legacies severally above nominated shall be payd and discharged, that house back side and gardens plots out of the Common enclosed in my liberty for the terme of his naturall life which Peeter Tyler[8] now lives in. And I do hereby constitute my deare Mother Jane Russell, Mr Bridges Nanfan of Morton,[10] William Betteworth of Sherridge in Lye Sinton,[11] Jhon Davis of Solihull[12] in the County of Warwick my Fefees in trust and my deare Mother Mrs Jane R[*ussell*] my executrice of this my will and testament. And in case of mortality, or either of the Fefees nominated shall refuse to take this charge upon them, that then it shall be lawful for the major parte of the Fefees to choose and nominate any other in the place or places of the parties deceased or refusing.

And that my will is also that my Fefees shall be all [*recompensed*] for all their charges and panes, in witness whereof I have hereunto put my hand and seal this 16th of July Anno Domini 1676

John Russ[ell]

1 According to Aileen Hodgson, this will was in the Lechmere Box but it is not there now. For the circumstances in which it was made see the Introduction, pp. xxxvii–xxxviii. Since it is so badly damaged, the original spelling has been retained, as in no. **170** above.

2 'Out*goings*' is recorded by 1622 and 'out*set*' in the same sense by 1764. 'Out*lay*' was Scottish and dialect until the nineteenth century. *OED*.

3 Francis was still receiving £30 18s a year in rents from Castlemorton in 1694; see no. **197**.

4 Thomas did 'dispose of himself to the service of the Church' as a Jesuit and returned to work in Worcestershire.

5 The first page ends here. The bottom of it is badly decayed, and so is the top of the second. Since Russell signed at the bottom of both the second and third pages, he may also have done so here. If he did, the space needed for the signature would mean that not much, if any, of the actual text is missing. The restoration here assumes that that is the case.

6 The leases which the trustees were empowered to make may have been for a longer or shorter term, but twenty-one years was common and has been supplied as a conjecture. In 1683, the year of his marriage to Elizabeth Greenwood, John Russell IV 'conveyed' Little Malvern to Charles Trinder and others: VCH *Worcs.*, III. 451. Trinder, who was Elizabeth's uncle and a distinguished lawyer, owned Holywell Manor in Oxford and Bourton-on-the-Water in Gloucestershire; Challoner, *Memoirs of Missionary Priests*, 552–3, prints a letter written to him by St John Wall from Worcester Castle on 18 July 1679.

7 The Dominican.

8 For Peter Tiler and Richard Wager see nos. **156**, **179**. In 1715 Henry Wager of Great Malvern was a papist: English, 'Worcestershire Nonjurors in 1715', 35.

9 The bottom of the second page, like the first, is much frayed, but the surname of the signature is still legible.

10 Bridges Nanfan of Birtsmoreton Court (1622–1704) was the elder son of John Nanfan (who succeeded his grandfather Giles in 1614 and died about 1677: see no. **131**) and of Mary Fleet of Worcester. He compounded for deliquency in 1651 and was MP for Worcestershire in 1680–81 and 1685. *Visitation of the County of Worcester, 1569*, 99; *Visitation of Worcestershire, 1634*, 73; VCH *Worcs.*, IV. 31.

11 Leigh Sinton, a village at the northern end of the Malvern Hills, six miles north of Little Malvern and five miles south-west of Worcester on the road to Hereford. Bette(s)worth has not been identified.

12 Solihull, where the Russells owned land, was a market town, now a metropolitan borough, in Warwickshire, eight miles south-east of Birmingham. Davies has not been identified.

197. *Accounts of John Russell IV*
1694
Berington (b. 705:24) 381 (1)

[p. 262]
My Rents in Little Malvern, 1694[1]
Nicholas Lane for the Mill meadow by the year £42.
John Lane for the Northfield by the year £52.
John Lane for his farm £30 by the year.
William Lane for his furlong and Tyler's by the year £9 10s.
William Nash for his tenement by the year 50s.

Richard Nash for his tenement by the year £5.
William Merick for his tenement for the year £6.
Francis Burford for the Mill Close 40*s*.
The Mill grounds and two orchards are worth by the year £50

[£199 0s 0d]

A little tenement in the parish of **Eldersfield** which is out for three lives
to William Davis and he is to pay only twelvepence a year, but when the
lives fall it is well worth 30*s* a year.   [£0 1*s* 0*d*]

[p. 263]
My rents in Warwickshire in the parish of **Solihull**
Are now set at thirty-nine pounds two shillings and fourpence by the
year.   [£39 2*s* 4*d*]

My farm at Coddington in Herefordshire is now set to John Guilding
at fifty-five pounds a year, and I am to be at all payments. It was formerly
set always at threescore and four pounds.   [£55 0*s* 0*d*]

[p. 264]
The Rents in Castle Morton 1694 as now set

William Pewtrice[2]	£5 5*s* 4*d*	
Widow Toms per annum	£6 8*s* 0*d*	[£11 13*s* 4*d*]

The Rents that follow in Castle Morton are my brother Frank's for
his life

William Pewtrice per annum	£9 18*s* 0*d*	
Widow Kings per annum	£21 0*s* 0*d*	[£30 18*s* 0*d*]

[pp. 265–7]
Tax to the King

Coddington is but eightpence a year to the King and fourpence for the
acquittance.

I pay out of my estate in Little Malvern every year to the Crown two-
and-twenty shillings and eightpence, and twelvepence a year for some
land in Coddington, which, with fourpence for the acquittance, makes
just twenty-four shillings. It is to be paid upon the 29th of September or
thereabouts.   [£1 4*s* 0*d*]

I pay yearly to the **parson for Little Malvern** for the Church service,
due and ending at Easter, as you may see by acquittances, five pounds
a year, and I give him forty shillings a year more, but that is not my bargain but my free gift.   [£7 0*s* 0*d*]

I am to pay thirty shillings a year to the **Constable** of Little Malvern
towards his charges, due upon the 25th of December, and this I put as
a memorandum to those that succeed me.   [£1 10*s* 0*d*]

Old John Lane is to pay me a mark a year for his tithes for house and lands which he holdeth of my Lady Strood, below my windmill in the parish of Little Malvern, and he hath a good bargain of it too ———

[13s 4d]

My cousin William Davis gathers up my rent at Solihull, for which I intend to give him twenty shillings a year, that is, ten shillings every half-year, if he brings it so or sends it: and this I think a sufficient gratuity.

[£1 0s 0d]

Mr Savage of Eldersfield is to pay me fourpence a year for chief rent, and so his heirs after him to mine successively   [4d]

[p. 136]
November 13 1694. Then paid, the year and day above mentioned, of the charity moneys which I receive yearly from my brother Greenwood to my uncle Martin[3] and Mary Cettle: twenty shillings.

[p. 268]
1708. Malvern estate in all is £350 a year as it is now set, 1708. The rents at Malvern are £213 a year, the rents at Morton[4] £40 a year, and at Solihull £40 a year and Coddington £55 a year.[5]

[1] For this list of tenants, cf. n. **179**.
[2] For the Pewtrices (Pewters, Pewtresses), see no. **109**.
[3] The Dominican: see nos. **182–3, 186, 190**.
[4] Castlemorton.
[5] This note was inserted by John Russell IV's widow Elizabeth (Greenwood): he had died in 1701, when his heir, John V, was only twelve.

198.   *Probate inventory of John Russell IV*[1]
           22 April 1701
           Berington 392

A true and perfect inventory of all and singular the goods and chattels of John Russell [*inserted*: late of Little Malvern in the county of Worcester] Esq. deceased, taken at Little Malvern the 22 of April Anno Dni 1701 and praised by John Lane, Nicholas Lane and James Hill as followeth:

Imprimis, his wearing apparel and ready money in his purse, £45 15s 0d
Item, in the Parlour, ten chairs, one great table and other lumber, £2 10s 0d
Item, in the Hall, one great table and two stools, 5s 0d
Item, in the Kitchen, four dozen and two plates, 13s 0d
Item, fifteen pewter dishes at £2 15s 0d
Item, twelve patty-pans and several other tin pans, 5s 0d

Item, the several kettles, pots, skillets and other utensils of brass, £5 0s 0d

Item, one jack, two spits, two dripping-pans and the fire-irons, £1 5s 0d

Item, one bell-metal mortar, 5s 0d

Item, seven flitches of bacon, £6 0s 0d

Item, other old lumber there, 2s 6d

Item, in the Larder, a cold still, shelves and other lumber, 2s 6d

Item, in the Cellar, thirteen hogsheads and other lumber, £3 7s 0d

Item, in the Dark House, fourteen hogsheads and two barrels, £3 5s 0d

Item, in the Brew-house, one furnace, several brewing vessels and tubs [*deleted*: and one malt-mill], £2 5s 0d

Item, in the Bolting-house, six hogsheads and other lumber, £1 12s 6d

Item, in the Dairy-house, several cheese-vats, a press and other things, 10s 0d

Item, in the old Store-Chamber, some old pieces of wooden lumber, 5s 0d

Item, in the Cheese Chamber, several cheeses at £2 0s 0d

Item, some more wooden lumber there, 4s 0d

Item, in the Servants' Chamber, the bed and some other old furniture, £1 10s 0d

Item, in the Chapel Chamber, old household stuff at £1 10s 0d

Item, in the Parlour Chamber, one chest-of-drawers at 15s 0d

Item, the bed and other furniture, £4 0s 0d

Item, in the Lower Chamber, the bed, glass and other furniture, £5 0s 0d

Item, in the Little Chamber, some old furniture there, £1 0s 0d

Item, in the Maids' Chamber, a bed and other furniture, £1 0s 0d

Item, in the High Chamber, the furniture there at £1 0s 0d

£94 1s 6d

The sum brought from the other side, £94 1s 6d

Item, in the Wool Chamber: the wool there at £2 0s 0d

Item, the linen of several sorts, £4 10s 0d

Item, one silver tankard and other small pieces of plate, £6 0s 0d

Item, eleven cows at £38 0s 0d

Item, six bullocks at £22 0s 0d

Item, four yearlings, £4 0s 0d

Item, one mare and colt and a little nag, £8 0s 0d

Item, eighty sheep and twenty-five lambs, £16 0s 0d

Item, three store pigs and one sow and four small pigs, £4 0s 0d

Item, two wains, a plough and other tack of team for husbandry, £5 0s 0d

Item, fourteen acres of oats now growing at £6 0s 0d

Item, in the granary, sixty bushels of wheat and ten bushels of maslin,[2] £10 0s 0d

Item, hay in the hay-loft, £3 10s 0d

Item, barley at the maltster's, £3 0*s* 0*d*
Item, rent due at Lady Day last, £31 4*s* 8*d*
Item, a debt due at Coddington for timber, £10 8*s* 0*d*

Sum Total, £267 14*s* 2*d*

The mark of John + Lane, Nicholas Lane, James Hill, Appraisers

¹ This inventory is also printed in Wanklyn, *Inventories of Worcestershire Landed Gentry*, 286–7.
² Rye and wheat mixed.

199.   *Mr Pollet's Recantation*¹
            1705
            British Library 1417 f.50

The Recantation of Mr. *Pollet*, A *Roman* Priest: Late Missioner and Popish Emissary in *Worcestershire, Glocestershire, Herefordshire, Flint-shire*, &c. and Popish Confessor and Chaplain to the *Roman* Catholick Families at *Hill-End*, at *Malvern* and *Blackmore Park*, and others, near the City of *Worcester*, and elsewhere; sent thither from the *English* College at *Rome*, and Authoriz'd by the Popish Bishop *Ellis* at Paris and Impower'd by the Popish Bishop *Gifford* at *Stafford-House*, behind St. *James*'s Park, London, &c. *Published for the further Discovery of Popish Intrigues against the State and Church of* England, *as well as for the Coversion* [sic] *of the Deluded* English *Papists, and their Conformity to the Protestant Church of* England. Printed in the Year 1705.

The Preface to the Reader

THE frequent Changing of Names is so essential to the Trade of Priests and Jesuits here in England, especially, that there is no possibility of carrying on that Emissary Employment without that necessary variety of multiplying Denominations as well as Protean Garbs, and other innumerable Shiftings of the Incognito Scene, in the rest of their invisible Legerdemain Conduct, for fear least Protestant Eyes of Intelligence should spoil their sports, and turn their Comedy and Masquerade into a Tragedy and a Penal Opera. And truly the same Reason often stands good to those also that leave of that Jesuitical Game, and obliges them, when they are converted to the Protestant Religion, frequently to continue the same Scene of Changing of Names, for another fear, not inferior, though quite contrary to the former, viz. least the Popish Interest and Jesuitical Policy should render their Conversion, not only suspected, but also odious, even to Protestantsm by spreading abroad under-hand, that these Converts are not sincere, being only turn'd, for the sake of Libertinism, or some private End, or Quarrel, or perchance a worse intent: So, that by such Jesuitical Aspersions, these poor Converts are often reduc'd to that unhappy Dilemma, either to hazard their Salvation by returning again to their Jesuitical Vomit, (and for those that are truly convicted to remain in their illegal Superstition) or to venture perishing for want of Subsistence and Business, in any Capacity, even of a menial Servant, (*experto crede Roberto*) a Word to the Wise is enough. By this cunning Resort of these Jesuitical Insinuations, Scandalous Aspersions and Unchristian Surmises, the Popish Policy shifts the Sail so dexterously, as to make often even Protestants unawares the Executioners, (as the Papists often brags [*sic*] and as a certain Berkshire Papish Gentleman threaten'd me not long ago, when his Lordship of Salisbury was making a Visitation last at Reading), as well as Prosecuters of their revenge upon these poor disconsolate Converts to the Protestant Religion; which proves a powerful Exhortation and Confirmation to all Papists in general, as well as a Spiritual Lesson, not without some diverting Entertainment to the Jesuitical Novices at Watton, and Leige [*sic*], with the rest of the Popish Seminaries at Rome, Paris and Doway, to my own certain Knowledge.

Now, the Jesuitical Interest having thus continually the Weather-gage of their Native Refugees upon all accounts and turns, I leave it to the Impartial Judgment of any Reader, (though Turk or Jesuit) whether 'tis not absolutely, that is, naturally, as well as morally Impossible, without Miracles, for these poor Popish Priests converted to the Protestant Religion, (who fly from Papists, and are fled from, and generally shun'd by most Protestants, especially as to familiarity, by reason of Poverty, and of the foremention'd Jesuitical Contrivances for the most part, as I charitably suppose) to compass any such Acquaintance that is either capable, willing or able, to give them any Recommendation, or Attestation, or Testimonials, or what else you are pleased to call it, especially since those poor Native Refugees, after their Conversion, are besieg'd with a constant pressing Necessity, (in spight of all Industry, which finds itself cram'd on all sides) and with an uncertain (at the best, if any at all, though ever so capable) and flying Business, (and that among the poorer sort, and even by them suspected to be what one was) as Soliciting in the Law, or Administrating a little Physick, or teaching of French, Italian, &c. sometimes in one place, sometimes in another; sometimes for a Week, sometimes for a Month or two, &c. without either fixt Place, Time or Company, according to the sudden starting Prospect of a little present Subsistence, &c.

And this they the rather and more willingly submit to, because they (I mean still our *Britannick* Refugees from Popery to their Native Protestancy) often find it otherwise impracticable to cover their Retreat and secure the Pass, since the continual Fire from the Politick Artillery and

Ambuscades of the implacable Jesuits giving a false Alarm (as if Enemies were coming) to the Protestant Camp; these poor converted Priests are often left in the middle between the two Camps, and expos'd unmercifully to the Batteries of both sides; which the crafty Jesuits (however Protestants look upon it) interpret to be a compleat Victory on their side, and fail not accordingly to have their *Te Deum* sung for it, if not by their Cousin, his Lordship's Grace of *Paris*, in *Notre Dame*, at least in as important Places, &c. *Verbum sapienti satis.*

As for the number of these Converted Priests, I am sure there have never been so many as the Church of *England* need to be thought overcloy'd or overburthen'd with them. And as for the want of Sincerity of some of those Native Refugees, by not answering the Protestant Expectation, besides the Ungenteelness (not to say Unchristianness) of the Objection, and the Uncertainty of the Matter of Fact, and the Occasion of it; if all those Converts hitherto had been so, it can have no other force in regard of the next Convert, than as a very uncouth Compliment for a seasonable put of, and trial of Tempers: whereas to the contrary, there have been and still are of those Converted Priests far more in number, who so fully maintain the Character of true Christian Converts, and truly Reform'd Protestant Ministers, that there scarce be any more Edifying and more Serviceable to the Church of *England* in their Stations. Though in good Logick this uncharitable Argument, from one to all, by proving too much, proves nothing at all; and consequently 'tis beneath Rationality as well as Christianity, to insist upon it. How inconsequential and hard soever upon the controverted Subject, such Objections may appear and prove, yet I hope the *Nouveaux* Converts in France, or those in this Asylum and Refuge, may have no preferable occasions to be envy'd as happier, and more encourag'd than the Native *Britannick* Refugees from Popery, into this Kingdom of rights and Privileges of Reform'd Consciences.

And again, I am in the Judgment of any *Candid Reader*, Whether a Popish Priest converted to Protestancy, cannot, and ought not, as well, if not better, be suppos'd to be sincere (without the least Probability or Influence of any sinister End or Interest) in his Conversion, or by a Self-conviction (with Reading and the inward Power of Grace) and private Conformity to the Protestant Religion for the space of six or seven Years (by endeavouring after a Livelihood with his own private Learning and Industry, and so putting his Conversion to a private Probation as preparatory to a publick One) before his making any Application to be publickly employ'd upon that account, than if he had at the very first Thoughts of Conviction, took the pompuous [*sic*] Method of a noisy Conversion by Addressing himself to Church or State (which Endeavours have often prov'd but imperfect Essays of the first, as well as second Thoughts) for a present Support and Employment in a Secular or Canonical Capacity.

To be understood is all I am at; the rest is Providence's Task, with my humble Province of an entire Resignation to Church and State.

I hope, by this time, unprejudic'd *Reader*, you are made sensible enough of the Romish Methods of Changing their Names, which was the reason (though my true Name is *Davies*) I went by the Name of Blount in all my Courses beyond the *Seas*, and by the Name of *Pollet* in my *Romish* Mission in *England, &c.*

¹ Miles Davies alias Blount and Pollet was born in Flintshire in 1662 and ordained in Rome in 1688: Anstruther, III. 47. His *Recantation*, printed in 1705, consists of three parts: a fulsome Epistle Dedicatory to Bishop William Beveridge of St Asaph's (6 pp.); this Preface to the Reader (2 pp.); and the sermon itself (18 pp.), which is a conventional denunciation of the Roman Church as the Whore of Babylon, based on Revelation 18:4. Towards the end of the Epistle, Davies mentions that he had 'often, some years ago, resorted as a private Hearer and Spectator' to Beveridge's sermons at St Peter's, Cornhill, which indicates that he had worked in London before coming to Worcestershire. Here are printed only the title-page, which gives valuable information about the houses where he had served, and the Preface to the Reader, which gives a vivid picture of his tormented state of mind. It appears that he had conformed 'six or seven years' before, eked out a miserable livelihood by teaching and other odd jobs and was now suspected (rightly or wrongly) of formally recanting merely to obtain preferment.

200. *Jacobite Verses on the White Rose*¹
        Berington 963

Why, fragrant Flow'r, does Beauty cease
    To Grace that lovely Hue?
Why should maligning Blights deface
    The snow that lives in you?

Raise thy fair Head, revive once more
    Diffuse thy Odours round;
With Hope enrich the British Shore
    And bless our Native Ground.

Blow soft, ye gentle Zephyrs, blow;
    And raise the drooping Flow'r
Wee Crave its Sweets, and Mourn our Woe
    To think we have [*inserted in pencil*: noe] Power.

Power to re[*deleted*: treeve; *inserted*: vive] each anxious Mind;
    Power to retrive what's lost;
Power to make angry Fortune kind
    And Power to rule the Roast.

This Rose transplanted might adorn
    The fairest Virgin's Breast

Vie with the Beauties of the Morn
And e'en [ ]*ispair* your [ ]est.

[1] See the Introduction, p. xxxix above. The title is that given to the poem in the Record Office catalogue, which assigns it to '[*c*.1750]'. The MS itself has no title, date, signature or endorsement: it is not clear even whether it came into the Collection through a Russell or a Berington.

APPENDIX I

THE PRIOR'S HALL

The Priory of Little Malvern was officially founded when Simon, Bishop of Worcester, gave it a charter some time between 1125 and 1151. It was always subject to Worcester and never belonged to Great Malvern, which depended directly on Westminster Abbey. However, there is a theory that Aldwin, founder of Great Malvern, retired from his priorate about 1100 and withdrew to Little Malvern, either because of domestic difficulties or because of the loss of an ascetic spirit in the house. This conjecture is supported by the fact that Walcher, the second Prior, died in 1125 and Aldwin did not die until 1140. Where did he spend his later years? The other theory as to the founding is that two monks of Worcester, Jocelyn and Aldred, obtained leave to go out from the priory at Worcester to found a hermitage in the wilderness of Little Malvern. The usual date given for the two brothers, 1171, is obviously too late, and they must have preceded the Simon charter. They may have found an already existing small building or chapel to serve as their hermitage.

The restored refectory of the priory must be studied as one entity with the church, for both were essential parts of the monastery. A guide to the church and a brief history is to be found in the church porch. The claustral buildings at Little Malvern, as was usual in Benedictine monasteries, were situated to the south of the church. The remains of them are incorporated into the fabric of the Court, which, as a dwelling-house, has had later alterations and additions in the 16th, 18th, 19th and the present century. The part that is now shown to the public is the prior's refectory. In the larger monasteries guests would be accommodated in a separate building, but in a small priory such as this the prior would entertain his guests in the Great Hall. Here also would be held the courts dealing with the affairs of the priory estates, as would be the manor courts when the monks' house became the house of the lord of the manor after the Dissolution.

The Hall forms the western boundary of the cloister yard. All traces of the actual cloisters have disappeared, but the site is marked by the wall to the south and the range of garages to the east, and the northern range would have run along the wall of the nave of the church. The door in the north-east corner of the yard made an easy entrance into the church from the eastern cloister and the dorter above it. The original entrance to the Hall was probably by a door and short stairway leading up from the south-west corner of the cloister. Formations in the stone and timber-work indicate that the present small room in that position was originally a covered porch over the stairway. The present entrance and outside steps were made only in the 18th century.

An undercroft of stone dating from the 12th century supports the superstructure of the Hall proper. The walls of the Hall are partly of stone but mostly of timberwork. They bear the traces of early repairs and alterations, some of which must have undoubtedly been the work of Bishop Alcock when in 1480 he undertook the restoration of the Priory 'because of the great ruin of the place and church'. In 1482, writing a letter of advice and admonition to the monks, he said, 'I have [re]builded your church and your place of your lodging is sufficiently repaired'.

The timbers of the roof are particularly fine, being in five bays with trefoil openings in the apex of the roof. In each bay, between the arches, are two rows of lateral arches. The design can be compared with that of the timber in the roof of Old Colwall church. All the timberwork is pinned with wooden pegs. A very complicated and exact restoration of the structure was lately undertaken by Mr Thomas Berington, the present owner of the house, helped by a strong team of experts. Decayed timber was replaced where necessary by careful lamination. The roof-trusses and tiling were removed and replaced. The fireplace is modern but on the probable site of the 16th-century hearth. The original fire may have been in the centre of the floor but no trace of a central hearth remains, although there is extensive blackening of the roof timbers. After the time of the monks, the Hall would have been used by the family as their central living space, as was usual in a Tudor manor-house.

The two sash-windows with their rather charming 18th-century Gothick lights were put in at the end of the 18th century, at the same time as the present outside door. The second sash-window, beyond the fireplace, has now been removed and an original 16th-century window discovered.

The dais would have been at the northern end, with a passage behind leading to the prior's room and possibly guest-rooms. The service screen stood at the southern end, and the service passage gives on to a stone newel stair leading down to the floor below and probably the kitchen. The small rooms at the end of the Hall, one with a stone fireplace, are contemporary with the Hall, the one on the left having original floorboards. The flooring of the main Hall is a replacement.

The preservation of this fine hall is due to the fact that the house, incorporating the domestic buildings of the Priory, has been in continual occupation by the same family from the time of the Dissolution. The Little Malvern community had never been large and on 31 August 1534 there were only Prior Bristowe and five monks to sign the Act of Supremacy. In 1537 it passed through the hands of Thomas Cromwell to the Crown. Then, after brief periods of lease-holding by various speculators, a twenty-one-year lease of the property was granted to John Russell of

Bedwardine, Worcester, a knightly family settled at Strensham since the 13th century. John Russell obtained his lease through the influence of his wife's brother-in-law Thomas Audley, though he himself was a person of some consequence, being a member of the Council of the Marches. A letter of Thomas Cromwell to 'my loving friend Mr John Russell' says, 'In your monastery I will do my best'. In 1554 his son, Henry Russell, secured a grant of the freehold from Mary Tudor, and from that time until the present day the place has been in the hands of the Russells and their descendants, the Beringtons.

[The text is that of a duplicated leaflet for visitors written by Aileen Hodgson in 1970. See also Alan Brooks and Sir Nikolaus Pevsner, *The Buildings of England: Worcestershire*, 2nd edn (London, 2007), 434.]

APPENDIX II

APPENDIX TO *SECOND REPORT OF THE ROYAL COMMISSION ON HISTORICAL MANUSCRIPTS* (LONDON, 1871)

The Original Charters, Papers, Deeds, and Letters of Charles Michael Berington, Esq., of Little Malvern Court

Joseph Stevenson

In the library of Charles Berington, Esq., is contained a very large collection of early documents, ranging from the time of King John to the end of the last century. The greater portion of the collection has reference either to the history of the various families of which their owner is the representative, or to the property of which these families were the proprietors and occupants. Within a comparatively recent period large masses of these papers (especially the earlier ones) have perished by damp and otherwise; the portions however which remain are very considerable numerically, and of great interest and value. Their importance consists not so much in the light which they throw upon the general history of the nation, as upon the illustrations which they afford of the inner life of the sixteenth and seventeenth centuries, and in this respect they are worthy of a careful examination. The entire series has recently been most liberally submitted to my inspection by the owner, who is most anxious in every way in his power to forward the interests of the Commission. But the collection is too extensive to be exhausted in the course of a single visit, and I find it necessary in my present report to limit my notice to a general statement of the nature of the papers as they were presented to me, reserving to myself the privilege of a more systematic examination at some future period.

In dealing with these documents it may be convenient to classify them under certain chronological divisions, commencing with the Charters and papers anterior to the death of King Henry VIII. The earliest Charters which have occurred among the bundles already opened are those which relate to grants made to the monastery of Little Malvern by Silvester, bishop of Worcester, and his successor in the same see, Walter de Cantilupe, confirmed by the Earl of Gloucester of the period.

[1] Charters relative to Presthemede, of the time of Edward I.

[2] Charters relative to tenements in Newcastle-under-Lyme, temp. Edw. III.

[3] Licence of Walter, abbot of Westminster, granting the request of John, prior of Little Malvern, to found an oratory at Bockebury, provided that the rights of the mother church of Longedone be not injured. Dated at Chaddeslye [Corbett], 13 kal. Jun. [20 May] 1289.

[4] Charters respecting lands and tenements in Pershore, temp. Hen. VI.

[5] Charters respecting lands in Leghe, granted by Alart Pepe of Leghe, temp. Edw. III.

[6] Lease of a tenement in Kersaltone [Carshalton], co. Surrey 'foranenst the cross', with a schedule of household necessaries left in the same (curious), dated 27 Hen. VII.

[7] Letters and papers connected with the proceedings of the Council appointed by King Henry VII for the management of the affairs of Prince Arthur and the Princess Catherine his wife, while resident at Bewdley. Among these may be mentioned the following:–

> A letter from 'H. Worcester' to the Princesse grace's counsail, without date [**10**];
> Letter of John Russell, secretary to the said council, in answer to the above letter;
> Letters (several) from John [Vesey], bishop of Exeter, to the same [**3, 5, 11, 14**];
> Letter (holograph) of Thomas Audley to 'his brother Russell, secretary with the Lady Princess' [**9**].

[8] Letters from the Commissioners for the pacification of the Marches of Wales [**7**].

[9] Rules for the pacification of the same [**2**].

[10] Various letters and papers of the time of Henry VIII.

[11] Letters of William, Lord Wyndesore, to his cousin Russell, 35 Henry VIII.

[12] Depositions respecting the will of Thomas Holgrave.

[13] Charters granted by the abbey of Gloucester, 28 Henry VIII.

[14] Letter (original) of Clement [Lichfield], abbot of Evesham, to 'Mr Secretary' [**13**].

[15] Depositions in a suit (23 Hen. VIII) betwixt Thomas Foliatt, Esq., and John Frauncis.

[16] Taxation of the subsidy for the first year, viz. 27 Hen. VIII in the limits of John Russell and William Gower, Esqrs.

[17] Various letters from Thomas Crumwell to Sir John Russell, Knight, and others, mostly undated, but one bearing the date 7 Dec. 30 Hen. VIII [1538] [**21, 23, 25–6, 31, 33**].

[18] Appointment of Henry Russell, Esq., to be 'Foster' of the late priory of Little Malvern, 23 Hen. VIII [1531/2], with drafts of his letter respecting the same.

[19] 'A device to make sure the manor of Hardwick'; two plans.

[20] Quietus given to John Russell, farmer, of Werepedyll [Wyre Piddle, Worcs.], 24 Hen. VIII [1532/3].

[21] Lease of land and tenements in Calais (5 Dec. 12 Hen. VIII [1520]) by Sir William Barber, Knt., to John Russell of the Frith, co. Surrey, 'squier'.

[22] Grant of tithes of corn in Besford [Worcs.] by 'Johannes episcopus Politensis, abbas Wigorniae', to John Russell, Esquire, for his good counsel, 29 Hen. VIII.

[23] Lease by the same abbot of Worcester to John Russell, vicar of St Andrew's of Pershore, of 'Pershore Myllys', 18 Hen. VIII.

[24] *Rentale terrarum et tenementorum nuper prioratus Minoris Malverniae.*

[25] Petition to the King for grant of restitution to Sir Richard Brunton and Joanna his wife, daughter and heir of William Stanley, esq., son of William Stanley, knt., of lands &c forfeited by him. No date.

[26] Letters testimonial embodying depositions respecting the will of Thomas Holgrave, gent., in 1527.

[27] Grant of lands in Solihull, co. Warwick, by Richard Boteler to Sir Edward Ferrers and others, 9 Hen. VIII.

[28] Documents connected with lands &c in Solershope [Hope Sollers], co. Heref., 24 Henry VIII.

[29] Account book containing the personal and private expenses of Thomas Holgrave, 15 Hen. VIII. (A curious volume.)

[30] Letters to and from the family of Brocton (or Broughton) of Henley, co. Salop, from the reign of Henry VIII.

[31] Letters and papers connected with the descent of tenements and lands in Berrowe, co. Wigorn., between Henry Russell and Charles Brocton, 1 & 2 Philip & Mary.

[32] Leases of lands in Ellefield [Eldersfield], temp. Philip & Mary.

[33] Letters patent of Philip & Mary granting to Henry Russell, esq., and Charles Brocton, gent., (in consideration of the faithful service rendered by the said Henry Russell and of £413 18*s* 6*d* paid by the said Henry Russsell and Charles Brocton) the demesne and manor of Little Malvern with its appurtenances &c, Barrowe &c. Dated at Westm., 26 Sept. 1 & 2 Philip & Mary. The original, with the royal seal appended.

[34] Household book of Henry Russell 'since the death of my mother'.

[35] General quit-claim by John Webb of London, gent., of all debts due to him by Rowland Russell of London, gent., 40 Eliz. [1597/8].

[36] Book of payment of Easter dues of Little Malvern, 37 Eliz. [1594/5].

[37] Another for A.D. 1609.

[38] Another for A.D. 1614.

[39] Letter from Richard Pigot 'from his chamber in Oriel College' to Mr Henry Russell, Little Malvern. [Cf. no. 58 below.]

[40] Letters from Mathew Berew to Henry Russell, Principal of Gloucester Hall, Oxford, 20 Eliz. [1577/8].

[41] Letters of William Berowe of Bullocks Hall, county Hants.

[42] Letters of John Higford, 1593.

[43] Letters of John Halsey, 1601, 1604. [**55, 64**]

[44] Letters of John Chapman, 1607.

[45] Letters of Thomas Chamberlain, 1639.

[46] Letters and papers relative to a suit about a farm in Long Wittenham, co. Berks, claimed by S. John's College, Oxford, 1583, among which are several letters of the Privy Council [**41**].

[47] Letters, chiefly domestic and personal, from members of the families of Russell, Packington, Grove, Waterhouse, Berkley, Leigh, Halsey, Uvedale, Walwyn, Monington, Throckmorton, Molyns, Gunton, ranging from about 1580 to 1680.

[48] Letters of Mary Cross, Frances Clifton and other inmates of the English Convent at Rouen to Mr Monnington and Mr Williams of Holywell, 1734–1795. (Interesting notices of the French Revolution.)

[49] Letters and papers respecting the relics of Queen Clementine Sobieski (with the relics themselves), given to 'this convent by Felix, bishop of Ipres, Oct. 4th, 1765'.

[50] Letter of Sister Mary Rosa Howard of Norfolk about the relics of Queen Clementina, dated Brussells, Aug. 29th, 1742.

[51] Attestation of relics presented by the said Sister Mary Rosa (with the relics themselves) by Joseph Habert, bishop of Ipres, dated 18 Sept 1772, the relics having been presented 12th May 1741.

[52] Attestation as to a portion of the hair shirt of St Thomas of Canterbury (with the relic itself) by Nicholas Leyburn, vice-president of Douai, Edward Everard, S.T.P., and Joseph Morgan, dated 9th March 1676.

[53] Papers of the very Rev. Prior Williams, last prior of the English Carthusians of Nieuport, Flanders (originally of Sheen), who died 2nd Jan. 1797 at Little Malvern.

[54] Papers relating to the temporalities of the English Carthusians at Nieuport.

[55] Proceedings of the Committee for sequestration of Papists and Delinquents as regarding Thomas Russell of Little Malvern, April 1649.

[56] Speech of Fr David Lewis, executed at Usk, Aug. 27, 1679.

[57] Documents connected with the period of the Commonwealth.

[58] Letters of Richard Pigot, Fellow of Oriel College, to Thomas Habington, the Worcestershire antiquarian. [Cf. no. 39 above.]

[59] History of the Priory of Little Malvern by Rowland Reade.

[60] Letters of Dorothy Lacon, 1607.

[61] Letters of J[ohn] Grove, 1605. [**72–5**]
[62] Letter of Edward Penant, Avignon, 1765.

Mr Berington permits me to state that he will be happy to afford every facility which I may require for the inspection of those portions of his papers which as yet remain unexamined; and further, that he is anxious to forward by every means in his power the objects contemplated by the Commission.

[The Commission did not in fact ever publish any further report on the Little Malvern MSS.]

THE BERINGTON COLLECTION: ITEMS EXHIBITED AT WORCESTERSHIRE RECORD OFFICE, 1958

[The items have been rearranged in chronological order and the nos. added.]

[1] Gift from King Stephen to the prior and monks of Worcester of land, fisheries, mills, tithes and appurtenances in Worcestershire and elsewhere, *c*.1140.

[2] Conveyance from John de Morton and Elizabeth his wife to Richard le Mercer of Worcester and Margaret his wife and to John, Richard's son, of the manor of Battenhall with appurtenances, 27 January 1303/4.

[3] Bill appointing Henry Russell as foster and keeper of the woods of the priory of Little Malvern, 16 February 1541/2.

[4] Inventory of the goods and chattels of Milborowe Russell of Little Malvern, 17th cent. [*sic*; 1575]. [**36**]

[5] The Boke and presentment of John Suffelde of Little Malvern, keeper of the Bruerne Walk in Malvern Chase, for and as concerning such taskements as he hath taken or appoynted upon the heades of such persons as have fallen woode within the said Chase in his vewe, 1576.

[6] Household account book of Henry Russell of Little Malvern. Bound in leaves from chant book with plainsong notation, *c*.1580.

[7] Letter from Henry Russell to Charles Russell, *c*.1586.

[8] Letters patent of Queen Elizabeth I, being a licence to Henry Russell, Esq., to alienate the site of the late priory of Little Malvern with lands and appurtenances to John Packington, knight, and Edmund Brode, gentleman, 2 September 1591.

[9] Notes made by Sir Michaell [Molyns] for [Rowland] Russell concerning a plot to separate Sir Francis [Willoughby] and his wife, *c*.1595.

[10] Letter from John Halsey to Henrie Russell containing a medical prescription, 22 October 1602. [**60**]

[11] Dressmaker's bill, 4 May 1604.

[12] Letter from Mary Abington (or Habington) of Hindlip to Mrs Russell of Little Malvern, early 17th cent. [**103**]

[13] Letter from Sir Henry Spiller to John Russell warning him of his indictment for recusancy, 10 September 1634. [**137**]

[14] Certificate by Charles Wright, Messenger and servant to the House of Commons, that he had made diligent search in the house of Thomas Russell of Little Malvern, Esq., for 'Jesuits, Romeish Priests;

all massinges stuff; Popeish Reliqkes; Popeish books; and Warlike Ammunition but did not find any such', 28 February 1641/2 [**152**].

[15] Orders of Prince Rupert respecting the City and County of Worcester and the conduct of the war against the Parliamentary forces, 10 February 1643/4. [**160**]

[16] Letter from Fr Anthony Turner, accused and put to death at Tyburn by Titus Oates, to Joan Russell, 17 March 1672/3. [**195**]

[17] Fragment of dissertation on the keeping of the running horse, c.1700.

[18] Jacobite verses on the White Rose, c.1750. [**200**]

[19] Account book of shipments of goods and slaves bought in Jamaica, 1774–1775.

[20] Invitation to the funeral of Elizabeth Williams, 5 March 1789.

[21] Three recipes, 18th–19th cents.

APPENDIX IV

THE LAWSUITS OF 1607–8

Letters **83–108**, from October 1607 to December 1608, are largely about two lawsuits. One was in Chancery between Humphrey Pakington and a Mr Newport: 'the variance between Mr Pakington and Mr Newport' (**87**), 'the controversy between me and Mr Newport' (**88**). The other was between John Grove and Sir John Hungerford, 'the base instrument of a Scottish beggarly gentleman' (**90**), concerning land near Ledbury (**58, 71, 107**). Sir John may or may not also be the knight referred to in a later letter of 2 March 1615/16, in which a Mr Hartland of Colwall was also concerned: 'Mr Hartland and his knight' (**124**; cf. **79, 105, 107, 109**). There are also references, sometimes in the same letters, but not connected with either of these suits, to land in Castlemorton, three miles from Little Malvern, which had been leased to a Mr John White by Henry and Sir Thomas Bartlett. In January 1607/8 Henry Russell bought the lease from White and wanted to buy the land outright from the Bartletts (**91**). But he died on 4 March, so that negotiations continued for the rest of 1608 between White, the Bartletts, John Grove, Humphrey Pakington and Elizabeth Russell on behalf of her elder son John (**101, 104–5, 108**). In the end the Russells did acquire the land, the rents from which were put at £40 in 1694 and 1708 (**197**).

A. Sir John Hungerford

Sir John Hungerford (1566–1635) of Down Ampney was the son of Anthony Hungerford (d. 1589) and Bridget, daughter of John Shelley of Michelgrove in Sussex. He was a descendant of the builder of Farleigh Hungerford Castle in Somerset and a connexion of Walter, Lord Hungerford (1502–1540), whose widow, Elizabeth, daughter of John, Lord Hussey, became the second wife of Sir Robert Throckmorton of Coughton (d. 1582).[1] Down Ampney, between Cirencester and Swindon, is just in Gloucestershire, but the boundary with Wiltshire ran through the kitchen of the fifteenth-century manor-house,[2] and Sir John's pedigree is in the Wiltshire Visitation.[3] A monument in the church there describes him as

---

[1] Cokayne, *Complete Peerage*, VI. 626 note (c).
[2] Samuel Rudder, *A New History of Gloucestershire* (Cirencester, 1779; repr. Stroud, 1977), 416; David Verey and Alan Brooks, *The Buildings of England: Gloucestershire*, I: *The Cotswolds*, 3rd edn (London, 1999), 327.
[3] *Wiltshire Visitation Pedigrees, 1623*, ed. G.D. Squibb, Harleian Society 105–6 (London, 1954), 89–95.

'serviceable to his King and country, liberal to his friends, charitable and courteous to all'; but Grove paints a rather different picture. Twice he makes contemptuous puns on the name, referring to 'Sir John *Hungri-fort*' (**109**) and 'the good knight who is *hungry for* my lands' (**107**). The dispute may have been over lands held by Grove on behalf of John Halsey, whose forfeitures for recusancy were granted away at Hungerford's request on 18 October 1611.[4] But the Hungerfords had other links with Worcestershire and Warwickshire. An Elizabeth Hungerford had married Roger Wintour of Huddington, great-grandfather of the Gunpowder Plotters;[5] another Elizabeth Hungerford married Robert Throckmorton (d. 1601) of Throckmorton Court, near Pershore.[6] In 1558 Sir John's grandfather inherited Suckley, seven miles west-south-west of Worcester, which he settled on his son Anthony (Sir John's father) when he married Bridget Shelley about 1565; in 1571 John and Anthony sold it to Edmund Colles of Leigh (d. 1606).[7] Sir John's eldest son by his wife Mary Berkeley was Sir Anthony Hungerford, whose first wife was Elizabeth, daughter of Sir Thomas Lucy of Charlecote, near Stratford-upon-Avon.

B. Newports

It is not easy to identify 'Mr Newport', since there were at least four local families of that name. First, there were the Newports of High Ercall in Shropshire, one of whom was Humphrey Pakington's mother Elizabeth.[8] Her brother Richard Newport married Margaret Bromley, who was a daughter of Lord Chief Justice Sir Thomas Bromley and so a sister of Sir Henry Bromley, who searched Hindlip in 1606.[9] After the Essex Rising, Sir Henry was committed to the Tower and Humphrey Pakington's cousin Sir Francis Newport (1557–1622) also came under suspicion.[10] Sir Francis owned land in Worcestershire at Croome D'Abitôt, which is now in Croome Park, three miles north-east of Upton-upon-Severn,[11]

---

[4] LaRocca, *Jacobean Recusant Rolls for Middlesex*, CRS 76, p. 41 n. 27.
[5] *Visitation of the County of Worcester, 1569*, 148; cf. pp. 70, 83 (Thomas Hugford and Isabel Hungerford; Anthony Ingram of Wolford in Warwickshire and Dorothy Hungerford). There is no Ingram pedigree in *Visitation of the County of Warwick, 1619*.
[6] VCH *Worcs.*, III. 356–7.
[7] VCH *Worcs.*, IV. 355; see further below.
[8] Lechmere Box B.77 is a fragment consisting of six notes of music and the words

> until you have geven v[s]
> all we your schollers desir[e]
> Magdeleyn Newport Ma[ ]
> Elizabathe pakingtone Ambr[ ]

[9] *Visitation of Shropshire, 1623*, II. 372–4.
[10] *Calendar of the Manuscripts at Hatfield House*, XI. 102, 103, 106.
[11] VCH *Worcs.*, III. 315.

and at Kempsey, between Worcester and Tewkesbury.[12] Secondly, in 1551 Humphrey's great-uncle Sir John Pakington left a legacy to a 'Mr Newport of [Droit]wich'.[13] Thirdly, there were John and Margaret Newport of Hanley Castle, who were recusants in 1593/4.[14] Fourthly, there was Edward Newport (d. 1619) of Hanley William, twelve miles north-west of Worcester.[15] According to their wills, both Sir John Pakington and his brother Robert (1495–1536) were born at Stanford-on-Teme, only two miles away;[16] and in 1548 their third brother, Humphrey I (d. 1556), paid for the building of a bridge across the Teme at Stanford.[17] A letter from John Bache to Humphrey Pakington mentions that 'Mr Newport of Hanley' and Mr William Chaunce of Bromsgrove are to be commissioners for an enquiry at Droitwich, but it is not clear whether this means Hanley Castle or Hanley William.[18] In no. **84** (which has the bottom missing and two large holes towards the top) John Grove notes that 'yesterday [14 November 1607] Mr Newport nor his kinsman *le* had not exhibited any Bill in Chancery'. But none of these Newports seem to have been related to any Lees or Leighs.[19]

C. Salways

Humphrey refers also to a Mr Salwaye or Sallawaye (**88**, **89**, **91**), who was his 'cousin' (**89**) and was concerned in the suit. At this time Stanford-on-Teme was owned by the Salways, who were related to the Pakingtons through the Washbournes; the Pakingtons had formerly owned land there.[20] So it seems likely that Humphrey's 'cousin' was

[12] VCH *Worcs.*, III. 432; *Visitation of Shropshire, 1623*, II. 373.
[13] Prerogative Court of Canterbury, 30 Bucke = *Index of Wills Proved in the Prerogative Court of Canterbury, 1383–1558*, II (Index Library 11, British Record Society, 1895), 399.
[14] Bowler, *Recusant Roll no. 2*, CRS 57, p. 197.
[15] VCH *Worcs.*, IV. 277. Edward Newport owned Hanley William by 1581.
[16] Prerogative Court of Canterbury, 30 Bucke (as above), 4 Dyngley = *Index of Wills Proved in the Prerogative Court of Canterbury, 1383–1558*, II. 399.
[17] Nash, *Collections for the History of Worcestershire*, II. 367. The inscription Nash quotes is now in the possession of Lord Hampton. The Pakingtons owned lands at Stanford (ibid.) and also at Buckland, Humber and Ferne Mawne and Brian's Mawne in Bodenham, all of which are about twelve miles south-west of Stanford, near Leominster. See Robinson, *History of the Mansions and Manors of Herefordshire*, 139 n., which is an abstract of Sir John's inquisition post mortem (C.142/93/102).
[18] Warwick Record Office, Throckmorton MSS (CR 1998), Box 52, unnumbered stitched set, [e]. Undated, but Bache refers to 24 May as 'the Thursday next before Whitsunday', which means that the year was either 1604 or 1610.
[19] The *Visitation of Worcestershire, 1634* has no pedigrees of Newport, Lee or Leigh.
[20] The Pakingtons impaled the Washbournes' arms with their own. The relationship is obscure, as early pedigrees of all three families are inaccurate and inconsistent. The materials are: *Visitation of the County of Worcester, 1569*, 101–2 (Pakington), 120–2 (Salway), 142–4 (Washbourne); *Visitation of Worcestershire, 1634*, 85 (Salway); Grazebrook, *Heraldry of Worcestershire*, II. 419–22, 490–91, 609–10; Habington, *Survey of Worcestershire*,

either Arthur Salway or his son Humphrey. Arthur had succeeded his father Thomas at Stanford between 1570 and 1603 and was succeeded there in 1616 by his son Humphrey, who married Anne Littleton and died about 1653.[21] There is a letter to Henry Russell of December 1607 from 'your loving kinsman and friend Humphrey Salwey', complaining that 'There was not any answer put in, . . . although I make no doubt but the bill was put in at the day agreed'.[22] This clearly refers to the proceedings mentioned in nos. **88–9**. But Stanford is (just) in Worcestershire, whereas Humphrey refers (**86**) to a verdict to be given by 'a *Herefordshire* jury'. It seems possible, therefore, that the 'lea ferme' (**85**) was a lease of Lea Green, just over the border into Herefordshire, which had been mentioned in 1525 in a deed of Sir John Pakington as 'Le' in Upper or Over Sapey.[23] Sir John, his nephew John and Humphrey himself were all patrons of the living at Sapey;[24] in 1591 Humphrey Pakington sold the manor there to Arthur Salway.[25] Lionel and Veronica Webster thought that this transaction was to raise money for recusancy fines,[26] but it could have been a device to transfer the nominal ownership before Humphrey's conviction and sequestration in October that year. In July 1607, just before the lawsuit began, the king granted to John Grove 'all manner of such forfeitures, sum and sums of money, penalties, damages and losses whatsoever' due for the recusancy of Humphrey Pakington and Christopher Cresacre More.[27] Could there have been a dispute about whether this included the revenues of Sapey or not? That would certainly explain the references in nos. **84–6** and **88** to 'the King's title'. In October 1605 Garnet had written:

> Every six weeks is a several court: juries appointed to indict, present, find the goods of Catholics, prize them; yea, in many places to drive away whatever they find *contra ordinem iuris* and put the owners, if perhaps Protestants, to

I. 297; the heraldic cartouches originally in the Great Chamber at Harvington and now at Coughton; VCH *Worcs.*, III. 471, 561–6; IV. 341–5. For the Pakington lands at Stanford, see Nash, *Collections for the History of Worcestershire*, II. 367.

[21] VCH *Worcs.*, IV. 343; *Visitation of Worcestershire, 1634*, 85. Thomas Salway had disinherited his eldest son Anthony in favour of Arthur (Harl. Soc. 27, p. 122). Was this Anthony the 'Thomas' Salway of the diocese of Worcester who was ordained at Soissons in 1588 (Anstruther, I. 298)? Arthur Salway's will (26 Cope) was proved in 1616: *Index of Wills Proved in the Prerogative Court of Canterbury, V: 1605–1619*, 390.

[22] Berington 562(40).

[23] British Library Add. MS 31314, ff. 41–2. Hugh Lea of the Lea died on 26 April 1622: John Duncumb, *Collections towards the History and Antiquities of the County of Hereford*, 6 vols. in 10 (Hereford and London, 1804–1915), II. 160.

[24] Duncumb, *Collections*, II. 159.

[25] VCH *Worcs.*, IV. 343; Duncumb, *Collections*, II. 157, 159; cf. Nash, *Collections for the History of Worcestershire*, II. 367.

[26] Anderton Webster and Anderton Webster, 'The Pakingtons of Harvington', 207.

[27] The National Archives, Patent Roll C.66/1739/3, printed in Daniel Shanahan, 'The Family of St Thomas More in Essex, 1581–1640', *Essex Recusant* 4 (1962), 60–62.

prove that they be theirs, and not of recusants with whom they deal. . . . If any recusant buy his goods again, they inquire diligently if the money be his own; otherwise they would have that too. In fine, if these courses hold, every man must be fain to redeem once in six months the very bed he lieth on.[28]

Although the emphasis here is on goods, it is not hard to see that such inquiries might easily extend to landed estates as well.

D. Leigh

Alternatively, was the 'lea ferme' a lease of the estates of Edmund Colles (1530–1606) at Leigh, which is further down the Teme, four miles west of Worcester and four miles north of Great Malvern?[29] Edmund's brother William had married Margery Pakington, Humphrey's aunt;[30] in 1570 Humphrey's father John Pakington stood godparent to a daughter of Bishop Sandys of Worcester, along with Mrs Anne Washbourne and Mrs Anne Colles.[31] According to Habington, 'Ley [was] surcharged with debte, which (as a snowball rowlinge downe from Malverne's hyll gatherethe greatnes) increased so with huge usery';[32] and after the death in 1615 of Edmund's son, also William, it was sold by his trustees to Sir Walter Devereux of Castle Bromwich, near Birmingham. This William and his wife Mary were convicted of recusancy in 1596;[33] their third son Thomas Colles (1596 – after 1633) was ordained in Rome in 1620 and arrested by the informer John Gee in London in 1624.[34] So the dispute may have arisen from the settling of the estates of Edmund Colles after his death in 1606, though in that case it is not clear how the Newports or the Salways might be concerned.

[28] Gerard, *The Condition of Catholics under James I*, 79–80.
[29] VCH *Worcs.*, IV. 103, 108, n.68.
[30] *Visitation of the County of Worcester, 1569*, 41, 102.
[31] Nash, *Collections for the History of Worcestershire*, II. 222. Cf. Hodgetts, 'Origins of Recusancy: The Pakingtons', esp. 12–13. (On p. 13, line 9, '*Hanbury* William' should be '*Hanley* William'.)
[32] Habington, *Survey of Worcestershire*, I. 329, quoted in VCH *Worcs.*, IV. 103.
[33] Bowler, *Recusant Roll no. 2*, CRS 57, p. 194.
[34] Anstruther, II. 67–8. There are monuments in Leigh church to Edmund Colles (1606) and to William (1615) and Mary (1602) Colles.

INDEX OF PEOPLE AND PLACES

Italic page numbers indicate material in appendices. Page spans may indicate repeated mentions rather than single entries. Letters are listed under names of senders and recipients and are located by page number, not letter number.

extension xv
granted to Henry Russell I xiv
location and description xi
looting xxxiv
Stuart relics xli
Little Malvern Priory xii–xiii, 34–5,
211–13
Littleton, Edward, Lord Keeper, to Sheriff
of Worcester 164
Littleton, Sir Thomas 166
Llantarnam, Monmouths 139
Locking, Berkshire 47
Lombard (Lumbard) Street, London 107
Long Parliament 163
Lord Chancellor Ellesmere 92, 117, 144
to [Francis Moore] 132–3
Lord Chief Baron 132
Lord Secretary 107
Lords of the Council 55
Lorimer, (wagoner) 74
Lorte, Thomas 50
Lowches Farm, Oxon. xvii–xviii
Lucies manor house, Herts. xxi
Luddington, Walter 189
Lumley, George xv
Lumley, Jane xv
Lumley, John xv
Lutley, Humphrey 150
to Thomas Russell I 176
Lutley, Mary xxviii, 58n, 140n
Lutley, Philip xxviii
Lutley, William 117
Lydney, Gloucs. 133, 137n
Lyford, Oxon. 47
Lygon, Hugh 48
Lyttelton, Gilbert 70
Lyttelton, Henry 167n
Lyttelton, Humphrey 92n
Lyttelton, Meriel xx
Lyttelton, Meriel (Bromley) 167n
Lyttelton, Sir John 167n
Lyttelton, Sir Thomas xxxiii, 163n, 167n
Lyttelton, Stephen 167n

McEvilly, Fr J. Denis xliv, xlvi, xlvii
Malvern Parva *see* Little Malvern
Marbury, Thomas xxvii, 123n, 127n, 131,
140n
Marcle, Much and Little, Herefs. 82, 133
Margery, sister to Frances Cowarne 85
Markham, Geoffrey xv
Markham, Griffith 98n
Markham, Griffith (Griffin) 98–9

Marshalsea Prison, London xxv
Marten, John 43
Martin, Mr xxix, 146
Mary; *see* Princess Mary
Mascall, Theophilus 189
Maskely, Mr 157
Mathew, Dr Tobie, Dean of Durham xviii,
55
Mathington, [unknown] 65
Maunder, George 189
Merick, William 202
Merionethshire 17–19
Merionethshire, Sheriff of 18
Mervyn, Hugh 21
Middlemore, Mr 48
Middlemore, Richard 153, 156
Middlesex, Clerk of the Peace 154–6
Middlesex, Under Sheriff 152
Middleton, Marmaduke, Bishop of St
David's 93n
Middleton, Richard 98
from Alderford Russell 93
Milan 191n
Mintridge, Elizabeth (Blount) 119n
Mintridge, James 44, 61, 119n
Mintridge, John 87n
to Elizabeth Russell 118–20
Mitre, The, Oxford 161
Moat Hall, Pontesbury, Salop. xlii
Montrose's army 184
[Moore, Francis], to Lord Chancellor
Ellesmere 132–3
Moore, William 179
Moor's Hall, Warks. 123
More, Frances 48
More, James 199n
More, Mistress 133
More, Prior William of Worcester, from
John Russell I 29–30
More, Rhys 48
More, Thomas 48
More, William, Prior 30n
Moreton, Herefs. 86
Morgan, Edward 138–9
Morgan, Peter 189
Morgan, Thomas 153, 156
Morris, David xxxvii
Morton, Thomas and Anne 65–6, 74
Mossey, William 15
Mr Tom's shop 188
Much Cowarne, Herefs. xlii
Munday, Anthony 49
Munster 73

SUBJECT INDEX